RICHARD NIXON'S AMERICA

The Legislative Record

GEORGE D. CAMERON III
Emeritus Professor of Business Law
Ross School of Business
University of Michigan

Van Rye
PUBLISHING

Cover design by Vila Design

Published by Van Rye Publishing, LLC
Ann Arbor, MI
www.vanryepublishing.com

ISBN: 978-1-957906-10-2 (paperback)
ISBN: 978-1-957906-11-9 (ebook)
Library of Congress Control Number: 2023934608

The evil that men do lives after them;
The good is oft interred with their bones;
So let it be with Caesar. The noble Brutus
Hath told you Caesar was ambitious.
If it were so, it was a grievous fault,
And grievously hath Caesar answer'd [for] it.

—Shakespeare, Julius Caesar, Act III
(from Mark Antony's funeral oration for Caesar)

Contents

Foreword

N EARLY FIFTY YEARS ON, the events and the personalities of the Nixon presidency continue to fascinate and confound us, even those of us who lived through it—or perhaps especially those of us who lived through it. President Nixon's spectacular foreign policy triumphs have been well-documented: among them, bringing China back into the community of nations and negotiating arms control and renunciation of nuclear solutions with the USSR. His China trip resulted in the PRC's emergence as a world economic power and the restoration of considerable economic—if not yet political—freedom for the Chinese people. His policy of détente with the Soviet Union and his use of the China opening to "triangulate" diplomacy avoided a nuclear exchange with the USSR and gave the tide of history a chance to wash away the Soviet Empire. With the benefit of forty-plus years of hindsight, the historical record seems clear that President Nixon's foreign policy was right, and his critics (of *both* the Right and the Left) were wrong.[1]

Somewhat less clear—perhaps—is the verdict on our long and bloody struggle to defend the people of South Vietnam and their independence. President Nixon's handling of this inherited war remains the subject of sharp controversy. Starkly differing assessments of what happened there and what it means are still held with passion and fervor. Suffice it to say at this point that he did end what was then the US' longest war and the draft, and he was successful in gaining the return of US POWs. (One of them, Air Force Captain David Gray, Jr., is quoted as saying: "A loving President preserved my honor. . . . Thank you, Heavenly Father. Thank you, President Nixon. . . . Thank you, America."[2]) Some critics think that the US should have stayed and fought on; others, that the US should have left sooner. As a result, there is considerable criticism of the Nixon legacy on this score. Here again, considerable wood pulp has been expended in presenting the pros and cons and the "what if" scenarios.

Of course, the summa cum laude of all the anti-Nixon diatribes is the series of events that proved to be the President's undoing: Watergate. On this point, there seems to be an all-but-unanimous consensus that President Nixon and various members of his administration were guilty of unforgivable crimes. The story has already been retold many times and nearly always with the same negative conclusions that the US Presidency was hijacked by a bunch of criminals and manipulators who could do (and did do) no good. The intense negativity surrounding the Watergate affair was surely reinforced by the sense of betrayal felt by many who had voted for Richard Nixon on four or five presidential ballots. (Just for the record, it's worth noting that only one other person in our history ever appeared on *five* national tickets for a major party and won four of five: Franklin D. Roosevelt. FDR, of course, won the presidency himself four times and lost as a vice-presidential candidate. Nixon was two for three as a presidential candidate, and he won both times as the vice president.[3] George H. W. Bush was three for four—two for two as vice president and one for two as president. No one else is even close to these totals, although William Jennings Bryan did *lose* three times as the Democrat candidate for president.)

Whether a more balanced evaluation of the tragic Watergate farce will ever be possible is hard to say, although the ongoing disclosures of the official lies about Franklin D. Roosevelt's and John F. Kennedy's health and their amorous adventures,[4] and the lengthy record of "sex-ploits" and ensuing lies of Bill Clinton[5] (and *his* impeachment) may change the equation a bit. (For many, much of the Donald Trump presidency was a replay of the Nixon saga—on steroids!)

President Nixon's personal biography has also been well-documented, both in print and on film. His hard work to overcome difficulties, his service in the US Navy, his tough political campaigns, his key role in the exposure and conviction of Soviet spy Alger Hiss, and his ultimate triumph at the polls in 1972—carrying 49 of 50 states!—have all been recounted many times.

All of the above aspects of "Nixon's America" having already been covered in some detail in prior works, what's left to justify another book on the subject? One significant part of the Nixon presidency seems to have been largely ignored: the legislative record.

Let's consider the situation. A minority-vote President (43 percent of the votes) takes office. His opposition controls both Houses of Congress—by substantial margins (57 to 43 in the Senate and 243 to 193 in the House of Representatives). He inherits our most unpopular (and then-longest) war. Draft cards are being burned; young men are fleeing to Canada. Tens of thousands of rioters and demonstrators are in the streets, university campuses are in chaos, and several cities have been burned and looted. A bit less than four years later, in the 1972 presidential election, that same man carries 49 of 50 states, with the largest national vote majority of any President in history! What happened? How could one of our most vilified Presidents have turned things around so completely and so quickly if, as his critics would have us believe, he was so totally evil and so totally misguided?

The answer is, of course, that we have been given a distorted picture. The words of the old song that say "accentuate the positive, eliminate the negative" have been reversed. We have been given only the negatives, and to be sure, there were enough of those. But fairness and accuracy demand a fuller exposition of the historical record. And while it's true that the Nixon/Kissinger reordering of the world is generally ranked as the greatest accomplishment of the Nixon presidency, significant advances were also achieved in several areas of domestic policy.[6] This book attempts to document some of them.

Introduction

A Re-Examination of the Legislative Record

THE MAJOR PREMISE of this book is that a great deal of valuable public policy was adopted during the Nixon administration. Perhaps not enough to balance off the sins of Watergate, but a considerable amount nonetheless. The final balancing is a matter for each of us to decide individually, and for future historians, and for a Higher Power.

President Nixon's efforts in three areas—protection of the environment, protection of workers, and protection of minorities—are especially worth noting. These are surprising areas, to be sure, given Nixon's status as the "heir" to Barry Goldwater's Conservative Revolution of 1964. And it's not always clear how much of this progress was the result of a conscious strategy of "doing the right thing" and how much was due to a pragmatic tactic of "taking what the other team will give you." (Remember that Nixon's Republican Party was a 49-to-75-seat minority in the House and a 10-to-14-seat minority in the Senate.)

Commentators have suggested both sides as dominant in the Nixon White House. Evans and Novak seem to indicate that President Nixon had little interest in domestic policy but rather concerned himself with the development of a grand strategy for international relations and the winning of the Cold War.[1] Domestic policy was left to subordinates—John Ehrlichman, Daniel Patrick Moynihan, and others.[2] Oliver Stone's film *Nixon,* on the other hand, has Nixon (played—improbably—by Sir Anthony Hopkins) promising his wife Patricia that they had a chance to "get it right this time"—i.e., by winning the presidency in 1968 and putting his progressive programs into effect. (One of the most surprisingly "progressive" of which was the "Family Assistance Plan," a form of guaranteed annual income that would have revolutionized the welfare system. Although applauded by many professionals, it lacked the political appeal and support necessary for passage.[3]) There are, of course, more factual and substantial pieces of evidence in the record—perhaps the most noteworthy of which (for our purposes) is Nixon's 1972 message to Congress, indicating the work still to be done on environmental protection. One also feels compelled to mention his promise to

Labor—to protect workers' retirement funds, which resulted in ERISA (passed twenty-three days too late for President Nixon to sign, although he was given full credit for it by his chosen—but unelected—successor, President Gerald Ford).

Wherever the true point is on this continuum, it seems clear that domestic policy was second priority to foreign affairs. After all, the USSR was at the height of its powers, the Vietnam War was consuming our young men and our resources, the long-unstable Middle East threatened to erupt at any time, and nuclear holocaust was a very real possibility. It was clearly a time for "first things first." If you inherit a house that's on fire, you probably don't make a leaky faucet your first priority! Given the then-existing world situation, President Nixon had no choice but to give foreign affairs most of his time and effort.

Whatever were the President's priorities and interests, and whatever level of delegation to staff was involved, the national statutes passed by the ninety-first Congress, the ninety-second Congress, and most of the ninety-third Congress were enacted on President Nixon's watch. Richard Nixon's signature is on those 1,664 Public Acts. (Seven additional statutes were passed by a two-thirds majority in each house of Congress, overriding a Nixon veto of the bill. Thirty-six of his vetoes were upheld by Congress; those bills did not become Public Acts.[4]) Those 1,664 statutes (or 1,671—depending on one's perspective) are the "Nixon legislative legacy."

We're obviously not going to reproduce or discuss all of those statutes here, even though any bill enacted into law presumably was adopted to promote some aspect of the "public interest." Statutes authorizing general appropriations for the various operating parts of the government were generally omitted from consideration in this book, even though some of those moneys would be spent in the areas being discussed here—Environment, Labor, Consumer Affairs, Minorities Policy, Veterans, and Health & Welfare. Acts that were amendments to existing statutes are included in this book where they extended coverage, duration, or funding for specific programs in these areas. Judgment calls have been made throughout this book's analysis, such as whether a particular "Development" Act does also seem to have some pro-environment aspects and thus deserves to be listed in the "Environment" chapter. Statutes that merely provided for the renaming of some project were not included in the numerical totals in this book, even when the renamed project was a park or a flood-control dam.

One basic point cannot be emphasized too strongly: the gross disparities in the size and scope of the 1,671 statutes. For many people, the word "statute" brings to mind the incredibly detailed several hundred pages of the Internal Revenue Code, or the two-hundred-odd pages of the Employee Retirement Income Security Act of 1974, or at least twenty or thirty pages of legislative craftsmanship. (For the author, after fifty-three years of teaching Business Law, "statute" immediately equates to the massive Uniform Commercial Code.) In fact, the majority—one is tempted to say "the vast majority"—of the 1,671 Acts under study in this book consist of only a few lines or two pages or less in the statute books. Each of these flyspeck efforts has—presumably—been processed through the entire legislative procedure: introduced as a bill in one of the two Houses of Congress, referred to the appropriate committee (and then perhaps to a subcommittee), investigated and discussed as felt necessary, reported back to the introducing House, scheduled for debate and voting on the floor, sent (after passage) to the other House, gone through the same steps, and then—after passage by the second House in identical form as in the first House—sent to the President for signature or veto.

One hundred Senators and 435 Representatives, plus numerous office and committee staff members, have potentially been involved in producing each of these tiny outputs. Even allowing for the obvious conclusion that massive pro-forma compliance with the niceties of legislative procedure must be occurring, this still seems to suggest a terrible waste of human (and temporal) resources. If one of the major criticisms of Congress is that it doesn't get anything done, the obvious response is that they are very busy dusting and sweeping the "house"—but without recognizing that the foundation of the "house" is crumbling away. This problem—or at least the perception of a problem—is, of course, well beyond the scope of the study in this book.

As it turns out, however, even the limited data-sets produced herein yield some interesting insights—again, even using the most elementary and unsophisticated levels of analysis. In a recent issue of the *International Public Management Journal*, the guest editors introduced a symposium on public management research by calling on scholars "to seek for novel and improved methods to produce research that lives up to scientific scrutiny and is valuable for practitioners."[5] Without trying to determine whether what is being discussed in this book belongs in the "public management" field, let me be brash enough to suggest that political discourse might benefit from additional information and analysis based on the study of actual outputs—statutes, regulations, and court cases—and a bit less emphasis on the intricacies of the processes and the personalities of the players.[6] It is surely useful to know the "who" and the "how" when it comes time to assign credit or blame, but let's at least first make sure that we know *what* got done. The objective here is to further clarify the "what" of Richard Nixon's years as President.

PART I

NIXON'S PARAMETERS OF POLICY

Chapter 1

Inheriting the Sixties

IT IS DIFFICULT to recall, today, just how completely the Vietnam War dominated our national consciousness and political debate in the US during those years. And if it is "difficult" for those of us who were there and old enough to appreciate what was happening, one can only imagine how difficult it must be for later generations to feel what we were feeling. (The author recalls giving a speech in 1954, as a freshman college student, advocating increased US support for the French troops battling to hold Indochina against the Communists. Only sixty-plus years later have I learned just how difficult—impossible?—their task was.[1])

By the mid-1960s, the Vietnam War was everywhere! We were treated to horrible images on what seemed like a daily basis—primarily on the TV news, but also in the press and the news magazines. It was clearly the dominant political issue of the time.[2] It had surely contributed to the warping of the 1964 presidential election. One remembers a sardonic joke circulating after that election: "They told me that I just *couldn't* vote for Goldwater. That if I did, there would be a half million US troops in Vietnam within a year. Well, I guess they were right. I did vote for Goldwater, and the half-million troops are there!"

Four years later, the war was the issue that ripped apart the Democrat Party and paved the way for Richard Nixon's election as President. When a relatively-obscure "back-bencher" Senator from Minnesota (Eugene McCarthy) parlayed an extreme anti-war stance[3] into a close-second finish against the sitting President in the New Hampshire presidential primary, LBJ saw the handwriting on the wall. He scheduled a special TV address to announce that he was dropping out of the race and that he would not even accept a draft by the Democrat convention. (The author remembers hearing the speech on his car radio on his way up William Street in Ann Arbor to the University of Michigan campus—probably to do research on his Political Science dissertation.[4]) Lyndon Johnson's vice president, Hubert Humphrey—the former Senator from Minnesota—picked up the fallen standard and announced that he was now a candidate for President.

Somewhere in this time frame, Robert Kennedy—the (transplanted) junior Senator from New York—decided to join the presidential derby. Also running on an anti-war platform, Bobby had just won the largest delegate prize (the June 6 California primary) when he was assassinated. One remembers his last public words: "Now, it's on to Chicago, and let's win theah!" What then transpired at the Democrats' Chicago convention was all but unimaginable. The anti-war (and other) groups' attempts to gather, march, and protest were resisted by the Chicago police. Insults were exchanged, missiles were hurled, violence flared, physical injuries were sustained, and mass arrests occurred.[5]

In the midst of this chaos, the Democrats nominated the "Establishment" candidate—Humphrey ("The Happy Warrior")—to the complete dismay and disaffection of the young and old activists who had enthusiastically embraced Gene McCarthy and Bobby Kennedy. The stage was set for the last great electoral battle of the Sixties, starring the resurrected Richard Nixon against the refurbished Hubert Humphrey.[6] With an at least somewhat reconstituted Republican Party facing a sharply divided band of Democrats, Nixon's chances of gaining the presidential prize seemed significantly enhanced. The initial polling figures so indicated, showing Nixon with a substantial lead. As the race progressed, however, the Nixon lead narrowed, and it appeared that Humphrey might yet pull out a win. He almost did, as many Democrats returned to the fold, and George Wallace carried several States that would otherwise probably have gone to Nixon. When all the votes were counted, Richard Nixon became the thirty-seventh President of the United States. This time, he won the "close one."

But what had Nixon inherited when he took the oath of office on January 20, 1969? What was left of the country he had known as he campaigned for the presidency the first time—in the first year of this agitated and uncertain decade? How did we get to 1968's package of results, after the glorious beginning of the 1960s—PT 109, Jackie, Camelot, Carolyn and John-John, "Ask not . . ."? What happened to the spectacular vision that was the US at the beginning of the decade? Where did we go wrong? How did we lose our way so badly? Of more direct relevance to the present study, how could Nixon be elected President when the voters overwhelmingly favored Democrats for Senators, Representatives, and Governors? What can possibly account for the massive ticket-splitting that must have occurred in the voting booths across the nation? What led voters to (narrowly) prefer Nixon over Humphrey for our highest office but nevertheless to continue to strongly favor Democrats for lesser offices?[7] (The size of that differential—in itself—is another question that's worth some additional investigation.)

Of course, we can examine the extensive documentary record of those years. There is considerable material available in aural and visual recording of events and of reactions to them. We can "re-view" and review the three assassinations (JFK, MLK, and RFK), the nightly TV news reports of the horrors in Vietnam, the rioting and burning in our cities, and the overall deluge of negativity that characterized those years. Historical post-mortems of that sort have been ongoing for some time; attempting to replicate or to summarize them would not seem to be the best use of this book's pages.

In an attempt to provide a slightly different focus, then, let us take a look at the Sixties through the eyes of a Nixon supporter: this book's author, who was a young man trying to build a life "back then." (This exercise is being attempted largely via a memory-bank now in its ninth decade of service and is therefore not guaranteed for exact factual accuracy.) This approach is clearly impressionistic and, of course, "unscientific." It's an attempt to correlate some of the major "events" of the decade with what one person who happened to be there was experiencing. Admittedly, this is only one example out of millions, but perhaps it still might be informative to someone who wasn't among us yet or was too young to appreciate much of what was occurring.

On January 1, 1960, our protagonist is twenty-four years old, married, and enrolled in his second year of law school. He is working part-time in one of the university's libraries (or soon will be) to supplement his wife's salary as a teacher. He supported the Eisenhower/Nixon tickets in 1952 and 1956, but he was too young to vote in 1952. As a strongly-committed Republican, he (probably) supports Nixon for President in 1960. He would prefer Lyndon Johnson over John F. Kennedy as the Democrat nominee, although it's not clear why he would.

As an undergraduate and graduate-school major in Political Science, our young man is generally aware of national and international developments, and he makes some effort to keep up-to-date with them. He is, however, relatively untouched personally by them. At this point, the levels of personal income taxation are not really of concern. He has been registered for the military draft since his eighteenth birthday in 1953, but the likelihood of his being called for military service is not great since the US' commitment in Vietnam is still quite tentative at this point. (He had been prevented by vision problems from enrolling in Air Force ROTC as an undergraduate.) No specific policy differentiation is recalled that would have made a "nickel's worth" of importance in choosing between the two parties.

In the summer of 1960, Nixon and Kennedy are named by their parties as the nominees, and the campaign for President intensifies. JFK has the glamour, the rhetoric, and the glowing press reviews. So, why isn't our budding lawyer swept up by the mystique; why is he still intending to vote for Nixon? No one can be absolutely sure about human motivations—even about one's own. The probability seems quite high that a major factor was what was identified by observers at that time (and which might have been a factor in Truman's shocking upset of Dewey in 1948—*and* which reoccurred with a vengeance in the 2016 election) as the "us/them" vote. For significant numbers of voters, the idea that Richard Nixon was "one of us" seemed important. He had struggled to achieve success, and many voters had similarly struggled during their lives—and were still struggling to maintain themselves and their families. Nixon understood our hardships in a way that JFK, Jackie, and the rest of "Camelot" never could, for all their shiny packaging.[8]

So, our man voted for the candidate whose biography paralleled his own (in many respects, at least). Both had tough childhoods. Both had to work their way through a college education. Both attended "elite," but not "Eastern-elite"—"Hahvahd" or "Yayle"—law schools. Nixon had settled for Duke—where he excelled. Our Nixon supporter had refused a Yale scholarship offer and opted instead for a leading Midwestern law school—where he had a very difficult first year. (After graduation, both would miss out on the "big-payoff" Wall-Street-law-firm jobs, and both would choose alternate "legal" careers.)

The likelihood of the "us/them" mindset as a significant factor in voters' decision-equations is enhanced when one considers the large variance in 1968 (and in 1972, for that matter) between the votes for Nixon and the votes for Republicans lower down on the ballot. He was "one of us"; by and large, that was not the perception many middle-class Americans had of the Republican Party. Despite its strong Midwestern roots, the Republican Party had become (or at least was perceived by many voters as having become) the party of the Eastern business establishment—bankers and managers, "the One Percent," and the Rockefellers and the Lodges.[9] Those Republican elitists were no more "one of us" than their counterparts in the Democrat Party—the media and film stars, the political and union bosses, and the left-leaning academics. All these "powers that be" were telling the rest of us how we should think and act and believe and were scoffing at our beliefs, opinions, and priorities (and still are). And further, that failure to think and act and behave as they prescribed somehow made us lesser human beings. The scope and depth of the anger and resentment that that attitude engenders are hard to describe, but it does seem to resonate politically.

So, when William F. Buckley, Jr., and his lesser-known but more profound co-worker Russell Kirk,[10] began the resuscitation of conservative philosophy, our nascent Nixon supporter immediately became an enthusiastic convert. We—the "lesser" humans, the outcasts—now had a clearly articulated belief system that validated our inner feelings and justified our political choices. Thus, when Nixon was "edged" out by JFK in the 1960 presidential race and was then humiliated in losing the 1962 California gubernatorial election, a new standard-bearer was needed. He emerged from the West. Arizona Senator Barry Goldwater would be the next President! (And there was at least a brief period when that perception seemed correct. Barry was able to beat back what seemed to be an endless series of "Stop-Goldwater" challengers in the Republican primaries and caucuses in 1964.)

Meanwhile, some of the JFK glow burned lower as domestic and international situations remained stubbornly resistant to a charm-and-press-blurb offensive. He had allowed the CIA-sponsored "invasion" of Cuba to proceed to its ignominious conclusion at the Bay of Pigs in April 1961. The charm-and-press-blurb approach was in full flower for his May/June visit to Paris—with Jackie. He followed that (PR) triumph with what was reported as a dismal performance in his two-day meeting with Soviet Premier Nikita Khrushchev in Vienna. One wonders how much impact Khrushchev's assessment of JFK's abilities had on the Soviets' decision to build the Berlin Wall some two months later.[11] In any event, they did build it—and there was not much of a response from the West. Again, one wonders how much that lack of any effective response contributed to Khrushchev's rather reckless decision to place offensive missiles in Cuba the next summer. Somehow, we managed to survive that most serious of all crisis, but the JFK foreign policy record was hardly outstanding.[12]

As the 1964 presidential-election year drew nearer, there were other potential problems clouding JFK's reelection bid. The truth about his health might leak out at any time. (He had reportedly received the "last rites" from a priest two or three times before Dallas.) His amorous adventures might have limited direct relevance to his qualifications to be President, but they nevertheless might be a serious negative for a number of voters. There were rumblings of a pending indictment of Vice President Johnson for various financial irregularities.[13] Texas Democrats were passionately divided, and JFK had barely won the State in 1960—or perhaps not won it at all, with an accurate vote-count. (Significant irregularities were also alleged in the 1960 vote counts from Mayor Daley's Chicago—enough to put Illinois in JFK's column, as well, and JFK won New York only by adding the votes he received as the candidate of the Liberal Party to those he got as the Democrat nominee.) Reportedly, a large part of the reason for President Kennedy's November 1963 trip to Texas was to mend some internal party fences in preparation for the 1964 election. He would need those electoral votes.

The November 22 Dallas assassination of JFK changed everything.[14] All bets were off. Whatever criticisms of JFK had been simmering beneath the surface now seemed unspeakable—almost treasonous. LBJ's pending legal difficulties burst like bubbles. He was the President!—for all intents and purposes, virtually indictment-proof. Massive waves of sympathy—for Jackie, Carolyn, John-John; for JFK's staff, administrators, and allies; and for JFK's Party and his program (whatever that was)—swept aside mere political differences for many voters. Poor Barry was overwhelmed by the emotion generated by the murder of JFK and the heart-rending images it produced: little John-John saluting as his father's coffin passed by, the bravery of Jackie, the burial ceremony, and the thousands upon thousands of sobbing citizens. How could we not vote for what was presumed to be a continuation of his policies and a certification of his legacy?[15] Barry Goldwater was portrayed as an extremist—one who might precipitate a nuclear holocaust at any time. (The point was made by inference in the vulgar TV commercial featuring a little girl with a flower being obliterated by an atomic explosion.) LBJ won by a large margin, and the Democrats had big majorities in both Houses of Congress.

LBJ was able to push the long-sought-after civil rights bill through Congress in 1964—a tremendous victory. And after his smashing election win that November, he followed the 1964 Civil Rights Act with another landmark statute: the Voting Rights Act of 1965. And he didn't stop there. In commencement speeches at two universities (Ohio University and the University of Michigan) in May 1964, Johnson made reference to building a "Great Society," including a goal of ensuring that every child received adequate nutrition and quality education. Several Acts had already been passed in 1964, and new programs had begun to deal with various economic and social problems.[16] The Democrats' legislative majorities were large enough to overcome the traditional reluctance to involve the national government directly in the education function. The Elementary and Secondary Education Act of 1965 did exactly that. It was followed in quick succession by the Higher Education Act of 1965, providing support for classrooms, libraries, technical institutes, research centers, and additional community colleges.[17]

Meanwhile, our budding Clarence Darrow-like[18] protagonist had graduated from law school in May 1961 and was studying for the state's bar examination—next scheduled for September. When no "regular" lawyer job turned up, he tried to enlist in the Air Force—Judge Advocate General Corps—but failed the physical (due to eyesight—again). Letters to several Midwestern universities, inquiring about a position teaching Political Science (with a B.A., LL.B., and all coursework for an M.A.), produced no offers. Through some now-forgotten circumstance, he happened to inquire—in person—at a nearby private business college. The response there was very positive—even enthusiastic. The main teaching subject, however, would be Business Law, with a section or two of Political Science. The regular class load was six fifty-minute classes per day, five days a week. Salaries ranged from $45 to $75 per class, per month, depending on credentials; our young Mr. Chips started at the $75 figure. The school was using a quarter-year schedule, so for a nine-month academic year, his salary was to be $4,050. (Extra income was available by teaching an additional class in the evening program or by teaching in the summer term.)

What sounds now like an impossibly heavy class load (five different preparations every day, five days a week, two sections of one class) is remembered as having gone quite well. The teaching of all those different legal topics was actually a great way to review for the bar exam. Having to respond—live—to student questions or admit that you don't know the answer but you'll try to find out turns out to be a strong mechanism for reinforcing what you do know and pointing out what you need to study further. And from a time standpoint, it's the "nth degree" of multi-tasking: earning your keep and reviewing for your coming exam at the same time.

It certainly helped to feel that we were all working for the same end, all on the same side. The administration and staff were very supportive, the faculty was a congenial group, and the students generally seemed appreciative of our efforts. It still seemed possible to discuss issues without vilifying each other. The main sentiment expressed in the faculty lounge during a 1961 critique on the Bay of Pigs, for example, seemed to be puzzlement at how things could have been fouled up so badly. It may have been the newcomer's lack of perception that missed subtle communications, but the remembered impressions of the college are quite positive.

After going through the classes the first time, there was also room for some research and writing, to finish the M.A. thesis. (It was accepted, and the M.A. was awarded in August 1962.) That same summer, the first class toward a Ph.D. in Political Science was taken—the start of a very long road through the 1960s and the Nixon years. (The degree was finally conferred in December 1975.)

Meanwhile, the "real world" outside our academic bubbles seemed more than a little schizophrenic. Domestically, after the excitement of the photo-finish 1960 presidential election, many of us seemed becalmed—satisfied to bask in the glow of Camelot (at least for a little while). For JFK & Co., however, the presidential "honeymoon" was incredibly brief. He had barely gotten moved into his new quarters when the Bay of Pigs debacle occurred in April 1961. The dust of that disaster had hardly settled when the busload of "Freedom Riders" arrived in Birmingham, Alabama, on May 14—to be greeted by mob violence. So, within four months of JFK's "bear any burden" inauguration speech, we had been treated to previews of two major "coming attractions": the major burdens of military misadventures and domestic violence. Each of these developments produced domestic divisions that neither political party nor any of the would-be national leaders seemed to be able to reconcile. Internationally, as noted above, the Cold War seemed headed toward a final Armageddon. Soviet Premier Khrushchev appeared determined to push a perceived advantage to the limit— building the Berlin Wall, putting missiles in Cuba, and pushing "liberation" movements.

Even as much of the world was recovering its equilibrium after the Soviets' Cuban gambit in 1962, another pair of what would be all-too-many US domestic "disturbances" broke out in 1963—in Birmingham, Alabama (May) and Cambridge, Maryland (June). In both cases, military units were called in to restore order. These two specific examples set a pattern that recurred throughout the decade. (Indeed, in a larger sense, it still continues—but now with one or two crazies killing batches of known or unknown persons—especially students.)

Then came November 22—"The Day The Music Died." JFK's assassination was, in a very real sense, the *coup de grace* of the entire decade. Even though over half the decade was still to come, the positive, hopeful spirit with which it had begun was badly deflated. "Camelot" was no more. LBJ tried his best—keeping on many JFK personnel and promising a "Great Society"—but it just wasn't the same. The magic was gone. The idea of greater national purposes and goals faded; "reality" set in; politics as usual began to reassert itself.

One possible response to the horror and tragedy of the murder might have been a re-newed determination and dedication to JFK's expressed visions and goals. But by and large, that did not seem to be a widespread reaction. Rather, the reverse: intensified social tensions. Each of the remaining years of the decade featured at least one reminder of the deep divi-sions that existed among us. Riots turned cities into war zones: (1964) Rochester and New York City; Chicago; Philadelphia; and Jersey City, Paterson, and Elizabeth, NJ; (1965) Los Angeles—"Watts" left 34 dead, some 1,000 injured, and +/– 4,000 arrested; (1966) Cleve-land, Chicago, and San Francisco; (1967) Detroit—"12th Street" produced 43 deaths, nearly 1,200 injured, and over 7,000 arrests. There were also recurring, specifically-targeted mur-ders of individuals—especially civil rights workers. In 1964, Michael Schwermer, Andrew Goodman, and James Chaney were killed, evidently by the KKK, and Viola Liuzzo was assassinated in 1965. And then, as noted earlier, election year 1968 saw the final curtains for Martin Luther King's pilgrimage and Robert Kennedy's quest for the presidency.

So, what was our budding academic doing while this madness and mayhem filled the TV screens and harmed so many people? In one sense, not very much—not nearly enough to try to solve the great problems of the day. A significant employment change occurred in 1963. Two friends teaching at the small business school were taking graduate work in the much larger state university in the same city, and they told our protagonist that a Business Law position might be available there. An interview produced a sort of "try-out" one-year ap-pointment as a "Visiting Lecturer." The Department of Business had been hiring local practi-tioners to teach part-time and had decided that it wanted to consolidate and coordinate its Business Law offerings with a full-time instructor. The timing was fortuitous since the De-partment quickly morphed into a new "College of Business" with five departments. (Thus, the "where were you when" memory of the JFK assassination in endnote 14 to this chapter.)

The next year (1964) saw the appointment changed to "Assistant Professor," followed by promotions to Associate Professor (1966), and finally Professor (1970). By 1969, all doctoral classwork had been completed; written preliminary examinations for the four sub-fields had been passed; and research and writing on the dissertation had been commenced. Much had also occurred on the personal side: a divorce (1962), a new marriage (1965), births of two children (son 1966, daughter 1969), and a house purchase (1967).

While there were life-changing personal and professional events during the 1960s, there are no memories of direct involvement in or contact with the strong currents and countercur-rents associated with that period. My closest connection to the issues during the 1960s was through my younger brother, who had enlisted in the Marines and was serving in Vietnam in the mid-60s. (I found it highly objectionable when one of my Ph.D. professors referred to our troops as "hired killers." Although only partially recalling the event, I don't think I protested that slur with sufficient vigor.) The Ypsilanti, Michigan schools where I was teaching were relatively quiet until 1970. There were protests and demonstrations in neighboring Ann Arbor during the 1960s, but I don't recall any serious violence and property destruction there until 1969. (The terrible riot in Detroit in 1967 did cause some concern in Ann Arbor; there was some speculation that the violence might spread to other nearby cities.)

Things finally did get a bit "hotter" in Ann Arbor in the summer of 1969. In what was clearly an intentionally violent and vicious act, a car bomb was set off outside North Hall on the main University of Michigan campus, where the university's Reserve Officers Training Corps program was located. (North Hall had originally been dedicated in 1900 for use as the U/M Homeopathic Medical College/Hospital. By 1940, with the homeopathic medical program having been terminated, the building was made available to the Navy's ROTC program, and it also housed the Army and Air Force programs in later years.) The explosion reportedly shattered some sixty windows in the building, started a fire, and did other physical damage. Fortunately, no one was physically injured—the bomb was detonated on a Sunday evening (June 1), with no classes in session. But that incident was the first act in a series of more ugly and threatening events that occurred over the following year and a half.

Barely two weeks after the bombing, what came to be known as "The Battle of Ann Arbor" was touched off by a police officer's attempt to ticket a motorcyclist who was doing "wheelies" on South University Street. ("South U" runs through a section of the main campus and then through a commercial district containing several student-patronized restaurants and bars.) Reports indicate that a crowd of about fifty "street people" gathered and began to argue with the officer; he called for assistance. When four police cars got there, the crowd had grown to almost 300—described as "increasingly hostile."[19] The police left without ticketing the cyclist, and the assembled citizens (now numbering 500 to 1,000) proceeded to barricade off a section of the street and celebrate—with drinking, dancing, fireworks, and motorcycle stunts. (Several newspapers, including the *Washington Post*, later reported that there had been at least one consensual sex act performed on the street.) There was almost no physical damage to property—only one or two broken windows and a few slogans painted on windows and parking signs. Perhaps the best indicator of this first night's activities is the fact that some of the young participants came back with brooms to sweep up the street after the party ended around 1 a.m. Reportedly, the city police took no action to suppress the "party" due to lack of manpower and/or because they felt any attempt to clear the street would have provoked a riot.[20]

The second night's "rerun" was a different story. Perhaps inspired by the prior month's efforts by radicals to commandeer a vacant lot in Berkeley, California, for a People's Park, the (Ann Arbor-based) White Panther Party issued a statement advocating the conversion of a section of South U into a pedestrian mall—a "people's park." Since some of the Monday night participants had indicated that they would hold another party there on Tuesday evening, word quickly spread that "big doings were on in Ann Arbor." About 200 city police and county sheriff's deputies also assembled, with officers from neighboring agencies on the way.

By 8 p.m., there were a thousand participants and observers in the street, dancing and blocking traffic, and the barricades had gone up again. The police ordered the crowd to clear the street and then advanced to do so when the order was ignored. The partiers responded with rocks, bricks, and bottles. Washtenaw County Sheriff Douglas Harvey had tear gas fired in response to the projectiles. After about an hour, South U was "cleared," with twenty-five people arrested for various offenses. The situation was relatively stable until a crowd of 800 or so gathered in front of the university president's house on South U. President Robben Fleming came out and attempted to mediate a peaceful resolution, but when an officer was hit by a thrown brick, the police and deputies again advanced to break up the crowd. As a result of the ensuing melee, another twenty-plus arrests were made.

After an on-campus rally of about 1,000 persons on Wednesday afternoon, at which there was (reportedly) a strong sentiment against the "South U pedestrian mall" idea, a free music concert was held that evening—attended by some 2,000 fans. South U was peaceful most of that evening, with some three hundred police in evidence, backed by an armored car and a hovering helicopter. When the police withdrew at about 11 p.m., however, a crowd began forming in the street, blocking traffic. Efforts by university faculty and local clergy to convince people to disperse were unsuccessful. Back came the police, who advanced from both east and west to clear the street. Some twenty more persons were arrested.

The "power elite" used a dramatically different approach on Thursday evening: "No Cops!" Although there were 175 officers on standby alert, the task of controlling pedestrian traffic and keeping South U open was assumed by faculty members and non-police city staff—and the White Panthers. It worked. A heavy rain around two o'clock washed out any thoughts of another late-night revel.

The university was back in session that September when disruptions of North Hall classes by protestors were reported on the 17th and the 19th, and a "sit-in" occurred on the 22nd/23rd. Two classes were also interrupted on October 15, the same day that several thousand U/M students and faculty celebrated the "national moratorium" against the Vietnam War.[21] And the violence continued into the winter semester of that academic year. "In February [1970], demonstrators broke into North Hall and did 'considerable damage' to breakable items."[22] There was another fire-bombing attempt on May 5, a "takeover" of the building on May 7, and a demonstration in front of the building on May 27. Rocks were thrown and windows were broken on June 23. (This "campaign" was apparently continued into the next school year: a Navy ROTC vehicle was fire-bombed on November 1, 1970.[23])

My own lack of personal involvement in the protest activities of the 60s was most assuredly not due to lack of opportunity. Living on the west side of Ann Arbor at the start of the decade, then for a few years on the east side, I was back west again for the last half—but never more than about two miles from the University of Michigan campus. And lots of headline-grabbing activity was occurring at "the U." As indicated in endnote 2 to this chapter, the decade in Ann Arbor began with the founding of the Students for a Democratic Society (SDS). (The SDS did not, however, fully endorse the political party using the same adjective, although at least some of that party's left-wing members were surely sympathetic to much of the SDS program.) Several SDS leaders and prominent members were U of M students, including Alan Haber, Sharon Jeffrey, Tom Hayden, Carl Oglesby, Bill Ayers, and Diana Oughton (who was killed in 1970 in a New York townhouse, with two of her Weathermen/terrorist co-conspirators, when the bomb they were making went off by mistake).

Deciding that the organization needed a clear statement of its concerns, criticisms, and program, the SDS leadership—at a December 1961 meeting in Ann Arbor—selected Tom Hayden to prepare a draft document for the membership's consideration. Having been the editor of U/M's student newspaper, the *Michigan Daily*, Hayden had graduated that year and was then living in New York. His draft was presented to the fifty-nine attendees at the SDS convention in June 1962, held in a United Auto Workers camp in Port Huron, Michigan—at the southern tip of Lake Huron, about an hour and a half of freeway driving northeast of Ann Arbor. (Reportedly, SDS was able to use the UAW facility because Sharon Jeffrey's mother was a UAW activist. In all fairness, it must be noted that there was considerable discussion in Hayden's draft of the need to improve the status of workers, along with some criticism of "Big Labor"—or at least parts of it.) While the adoption of the Port Huron manifesto was clearly an important moment in the growth of the SDS, I do not recall having any particular reaction to it at the time (or later, for that matter). Here again, I would have to have been aware of the event, but I must have thought it was of limited relevance to my life and work.

The assassination of our President was, of course, an event of an entirely different nature, with consequences for all of us—indeed, for the whole world. One man with a rifle profoundly changes history! How could it happen—here? Did he really act alone? Questions continue to be asked after six decades and several investigations. Somehow, life went on for the rest of 1963 and the rest of the decade. For most of us, it was a sadder life, and for many, an angrier life. An extremist wing—the Weathermen—broke away from SDS and set off a few bombs; in the end, most of the "Weathers" tried to return to more "normal" lives, even if they had to change their identities.[24] As noted earlier, the mid-60s were also characterized by a series of urban riots, many sparked by similar concerns but (evidently) not otherwise "connected."

Two years after the LBJ landslide, in the 1966 "off-year" (i.e., non-presidential) elections, politicking looked surprisingly normal at my university in Ypsilanti, Michigan. A crowd estimated at over 3,000 gathered that November to hear Senator Bobby Kennedy endorse Zolton Ferency for Governor and former Governor G. Mennen "Soapy" Williams for US Senator. The university's record of the occasion states that Bobby "was greeted by screams, cheers, and a few youthful squeals."[25] Earlier that Fall (September 27), Stokley Carmichael—chair of the Student Nonviolent Coordinating Committee—had spoken at the University of Michigan in Ann Arbor, but the brief historical note in the *University Record* of September 24, 2018, does not indicate the subject/s of his remarks.[26] (This book's author has no recollection of attending either of these events, nor of the "national moratorium against the war in Vietnam," in which "thousands of [U/M] students and faculty" participated on October 15, 1969—according to the *University Record* of October 14, 2019.)

Although out of office since 1960 and having lost two elections in a row, Richard Nixon was still a "big name" in the Republican Party. Michigan Congressman Gerald Ford had invited him to Grand Rapids to speak in support of Ford for reelection and of former Congressman Robert Griffin, who had been appointed by Governor George Romney to fill a vacant Senate seat and was running against Soapy Williams for a full six-year term. Since Romney was a potential candidate for the 1968 Republican presidential nomination, his welcome of Nixon to the State was not especially "warm."[27] In any event, Romney did not particularly need any help in his reelection campaign against Zolton Ferency. Gerry Ford was also a probable winner. Griffin and Williams, however, were in a tight race. It's, of course, hard to know all the conflicting motivations of the voters or the net positive or negative influences of Nixon's and Kennedy's endorsements of their respective candidates. The bottom line is that Nixon's man won—even though the other fellow had been praised by the inheritor of the JFK mystique! That must have been quite satisfying to Mr. Nixon as he thought about a possible rematch in 1968.

Whatever slight breath of "normalcy" may have characterized the 1966 elections, it was certainly overpowered in Michigan by the 1967 Detroit riot. We were still a long way from any solutions to our major societal problems—racism and Vietnam. Then came 1968, with LBJ's non-candidacy announcement and the assassinations of Dr. King and Bobby Kennedy.

Politically, as already discussed, the sadness and anger so many felt culminated in the mass demonstrations in Chicago, at the Democrat Party's 1968 national convention to nominate its candidates for President and Vice President. But even after that orgy of shouting, rock-throwing, tear-gassing, and clubbing, presidential campaigning was conducted—largely without violence. And, as also noted earlier, there were indications toward the end that many sad and/or angry Democrats might be "coming home" to their party. For all the liberal/left's convention disappointments, Humphrey did come within a whisker of winning the presidency.[28]

So, what conclusions, if any, can be drawn from this somewhat random, highly impressionistic review of "the Sixties"? It's clear that the nation President Nixon inherited was less optimistic, sadder, (perhaps) wiser, and more deeply divided than it had been in 1960. There was certainly hope for some sort of "fresh start," but, of course, nothing like the euphoria that had greeted JFK, Jackie, and "Camelot." Many of us who lived through those years remember rather "normal" lives—going to work, raising our kids, attending church, partying with friends and family, and paying our bills. We may have been inundated with negative "news" images, but they did not seem to dominate our lives or our feelings. Somehow, most of us managed to "muddle through." Many of us became part of Nixon's "great silent majority"—approving (or at least tolerating) the policies he was working out with the Democrat-controlled Congress and hoping that a degree of "normalcy" would be restored. We were certainly aware that our nation faced significant problems—at home and abroad—but hoped that they could be dealt with more rationally. We didn't need or want the "bread and circuses" approach to public policy. Given President Nixon's landslide reelection victory, a lot of us must have been satisfied with his performance. We may even have been impressed by the fact that he had gotten so much done, in so little time, facing so many problems, with so tenuous political resources. Some of us may also have felt that he deserved a chance to pursue further some of his un-achieved objectives (the guaranteed income, for example).

As of November 1972, of course, we were generally unaware of most of the negative actions that had already taken place or were still taking place. It was hard for a lot of us to believe the disclosures when they were made. We didn't want to believe them—to abandon "our" President. Even five decades later, while we may have some understanding of why he did what he did, it is still a reality that is difficult to accept.

Chapter 2

Legislating and Litigating in the United States

A S A PRELUDE to our discussion of the legislative record during the Nixon presidency, it seems necessary to explain—however briefly—both the place of statutes in the US legal system and the place of Congress in our constitutional framework. Since statutes are subject to review by the courts—as part of the enforcement mechanism—an overview of the litigation process also seems worthwhile.

A Common Law System

Even though it is not widely publicized or understood, the US has what is described as a "common law" legal system. As derived from the English system, the great body of our laws in the US is to be found in the rulings of appellate courts in actual cases that have been decided. General rules are created by examining what rules were used to decide specific disputes. The working assumption is that the dispute at issue today should be decided using the same rule as was used for the same sort of disputes in the past. This consistency thus provides a basis for determining what conduct is permissible and what is not—at least not without the possibility of court-imposed sanctions of some type.

Of course, the functioning of our system in the US is not nearly as neat and simple as the meager paragraph above might imply. Lawyers and judges often disagree about exactly what the "rule" was that a prior court used to decide its case. They may also disagree on which case is or cases are enough like the one to be decided to serve as examples ("precedents," in legal jargon). Or even if a prior case does seem to involve the same legal question, there may be other facts present that provide a basis for arguing that the present case (or the claimed precedent case, for that matter) should be treated as an exception to the general rule.

More rarely, a lawyer whose client's position is on the wrong side of the acknowledged legal rule may try to argue that the established rule should no longer be followed—that the precedent should be "overruled." Judges are replaced, and not all judges think the same way about all issues. Those truisms are, in fact, part of the rationale underlying the "doctrine of precedent." A case should not be decided based on the idiosyncrasies of an individual judge but rather on the basis of generally applicable and accepted rules. Decisions of individual judges are thus not considered to be "precedents"—but they may be persuasive examples.

There is a very strong working presumption that existing rules should be followed, and courts are generally quite reluctant to overturn precedents in most areas of the law. Especially on those topics where persons may have relied on courts' announcements as to what the law is and then planned their conduct accordingly, a court asked to overrule a precedent may expressly defer to the relevant legislative body. Justice Blackmun's majority opinion for the US Supreme Court in *Flood v. Kuhn*, 472 US 258 (1972), refusing to overturn the 1922 Supreme Court ruling that professional baseball is not part of "interstate commerce" and therefore cannot be regulated by Congress, is a classic example of this "buck-passing"—to Congress! Suggesting that Congress can solve the problem by amending the Sherman Antitrust Act is a bit nonsensical in this instance since Justice Holmes and a unanimous Supreme Court ruled in 1922 that the performances of major league baseball players did not constitute "commerce" within the meaning of the Constitution and therefore could not be regulated by Congress. If the Supreme Court is not willing to change its mind and overrule that 1922 decision, the only way to get a different result is to pass a constitutional amendment.[1] On the other hand, if all the Court said in 1922 was that Congress did not "intend" to cover baseball with the Sherman Act's provisions, even though it *was* "commerce," then Congress could indeed change the 1922 result by simply amending the Act so as to correct Justice Holmes's misperception.

Legislation

So, in our legal system in the US, the courts are primarily a provider of continuity, and legislatures are the vehicles for change. Courts cannot themselves initiate lawsuits; they must wait for a perceived problem to be brought to them. Legislatures, by contrast, generally have the power to investigate what they wish, report their findings, and then develop, debate, and enact legislation to deal with the problem as they think best. Moreover, they are not bound in any way by past practices and customs. They are free to experiment with new ideas and policies, limited only by the guarantees in the national Constitution and that of their State. Since they are elected, they are, of course, at risk of alienating voters and losing their positions if their "experiments" fail to work—or produce an unacceptable measure of "collateral damage." Constitutional provisions or legislative rules may require some kind of supermajority or other special procedure to enact certain fundamental changes. Amendments to the national Constitution, for instance, must be passed by a two-thirds majority in each House of

Congress and then ratified by three-fourths of the States.

The proposed Equal Rights Amendment (ERA) provides an instructive case-study of the process. First introduced in Congress in the 1920s, the ERA's guarantee of equal rights regardless of sex was opposed by many working women, who feared it would eliminate all the laws that protected them against oppressive working conditions. It languished for nearly fifty years, until Michigan Representative Martha Griffith reintroduced it in 1971. It was passed by the House and Senate by the required two-thirds majorities, and it was presented to the State legislatures for ratification.

Congress set a ratification deadline of March 22, 1979. Thirty-five of the required thirty-eight States had ratified by the end of 1977. But Idaho, Kentucky, Nebraska, and Tennessee voted to revoke their ratifications, before the 1979 deadline, and South Dakota had provided that its ratification would expire on the deadline date. Congress had passed, by a simple majority vote, and President Carter had signed, an extension of the deadline to June 30, 1982. Many were prepared to read "last *rites*" for the ERA. But pressed on by the new enthusiasm for "equality," Nevada ratified the ERA in 2017, Illinois in 2018, and Virginia in 2020, equaling . . . thirty-eight ratifications?! Has Lazarus been resurrected? Stay tuned! Can a State revoke its prior ratification of a proposed constitutional amendment? Can Congress extend a ratification deadline by a simple majority vote—rather than the constitutional two-thirds? Could Congress now retroactively rescind its ratification deadlines? These appear to be live issues.

Typically, the Act passed by the legislature does not become law unless signed by the executive—the President, for Acts of Congress; the State's Governor, for State legislation. If the executive is of a different political party than one or both of the legislative majorities, that can, of course, introduce a whole additional range of complications into the legislative process. A veto by the executive can be a death sentence for legislation that does not have overwhelming support since votes to override a veto typically take a supermajority (two-thirds of the votes, e.g.).

Both Congress and the State legislatures have been enthusiastic producers, enacting many pages of new national and State laws. (Our final chapter shows a disturbing trend to increase the number of pages produced under succeeding Presidents.) There has been a questionable increase in the federal criminalization of conduct. There has also been a long-term effort to legislate uniformity of commercial rules among the States (generally viewed as a positive development).

Perhaps even more disturbing, there has been increasing use of independent or semi-independent administrative agencies to regulate major economic and social sectors. Congress (with presidential approval) creates the agency, defines its mission, and gives it the power to adopt rules having the force of law. In theory, this is a logical response to the increasing complexity of modern society and the pace of change that is occurring. In practice, the continuing addition of hundreds—or thousands—of pages of regulations having the force of law raises serious questions of legitimacy and accountability.[2]

Constitutional Power to Legislate

Article I. Section 1 of the Constitution states the principle briefly and clearly: "All legislative Powers herein granted shall be vested in a Congress of the United States, which shall consist of a Senate and a House of Representatives." Notice that it says "*all*"! Neither the Courts nor the President is to have any *legislative* power—the power to *make* law. The President is given *executive* power by Article II. Section 1. [1]—the power to implement and enforce the law. The *judicial* power—the power to interpret the law and apply it to resolve specific disputes—is entrusted to a supreme Court and "such inferior Courts as the Congress may from time to time ordain and establish."

Section 8 of Article I consists of eighteen numbered subsections, listing the subjects on which Congress has the power to legislate. Heading the list in subsection [1] is the "Power to lay and collect Taxes, Duties, Imposts, and Excises. . . ." [2] authorizes Congress to borrow money. [3] provides the endlessly-litigated power "To regulate Commerce with foreign Nations, and among the several States, and with the Indian Tribes." [11] gives Congress—*not* the President—the power to declare war (hence, FDR's memorable request for a declaration of war after the surprise attack at Pearl Harbor on December 7, 1941). [12] says Congress can "raise and support arm*ies*," and [13] adds "provide and maintain *a* navy." Just in case they forgot to put something on the list, and to make sure Congress could provide for effective implementation of all the listed powers of the national government, the drafters of the Constitution included in subsection [18] the power "To make all Laws which shall be necessary and proper for carrying into Execution the foregoing Powers, and all other Powers vested by this Constitution in the Government of the United States, or in any Department or Officer thereof." (This "necessary and proper clause" has indeed been used to justify legislation that did not seem to be unambiguously covered by any language in the other seventeen subsections.)

Congress

At the risk of restating more already-known information, another brief review seems in order. The theory of the Constitution is that the Senate and the House of Representatives are co-equal bodies but are chosen to represent different constituencies. The Senators are chosen to represent the peoples of entire States—with all their diverse interests and characteristics. Representatives are mostly selected from geographically smaller, and therefore generally

17

more homogeneous, areas. Basic legislative equality between the House of Representatives and the Senate is shown by the fact that each of them must agree to the exact same language in order for a bill to become law. Neither has the power to override the other. Which body's views prevail if there is a disagreement depends on the relative size of the vote margins in each, the party alignments, the President's position, perceived popular support, and other such factors (including perhaps the persuasiveness of each side's negotiators). If the House and Senate cannot agree on the final language, the bill simply does not pass.

Recognizing the House's and Senate's fundamental equality in the lawmaking process does not, however, make them mirror-images of each other. Structural differences are stated in the Constitution, such as the qualifying age: twenty-five years old, for Representatives; thirty years old, for Senators. Senators are elected for six-year terms, with one-third elected every two years; all Representatives are elected every two years. Section 3 of Article I provided that Senators were to be chosen by the various State legislatures, but the ratification of the Seventeenth Amendment in 1913 provided for direct popular election. That surely lessened, but did not eliminate, the electoral differentiation between the two bodies.

An additional structural variant can be seen in the selection of the House's and Senate's presiding officers. The Representatives choose the "Speaker of the House" by majority vote. Section 3 of Article I states: "The Vice President of the United States shall be President of the Senate, but shall have no Vote unless they be equally divided." The Senate instead chooses a "President pro tem" to preside in the Vice President's absence. Of course, the vast difference in the numerical size of the two bodies necessitates differences in their procedural rules. Some liberalities and informal arrangements that are still possible with 100 members (in the Senate) would be impossibly difficult to allow with 435 (in the House of Representatives). The fourth paragraph of Section 2 of Article I originally allocated sixty-five House seats among the thirteen States—from Virginia's ten Representatives to one each for Delaware and Rhode Island. With the twenty-six Senators, there were thus fewer than 100 persons in the whole of Congress. We can hardly expect legislative business to be conducted at the same level of one-on-one personal interchanges among a body with nearly six times the combined membership. More detailed rules are necessary.

Moreover, there are even some significant distinctions in the legislative powers of the two Houses. Perhaps because of the original process of indirect selection of Senators by the States' legislatures, Section 7 of Article I provides that "All bills for the raising of Revenue shall originate in the House of Representatives, but the Senate may propose or concur on Amendments as with other Bills." (Since one of the major rallying cries of the Revolution had been "No taxation without representation!," the Constitution's drafters were careful to ensure that only the "People's House" could propose new or increased taxes.) But of course, the Senate still has to agree—exactly—with any revenue bill proposed by the House and can offer its own amendments.

Perhaps intended as a kind of balancing-off for the special revenue power given to the House, the Senate is given two extremely important powers in Section 2 of Article II (dealing with the President's authority). The Senate's "Advice and Consent" is required for appointments of Ambassadors, Supreme Court Justices, "and all Officers of the United States, whose Appointments are not otherwise provided for. . . ." While it may not have been fully appreciated in 1787, this check on presidential appointments has become a major role for the Senate—and a major factor in Senate elections.

A close reading of the Constitution appears to make the companion "Advice and Consent" role of the Senate—to ratify treaties made by the President, "provided two-thirds of the Senators present concur"—of at least equal importance. The importance of this function is derived from the second paragraph of Article VI: "This Constitution, and the laws of the United States which shall be made in Pursuance thereof, and all treaties made, or which shall be made, under the authority of the United States, shall be the supreme Law of the Land; and the Judges in every State shall be bound thereby, any Thing in the Constitution or Laws of any State to the contrary notwithstanding." Contrary to the foundation statement in Article I that *all* legislative power is vested in Congress, Article VI gives the President, with consent of two-thirds of the Senators "present," the power to create binding "supreme Law" for the United States by negotiating a treaty!

One could have argued that the Article I principle was still being observed since a treaty is not valid national law in the US unless two-thirds of the Senators "present" concur. That was certainly a strong argument until the Supreme Court decided a series of cases in the 1930s involving so-called "executive agreements." *United States v. Belmont*, 301 US 324 (1937), is a clear example of the Court's handiwork.[3]

The issue for the Court was dreadfully simple: Were agreements that the President reached with foreign leaders but did not submit to the Senate for ratification as a treaty also part of the "supreme Law of the Land"? Perhaps wishing to avoid the terrible fate of President Woodrow Wilson and his prized Versailles Treaty, FDR had not submitted his 1933 "Litvinov Agreement" (a claims settlement with the USSR) to the Senate. The US government sued in US District Court in New York to collect one of the claims that had been transferred to it by the Soviet Government. That Soviet claim was based on the USSR's nationalization of the assets of the Petrograd Metal Works, a Russian company that also had assets held by Belmont's bank in New York. Since the uncompensated taking of private property would violate the Constitutions of both New York and the United States, the District Court held that the claim was invalid and dismissed the case. The US Second Circuit Court of Appeals affirmed, and the US Government appealed.

Justice Sutherland's opinion for the Court focused on the fact that the national government had exclusive powers to conduct the country's foreign relations and that States' conflicting policies had to give way. As a general proposition, that is, of course, correct. But that is not the precise point at issue here. The question is whether the President—acting alone, without the Senate's confirmation—has the power to create "supreme Law" *inside* the United States. Article VI makes *treaties* "supreme Law," and Article II conditions the President's power to make *treaties* on their confirmation by two-thirds of the Senate. "Treaty" is the term specifically used in the Constitution, and the President's power to negotiate them is specifically limited. The term is presumably intended to mean the same thing in both Articles. Neither adds a phrase such as "and other international agreements."

That may seem to be too fine a legal point for Justice Sutherland[4] and the Court, but it is, in fact, precisely the difference that we thought existed between the two parties to the agreement under litigation in this case. When "good old Uncle Joe" Stalin said "Jump!," everyone in the USSR said "How high, Your Greatness?"—if they wished to go on living.[5] Stalin did indeed have the power to "make Law" in the USSR—all by himself. FDR did not—or at least that is what the US Constitution literally said—in Article I, Article II, and Article VI.

FDR acknowledged as much when he made that tremendous physical effort to come to Congress on December 8, 1941, and personally deliver his stirring *request* for a declaration of war. He did not do the declaring; he asked Congress to do it—as specified in the Constitution! The decision to go to war is surely the ultimate "international relations" decision, and as Justice Sutherland tells us, the "national government" has exclusive power to conduct such business. Yet that does not necessarily mean that the President *alone* has the exclusive power to conduct such business. He and "Uncle Joe" (or "Winnie" or "Chiang") can make whatever arrangements they like, but that does not necessarily mean that the provisions of their executive agreements automatically become "supreme Law" *within* the United States. The President is constitutionally the commander-in-chief of our armed forces, but FDR also had to ask Congress for the funds to pay, train, and equip the armed forces, or he had nothing to command.

Belmont was one of the last bequests of the Court of the "Nine Old Men" that had plagued FDR and which he was about to (almost) completely restaff. In fact, he started the process later in that same year, 1937, by replacing Justice Van Devanter with Hugo Black. Justice George Sutherland (our *Belmont* author) and Justice Cardozo were succeeded in 1938 by Justices Reed and Frankfurter. Two more left in 1939: Brandeis and Butler, replaced by Douglas and Murphy. It is, of course, impossible to say with certainty that the result would have been different if the *Belmont* case had been delayed two or three years, but that certainly seems possible. It's difficult to believe that the blatant violation of the bedrock principle of legislative exclusivity in Article I would have escaped a painstaking constitutional analysis by Justice Frankfurter and the "liberal" predilections of Justices Black and Douglas. Whatever might have been "if," we have, in fact, been forced to deal with the *Belmont* principle.

And there is yet another similar breach of Article I's exclusivity rule. Section 2 of Article II gives the President, with the consent of two-thirds of the Senators "present," the power to make "supreme Law" within the United States by negotiating a treaty. Suppose it later becomes better policy to terminate the negotiated—*and ratified by the Senate*—treaty? Who has the authority to do that, and by what process? It's worth noting here that amending the Constitution also requires a special procedure, with supermajorities: proposal by two-thirds of each House of Congress and ratification by two-thirds of the States. When it came time to change our "prohibition" policy established by the Eighteenth Amendment, we adopted the Twenty-First Amendment to do so. By analogy—and simple logic—it would seem that a decision to undo the adoption of a policy that required Senate ratification to establish would also require Senate ratification.

Unfortunately, for both logic and constitutional consistency, that was not the decision reached in (Senator Barry) *Goldwater v.* (President Jimmy) *Carter*, 617 F.2d 697 (DC Cir. 1979); 444 US 996 (1979). Senator Goldwater and others challenged the legality of President Carter's unilateral decision to terminate the 1954 Mutual Defense Treaty with the "Republic of China" (ROC). The ROC was Chiang Kai-shek's Nationalist Government of China that had retreated to the island of Taiwan in 1949, after having been defeated by the Chinese Communists in the Chinese civil war. The United States had been generally supportive of Chiang's efforts to unify a badly fractured Chinese nation, but the relationship was extremely complicated. Chiang had been fighting the Japanese since 1931, when Japanese troops staged a fake "incident" at Mukden as a pretext for invading Manchuria. Meanwhile, Mao Tse-tung and the Chinese Communists, with Soviet Russia's support, had been conducting a civil war against Chiang's Nationalist Government. Chiang and the Nationalists fought virtually alone against the powerful Japanese invaders for ten years—until Pearl Harbor and Japanese aggressions against colonial holdings in Asia forced the US and the European colonials into the Asian half of the Second World War.

As the tide gradually turned in favor of the Western Allies—against Japan—greater western support came to the Nationalists. But Chiang's insistence on maintaining Chinese commanders for his troops alienated some US generals, in much the same way as US General Pershing's similar stubbornness had peeved the British and French generals in World War I. The official policy of recognizing Chiang as a member of the "Big Four" Allies was seriously undermined by the China "experts" in the US Government agencies and the media. High-level US support for Chiang's Government was frustrated by lower-ranking Communist sympathizers. Chiang was denied effective military, diplomatic, and moral support by the US. Mao's forces received significant deliveries of weapons and supplies taken from the defeated Japanese troops in northern China by the (late-arriving) Russians. Momentum shifted sharply in favor of the "Reds."[6]

The results were to be expected. Mao's Communists won the long-standing civil war in 1949 and established the People's Republic of China (Chiang and his surviving supporters having retreated to Taiwan). With Chinese and Russian support, North Korea invaded South Korea in June 1950. Not waiting for a declaration of war by Congress, but calling his commitment of US military units a "police action," President Truman stretched his powers as commander-in-chief to the limit—perhaps beyond. After the UN condemned the North Korean aggression, its "UN forces" (primarily US troops, weapons, and supplies) forced the North Koreans back near their border with Communist China. Massive Chinese forces then entered the conflict and drove the UN troops south again. A stalemate eventually developed, close to the original dividing line of the thirty-eighth parallel, and a truce agreement was signed in July 1953. Thus, the logic behind the 1954 treaty with the Nationalist Chinese on Taiwan—and similar pacts with other nations in Southeast Asia, and a "democratized" Japan.

By 1972, President Nixon and his close foreign policy collaborator Henry Kissinger had decided that it would be in the US' interest to enter into a rapprochement with Red China, playing the one competing communist giant against the other (the USSR). With its supply of nuclear missiles, the latter was viewed as the chief threat to the US. Anything that lessened its relative power—or even diverted its attention from us—was viewed as an advantage to us. Hence, the world-changing Nixon trip to China. Part of this Asian détente was our "acceptance" of the UN's decision to recognize Mao's China as the holder of "China's" seat in the UN Security Council and General Assembly. Mao's claim to Taiwan was also implicitly recognized, in that each of the "two Chinas" claimed to represent both the mainland and Taiwan. Mao insisted that full mutual diplomatic recognition could not occur until the US terminated the 1954 treaty and other agreements with the ROC.

In September 1978, President Carter signed the International Security Assistance Act, Section 26 of which stated: "It is the sense of the Congress that there should be prior consultation between the Congress and the executive branch on any proposed policy changes affecting the continuation in force of the Mutual Defense Treaty of 1954." Nonetheless, three months later, he announced that the US would withdraw recognition of the ROC as the "Government of China," in favor of Mao's "People's Republic of China"—and that the US would terminate the 1954 Mutual Defense Treaty. The State Department gave the required one-year notice of termination to the ROC on December 23, 1978, with termination as of January 1, 1980.

Senator Goldwater and the other plaintiffs had already filed their lawsuit in US District Court on December 22, 1978, asking for an injunction to prevent the termination of the Treaty without Senatorial or Congressional consent. The lawsuit was dismissed on June 6,

1979, with the court noting that three resolutions—any one of which might resolve the problem—were pending in the Senate. Within hours, the Senate amended one of them, by a vote of 59 to 35, to read: "It is the sense of the Senate that approval of the United States Senate is required to terminate any mutual defense between the United States and another nation." Unable to agree on whether the amended resolution would apply retroactively or only prospectively, the Senators did not pass it, so the Majority Leader put it back on the Senate's calendar. But the plaintiffs, using the vote on the amendment as evidence of an existing controversy, got the court to reinstate their case. After ruling that the case was not a "political question" beyond the jurisdiction of the judiciary, the District Court issued a summary judgment for the plaintiffs. President Carter appealed to the DC Circuit.

A three-judge panel of the DC Circuit affirmed the District Court decision, and Jimmy appealed for review by the full DC Circuit Court (an "*en banc*" review—by all eight judges). All eight did hear oral arguments on November 13, 1979, and participated in subsequent discussions, but Judge Harold Leventhal died of a heart attack on November 20.[7] The court's "*per curiam*" opinion (no specific judge being identified as the author) thus represented only seven judges. The seven did agree that the case presented a constitutional question that they had the power to decide, rather than just a "political" question for the other two branches of the national government. The decision to terminate the treaty was certainly a political one, but the issue in the case was not specifically that decision but rather which of the political branches had the power to make it. But Chief Judge Wright and Judge Tamm felt that the plaintiffs did not have "standing" to bring the lawsuit and voted to reverse the District Court on that basis alone. Goldwater and associates may have been personally offended by Carter's treaty cancellation, but Carter was not defying Congress in doing so—since Congress had not taken specific action to challenge his decision. The plaintiffs had therefore suffered no special personal injury distinct from any US citizen who did not agree with Carter's decision.

The other five judges felt that there was a sufficient direct controversy to justify the lawsuit and that they therefore could and should decide the merits of the case. Four of them ruled that the President had the authority to exercise the cancellation option that the treaty provided for each party. Since there was no explicit constitutional provision on the cancellation of treaties and since the President had been given general executive power, he was impliedly authorized to cancel (at least if Congress had made no contrary decision). Judge MacKinnon dissented, issuing a lengthy review of relevant precedents and historical examples. His major point was a powerful one: Since the Constitution makes a treaty part of the "Law of the Land," it can only be amended or repealed "in the same manner as any other 'law' by a formal act of Congress approved by the President." The plaintiffs requested Supreme Court review.

All nine Justices agreed to the grant of "*certiorari*" (the requested review), but the Court then summarily vacated the judgment of the DC Circuit Court—and remanded the case to it, with instructions to dismiss the complaint. The "opinion" consisted of a scattering of brief notes from the various Justices. "Mr. Justice Marshall concurs in the result." Justice Powell filed a two-page concurrence echoing the DC majority: "If the Congress chooses not to confront the President, it is not our task to do so." Joined by Justices Stewart, Stevens, and White, Chief Justice Rehnquist's page-and-a-half contribution expressed the belief that the case did, in fact, present a "nonjusticiable" political question and thus should be dismissed for that reason. Justice Blackmun's single paragraph stated that he would have heard the parties' arguments and decided the case on the merits; Justice White agreed with him. Justice Brennan took three paragraphs to express his dissent; he would simply have affirmed the DC Appeals Court's decision on the merits.

The mishmash of judicial views at both levels of appeal, and the ultimate non-decision of the important constitutional question, certainly do a disservice to the rule of law. President Carter clearly won this round since his cancellation of the treaty was not prevented by the courts. But it is by no means clear that there is a solid precedent for that result in a future replay of the issue. And, in terms of the bottom-line finale, what seems to be the prevailing sentiment at both levels is that the President can not only make the "Law of the Land" by negotiating unratified treaties and international agreements, he can also "un-make" laws by canceling them without any action by Congress. Both powers seem blatantly violative of Article I's express statement of exclusivity. Thankfully, subsequent Supreme Court decisions have substantially limited the worst implications of the *Belmont/Goldwater* rulings.[8]

Congressional Procedure

Since we are concerned here with the output of Congress during the Nixon presidency, we focus here on those procedures, without also examining the variances that may exist in the State legislatures. (The most obvious and widely-known difference is, of course, the unicameral [one-House] legislature of Nebraska, which greatly simplifies the process.) Allowing for the rather considerable differences among the fifty States—geographical, historical, economic, and cultural—the basics of their separate legislative practices would probably not seem all that different to a legislator from another State. (Louisiana might seem a bit stranger, due to its reliance on the Civil Code of France—the "Code Napoleon"—adopted when Louisiana was still a French colony, before President Jefferson bought it and added it to the US.)

The legislative procedures for the House of Representatives and the Senate are quite detailed and complex. What follows is a brief overview, based primarily on *How Our Laws Are Made* (House Document 110-49), as updated and revised by John V. Sullivan (the House Parliamentarian), July 2007. Although it is a "House Document," issued by their officer, it does also include six pages (of some twenty-one text pages) discussing Senate procedures. (Sullivan notes that there is considerable overlap in the two sets of rules.) Several specific examples—some rather lengthy and involving litigation—have been included to illustrate both the importance of the rules and the significance of the courts as the final decider of what they mean in actual situations.

Proposals for Legislation

Individual members may themselves propose bills to deal with problems they perceive. Their constituents—or professionals hired by some of their constituents ("lobbyists")—may prompt them to do so. Proposals may come from the President, especially in the annual "State of the Union" message, or from one of the Cabinet members (tax changes from the Secretary of the Treasury, for example), or from the head of an agency (such as added pollution limitations requested by the Chairman of the Environmental Protection Agency). A State may pass a resolution asking Congress for legislation. The various House and Senate committees may conduct studies of perceived problems and recommend legislation.

Introduction of a Bill

Whatever the source of the idea, the proposal must be stated in appropriate legislative form. The House and the Senate each have a "Legislative Counsel" to assist with the drafting of bills. The sponsoring member or members must sign the bill. It is officially submitted in the House by being placed in the "hopper"—a container at the side of the Clerk's desk. Senators usually introduce their bills by giving them to a clerk at the presiding officer's desk, but they may also introduce them from the floor.

Most proposals are submitted in the form of a "bill" captioned with "For the establishment . . . (whatever)" or "Be it enacted . . . (whatever)." The "joint resolution" is an alternate form, with slightly different introductory headings: "Authorizing . . ." or "Resolved by . . ." The official House document *How Our Laws Are Made* indicates that there is little substantive difference between these two forms, except that a joint resolution proposing a constitutional amendment is not sent to the President but to the US Archivist—for transmission to the States.

"Concurrent resolutions" are merely expressions of opinion, purposes, principles, or facts believed by the House and Senate members. "Simple resolutions" from either House concern the operations and rules, or the opinions of only one of the two parts. Neither has any legislative effect as "the Law."

Referral to Committee

In nearly all cases, the most intensive and detailed consideration of the proposed bill occurs at the committee level. The Speaker of the House may refer the bill to several of the twenty Standing Committees of the House if it contains subject-matter within their areas of authority, but s/he must designate one of them as the primary committee. The committee/s will usually request input from the federal agencies whose regulatory jurisdictions concern the topics to be affected by the bill. They may likewise ask the Government Accountability Office for an advisory report on the need for the bill. The rules of many committees require assignment of the bill to an appropriate subcommittee for initial study, unless the full committee votes to retain it. If the bill is sent to a subcommittee, most of the review and study will be done at that level.

If the bill is thought to be sufficiently important, the committee (or subcommittee) may schedule public hearings—to provide an opportunity for public input. One week's public notice of the time and place for the hearing must be given, unless the committee chair and its ranking member of the minority party otherwise agree or a majority of the committee votes for an earlier date. Committees also have the power to force persons to provide testimony and documents relevant to their investigations—by issuing subpoenas. A majority of the members present at a meeting of the committee or subcommittee can authorize the issuance of a subpoena, which must be signed by the chair or by a designated member. Minority party members also have the right to call witnesses to testify. Recognized evidentiary privileges apply to witnesses in these proceedings (self-incrimination, attorney-client, and the like).

The saga of the Senate's McClellan Committee provides us with a classic example of the committee investigative power. Chartered in January 1957 as the "United States Senate Select Committee on Improper Activities in Labor and Management," it was a major player in DC until it was terminated on March 31, 1960. Its body of work included a reported 253 investigations, some 8,000 subpoenas ordering testimony or documents, 270 days' worth of hearings, and 1,526 witnesses—providing testimony totaling almost 150,000 pages. (343 of the witnesses reportedly claimed the constitutional Fifth Amendment privilege against having to make self-incriminating statements.) As the committee's activity peaked in 1958, it employed over 100 persons.

The Democrats regained control of the Senate in the 1954 elections, and Arkansas Senator John McClellan became chair of the Committee on Government Operations and its Permanent Subcommittee on Investigations. Bobby Kennedy, the younger brother of Massachusetts' junior Senator John F. Kennedy (JFK), became the Committee's chief counsel. A struggle for the leadership of the very powerful Teamsters Union had been ongoing since the mid-1950s, between its president Dave Beck and midwestern rival Jimmy Hoffa.

Rumors and charges of falsified local unions, financial irregularities, and mobster influence brought on investigations by the Justice Department and the Committee on Government Operations (CGO).

Beck and other Teamsters objected to the CGO's activities, claiming that the Labor and Public Welfare Committee (the LPWC, chaired by JFK) had been given authority over union activities. To meet that claim, the Senate created the "Select" Committee with half CGO Senators and half LPWC, and half Democrats and half Republicans—but with McClellan as chair rather than JFK from the LPWC. As it turned out, though, five of the eight Senators did not view unions favorably. And when McClellan named Bobby Kennedy as the Select Committee's chief counsel and investigator, the die was cast for a bitter struggle with the Teamster's leadership.

Bobby subpoenaed Beck in 1957 for examination about $332,000 in missing Teamster funds, and Beck asserted his Fifth Amendment privilege 117 times. He did not run for reelection as Teamster president in 1957. He was convicted in 1959 by the state of Washington for embezzling $1,900 derived from the sale of a union-owned Cadillac and convicted by the IRS for income tax evasion. He served thirty months of a (reduced) three-year sentence in state prison, was paroled, and was then pardoned by the state governor. President Gerald Ford also pardoned him for the tax violations. Some twenty other persons were also convicted as the result of the Select Committee's disclosures concerning the Teamsters, other unions,[9] and various corporations.

Continuing investigation of Hoffa and the Teamsters produced further evidence of mob connections and corruption, and it led to the union's expulsion from the AFL-CIO in December 1957. McClellan asked for and received from the Senate a one-year extension for his committee in January 1958. At the insistence of several Republican Senators, the Select Committee turned its attention to the United Auto Workers (UAW) but found no irregularities in the UAW's finances or administration. An interim committee report, highly critical of Hoffa and the Teamsters, was issued in March 1958, and a few follow-up hearings were held in August.

After receiving still one more year's authorization, McClellan spent most of 1959 investigating organized crime. But a second report, in August 1959, was basically a rehash of the Hoffa/Teamster charges. Bobby Kennedy resigned from the committee staff in September 1959 to become his brother's campaign manager in JFK's successful bid for the US presidency. Still a free man—and Teamster president—when the Select Committee disbanded in 1960,[10] Hoffa was eventually convicted of jury-tampering (in March 1964) and then of conspiracy and mail and wire fraud (in July 1964). After spending nearly five years in prison, he was released in December 1971, after an agreement was reached for a commutation of his sentence. He had resigned as union president on June 19, 1971. Hoffa disappeared from the Detroit area on or about July 30, 1975. Legend has it that "the mob" disposed of him.

The bottom line for our purposes here is that the tremendous expenditure of time, effort, and funds summarized above did not go for naught. Documentation of the abuses and irregularities in the administration of unions and the tremendous funds they were accumulating provided the basis for congressional action. A Senate bill was introduced in 1958, but it did not pass. Reintroduced by JFK in 1959, it was amended at Republican insistence to include a management "bill of rights" as well.

The Eisenhower administration sponsored its own bill, introduced in the House by Phillip Landrum of Georgia and Robert Griffin of Michigan. The Landrum-Griffin Bill contained stronger financial reporting and fiduciary restrictions on unions as well as additional limitations on union tactics. It was passed by the House on August 13, 1959: 95 Democrats joined 134 Republicans to do the job. In opposition were 17 Republicans, 183 Democrats, and one independent. Voting "present" were four Democrats and two Republicans. The two bills were sent to a conference committee, which came up with a product that was largely Landrum-Griffin content. That version was accepted by the Senate on September 3 by a vote of 95 to 2, with three Senators not voting. The House approved the next day, 352 to 52, with one voting "present" and 30 not voting. President Eisenhower signed the Labor Management Reporting and Disclosure Act of 1959 on September 14. The crusaders had actually found (or rather, produced) a grail.

Passage by the House of Representatives

Our historical example above has the Senate acting on the proposed legislation first. The procedure is essentially the same whichever House acts first. However, as noted above, section 7 of Article I of the Constitution states that "All bills for raising Revenue shall originate in the House of Representatives," so the sequence of action is established for those items. (We have likewise used that sequence for our brief discussion here.)

The staff of the committee reporting the bill for action files a report indicating the scope and purpose of the bill and the reasons why it is recommended for approval as well as its "general goals and objectives." Any new budget authority it provides must be stated as well as a cost estimate from the Congressional Budget Office director. Also required are the constitutional sections authorizing Congress to enact the measure and the committee's estimate of the cost to implement the bill in the current year and the next five years.

The reported bill is placed on one of the four House calendars for business. The "Union" calendar (for "the Committee of the Whole House on the State of the Union") is used for bills raising revenue, appropriating funds, authorizing expenditure from prior appropriations, or disposing of property. Meeting as the "Committee of the Whole" allows business to be done with a quorum of 100 members present, rather than a majority of the whole House—

218. The House Committee on Rules, with jurisdiction over the order of business in the House, reports a "rule" providing for consideration of the bill by the Committee of the Whole. When the House adopts that rule, the Speaker can then announce that the House is so operating, appoint a Committee Chair to preside, and turn the assembly over to that member.

The "House" calendar lists all non-financial public bills and resolutions. The "Private" calendar is taken up on the first and third Tuesdays each month, for such matters as individualized financial claims against the Government or immigration/naturalization claims. If any two House members object to consideration of one of these Private bills, the bill is referred back to the reporting committee. Each of the two parties appoints three members as official "objectors" to ensure that no improper measures pass through this way. A special "Calendar of Motions to Discharge Committees" exists to schedule such actions when thought necessary. (This procedure allows a majority of the House to call up a bill for debate and action after it has been under committee discussion for a minimal period and not been reported to the House for action, preventing legislation that may be disfavored only by a majority of members of that particular committee.)

Bills are not necessarily taken up for action in the sequence in which they were placed on the calendar. There are special procedures for taking up bills felt to require priority. The Rules Committee can propose a "rule" providing for special procedural handling. For example, there might be a provision limiting or prohibiting amendments to the bill—a "modified closed rule" or "closed rule." A two-thirds vote is required to consider a bill on the same day it is reported by its committee. Usually, the bill stays on the calendar for at least one legislative day. If it is not called up for House action within seven days by the member who reported it, any member of the Rules Committee may do so after giving one day's notice.

In contrast to the Senate, discussion of a bill continues only so long as a majority of the House wishes. When the Rules Committee issues a "rule" authorizing consideration of a bill, it usually also indicates the maximum length of the discussion. The House adopts the general procedures for its debates at the beginning of each numbered two-year Congress. The House also recognizes the set of procedures Thomas Jefferson adopted as President of the Senate from 1797 to 1801. The leaders of the two parties generally agree on the schedule for the speakers for and against the bill.

After the general debate on the bill, there is a "second reading"—section by section—at which time amendments to the various sections may be offered. If the House has voted for an "open rule" for the discussion of the bill, the member proposing the amendment is given five minutes to explain the proposal, and then the first member recognized by the chair is given five minutes to explain why it should not be adopted. Members may also offer amendments to the initial amendment, with the five-minute each pro and con discussion. Each proposed change is voted on by the "Committee of the Whole," unless the House has provided a special rule that certain amendments will be automatically adopted. By unanimous consent, the House can change the open rule by adopting an agreed list of amendments—for example, a lengthy list of pluses or minuses to a general appropriation bill for a major department or agency. At any time, a majority of the Committee of the Whole can decide to close debate on an amendment or the section or the paragraph of the bill being discussed. If that happens, however, the member who has provided for advance publication in the *Congressional Record* of a proposed amendment to that section or paragraph must be given the required five minutes to explain it, and an opposing member an equal five minutes to present the negatives.

When this discussion ends, the Committee of the Whole "rises" (reverts back to its status as the House, with the Speaker resuming the chair), "reporting to the House" the bill with any adopted amendments. If a rising occurs before the amendment discussion is completed, the bill will have to be returned to the Committee of the Whole at a later date. Thus, a motion to rise, if passed, postpones final action on the bill by the Committee of the Whole, just as a motion to adjourn—if passed—would postpone consideration of a bill being considered by the House.

Having been reported back to the House for further consideration, debate on the bill can be ended at any time by a majority vote of the members present (assuming there is a quorum). A member moves "the previous question," and if a majority agrees, the Speaker calls for an immediate vote. The bill is read, and the House then votes to pass it or reject it. (The Speaker does have the option of postponing the final vote for up to two legislative days.)

Even after "the previous question" has been ordered, the Speaker can recognize one member (giving preference to a minority party member opposed to the bill) to offer a motion to recommit the bill to a committee. That motion is not debatable, unless it is a motion to recommit with instructions to the committee, which requires a ten-minute debate. And in that case, the majority floor leader can demand a one-hour debate.

Measures that do not have to proceed through the Committee-of-the-Whole procedure are subject to whatever time limitations are provided by the Rules Committee in its "rule" allowing discussion. Lacking such specifications, the "hour rule" applies: no member may "occupy" more than sixty minutes in the debate on a particular measure. The Speaker also can rule that a motion is out of order as "dilatory." After a bill has been adopted, a motion to reconsider is made and then "laid on the table" (i.e., postponed) by unanimous consent, to prevent a similar motion from being made in the future, when there might be a different majority. (A House vote to adopt is not considered final until there is an opportunity to reconsider it.)

Votes are taken by various procedures. In a voice vote, the Speaker determines whether the "Aye" or the "No" responses are the loudest. If that decision seems difficult, either a member may demand or the Speaker may decide to use a "division" (a count of the standing proponents versus the standing opponents). If any member requests and is supported by at least one-fifth of a quorum of the House (forty-four members)—or twenty-five members of the Committee of the Whole—electronic voting is used. The Constitution requires the support of one-fifth of the House members for a roll-call vote ("the yeas and the nays"), and the roll-call procedure is also used for quorum determinations. Time limits are set for the counting of electronic votes. No one but the member can cast that member's vote.

Each of the two bodies has an "Enrolling Clerk," whose function is to prepare an official copy of the bill as passed—with all amendments. This final copy (on blue paper) is then given to the Clerk of the House, for signature and transmission to the Senate.

Action by the Senate

Acting on behalf of the Vice President (the "President of the Senate"), the Senate Parliamentarian refers the House bill to one of the sixteen standing Senate committees. Copies are immediately printed and made available in the document rooms of both bodies. The committee studies the bill, holds hearings as felt necessary, and issues its report to the Senate. If the report is favorable, there may or may not be recommended amendments. If there are such, added language is shown in italics, and deleted language is lined through. There may also be one or more committee members who disagree and file a minority report.

According to the official House document *How Our Laws Are Made*, "The Senate relies heavily on the practice of obtaining unanimous consent for actions to be taken." So, for example, the Majority Leader may ask for unanimous consent to immediately consider a committee-reported bill, and non-controversial measures can be taken up and passed with minimal debate. Such agreements often include limits on debate time and possible amendments.

If unanimous consent cannot be obtained, the bill must be placed on the appropriate calendar for one "legislative day." (There are two Senate calendars—the Executive Calendar, for treaties and nominations referred by the President, and the Calendar of Business, for legislation.) A "legislative day" is not the same as the normal twenty-four-hour period but rather means the time from one adjournment of the Senate until the next one. It may thus extend for several weeks—or months. When it is in session, the Senate does not normally "adjourn" at the end of each working day but rather "recesses" until it comes back to conduct business again. Modern practice is to obtain unanimous consent for waiver of a call of the calendar at the start of a new legislative day. If the calendar is called, bills are taken up for discussion in the order they appear on the calendar, with each Senator allowed to speak only once—for five minutes—on each bill considered.

When the Senate has adjourned, the first two hours of the following new legislative day are called the "morning hour." (Senate Rule XXX sets the start of each session day at noon, unless otherwise noted.) "Morning business" is a reserved period within those two hours to deal with the items specified in Rule VII: receiving various communications from the President, executive departments, and the House—to the Senate or its committees; filing committee reports; introducing bills; submitting resolutions; and receiving petitions. In fact, the Senate handles such matters as they come up in any session day—and also sets the new legislative day's schedule—by unanimous consent.

After the close of morning business on any day except a Monday that begins a new legislative day, any Senator can move to consider any bill on the calendar out of its regular sequence. (This option is usually exercised by the Majority Leader.) The five-minute limits do not apply to bills taken up in this manner. Debate continues until the Presiding Officer closes business for that day. If debate has not finished, the bill goes back on the calendar and can be called up again for further discussion and action.

A bill that has been passed over can be called up by the Majority Leader, after consulting with the Minority Leader. If made after the morning hour, the motion is debatable. A Senator who is recognized by the Presiding Officer may speak as long as s/he wishes and—unless there has been a unanimous consent agreement limiting the length of the debate—loses the floor only by yielding it or by taking some action regarded as forfeiting it. A Senator may not speak twice on the same question in the same day without consent of the Senate. Debate ends when a Senator yields the floor and no other Senator seeks to be recognized to speak or when any agreed time limit expires.

The Senate has a long history of permitting unlimited debate on issues. Its original rules permitted a majority to end debate by passing a motion to call the "previous question"—to end debate and vote immediately on the issue. Aaron Burr, Vice President and thus constitutionally "President of the Senate" from 1801 to 1805, proposed that the motion was redundant and should be removed from the Senate's Rules. The Senate did so in 1806, without providing any specific alternative mechanism to terminate debate. Whig Party Senators engaged in a kind of "filibuster" against Democrat President Andrew Jackson in 1837. The shoe was on the other foot in 1841, when Whig Henry Clay attempted to close debate on a bill creating a new national bank—by majority vote. Democrat Senator William King threatened a filibuster, and Clay withdrew his proposal.

In 1917, after a filibuster by twelve anti-war Senators had blocked a bill allowing President Woodrow Wilson to arm merchant ships for defense against German submarines, Wilson (a political scientist by training) urged the Senate to adopt a rule for ending debate. The Senate did so, by a vote of 76 to 3, allowing two-thirds of the Senators voting in favor of a motion for "cloture" (closure) to close debate. As is too often the case, the "democratically-inspired" reform produced significant collateral damage. The first vote using the Senate's new rule on cloture ended the 1919 Senate debate on Wilson's cherished Versailles Treaty, and the resulting vote on the treaty itself rejected it!

The next thirty years averaged about one such cloture vote per year. As pressure increased in the 1950s and 1960s for civil rights legislation, filibusters were one significant tactic used by opponents. The serious impact of a filibuster was that it prevented the Senate from conducting any other business for as long as it could be sustained. The downside of that rule was that a general stoppage of the national legislative function was undoubtedly harder for the filibuster's supporters to justify. Thus, in 1970, the Senate leadership was able to muster support for a change in the rules so as to allow a "two-track" system. This procedural device allows the Senate to have two or more main motions under discussion at the same time, if the Majority Leader can get unanimous consent or the agreement of the Minority Leader.

Subsequently, there have been further changes to the cloture rules. In 1975, the vote requirement was raised to three-fifths of the *total* Senators, or 60 votes out of 100. In 2013, in what was a more widely-publicized and controversial move, the Democrat majority (3 disagreed, along with all 45 Republicans) eliminated the filibuster for executive appointments and for all judicial appointments—except the Supreme Court. In 2017, in a kind of political tit-for-tat, 52 Republicans outweighed 48 Democrats to eliminate filibusters against Supreme Court nominations, to allow Judge Neil Gorsuch—and then Judge Brett Kavanaugh and Judge Amy Barrett—to be confirmed to the Supreme Court by Republican majorities.

The Senate's modifications of the filibuster rules thus provide us with two nice examples of the importance of procedural rules and two cautionary tales for Senate majorities: "Think very carefully about what you vote for; how would it affect you if you were the minority?"

Referral to Conference Committee

Since both Houses must accept identical language, any differences between the bills passed by the House and the Senate must be eliminated. Either one may simply accept the language in the other's version of the bill. This would seem to be easier to do if the same political party controls both Houses since the opposition party would still get little or no credit (or blame) for passing the legislation. That easier solution might also be indicated where, for example, the Senate bill was passed with only a small majority but the House version by a large margin.

Either House may amend the other's bill (so that it agrees with the amender's) and then request that a "conference committee" be appointed to try to negotiate the differences. There are detailed procedures governing this process. Typically, each chamber appoints five conferees, chosen in accordance with specified criteria. While the two sets of conferees meet and discuss the differences together, each unit votes separately on proposed compromises. They are generally limited to resolving variances between the two versions of the bills, and they do not have the authority to go beyond those provisions.

The conferees are subject to a time limit within which to report, and further procedural steps may be taken if they fail to do so. Most such conferences result in a recommendation that one House agree to some or all of the other's amendments to its version of the bill. If and when the bill has been passed in identical form by both Houses, a final version is "enrolled," meaning printed and certified—by the Clerk of the House, if the bill originated there; by the Secretary of the Senate, if it was a Senate bill. By custom, the Speaker of the House signs the bill first, then the Vice President (as "President of the Senate") or the Senate's "President pro tem." A House-originated bill is presented to the President by the House Clerk; a Senate bill, by the Senate Secretary.

Action by the President

The enrolled bill (a congressionally, at least, "finished product") comes to the President for his (or "her"—sometime) signature. This requirement of presidential approval in Section 7 [2] and [3] of Article I means that the President is also part of the *legislative* (law*making*) process. Constitutionally, he himself has no lawmaking power, but Congress can't make any law without his approval. Unless there is at least 2-to-1 support—in each House of Congress—for the bill, its content must be such that the President is willing to accept it, even if it's not exactly what he would prefer. Thus, the President has considerable leverage in negotiating with congressional leadership about what gets passed and presented to him for signature, even if Congress is controlled by the other political party (as was, in fact, the case with President Nixon).

If the President does not respond within ten days after the passed bill has been presented to him, Section 7[2] says that his silence will be taken as his agreement—just as if he had signed it. (That presumption is consistent with an ancient rule of the English common law: silence by one who has a legal duty to speak is equated to an assent to the contents of the unanswered communication.[11]) However, if Congress adjourns within the ten-day period, so that the President cannot return the bill to them if he objects, the unsigned bill does not become law. This nonaction by the President is called a "pocket veto." (He keeps it in his pocket, unsigned—and lets Congress kill it by adjourning before the ten days are up.)

Overriding a Veto

As noted above, Section 7[2] of Article I of the Constitution requires a two-thirds vote by each of the two bodies to override a President's veto. (And it also requires that the Yea or Nay vote of each person be recorded.) That supermajority requirement ensures that the congressional position has a strong level of support in order to prevail over the President's objection.

The override of President Harry Truman's 1947 veto of the Taft-Hartley Act provides an interesting example for us. A wave of strikes in the immediate post-war years had alerted the nation to the power that labor unions had over the economy—and the society at large. A coal miners' strike had threatened the supply of winter heating fuel for millions of people. In the November 1946 elections, the Republicans had won control of both Houses of Congress, for the first time since the early 1930s. Ohio Senator Robert Taft and New Jersey Representative Fred Hartley introduced bills to rebalance the management/labor relationship. Taft's bill passed the Senate 68 to 24; Hartley's bill, the House 308 to 107. Calling it a "slave labor bill," Truman vetoed the conference committee's product. The override vote was 331 to 83 in the House and 68 to 25 in the Senate. The intensity of feeling on this issue is shown by the fact that 106 of 177 Democrat members of the House and 20 of 42 Democrat Senators voted against "their" President. He actually lost twenty-four of the House members who had voted against the bill originally but then voted to override his veto of it!

Court Review of Legislation

Understanding of the operations of the "Third Branch"—the Judiciary—is also important because a number of social problems seem to have a solution that is evasive, at best, and perhaps impossible, at worst. The executive and legislature can adopt policies intended to deal with the problem or at least to minimize its consequences. The well-intentioned policies may themselves have unforeseen negative effects, or the problem may morph into a new form. Rarely—if ever—is there a perfect solution, one that completely eliminates the problem and leaves all interested parties satisfied. For present purposes, what this means is that persons feeling aggrieved by the incomplete solution to a problem, or by the attempted solution itself, may still resort to legal action.

Thus, many of the toughest problems appear as litigations, with groups or individuals claiming that their legal rights have been violated—by other private parties or by governmental agencies themselves. Significant areas of public policy are thus decided, at least temporarily, by judges rather than legislators or administrators. Judges in the national ("federal") courts are appointed, rather than elected; so are some state-court judges, and vacancies on state courts are typically filled by appointment—at least until the next election cycle. The public officials *least* directly accountable to the people are thus making many of the rules governing our social interactions.

Two Court Systems

Several other countries have federal systems of government, with national agencies and parallel regional agencies. In most of them, however, the only national court is a supreme court, with authority to resolve differences among regional courts as to interpretation of national law. That is not the case in the US, which has not only its national Supreme Court but also a complete set of national trial and intermediate appellate courts—and several special courts.

Criminal cases must be tried in the courts of the governmental jurisdiction whose criminal law has allegedly been violated, using the criminal procedure rules of that jurisdiction. Alleged violations of national criminal law must be tried in national courts—generally, a US District Court in the State where the alleged misconduct occurred. If the defendant is charged with violating the criminal law of a particular State, the trial must be held there, using its criminal procedure. Those rules may include specifications as to which offenses can be tried in which courts within that State, if there are different levels or types of courts.

Cases involving claims by private persons—individuals or organizations—against one another ("civil cases") often have more than one possible trial location. In our age of world travel and telecommunication, many private relationships and interactions involve persons from different States (or from a US State and persons from one or more foreign nations). If a dispute arises from such a combination of parties and involves *more than* $75,000, either party may sue the other in a US District Court that has a sufficient connection to the dispute—even though the dispute itself does not involve any question of national law.[12] In such "diversity of citizenship" cases, the US court will be using the national rules of civil procedure for conducting the trial but is applying State law defining the rights of the parties in the kind of interaction involved in the dispute. Some civil cases arising under national law may be tried only in national courts, but there are also some that can be tried in State courts if the parties wish to do so. In that latter case, it is the State court that is applying its State's rules of civil procedure, but it does so using the relevant national law defining the rights of the parties.

Use of the simplistic "federal" dichotomy between national and State courts is actually quite misleading since there are fifty separate and independent State court systems. Thus, the litigants' possible choice is not just between national and State courts but also may be between and among several combinations of the various States—with or without the added possibility of one or more US District Courts in different States.

Fifty Versions of "State Law"

To add to the complications and confusion (and therefore also to the possibility of litigations to resolve the resulting differences of opinion), most "civil law"—the rules governing private relationships—is State law, determined by State governments. And most of it is case law, based on court decisions rather than statutes produced by the State's legislature. A State's legislature and governor can change the case-law rule by passing a statute or by amending the State's constitution. But until they do so, the last word in that State on what "the Law" is comes from that State's highest court. The US Supreme Court can overrule State courts on points of *national* law but **not** on points of *State* law. So, for example, there are potentially fifty different sets of rules as to what it takes to create a binding contract between persons or what implied powers an agent has to obligate the person represented to third parties.

Fortunately, the actuality is far simpler than the theoretical possibilities. There is considerable congruence among the States on most of the rules for most private-law subjects. Large-scale operations have been under way for some years to unify the States' legal rules, especially in commercial law. The American Law Institute has organized and summarized the case law on various topics in its *Restatements of the Law*. Similarly, the Uniform Law Commission has developed uniform statutes and recommended their adoption by the State legislatures. The Uniform Commercial Code, for example, has been adopted in all fifty States (perhaps not totally in Louisiana)—and by Congress, for the District of Columbia.

Conflict of Laws

A separate topic of law school study, "Conflict of Laws," has been developed to convey the complex set of rules on whose law applies to determine the rights of the parties in various types of legal disputes. For example, the validity of a contract is usually to be determined according to the law of the place where it was "made"—and that is usually the place where the last act necessary to form the agreement takes legal effect—and that is usually defined as the acceptance of the offer to do business—and in the US and the UK, but not in all nations, an acceptance by mail is presumed to be legally effective to form the contract when it is "mailed." The obvious questions about whether the "sending" presumption also applies to the various forms of electronic communication now available are not yet fully resolved.

Jurisdiction

In order to issue a valid judgment, a court must have both the power to hear the kind of dispute involved in the case and the power to determine the rights of the parties concerned. Jurisdiction to decide certain types of cases ("subject-matter jurisdiction") is conferred by the constitution or statute creating the court and defining its workload. The parties involved in the case cannot endow a court with the authority to hear their case, even if they both agree. But they can agree to have their dispute heard and settled by arbitration or some other alternate method of resolution.

The parties can, by agreement, consent to have their rights determined by the court ("personal jurisdiction"). The plaintiff normally "consents" by filing the lawsuit requesting the court to remedy the injury alleged. (There may be some question as to whether the filing also implies consent to have the defendant's counterclaim decided by that same court.) Typically, the defendant being sued is not willing to consent, particularly if the plaintiff has chosen a location seeming to favor that side of the dispute. The suit can be filed without such consent in the defendant's domicile. Likewise, the lawsuit can proceed if the defendant can be served with court process (a summons to appear and a copy of the plaintiff's complaint) within the geographical area subject to the court's authority. These three alternative bases for personal jurisdiction—consent, domicile, and presence—are available for most civil lawsuits.

Because many disputes involve claims against parties outside State or national boundaries, those three historical bases for personal jurisdiction were found to be grossly inadequate to deal with the realities of modern-day trade and commerce. To avoid the unfair result that no local remedies would be available to injured parties, States began to recognize that some local actions by nonconsenting out-of-staters would justify their being "haled into court" there, if they were properly notified that the lawsuit had been filed. Surely it was fair to force anyone who caused injury in the State to defend a lawsuit filed where the injury had occurred. Likewise, anyone who had agreed to perform services or deliver goods there and then failed to do so. A nonresident owner of real estate or tangible things in the State that caused injury there ought to be suable there. A person serving as an officer or director of a corporation or other legal person organized in the State or having its principal place of business there should be required to appear there to defend charges of nonperformance of those duties. Agreeing to become a director of Ford Motor Company (a Delaware corporation, with its principal place of business in Michigan) does not mean that one is now liable to be sued in Delaware and Michigan for anything and everything—but only for claims relating to service as a Ford director. The various States, of course, have different combinations of these and other bases for "*limited* personal jurisdiction."

Supreme Court as Referee and Guarantor

The US Supreme Court has appeared several times in the above paragraphs. The highest of the national courts, it is the overseer of the system, with certain administrative functions. As the final level of review of lower court decisions, it has the last word on the meaning of national law in the context of particular situations, and it is thus able to resolve conflicting interpretations among lower courts on these points. But it also seems necessary to re-emphasize the important point that the Supreme Court does *not* have the last word on points of State law—that power belongs to the highest court in each of the fifty States. Congress can "overrule" the Court's interpretation of national statutory or case law by amending a statute or passing a new one, but the Court's decisions on constitutional issues are binding until a new Court majority changes the interpretation—or the Constitution is amended.

The "referee" function is the Supreme Court's power to declare actions of Congress and the executive branch unconstitutional: "out of bounds," in the language of many sports. As illustrated by the *Goldwater* case, the Court defines the boundaries between the three branches of government and between the national government and the States. With electronic relationships increasing exponentially in number and complexity, that function becomes more important than ever.

Just as has been true from the beginning, and was the reason for the insistence on a "Bill of Rights" being added to the body of the Constitution, the Supreme Court's ultimate *raison d'être* is its function as "guarantor": the guardian of the basic rights of the people—to make sure that no governmental action can take away or impede the exercise of the rights gained by an intense and bloody revolution of six-and-a-half years. Arguably, this is the Court's major task: to make "the Law on the books" come alive as "the Law in action"!

(How well the Court has been performing these functions under the various combinations of Justices is the subject of the second volume in this series on the Nixon presidency: *Richard Nixon's Court*.)

PART II

NIXON'S LEGISLATIVE LEGACY

Chapter 3

Nixon Protecting the Environment

ENVIRONMENTAL POLICY IS PERHAPS a bit surprising to use as a starting point in the re-evaluation of the legislative record of the Nixon presidency. The reason for doing so is quite simple: environmental policy provides a clear and unarguable example of the contrast between Nixon's "public image" and his actual accomplishments as President. (As a rather strong supplementary argument, "environmental protection" statutes are clearly the numerically predominant category of the five specific types identified. Their 223-Act total is about twice that of "workers' protection" [89], "minorities' protection" [118], "veterans' protection" [93], or "consumers' protection" [85].) Even the generic "citizens' protection" category (i.e., the public at large) is only *very* slightly more numerous: 229 Acts so identified.

Theodore Roosevelt has established a well-deserved (and positive) reputation as a "conservationist" as a result of his efforts to set aside large tracts of land for government-owned parks and recreation areas. Clearly, the setting-aside of natural areas to prevent environmental damage as a result of "development" is an important sub-part of protecting the environment. Implementation of TR's conservation program certainly involved some battles with interests that wished to use the same lands for various economic purposes. For his efforts, TR was recognized in 2012 as the "greenest" President, by a group of twelve leading environmental groups—including the National Resources Defense Council, Friends of the Earth, the Sierra Club, Greenpeace, the Union of Concerned Scientists, World Wildlife Fund, and Public Citizen.[1]

That same collection named *Richard Milhouse Nixon* as "Number Two"! One could certainly argue that implementing rules that require significant (and costly!) changes to *existing* methods of operation will surely provoke stronger and more widespread opposition than imposing rules which merely stop the extension of present operations to new geographical areas. It's one thing to set aside large tracts of unoccupied and unspoiled land as nature preserves, for the future enjoyment of those who may wish to visit them. It's quite another matter to impose new, significant limitations on the activities of individuals and businesses, so that *all* of us throughout the nation—*and* future generations—can live healthier, happier, and safer lives. In other words, environmental *regulation* is generally going to be a much harder sell than "conservation."[2]

A good part of the 2012 "One/Two" rankings may be due to the fact that we perceive TR as the more consistent and enthusiastic initiator/advocate of his (conservation) program. And Nixon did veto the 1972 amendments that came to be known as the Clean Water Act of 1972—because he said they "would provide for the commitment of a staggering, budget wrecking $24 billion" on top of "the nearly tenfold increase in my budget for this purpose during the past four years."[3] In any event, President Nixon's #2 "environmental protector" ranking—by a collection of persons one would hardly identify as his strong supporters— speaks volumes about the misperception and misevaluation of his presidency.

Environmental regulation did not at the time seem to be a hot issue on many voters' "wish lists."[4] The serious pollution problems were there, to be sure—dramatically illustrated by the 1969 burning of the surface of the Cuyahoga River in Ohio.[5] (The City of Cleveland became "the mistake on the lake.") It is rather surprising, then, that President Nixon "launched the most advanced environmental program in American history, and both air and water were being rid of filth."[6] What follows here are some legislative examples of that "most advanced" program. Many of these Public Acts are, of course, amendments that extend or expand prior laws or provide additional funding for them. Many are, therefore, quite brief and—presumably—not controversial: fine-tuning or updating of already-passed legislation. There are also, however, several significant new initiatives. (It might be argued that even the "fine-tuning"/"updating" shows a continuing congressional—and *presidential*— commitment to the environment and to policies and programs designed to protect it.) The following list gives some indication of the scope and depth of the successful efforts during the Nixon years to protect—and *improve*—our environment.

Protecting the Environment—the Nixon Legislative Record

91st Congress, First Session (1969)

- PL 91-15: amends Marine Resources and Engineering Development Act of 1966

- PL 91-42: appropriation for Padre Island National Seashore

- PL 91-43: authorizes appropriations for saline water conversion

- PL 91-52: consents to WY/NE compact for upper Niobrara River

- PL 91-58: designates the Ventana Wilderness in Los Padres National Forest, CA

- PL 91-60: establishes the Florissant Fossil Beds National Monument, CO

- PL 91-81: authorizes water-resource feasibility studies by Secretary of the Interior

- PL 91-82: designates Desolation Wilderness, in Eldorado National Forest, CA

- PL 91-88: amends boundaries and authorizes added land for Everglades National Park, FL

- PL 91-108: authorizes road construction at Great Smoky Mountains National Park, NC

- PL 91-109: establishes Frederick Douglas's home as part of National Park System, DC

- PL 91-118: amends 1956 Soil Conservation and Domestic Allotment Act—adds the Great Plains

- PL 91-132: establishes William Howard Taft National Historic Site, OH

- PL 91-133: establishes Eisenhower National Historic Site, Gettysburg, PA

- PL 91-134: establishes Lyndon B. Johnson National Historic Site, Stonewall, TX

- PL 91-135: no importation of endangered species; no interstate transfer of illegally taken wildlife

- PL 91-137: amends Clean Air Act—extends research authorization for one year; provides funds

- PL 91-144: public works appropriations for water, pollution control, et al.

- PL 91-146: appropriation for Fort Donaldson National Battlefield, TN

- PL 91-148: authorizes the Tahoe Regional Planning Compact between California and Nevada

- PL 91-150: Chickamauga and Chattanooga National Military Park, GA—land transfer

- PL 91-158: consents to the renewal of the interstate compact to preserve oil and gas

- PL 91-162: waives acreage limits for conveyance of land to Valley of Fire State Park, NV

- PL 91-190: the National Environmental Policy Act of 1969

91st Congress, Second Session (1970/71)

- PL 91-218: authorizes appropriations for Missouri River Basin project

- PL 91-221: FY 1971 appropriations for saline water conversion program

- PL 91-223: authorizes appropriation for Point Reyes National Seashore (CA) land acquisition

- PL 91-224: amends Federal Water Pollution Control Act

- PL 91-236: Joint Resolution—authorizes President to proclaim 1970 National Arbor Day

- PL 91-239: establishes an international animal importation quarantine system, for breeding stock

- PL 91-243: amends 1966 Act by extending historic properties preservation program

- PL 91-249: amends Anadromous Fish Conservation Act of 1965—to encourage joint research

- PL 91-252: establishes the Cape Cod National Seashore

- PL 91-270: authorizes Secretary of the Interior's Merlin division of OR Rouge River project

- PL 91-282: authorizes appropriations for certain comprehensive river basin projects

- PL 91-288: establishes Ford's Theatre National Historical Site

- PL 91-293: amends 1948 Act relating to Independence National Historical Park

- PL 91-308: amends the Land and Water Engineering Fund Act of 1965

- PL 91-315: consents to the amendment of the Pacific Marine Fisheries Compact

- PL 91-316: amendments to Clean Air Act and Solid Waste Disposal Act

- PL 91-332: commemorates 100th anniversary of Yellowstone National Park, WY-MT-ID

- PL 91-343: authorizes Secretary of Agriculture's financial assistance for land conservation

- PL 91-349: amends the Marine Research and Engineering Development Act of 1966

- PL 91-357: authorizes Secretary of the Interior's establishment of volunteers in parks program

- PL 91-372: extends boundaries of Toiyabe National Forest, NV

- PL 91-378: establishes Youth Conservation Corps

- PL 91-383: improves Secretary of the Interior's administration of national park system

- PL 91-387: extends term during which Secretary of the Interior can make fisheries loans

- PL 91-389: authorizes operation of the Narrows unit in the Missouri River basin project, CO

- PL 91-390: consents to the Falls of the Ohio Interstate Park Compact

- PL 91-407: consents to amendments to compact for Potomac Valley Conservancy

- PL 91-408: authorizes construction of added facilities at Yuma Mesa Irrigation District, AZ

- PL 91-409: reauthorizes aspects of the Missouri River Basin project

- PL 91-411: adds Freeman School to the Homestead National Monument of America, NE

- PL 91-414: continues the National Council on Marine Resources and Engineering Development

- PL 91-415: authorizes operation of Minot extension in Missouri River Basin project, ND

- PL 91-424: establishes the Apostle Island National Lakeshore, WS

- PL 91-425: authorizes feasibility study for national lakeshore at Lake Tahoe, NV & CA

- PL 91-427: protects Pacific island coral reefs

- PL 91-428: amends boundaries and authorizes added land for Everglades National Park, FL

- PL 91-429: authorizes fire protection contracts for public lands

- PL 91-435: amends 1944 Act for aerial services and facilities of the Forest Service

- PL 91-439: appropriations for water, pollution control, et al. (FWQA & other agencies)

- PL 91-451: appropriations for jellyfish control

- PL 91-457: establishes Fort Point National Historic Site, CA

- PL 91-462: authorizes feasibility study for national park at Cherokee Strip, KS & OK

- PL 91-465: authorizes Andersonville National Historic Site, GA

- PL 91-476: establishes King Range National Conservation Area, CA

- PL 91-479: appropriations for Sleeping Bear Dunes (MI) park

- PL 91-485: amendments to Land and Water Conservation Act of 1965

- PL 91-503: amends Wildlife Restoration Act of 1937 and Fish Restoration Act of 1950

- PL 91-504: designates additional wilderness areas

- PL 91-512: Resources Recovery Act of 1970 (amends Solid Waste Disposal Act)

- PL 91-514: strengthens penalties for illegal fishing in US territorial waters

- PL 91-516: Environmental Education Act (authorizes the establishment of such programs)

- PL 91-548: authorizes revision of Minute Man National Historical Park boundaries

- PL 91-554: amends 1960 act establishing Wilson's Creek Battlefield National Park

- PL 91-559: provides for conservation of surface water and wildlife habitats

- PL 91-575: consents to Susquehanna River Basin compact

- PL 91-577: encourages development of new plant varieties

- PL 91-581: Geothermal Steam Act of 1970—authorizes disposition of such resources

- PL 91-594: authorizes presidential proclamation of "Clean Waters for America Week"

- PL 91-601: Poison Prevention Packaging Act of 1970—requires childproof packaging

- PL 91-604: amends Clean Air Act to provide a more effective program

- PL 91-609: Housing and Urban Development Act of 1970—a national urban growth policy

- PL 91-611: River and Harbor Act of 1970—public works for navigation and flood control

- PL 91-660: establishes Gulf Islands National Seashore, FL & MS

- PL 91-661: authorizes Voyagers National Park, MN

- PL 91-664: establishes Chesapeake and Ohio Canal National Historical Park

- PL 91-695: Lead-Based Paint Poisoning Prevention Act

92nd Congress, First Session (1971)

- PL 92-27: amends Water Resource Planning Act (increased appropriations)

- PL 92-50: Federal Water Pollution Control Act (extends authorization)

- PL 92-60: Saline Water Conversion Act of 1971 (expands and extends program)

- PL 92-73: appropriations for Agricultural-Environmental & Consumer Protection programs

- PL 92-82: authorizes cooperation with local law enforcement officials regarding national parks

- PL 92-87: amends Northwest Atlantic Fisheries Act of 1950

- PL 92-125: establishes National Advisory Committee on Oceans and Atmosphere

- PL 92-127: establishes Lincoln Home National Historic Site, IL

- PL 92-137: extends Federal Water Pollution Control Act

- PL 92-146: authorizes operation of the Kortes Unit of the Missouri River Basin project, WY

- PL 92-154: revises boundaries of Canyonlands National Park, UT

- PL 92-155: establishes Arches National Park, UT

- PL 92-159: amends 1956 Fish & Wildlife Act (penalties for shooting wildlife from airplane)

- PL 92-175: amends Water Resource Research Act of 1964 (provides increased appropriations)

- PL 92-195: protects wild horses and burros

- PL 92-199: authorizes feasibility studies for water resources development projects

- PL 92-207: establishes Capitol Reef National Park, UT

- PL 92-219: amends 1967 Fishermen's Protective Act—international conservation of fish

- PL 92-222: added appropriations for certain comprehensive river basin projects

92nd Congress, Second Session (1972)

- PL 92-230: designates Pine Mountain Wilderness, Prescott National Forest, and Tonto National Forest, AZ

- PL 92-237: establishes Buffalo National River, AK

- PL 92-240: extends Federal Water Pollution Control Act

- PL 92-241: establishes Sycamore National Wilderness, et al., AZ

- PL 92-260: establishes Oregon Dunes National Recreation Area, OR

- PL 92-263: authorizes payment of DC's share of Potomac River reservoir costs

- PL 92-272: provides appropriation increases and boundary changes for certain national parks

- PL 92-273: FY 1973 appropriations for saline water conversion program

- PL 92-275: amends 1971 Gulf Islands National Seashore Act

- PL 92-276: authorizes presidential proclamation of "National Arbor Day"

- PL 92-288: supports cooperative forestry programs of Department of Agriculture

- PL 92-300: authorizes program for volunteers in national forests

- PL 92-308: consents to Kansas-Nebraska Big Blue River Compact

- PL 92-319: release of condition in deed of land to Arkansas Fish & Game Commission

- PL 92-322: consents to renewal of interstate compact to conserve oil and gas

- PL 92-326: establishes Tinicum National Environmental Center, PA

- PL 92-330: establishes San Francisco National Wildlife Refuge

- PL 92-340: Ports and Waterways Safety Act of 1972

- PL 92-346: authorizes feasibility study for Honokohau National Historical Landmark, HI

- PL 92-362: facilitates the preservation of historic monuments

- PL 92-364: designates wilderness land in Cedar Keys National Wildlife Refuge, FL

- PL 92-367: authorizes National Dam Inspection Program by Secretary of the Army

- PL 92-370: increases appropriations for Upper Colorado River Basin project

- PL 92-371: increases appropriations for Missouri River Basin project

- PL 92-388: establishes Puukohola Heiau National Historic Site, HI

- PL 92-395: defines Scapegoat Wilderness and Helena, Lolo, and Lewis & Clark National Forests, MT

- PL 92-396: increased appropriations for Water Resources Planning Act

- PL 92-399: appropriations for Agricultural-Environmental and Consumer Protection programs

- PL 92-400: establishes Sawtooth National Recreation Area, ID

- PL 92-401: amends Natural Gas Pipeline Safety Act of 1968

- PL 92-406: establishes Grant-Kohrs Ranch National Historical Site, MT

- PL 92-408: establishes Seal Branch National Wildlife Refuge, CA

- PL 92-421: provides accelerated tree-planting needed in national forests

- PL 92-432: amends 1948 Act regarding use of real property for wildlife conservation

- PL 92-444: Central, Western, and South Pacific Fisheries Development Act—tuna, et al.

- PL 92-465: modifies boundaries for Santa Fe, Gila, Cibola, and Carson National Forests

- PL 92-471: amends North Pacific Fisheries Act of 1954

- PL 92-474: authorizes land exchanges in Carson and Santa Fe National Forests

- PL 92-475: establishes the Longfellow National Historic Site, MA

- PL 92-476: designates the Stratified Primitive Area as part of the Washakie Wilderness, WY

- PL 92-478: authorizes feasibility study for protecting Great Dismal Swamp, NC & VA

- PL 92-493: designates Black Lava Flow and Schonchin Lava Flow areas, CA as wilderness

- PL 92-500: Federal Water Pollution Control Act Amendments of 1972

- PL 92-501: addition to Sitka (Alaska) National Monument

- PL 92-502: amends Fish and Wildlife Act of 1956 (enforcement against air shooting of wildlife)

- PL 92-504: amends Sockeye Salmon or Pink Salmon Fishery Act of 1947 (restores and extends)

- PL 92-510: designates as wilderness certain areas in Lassen Volcanic National Park, CA

- PL 92-516: Federal Environmental Pesticide Control Act of 1972 (amends FIFR Act)

- PL 92-520: provides for the Dwight D. Eisenhower Memorial Bicentennial Civic Center, DC

- PL 92-521: authorizes additional wilderness areas adjacent to Eagle Cap Wilderness, OR

- PL 92-522: Marine Mammal Protection Act of 1972 (sets up the Marine Mammal Commission)

- PL 92-524: establishes the Thaddeus Kosciuszko Home National Historic Site, PA

- PL 92-525: establishes the Hohokam Pima National Monument, AZ

- PL 92-527: provides administration for Mar-A-Lago National Historical Site, FL

- PL 92-528: authorizes review of Indian Peaks Area, CO for wilderness designation

- PL 92-532: Marine Protection, Research, and Sanctuaries Act of 1972 (ocean waste-dumping)

- PL 92-533: authorizes additional funds for land acquisition at Piscataway Park, MD

- PL 92-534: ends certain restrictions on adding land for recreation and natural resource protection

- PL 92-535: increases penalties for killing bald eagles or golden eagles

- PL 92-536: establishes Cumberland Island National Seashore, GA

- PL 92-537: establishes Fossil Butte National Monument, WY

- PL 92-558: additional funds for wildlife restoration projects

- PL 92-560: designates portion of Saint Croix River, MN & WI, as wild and scenic

- PL 92-567: increases funds for National Advisory Committee on Oceans and Atmosphere

- PL 92-574: Noise Control Act of 1972

- PL 92-575: increases land for Delaware Water Gap National Recreation Area

- PL 92-577: authorizes feasibility studies for potential water resource developments

- PL 92-583: amends Marine Research and Engineering Development Act of 1966 (coastal zones)

- PL 92-589: establishes Golden Gate National Recreation Area

- PL 92-590: extends Commercial Fisheries Research and Development Act of 1964

- PL 92-592: establishes Gateway National Recreation Area, NY & NJ

- PL 92-593: establishes Glen Canyon National Recreation Area, AZ & UT

- PL 92-597: amends Youth Conservation Corps Act of 1970—expands pilot program

- PL 92-598: approves US participation in the International Exposition on the Environment (WA)

- PL 92-601: prohibits certain small vessels in US fisheries

- PL 92-604: provides appropriations for jellyfish control

- PL 92-605: declares a portion of Delaware River in PA to be non-navigable

93rd Congress, First Session (1973)

- PL 93-14: extends Solid Waste Disposal Act; provides appropriations

- PL 93-15: extends Clean Air Act; provides appropriations

- PL 93-18: Joint Resolution—establishes National Clean Water Week (4/15/73 to 4/22/73)

- PL 93-36: added appropriations for Department of Environmental Quality

- PL 93-51: Saline Water Program—funds for Saline Water Conversion Act of 1971

- PL 93-54: establishes a program for acquisition of additional historical properties

- PL 93-55: amends Water Resource Planning Act; provides appropriations

- PL 93-81: Land and Water Conservation Fund—provides for recreational use fees

- PL 93-97: appropriations for water and power development projects

- PL 93-119: Oil Pollution Act Amendments of 1973 (amending Oil Pollution Act of 1961)

- PL 93-122: authorizes four feasibility studies for projects in four Western states

- PL 93-135: appropriations for agricultural-environmental and conservation programs

- PL 93-151: Lead-Based Paint Poisoning Prevention (amends 1971 Act—PL 91-695)

- PL 93-152: consents to Arkansas River Basin compact (AR & OK)

- PL 93-188: appropriates $40 million for US participation in UN Environmental Fund

- PL 93-205: Endangered Species Act of 1973

- PL 93-206: authorizes agreements with non-federal agencies to replace American Falls Dam (ID)

- PL 93-207: amends Federal Water Pollution Control Act

- PL 93-211: Joint Resolution—establishes Lyndon Baines Johnson Memorial Grove, DC

- PL 93-242: Offshore Shrimp Fisheries Act of 1973 (extends international agreement to Brazil)

- PL 93-243: amends the Federal Water Control Act

93rd Congress, Second Session (1974)

- PL 93-248: Intervention on the High Seas Act—for oil pollution occurrences

- PL 93-251: Water Resources Development Act of 1974—projects for flood control, navigation

- PL 93-254: amends Marine Protection, Research, and Sanctuaries Act of 1972

- PL 93-271: amends Fish and Wildlife Act of 1956; abolishes office of Commissioner

- PL 93-278: extends Environmental Education Act for three years

- PL 93-279: National Wild and Scenic Rivers System Act amended by adding rivers

- PL 93-280: agency loans of personnel and equipment to Bureau of Sport Fisheries and Wildlife

- PL 93-300: Migratory Birds Treaty extended to include Japan

- PL 93-303: amends Land Water Conservation Fund Act (user fees at additional campgrounds)

- PL 93-304: International Ocean Exposition Appropriations Authorization Act of 1973

- PL 93-313: delays funds for certain wildlife restoration projects for six months

- PL 93-319: Energy Supply and Environmental Coordination Act of 1974

- PL 93-320: Colorado River Basin Salinity Control Act—authorizes public works therefor

- PL 93-338: provides for availability of funds for forest highways

- PL 93-339: Fisheries Conservation—authorizes US participation in international program

- PL 93-341: establishes Egmont Key National Wildlife Refuge, FL

- PL 93-342: Saline Water Conversion Act of 1971—appropriations to expand the program

- PL 93-362: amends Anadromous Fish Conservation Act; extends appropriations therefor

President Nixon's resignation took effect on August 9, 1974. Public Law 93-362 was approved on August 7. Public Law 93-370 was approved on August 10, so it and all later legislation enacted by the 93rd Congress occurred during the Presidency of Gerald Ford. Our listing of the environmental legislation of the Nixon years thus ends with PL 93-362.

Total output? As listed above, 223 "environmental" bills (13-plus percent of the 1,671 total) ground through the legislative mill during President Nixon's five-plus years in office. Even allowing for possible differences in one's classification of specific statutes as "environmental" or not, there would seem to be little question that the legislative output on this subject was very substantial during the Nixon presidency. As described by the 2012 study cited earlier: "The list of environmental bills put into law during Nixon's presidency is almost numbing. . . . [T]he evolution of these core Nixon-era laws and institutions has set the course for US environmentalism ever since."[7] A detailed examination of each of these laws is, however, far beyond the scope of our purpose here. That sort of study would require a book of its own. We will therefore have to be satisfied for now with an overview of the types of laws passed and a closer look at several major examples, but even an abbreviated sampling of the 200-plus acts signed by President Nixon clearly establishes him as THE "*Environmental* President."[8]

Environmental Statutes—a Closer Look

What were the environmental conditions/problems at which these various statutes were aimed? Based on their titles and/or stated purposes, most of the acts fall into one of four categories: conservation—including the establishment/expansion/management of national parks, forests, sites, and refuges (102); water regulations (54); species protection (30); or general environmental policies (23). Congress gave legislative consent to seven interstate agreements ("compacts") dealing with various environmental problems and policies. Six statutes targeted specific problem areas that were dealt with only once or twice—noise pollution (1), poison control (1), pesticide safety (1), lead-based paint safety (2), and gas pipeline safety (1). Air pollution was addressed specifically only four times. (Two statutes passed by the 92nd Congress dealing with "oceans and atmosphere" were counted in the "water regulations" category but could have been tallied in the "air pollution" group.)

The results for both the 91st Congress (1969–1970) and the 92nd Congress (1971–1972) were heavily skewed in favor of acts dealing with conservation policies (46 of the 89 acts passed by the 91st and 49 of 97 from the 92nd). Water policy was the largest category for the 93rd Congress (15 of the 40 environmental acts it passed prior to President Nixon's resignation on August 9, 1974). Water policy was also the second-favorite target for both the 91st and 92nd Congresses (17 of 88 for the 91st and 22 of 96 for the 92nd). Species protection had the second-largest count for the Nixon portion of the 93rd Congress (8 of 40 acts) and was the third-largest category for the 91st (9 of 88 acts) and the 92nd (13 of 96 acts).

General Environmental Policies

Much of the support for President Nixon's high marks as a protector of the environment surely—and deservedly—rests on the 1969 passage by the first session of the 91st Congress of PL 190: "NEPA"—the National Environmental Policy Act. Although many (most?) of us were not aware of it at the time, NEPA turned out to be a real game-changer—not only in the US but worldwide as well. In effect, NEPA put a national-government "thumb" on the scales of justice—on the environmental side of the scale. The foundation was laid for a whole new body of law dealing with environmental degradation.

The traditional rules of the Anglo-American common law were weighted rather heavily in favor of landowners. The owner's rights were stated as extending from the center of the earth to the heavens: the "*ad coelum*" doctrine.[9] The landowner was generally free to use the land as s/he saw fit, subject only to the claims of others who also had rights in the same property. (For example, landlords and tenants, as to each other; or holders of a life interest in the land, as to the owner of the residuary interest; or mortgagors who had pledged their lands as collateral to mortgagees.)

Where the landowner's activities caused injury to other persons, s/he could be held liable for damages caused by the owner's negligence in conducting those activities. Proving "causation" in such cases is, however, often quite difficult. Alternatively, liability might be imposed if the injured party could prove that the landowner's activities constituted a "nuisance"—the unreasonable use of one's property in such a way as to interfere with the others' rights to use and enjoy their properties. Under either theory, the costs involved in pursuing the litigation alternative—temporal and psychological, as well as financial—need to be weighed in making the decision to sue. Moreover, legal doctrine generally favors the remedy of "damages" (i.e., money paid for injuries proven to have been caused or which will be caused by the defendant's conduct), rather than an injunction—a court order to the defendant to stop the offensive conduct. Thus, in many cases, the "winning" plaintiff cannot get the wrongful conduct ended but only receives whatever dollar price a jury puts on the injury sustained or to be sustained.

If negligence can be proved, and damage to others is caused thereby, the financial liability, at least, seems clear. The courts have had much more difficulty in balancing the user rights of a non-negligent owner against the rights of other owners to clean air and water and to the absence of annoying odors and noises. In an early "nuisance" case, the Kentucky Supreme Court stated a clear—but rather extreme—position: "The doing of a lawful thing in a careful and prudent manner cannot be a nuisance."[10] By 1960—Nixon's last year as Vice President and his first as candidate for President—the Kentucky court had substantially modified its "nuisance" analysis:

[W]e accept the proposition that the existence of a nuisance must be ascertained on the basis of two broad factors, neither of which may in any case be the sole test to the exclusion of the other: (1) the reasonableness of the defendant's use of his property, and (2) the gravity of harm to the complainant. Both are to be considered in the light of all the circumstances of the case, including the lawful nature and location of the defendant's business, the manner of its operation, and such importance to the community as it may have; the kind, volume, time, and duration of the particular annoyance; the respective situations of the parties; and the character (including applicable zoning) of the locality. The extreme limits are therefore, on the one hand, the reasonable use causing unreasonable damage and, on the other hand, the unreasonable (or negligent) use causing damage that is more unnecessary than severe.

In the suit for damages alone the application of these broad considerations to the facts of the case is for the jury, subject to the general principle that there must be sufficient evidence of an over-all inequity to the complainant in order to justify its submission. That the minimum sufficiency of the evidence is a difficult line to draw may be conceded, and in that respect each case must be judged on its own facts, recognizing that no matter what else might be said, in the final analysis the question of what constitutes a private nuisance is a matter of degree anyway.[11]

Thus, by the 1960s, there had already been some reformulating by State courts of the legal doctrine of nuisance, so as to increase the "environmental-protection" rights of those adversely affected by landowner activities.

The legal remedies for negligence and nuisance were primarily after-the-fact attempts to deal with environmental injuries already caused, although injunctions could be granted to prevent threatened future harms. Many local governments in the US also took a proactive stance and attempted to prevent or minimize land-user conflicts by segregating types of land-user activities. Human settlements were the collective result of millions of individual decisions; cities and towns grew "organically," that is to say, haphazardly. Since lakes and rivers were important means of transportation, as well as sources of the water required for habitation, agriculture, and industry, many communities were located on or near them. Various land uses were often clustered together so that the homes of workers in mines and factories might be subjected to the inevitable noises, odors, and waste of industrial processes. With the onset of the automobile came a new set of adverse environmental effects—fumes, noise, damage to land, danger of personal injury, etc.

"Zoning" provided an overall land-use plan for the community, with designated uses for various areas. Industrial plants were typically permitted only in a designated section; retail stores and office buildings in another; and residences—often subcategorized into single-family and multi-family—in still another. The enactment of local zoning ordinances did not eliminate land-use disputes, of course; the 1960 Kentucky case cited above itself acknowledged that "nuisance" claims of residence owners just over the dividing line from industrial plants presented some of the most difficult decisions for the courts. And the zoning ordinances themselves were subjected to constitutional challenges for their interference with constitutionally-guaranteed property rights. One of the early cases to reach the US Supreme Court involved a realty company's claim against the Village of Euclid, Ohio.[12] By a 6-to-3 vote, the Court held that the zoning ordinance was a valid exercise of Euclid's "police power" to regulate activities so as to protect the health and safety of the community:

> **The serious question in the case arises over the provisions of the ordinance excluding from residential districts, apartment houses, business houses, retail stores and shops, and other like establishments. This question involves the validity of what is really the crux of the more recent zoning legislation, namely, the creation and maintenance of residential districts, from which business and trade of every sort, including hotels and apartment houses, are excluded. Upon that question, this Court has not thus far spoken. The decisions of the state courts are numerous and conflicting; but those which broadly sustain the power greatly outnumber those which deny altogether or narrowly limit it; and it is very apparent that there is a constantly increasing tendency in the direction of the broader view. . . .**

> **The decisions enumerated . . . agree that the exclusion of buildings devoted to business, trade, etc., from residential districts, bears a rational relation to the health and safety of the community.[13]**

A different (and perhaps more compelling) constitutional argument relates to the application of a zoning law to already-existing uses that are not to be permitted in that area. It's one thing to prevent a landowner from erecting a structure in a zoning area that does not permit the type of structure proposed. But an after-the-fact application of the law, to terminate operations that were legal when begun in that location, would seem to violate the national Constitution's prohibition against "ex post facto" laws—criminalizing today what was lawful yesterday.

The counter-argument, of course, is that the landowner is not being penalized for *past* conduct but merely being told not to *continue* conduct that is now unlawful. If that response is accepted as valid, it would seem to leave the offending structure(s) still in place, even if the prohibited manufacturing or other commercial activities ceased. Many zoning ordinances seem to finesse the problem by allowing preexisting businesses to continue their otherwise nonconforming uses—a so-called "grandfather" clause. When the preexisting business is terminated, however, the land in question is subject to the then-existing zoning rules.

Much more recently, another layer of complexity was added to the land-use debate by the US Supreme Court decision in *Lucas v. South Carolina Coastal Council*.[14] David Lucas had purchased two island lots for $975,000, on which he intended to build single-family homes. The State passed an act prohibiting construction of occupiable dwellings within twenty feet of the coast at any point where erosion had occurred in the last forty years. The majority opinion by Justice Scalia indicated that a governmental regulation that prohibited the landowner from making *any* economically productive use of the land amounted to a "taking" of the property for which the national Constitution required compensation:

> **[A]ffirmatively supporting a compensation requirement is the fact that regulations that leave the owner of land without economically beneficial or productive options for its use—typically, as here, by requiring land to be left substantially in its natural state—carry with them a heightened risk that private property is being pressed into some form of public service under the guise of mitigating serious public harm. . . .**

> **We think, in short, that there are good reasons for our frequently expressed belief that when the owner of real property has been called upon to sacrifice *all* economically beneficial uses in the name of the common good, that is, to leave his property economically idle, he has suffered a taking. . . .**

> **The trial court found Lucas's two beachfront lots to have been rendered valueless by respondent's enforcement of the coastal-zone construction ban. Under Lucas's theory of the case, which rested upon our "no economically viable use" statements, that finding entitled him to compensation. . . .**

> **Where the State seeks to sustain regulation that deprives land of all economically beneficial use, we think it may resist compensation only if the logically antecedent inquiry into the nature of the owner's estate shows that the proscribed use interests were not part of his title to begin with.[15]**

So, environmental restrictions on land use were not unknown prior to the 1969 NEPA, and both national and State courts have continued—after NEPA—to refine and adjust environmental law (including, of course, the newer environmental statutes—as discussed later in this chapter). So, why all the fuss about NEPA? What accounts for its significance and its recognition as being significant? Why is this short and simplistic statute so important?

For openers, the US national government owns more than one-quarter of all the 2.27 billion acres of land in the US. So, the (by far!) largest landowner in the country is now committed to considering the environmental effects of any of its physical activities—such as the construction or modification of roads, bridges, canals, levees, buildings, military installations, whatever—or of its far-flung operations. The wide scope of this legal commitment is illustrated by a 1993 case from the US Court of Appeals for the District of Columbia: *Environmental Defense Fund v. Massey.*[16]

The National Science Foundation (NSF—a US government agency) operated a research station in Antarctica. At one point, it decided to resume burning the food wastes generated by the occupants of the station. It did not prepare and file an "environmental impact statement"—as required by NEPA. Claiming that the NSF had violated NEPA's requirements, the EDF (a nonprofit corporation established to protect the environment) filed a lawsuit in US District Court against the NSF and its director—Massey—to prevent the waste-burning. The NSF argued that NEPA did not apply because there was a presumption against acts of Congress having international effect and/or because NEPA itself did not specify such broad application. Based on those arguments, the US District Court dismissed the lawsuit, and EDF appealed.

The DC Court of Appeals agreed with the EDF, stating (in part):

We reverse the district court's decision, and hold that the presumption against the extraterritorial application of statutes . . . does not apply where the conduct regulated by the statute occurs primarily, if not exclusively, in the United States, and the alleged extraterritorial effect of the statute will be felt in Antarctica—a continent without a sovereign, and an area over which the United States has a great measure of legislative control. We therefore remand to the district court for a determination of whether NSF actually failed to comply with Section 102(2)(C) of NEPA, as EDF alleges in its complaint. . . .

Section 102(2)(C) lies at the heart of NEPA and is often considered the "action-forcing" element of the statute. . . . This section requires "all agencies of the Federal Government" to prepare a detailed environmental impact statement for every "major Federal action[ ]" which has the potential to significantly affect the human environment. . . . Section 102(2)(C) binds only American officials and controls the very essence of the government function: decisionmaking. Because the decisionmaking processes of federal agencies take place almost exclusively in this country and involve the workings of the United States government, they are uniquely domestic. . . .

Section 102(2)(C), on its face, is clearly not limited to actions of federal agencies that have significant environmental effects within US borders. This Court has re-

peatedly taken note of the sweeping scope of NEPA and the EIS requirement. . . . ("The sweep of NEPA is extraordinarily broad, compelling consideration of any and all types of environmental impact of federal action."); . . . ("[NEPA] was designed explicitly to take account of impending as well as present crises in this country and *in the world as a whole.*") (emphasis added).

Far from employing limiting language, Section 2 states that NEPA is intended to "encourage productive and enjoyable harmony between *man and his environment*" as well as to "promote efforts which will prevent or eliminate damage to the environment and *biosphere.*" . . . (emphasis added). Clearly, Congress painted with a far greater brush than NSF is willing to apply. . . .[17]

The lower court's dismissal of the case was reversed—NEPA did apply to the NSF's decision, and thus NSF was required to prepare and file an EIS. The case was sent back ("remanded") to the lower court to confirm that the NSF had indeed failed to meet this requirement. If so, the NSF's "resume burning" decision was invalid, and waste-burning would have to cease—at least until the EIS had been filed and evaluated and the environmental consequences of the burning factored into the decision on resumption.

And so, any and every decision by agencies of the national government is potentially subject to this sort of challenge and court review! NEPA specifies that every recommendation or report on proposals for national legislation or other major actions "significantly affecting the quality of the human environment" must include "a detailed statement" on: "(i) the environmental impact of the proposed action, (ii) any adverse environmental effects which cannot be avoided if the proposal is implemented, (iii) alternatives to the proposed action, (iv) the relationship between local short-term uses of man's environment and the maintenance and enhancement of long-term productivity, and (v) any irreversible and irretrievable commitments of resources which would be involved if the proposal is implemented." And NEPA further requires that "the responsible Federal official," prior to filing the required EIS, *shall* "consult with and obtain the comments of any Federal agency which has jurisdiction by law or special expertise with respect to any environmental impact involved." NEPA thus ensures that the agencies with environmental expertise are alerted to, and involved in, the decision to undertake any such "major action." The forewarning does not necessarily give the environmentalists a veto on the proposed action, but it does seem to indicate that any serious environmental effects will at least be presented—and factored into the decision on whether to proceed with the action or not.

The other twenty-two statutes included in this "general environmental" category can be further sorted into several subgroups, the most numerous of which is "environmental education and research": PL 91-516, PL 92-326, PL 93-278, PL 93-319, and PL 93-322. "International" concerns are expressed by PL 92-598 (allowing US participation in an international exposition) and PL 93-188 (contributing to a UN environmental fund). "Reclamation" is the subject of PL 91-502 and PL 92-167, and "solid waste" is the subject of PL 91-512 and PL 93-14. There are three Acts dealing with "agricultural-environmental and consumer protection programs": PL 92-73, PL 92-399, and PL 93-135. If one needed any further evidence of the "long arm" of the national government, its power to reach a vast multitude of activities and subject-matters, one need only consider PL 91-451 and PL 92-604—providing funding for "jellyfish control"! On a more prosaic level of "administration," PL 93-36 provides appropriations for President Nixon's new Office of Environmental Quality, and PL 92-319 authorizes the transfer of certain land in Arkansas. Two minuscule Acts—PL 91-236 and PL 92-276—authorize the proclamation of "Arbor Day" (an official reminder to take care of the environment).

In addition to NEPA (PL 91-190), there are two other "new initiatives" in this "general environmental" grouping. PL 91-581 (the "Geothermal Steam Act of 1970") authorizes the Secretary of the Interior to arrange for disposition of the naturally-occurring energy resource. This would seem to indicate "one small step for man" toward the development of alternative energy options. Finally, PL 91-609 (the "Housing and Urban Development Act of 1970") provides—along with many other plans and objectives—for "the establishment of a national urban growth policy, to encourage and support the proper growth and development of our States, metropolitan areas, cities, counties, and towns." This is surely a most ambitious and comprehensive program statement, and certainly "forward-looking." Indeed, it might seem to be a call for a system of national "zoning laws"—analogous to what local communities had been doing since the early 1900s.

Conservation (including Parks, Forests, Historic Sites, Refuges)

"Conservation" turned out to be the numerically largest subcategory of the "environmental protection" statutes produced during the Nixon presidency. Included here are eighty Acts establishing, designating, or managing specific parks, forests, wildernesses, rivers, wildlife refuges, and historical sites—"conservation" in the Theodore Roosevelt tradition. Many of these pieces of legislation are very brief—one page or less in the annual volume of Public Acts. (Excluded from the count are any Acts which merely renamed one of these public places; counting such items as "protection" seemed a bit excessive.) Also excluded from the analysis were any mentions of such public places in general appropriations bills, although specific Acts providing funds for specific places were included (e.g., PL 92-272, appropriating additional funds for certain national parks, and PL 92-333, authorizing added funds for land acquisition in the area of Piscataway Park, MD).

Twenty-two other Acts seemed to be more generally focused. Like most of the eighty

Acts creating or expanding specific public places, even these more generally worded statutes are very short in length: fourteen of them are less than a page in length; the other six are each from one to two pages long. Nine deal with management of these sorts of public areas: PL 91-383, improving park administration by the Secretary of the Interior; PL 91-429, authorizing contracts for fire protection of public lands; PL 91-435, authorizing contracts for aerial services for public forests; PL 92-82, authorizing cooperation by park management with local law enforcement officials; PL 92-421, providing for accelerated tree planting for reforestation; PL 92-534, ending some restrictions on land acquisition for recreation and resource protection; PL 93-338, extending fund availability for forest highways; and PL 91-378 and PL 92-597, establishing—and then renewing—a Youth Conservation Corps.

Of the remaining thirteen Acts, five refer specifically to "land and water conservation," and so they are identified as a separate subcategory. PL 91-118 amends a 1956 Act promoting soil conservation on the Great Plains. PL 91-485 amends the Land and Water Act of 1965. PL 92-432 amends a 1948 statute regulating land use for wildlife conservation (a *one-word* amendment!) And the 93rd Congress passed two bills imposing fees on persons using some of these public facilities—PL 93-81 and PL 93-303.

Two Acts authorize the Secretary of Agriculture to cooperate in implementing conservation programs: PL 91-343 (land conservation) and PL 92-288 (forestry). "Volunteer" programs are authorized for parks (by PL 91-357) and for forests (by PL 92-300). Both PL 91-243 and PL 93-54 extend the national government's program to preserve historical sites. PL 91-390 might have been placed in the "Interstate Compacts" category, but it is included here because the compact had to do with the establishment of the "Falls of the Ohio Interstate *Park*." (The "park establishment" subject-matter seemed more important than the interstate-agreement procedure by which it is to be created.)

Finally, even in this category, there was one Act with an (immense) international dimension—PL 91-427. In a mere three-quarters of a page, the Secretary of the Interior and the Smithsonian Institution are authorized "to expend certain sums, in cooperation with the territory of Guam, the territory of American Samoa, the Trust Territory of the Pacific Islands, other United States territories in the Pacific Ocean, and the State of Hawaii, for the conservation of their protective and productive coral reefs." (PL 91-427 would seem to be strong support for the earlier comment that President Nixon proposed "the most advanced environmental program in American history"—and that he delivered on much of it!)

Water Regulation (including Pollution Control, Resources, River Basins, Desalinization)

Perhaps the most surprising feature of this category of fifty-three Public Laws is that only

eight of them—91-144, 91-224, 91-439, 92-50, 92-137, 91-240, 92-500, and 93-207—
seemed to merit inclusion in the "pollution control" subgrouping.[18] (There are several others
with some "pollution" connection but which also had other specific features that led to an
alternate classification.) Both 91-144 and 91-439 involved appropriations, at least some of
which were for water pollution control. Act 91-224—the Water Quality Improvement Act of
1970—was a set of substantial amendments to the Federal Water Pollution Control Act of
1948. Further significant changes came in the 92nd Congress—twenty-five pages of them,
PL 92-500. The complex and lengthy negotiations leading up to 92-500 were evidently
responsible for the passing of three short-term extensions—92-50, 92-137, and 92-240—of
parts of the earlier statutes. As noted at the beginning of this Chapter, President Nixon's veto
of 92-500 was one of seven overridden by Congress; thirty-six Nixon vetoes of other legislation were sustained by Congress. (The vote to override on Act 92-500 was 52 to 12 in the
Senate and 247 to 23 in the House. The Democrats had a 55 to 45 majority in the Senate and
255 to 180 in the House. Obviously, not everyone voted, and not every Democrat voted to
override.) PL 92-207 added some relatively minor "fine-tuning" changes to the water-
pollution regulations.

The largest subcategory consisted of statutes dealing with "water resources"—Acts relating to their identification and development. PL 91-81, PL 92-199, PL 92-577, and PL 93-122
were less than one-page authorizations of feasibility studies for various water-development
projects. PL 93-97 and PL 93-251 actually authorized such projects—in some detail (eleven
pages in the former, thirty-eight pages in the latter: the "Water Resources Development Act
of 1974"). The other nine Acts in this subcategory are amendments to earlier statutes; all
except PL 92-583 consist of less than a page each. PL 91-308 amends the Land and Water
Conservation Fund Act of 1965, which uses revenues from offshore oil and gas leases for
conservation purposes. PL 92-27, PL 92-175, PL 92-396, and PL 93-55 are brief amendments to the Water Resources Planning Act of 1965. The Marine Resources and Engineering
Development Act of 1966 is amended by PL 91-15, PL 91-349, PL 91-414, and the afore-
mentioned PL 92-583—which uses nine-plus pages to outline policies for the development
and use of the US' coastal zones.

The next-largest subcategory under "water regulation" is "river-basin development"—a
closely-related subject but with a slightly different geographical focus.[19] Ten Acts fall into
this group: 91-218, 91-270, 91-282, 91-381, 91-409, 91-415, 92-146, 92-222, 92-370, and
92-371. All ten are quite brief—four are less than one page in length; four are from one to
less than two pages long; one is three-plus pages; and one is four-plus pages. The "river-
basins" involved range from the Rogue River basin in Oregon (PL 91-270) and the Upper
Colorado River basin (PL 92-370) to the huge Missouri River basin—covering a number of
States (PL 91-218, PL 91-389, PL 91-409, PL 91-415, PL 92-146, and PL 92-371, with this

last Act authorizing appropriations "for completing work in the Missouri River Basin by the Secretary of the Interior"). General appropriations authorizations for several projects—some dating back to statutory beginnings in the 1940s—are found in Acts 91-282 and 92-222, the latter putting a $628,000,000 cap on additional expenditures for the fourteen river-basin projects listed in its first subsection. (These last two Acts are the longest in length in this subcategory.) By comparison, the average length of the two Acts in the "ports and waterways" subcategory (PL 92-340: the "Ports and Waterways Safety Act of 1972"—at seven-plus pages—and PL 91-611: the "River and Harbor Act of 1970"—at seventeen-plus pages) is larger than the *total* length of the ten Acts constituting the "river-basin" group.

Three subcategories—"oceans," "desalinization," and "miscellaneous"—contain six or seven Acts each. The continuing efforts during the Nixon presidency to promote research on desalinization seem particularly forward-looking. Many of the world's inhabitants lack convenient access to clean water. While the US is blessed with large bodies of fresh water (e.g., the Great Lakes and the Mississippi-Missouri River system), shortages have occurred even here. President Nixon recognized these realities, too—outlining a plan in his 1972 environmental message to Congress to set aside some 547,000 acres as the "Big Cypress National Freshwater Reserve." The seven desalinization statutes—PL 91-43, PL 91-221, PL 92-60, PL 92-273, PL 93-51, PL 93-320, and PL 93-342—thus have a continuing relevance, which seems destined to intensify as the world's population continues to increase, along with the concomitant increases in industrial and agricultural activities. (PL 92-60 "expands and extends" the research program; and PL 93-320 is specifically directed at controlling the salinization of the Colorado River, a major water source for California and Arizona as well as Colorado. The other five Acts provide continued funding for desalinization efforts.)

The "oceans" subcategory—PL 92-125, PL 92-532, PL 92-567, PL 93-119, PL 93-248, PL 93-254, and PL 93-304—illustrates again the "international" dimensions of the Nixon presidency's environmental activities. In 1971, President Nixon had requested action by Congress to regulate ocean-dumping of wastes. Congress had discussed several proposals, but no legislation had resulted. His efforts came to fruition in the 92nd Congress. The first session merely established the National Advisory Committee on Oceans and Atmosphere (PL 91-125). The second session, however, did pass PL 92-532: the "Marine Protection, Research, and Sanctuaries Act of 1972," which did indeed regulate the ocean-dumping of wastes—as President Nixon had requested. PL 92-567 increased the appropriation for the National Advisory Committee on Oceans and Atmosphere. PL 93-119 amended the Oil Pollution Act of 1961, and PL 93-248 authorized US "intervention" on the high seas when there was an oil pollution "occurrence." PL 93-254 amended the 1972 Marine Protection, Research, and Sanctuaries Act. PL 93-304 merely provided funds for the US' participation in the International Ocean Exposition. Here again, these early efforts during the Nixon administration anticipated the increased importance of seaborne trade, as international commerce increased exponentially in later years.

The last six Acts in the "water regulation" category certainly merit their categorization as "miscellaneous"—a "mixed bag" if ever there was one. PL 91-408 authorizes additional construction at the Yuma, AZ irrigation project. PL 91-514 increases the penalties for illegal fishing in US territorial waters. PL 92-367 and PL 93-206 have to do with dams; the former sets up an inspection program under the Secretary of the Army, and the latter authorizes the Secretary of the Interior to contract with non-federal agencies for the replacement of the American Falls dam in Idaho. PL 92-263 authorizes payment of DC's share of the Potomac River reservoir's costs. Finally, PL 93-18 (a joint resolution) recognizes April 15–22, 1973 as "National Clean Water Week."

Species Protection

As indicated in this section's introductory overview, "species protection" was the third most numerous category of environmental legislation during President Nixon's tenure in office. By our count, the 91st Congress passed nine such Acts (one in its first session, eight in its second), the 92nd Congress passed thirteen (four and nine), and the 93rd passed eight (two and six).

What form did these various "protections" take? Even the single, initial effort by the first session of the 91st Congress contained a warning that there was "a new sheriff in town" and that serious consequences might flow from environmental violations. PL 91-135, approved on December 5, 1969, occupies a modest eight-plus pages in volume 83 of the US Statutes at large. Its brief introductory description says that its purpose is to prohibit the importation of any endangered wildlife species and the interstate shipment of any wildlife "taken contrary to State law." The Secretary of the Interior makes the determination of "endangered" status— "based on the best scientific and commercial data available to him" and after consulting with officials in the nations which are the normal habitats of such wildlife. The strong message of "serious business" comes in the penalty sections of the Act: forfeiture of the prohibited items *and* a "civil penalty" of up to $5,000—*per offense*, with each violation considered as a separate offense. (Ten illegal items = a total penalty of up to $50,000; 100 items = $500,000 is at stake!) The Act does require notice to the offender and an opportunity for a hearing, and the Secretary may "compromise" any such penalty—but the intended deterrence still seems quite clear. Especially so since the *criminal* penalties provided for persons convicted of "knowingly and willfully" violating the Act include a $10,000 fine and/or imprisonment for up to one year.

There is considerable length-variation among the other twenty-nine Acts in this category. Twenty-three of them are brief enough to fill fewer than four pages each, with eleven of those being less than one full page in length. Three Acts consist of four to seven pages each: PL 92-471 (amending the North Pacific Fisheries Act of 1954), PL 91-503 (amending the Federal Aid in Wildlife Restoration Act of 1937 and the Federal Aid in Fish Restoration Act of 1950), and PL 93-242 (the Offshore Shrimp Fisheries Act of 1973, which extends an existing international agreement to include Brazil). PL 91-577 takes some eighteen pages to "encourage the development of novel varieties of sexually reproduced plants." The 92nd Congress used nineteen pages in PL 92-522 to protect marine mammals, and the 93rd Congress protected endangered species in the twenty pages of PL 93-205.

In addition to 91-577, the 91st Congress passed one other "developmental" measure: PL 91-239, which needed only one page to establish an "international quarantine station," through which animals could be imported "from any country" for the purpose of improving livestock breeds. Besides the Brazilian shrimp agreement (PL 93-242), the 93rd Congress produced two other Acts which were clearly "international" in character: PL 93-300, which extended the international treaty on migratory birds to Japan, and 93-339, which authorized US participation in an international exposition on fisheries conservation. The 93rd Congress also concerned itself with several "administrative" decisions, passing brief Acts replacing the "Commissioner" of Fish and Wildlife with a "Director" of that "Division" in the Department of the Interior (PL 93-271), authorizing the various national government departments to "loan" personnel and equipment to Interior's Bureau of Sport Fisheries and Wildlife (PL 93-280), and delaying funds for certain wildlife restoration projects (PL 93-313).

The "special interest" of the 92nd Congress was the shooting of game from airplanes! It passed two abbreviated (one-plus page each) pieces of legislation dealing with the topic: PL 92-249, which amended the Fish and Wildlife Act of 1956 so as to prohibit using an "aircraft" to shoot or harass "any bird, fish, or other animal" and PL 92-502 (passed eleven months later, in the second session of the 92nd Congress), which added further enforcement provisions. The first amendment of the 1956 FWA had included a $5,000 fine and/or imprisonment for up to one year for violations; PL 92-502 added forfeiture of any animals taken in violation of the statute and added civil forfeiture of any guns, aircraft, or equipment used during the violation. In addition, the Secretary of the Interior was given the power to promulgate regulations, and the forfeiture regulations for customs violations were to be applied to actions under this statute, with the Interior Secretary to exercise the same authority here as the Treasury Department has in enforcing the customs laws.

The most numerous subcategory under "species protection" had to do with "fisheries"—protection of the fishing industry by managing the fish "stocks" in which the US has an interest. Twelve of the thirty "species protection" category Acts concerned "fisheries": 91-249, 91-315, 91-387, 91-514, 92-87, 92-219, 92-444, 92-471, 92-504, 92-590, 92-601, and 93-362. The first and the last of these were aimed at protecting "anadromous" fish—which

Wikipedia tells us are fish that spawn in fresh water but mature in salt water (salmon, e.g.). PL 91-249 encouraged the States to engage in joint research and development of this research; PL 93-362 targeted the sea lamprey threat to these fish and increased the national government's funding from $10 million to $20 million.

Eight of the other ten "fisheries"-related Acts are also relatively brief (six of the eight are less than two pages in length) renewals/extensions/updates of previously-existing programs. PL 92-87 takes three-plus pages to amend the Northwest Atlantic Fisheries Act of 1950; PL 92-471 uses a bit more language to update the North Pacific Fisheries Act of 1954. By contrast, PL 92-444 (the "Central, Western, and South Pacific Fisheries Development Act") needs less than one page to authorize a new program for the controlled development of the fishing industry in the vast oceanic expanse designated in its title. (An interesting parallel to PL 91-427!) In less than two pages, PL 92-601 imposes a set of new restrictions on fishing in ocean areas subject to US jurisdiction: a five-year prohibition on the transfer at sea or the direct importation into the US of "prohibited fish" by a "prohibited vessel." ("Prohibited vessel" means any ship of less than five net tons which was constructed in a foreign country, and used in a fishery there, and subsequently barred from use there. "Prohibited fish" is defined as any marine animal or plant that the vessel was authorized to catch before being barred from doing so.) A civil penalty of up to $1,000, plus forfeiture of the prohibited fish—"in addition to any other penalty provided by law"—may be imposed for violation.

While much (if not all) of the "fisheries" legislation had a distinct economic tinge ("protecting" the fish stock to try to make sure that the fishing *industry* remained viable), the species "conservation" motive behind our last subcategory seems purer. In addition to PL 91-135 (already discussed), seven other Acts were placed in this grouping: 91-503, 91-559, 92-195, 92-522, 92-535, 92-558, and 93-205. As a group, these eight Acts are the most innovative subcategory of the 220-odd statutes in this pro-environment Chapter. They are thus also the most substantial (i.e., the longest—the top two and four of the top six Acts in the "species protection" subcategory of thirty, and three of the nine longest among the entire environmental set of 220+).

Three of these Acts (91-503, 91-559, and 92-558) are directed at wildlife restoration generally, including habitat protection. Two provide protection for a specific wildlife subset: PL 92-195 (wild horses) and PL 92-535 (eagles). PL 92-522 contains a rather comprehensive set of protections (nineteen-plus pages' worth) for marine mammals. And last—but by no means least—we come to PL 93-205: the Endangered Species Act (ESA). A game-changer: twenty pages of legislative U-235! It is a governmental commitment to try to prevent the extinction of additional species, by modifying or terminating government activities that may interfere with the continued viability of the threatened plant or animal life. President Nixon had such a law on his 1972 "wish-list" message to Congress; he got this "wish" when he signed 93-205 into law on December 28, 1973.

As interpreted by the courts, the ESA has proved to be a serious barrier to human activities which have potentially adverse effects on endangered fauna or flora. The 6-to-3 decision by the US Supreme Court in *Tennessee Valley Authority v. Hill*, 437 US 153 (1978) is probably the leading example of the intent and scope of the ESA.

The Tennessee Valley Authority (TVA) started construction on the Tellico Dam/Reservoir project in 1967. By 1973, when the ESA became law, the project was "nearly completed," at a cost of over $100 million dollars. Having determined that a small fish called the "snail darter" was an endangered species and that its "critical habitat" in the Little Tennessee River would be destroyed by the completion of the dam and the filling of the reservoir, the Secretary of the Interior ruled that all federal agencies had to avoid that result. As authorized by the ESA, several concerned citizens then filed a lawsuit in the US District Court in Tennessee, asking that the TVA be enjoined from completing the Tellico Dam. While the District Court refused to issue the injunction, the Sixth Circuit Court of Appeals reversed that ruling and ordered the issuance of a permanent injunction prohibiting the TVA from completing the dam. The TVA asked for review by the US Supreme Court. Six Justices of the Supreme Court agreed with the Sixth Circuit. Writing for the majority, Chief Justice Burger quoted with approval parts of the Sixth Circuit's explanation of its decision:

Current project status cannot be translated into a workable standard of judicial review. Whether a dam is 50% or 90% completed is irrelevant in calculating the social and scientific costs attributable to the disappearance of a unique form of life. Courts are ill-equipped to calculate how many dollars must be invested before the value of a dam exceeds that of the endangered species. Our responsibility under § 1540 (g)(1)(A) is merely to preserve the status quo where endangered species are threatened, thereby guaranteeing the legislative or executive branches sufficient opportunity to grapple with the alternatives. . . .

It is conceivable that the welfare of an endangered species may weigh more heavily upon the public conscience, as expressed by the final will of Congress, than the writeoff of those millions of dollars already expended for Tellico in excess of its present salvageable value.

Burger then indicated that he thought the ESA had to be applied as it was written:

It may seem curious to some that the survival of a relatively small number of three-inch fish among all the countless millions of species extant would require the permanent halting of a virtually completed dam for which Congress has expended

more than $100 million. The paradox is not minimized by the fact that Congress continued to appropriate large sums of public money for the project, even after congressional Appropriations Committees were apprised of its apparent impact upon the survival of the snail darter. We conclude, however, that the explicit provisions of the Endangered Species Act require precisely that result.

Dissenting, Justices Powell and Blackmun did not think that the ESA could reasonably be applied to a project that was completed or substantially completed when its threat to an endangered species was discovered. Justice Rehnquist also dissented—separately—"on the ground that the Endangered Species Act did not prohibit the District Court from refusing, in the exercise of its traditional equitable powers, to enjoin completion of the dam." (Interestingly, the three dissenters were all Nixon appointees—as was Chief Justice Burger, who wrote the opinion for the majority!)

While the exact timing sequence of the TVA case will not recur, it is clear that the Supreme Court has decided that any "balancing" of the worth of a project and the worth of an endangered species has already been done by the 93rd Congress in passing the Act—and by President Nixon in signing it. The courts do not have the authority to do their own "balancing" as alleged violations of the Act are brought to their attention. Needless to say, lawsuits claiming violations of the ESA have proliferated, and much legal time and effort (and cost) has been expended in determining their validity. It should also be obvious that there are strongly-held differences of opinion as to just where the "balance-line" between species protection and development projects should be drawn. As to one basic point, however, there can be no doubt: this particular piece of Nixon-era environmental legislation has had a profound effect on our society.

Recent developments suggest that the Burger Court's snail-darter decision may not be the last word after all. The August 13, 2018, issue of *Time* magazine reported (page 14) that: "In 118 pages of technical documents, the Department of Interior proposed making it harder to protect new land, adding rules that might allow regulators to ignore the effects of climate change and, perhaps most significantly, removing the ban on factoring in cost when deciding how and whether to protect a species." It also noted that Congress is considering legislation "that would defang [*sic*] the law and, in some cases, explicitly remove some animals from the endangered-species list." If adopted by the Department of the Interior, such regulations could—and presumably would—be challenged in the courts. The stakes here are, of course, enormous: billions of dollars in costs—and "benefits." (The same article stated that the National Fish and Wildlife Foundation valued the "lifestyle" benefits resulting from the ESA at "about $1.6 trillion annually in the US.")

Interstate Compact Consent

Although there were only seven such pieces of legislation during the Nixon presidency, their nature seemed different enough to identify them as a separate category. Four such "compacts" were consented to by the 91st Congress (91-52, 91-148, 91-158, and 91-575), two by the 92nd (92-308 and 92-322), and only one by the 93rd (93-152). As a group, these seven Acts have an average length (at about ten pages) considerably longer than the other categories. The average is considerably raised by PL 91-575's thirty-two pages (the fifth-longest of the 220-plus Acts), but none of the other six contains fewer than four pages (there are no minuscule items of one-third or one-fourth of a page).

PL 91-575 not only gives congressional approval to the Susquehanna River Basin Compact between New York, Pennsylvania, and Maryland, but it also makes the US national government a party to the Compact—by enacting it into national law. (Hence the entire thirty-two-page text of the Compact is reproduced.) Four other Acts also approve multi-State conservation/development efforts but without necessarily making the US itself a party to the compact involved. PL 91-52 approves the joint efforts of Wyoming and Nebraska for the Upper Niobrara River; PL 91-148, the coordination of Nevada and California as to the Lake Tahoe area; PL 92-308, the Big Blue River project of Kansas and Nebraska; and Act 93-152, the agreement of Arkansas and Oklahoma for the Arkansas River.

PL 91-158 and PL 93-152 represent a different sort of concerted State action. In Dallas, Texas, in February 1935, representatives of the States of Oklahoma, Texas, California, and New Mexico agreed to an oil-and-gas compact. Article II of the compact states: "The purpose of this compact is to conserve oil and gas by the prevention of physical waste thereof from any cause." Signatory oil-producing States agreed to avoid extraction processes that resulted in waste of these resources. The original compact was to expire in 1937, but it could be renewed. Congress has evidently given its approval to each such renewal. Additional oil-producing States signed on over the years—twenty-nine States were listed in each of these renewal Acts. PL 91-158 consented to a renewal of the Compact until September 1, 1971, and PL 93-152 agreed to an extension until September 1, 1974.

Air Pollution Regulation

Most surprising, at least to the author, was the discovery that the Nixon "environmental revolution" contained only four statutes dealing with air pollution—and three of those consisted of less than a half page each! PL 91-137 takes less than one-third of a page to extend air-quality research authorization for one year and provide the funds therefor. PL 91-316 uses slightly more space to extend for two months the availability of funding authorizations for the Clean Air Act and the Solid Waste Disposal Act. PL 93-15 takes the same length to extend funding for the Clean Air Act from June 30, 1973, to June 30, 1974.

Which leaves us with the fourth "air regulation" statute (PL 91-604)—the thirty-eight-page assemblage of several significant air-quality initiatives, including State responsibilities in maintaining air quality and national gas-mileage standards for motor vehicles. With the benefit of thirty years of hindsight, one commentator observed: "The Clean Air Act of 1970 was the most sweeping measure of its kind ever written. . . ."[20]

What-all does that Act contain, then? The first order of business here is a necessary clarification: PL 91-604 is officially titled the "Clean Air Amendments of 1970." It is a set of amendments to the preexisting air pollution legislation already found in volume 42 of the US Code as sections 1857–1857g and referred to as the "Clean Air Act." The initial statute—the Air Pollution Control Act—was passed during the Eisenhower administration (in 1955). It had been amended several times, most notably by the Clean Air Act of 1963 (PL 88-206), the 1965 Motor Vehicle Air Pollution Control Act, and the 1967 Air Quality Act. As each amended Act becomes law, the changed wording is reflected in the appropriate US Code volume and section. Thus, PL 91-406 says it is amending "42 USC 1857, et seq. [and following]"—the "Clean Air Act." Its thirty-eight pages significantly expanded the activities of the Environmental Protection Agency and provided some additional, powerful enforcement mechanisms.

The 1970 Act begins by setting forth an expanded research program, giving "special emphasis to research on the short- and long-term effects of air pollution on public health and welfare." For this purpose, it authorizes contracts up to ten years in length and appropriation of $15,000,000.

Second, it sets up an arrangement for cost-sharing grants to "air pollution control agencies" to assist them in developing and implementing programs to meet national air quality standards. Such grants could cover "up to three-fourths of the cost of planning, developing, establishing, or improving, and up to three-fifths of the cost of maintaining" plans applying to areas including two or more municipalities, whether in the same State or two different States. For plans governing designated "interstate air quality control regions," grants to the applicable control agency can be for 100 percent of the costs for two years and for three-fourths of the costs thereafter.

Third, the Act adds eight new sections that establish "ambient air quality and emission standards." Section 107 imposes on "[e]ach State" . . . "the primary responsibility for assuring air quality within the entire geographic area comprising such State by submitting an implementation plan for such State which will specify the manner in which national primary and secondary ambient air quality standards will be achieved and maintained within each air quality control region in such State." The "regions" covered here include those already established prior to the 1970 amendments and those subsequently designated by the EPA Administrator under the authority given by subsection (c) of Section 107. (All by itself, this section thus represents a massive increase in the regulatory power of the national government.)

Seven more new statutory sections flesh out this comprehensive attack on air pollution. Section 108 outlines "Air Quality Criteria and Control Techniques." Section 109 establishes "National Ambient Air Quality Standards." Section 110 describes the required "Implementation Plans." Section 111 specifies "Standards of Performance for New Stationary Sources" (of air pollution); Section 112 outlines "National Emission Standards for Hazardous Air Pollution." Section 113 provides for "Federal Enforcement"—through orders by the EPA Administrator or by filing a civil action in US District Court. (Such lawsuit may be filed in the district "in which the defendant is located or resides or is doing business." For a first offense, punishment is by fine of up to $25,000 *per day* or prison for up to one year, or both; for subsequent convictions, the fine is up to $50,000 per day, up to two years in prison, or both.) Section 114 gives the EPA powers for "Inspections, Monitoring, and Entry [to premises]."

Section 115 (renumbered) is retitled and reworded to provide for "Abatement by Means of Conference Procedure in Certain Cases" and Section 116, to reaffirm "Retention of State Authority." Renumbered and amended Section 118 ("Control of Pollution from Federal Facilities" is of special significance: "Each department, agency, and instrumentality of the executive, legislative, and judicial branches of the Federal Government (1) having jurisdiction over any property or facility, or (2) engaged in any activity resulting, or which may result, in the discharge of air pollutants, shall comply with Federal, State, interstate, and local requirements respecting control and abatement of air pollution to the same extent that any person is subject to such requirements." That is a truly breathtaking commitment—both in its scope and in its equity! Having imposed on the States "the primary responsibility" for air quality within their borders, Congress and the President now commit themselves *and the national Judiciary* to obeying whatever rules State and local governments adopt to meet that requirement!

A fourth major section of the 1970 amendments deals with "Motor Vehicle Emission Standards." There are nearly thirteen pages of changes dealing with such matters as the establishment of standards, enforcement, penalties, compliance testing and certification, regulation of fuels, and development of low-emission vehicles. (Interestingly, one of the criteria for certification as a "low-emission vehicle" is: "[vi] its noise level . . .") A new "Part B—Aircraft Emission Standards" is added to Title II of the Clean Air Act, and a new subsection on "Aviation Fuel Standards" is added to section 601 of the Federal Aviation Act of 1958.

Several of the 1970 Act's "General Provisions" seem worth mentioning. "Citizen Suits" are permitted by a new "Sec. 304": "any person may commence a civil action on his own behalf" against any other person—including the United States or any other governmental agency—who is alleged to be violating an emission standard or an EPA or State order relating thereto. Suit can also be filed against the EPA Administrator for failure to perform a nondiscretionary duty under the Clean Air Act. Under the new section 306, no Federal agency can enter into a purchase contract with a person convicted of certain violations of the Act "until the Administrator certifies that the condition giving rise to such a conviction has been corrected." If the Attorney General determines that a product or process protected by a patent is necessary for compliance with an environmental requirement and that there are no reasonable alternatives (so that the patent owner would be the only person able to supply—lawfully—the pollution-producing good or service), the Attorney General may request a US District Court order requiring the owner to license use of the patented item.

The 1970 Act also adds a very brief "Title IV—Noise Pollution" at the end of the (overall) Clean Air Act. It requires the EPA Administrator to establish "an Office of Noise Abatement and Control" and to conduct "through such Office a full and complete investigation and study of noise and its effect on the public health and safety." (The 1972 noise statute discussed later in this Chapter was clearly a product of this "investigation and study.") Some three-plus pages of "Technical and Conforming Amendments" complete the Act.

The EPA Administrator is given considerable discretion in setting standards for meeting the requirements of the Clean Air Act, as illustrated by the Supreme Court's decision in the *Chevron* case,[21] excerpted in the following paragraphs. EPA regulations permitted States to consider all pollution-emitting devices within the same industrial grouping to be treated as one unit (one "bubble") for purposes of deciding if a permit should be issued to allow modification of facilities. That regulation was challenged by several environmental groups. The US District Court held that the regulation was valid, but that decision was reversed by the US Circuit Court for the District of Columbia. Chevron requested Supreme Court review. All six participating Justices agreed that the EPA Administrator's ruling was a permissible interpretation of the amended CAA. Justice Stevens's opinion for the Court contains a classic statement of the relationship between courts and administrative agencies:

The arguments over policy that are advanced in the parties' briefs create the impression that respondents are now waging in a judicial forum a specific policy battle which they ultimately lost in the agency and in the 32 jurisdictions opting for the "bubble concept," but one which was never waged in the Congress. Such policy arguments are more properly addressed to legislators or administrators, not to judges. . . .

In these cases the Administrator's interpretation represents a reasonable accommodation of manifestly competing interests and is entitled to deference: the regulatory scheme is technical and complex, the agency considered the matter in a

detailed and reasoned fashion, and the decision involves reconciling conflicting policies. Congress intended to accommodate both interests, but did not do so itself on the level of specificity presented by these cases. Perhaps that body consciously desired the Administrator to strike the balance at this level, thinking that those with great expertise and charged with responsibility for administering the provision would be in a better position to do so; perhaps it simply did not consider the question at this level; and perhaps Congress was unable to forge a coalition on either side of the question, and those on each side decided to take their chances with the scheme devised by the agency. For judicial purposes, it matters not which of these things occurred.

Judges are not experts in the field, and are not part of either political branch of the Government. Courts must, in some cases, reconcile competing political interests, but not on the basis of the judges' personal policy preferences. In contrast, an agency to which Congress has delegated policymaking responsibilities may, within the limits of that delegation, properly rely upon the incumbent administration's views of wise policy to inform its judgments. While agencies are not directly accountable to the people, the Chief Executive is, and it is entirely appropriate for this political branch of the Government to make such policy choices—resolving the competing interests which Congress itself either inadvertently did not resolve, or intentionally left to be resolved by the agency charged with the administration of the statute in light of everyday realities.

When a challenge to an agency construction of a statutory provision, fairly conceptualized, really centers on the wisdom of the agency's policy, rather than whether it is a reasonable choice within a gap left open by Congress, the challenge must fail. In such a case, federal judges—who have no constituency—have a duty to respect legitimate policy choices made by those who do. The responsibilities for assessing the wisdom of such policy choices and resolving the struggle between competing views of the public interest are not judicial ones: "Our Constitution vests such responsibilities in the political branches. . . ."

We hold that the EPA's definition of the term "source" is a permissible construction of the statute which seeks to accommodate progress in reducing air pollution with economic growth. "The Regulations which the Administrator has adopted provide what the agency could allowably view as . . . [an] effective reconciliation of these twofold ends. . . ."

The judgment of the Court of Appeals is reversed.

Quite recently (2011), the Supreme Court has issued an important opinion,[22] excerpted in the following paragraphs, dealing with the legalities involved in activities generating so-called "greenhouse gases" and the "global warming" that most scientists believe occurs as a result. Justice Ginsburg wrote the opinion for the eight Justices who participated in the decision (two of whom did not entirely agree with it but did "concur"—agree, with the judgment/decision). Note that the basis for the Court's decision is the *Clean Air Act* (as subsequently amended, of course):

We address in this opinion the question whether the plaintiffs (several States, the city of New York, and three private land trusts) can maintain federal common-law public nuisance claims against carbon-dioxide emitters (four private power companies and the federal Tennessee Valley Authority). As relief, the plaintiffs ask for a decree setting carbon-dioxide emissions for each defendant at an initial cap, to be further reduced annually. The Clean Air Act and the Environmental Protection Agency action the Act authorizes, we hold, displace the claims the plaintiffs seek to pursue. . . .

In *Massachusetts* v. *EPA* . . . this Court held that . . . the Clean Air Act . . . authorizes federal regulation of emissions of carbon dioxide and other greenhouse gases. . . . Responding to our decision in *Massachusetts*, EPA undertook greenhouse gas regulation. . . .

EPA and the Department of Transportation subsequently issued a joint final rule regulating emissions from light-duty vehicles . . . and initiated a joint rulemaking covering medium- and heavy-duty vehicles. . . . EPA also began phasing in requirements that new or modified "[m]ajor [greenhouse gas] emitting facilities" use the "best available control technology." . . . Finally, EPA commenced a rulemaking . . . to set limits on greenhouse gas emissions from new, modified, and existing fossil-fuel fired powerplants. Pursuant to a settlement finalized in March 2011, EPA has committed to issuing a proposed rule by July 2011, and a final rule by May 2012. . . .

The District Court dismissed both suits as presenting nonjusticiable political questions . . . but the Second Circuit reversed. . . . On the threshold questions, the Court of Appeals held that the suits were not barred by the political question doctrine . . . and that the plaintiffs had adequately alleged Article III standing. . . .

Turning to the merits, the Second Circuit held that all plaintiffs had stated a claim under the "federal common law of nuisance." . . .

The plaintiffs argue, as the Second Circuit held, that federal common law is not displaced until EPA actually exercises its regulatory authority, *i.e.*, until it sets standards governing emissions from the defendants' plants. We disagree. . . .

The Clean Air Act is no less an exercise of the Legislature's "considered judgment" concerning the regulation of air pollution because it permits emissions *until* EPA acts. . . . The critical point is that Congress delegated to EPA the decision whether and how to regulate carbon-dioxide emissions from powerplants; the delegation is what displaces federal common law. Indeed, were EPA to decline to regulate carbon-dioxide emissions altogether at the conclusion of its ongoing § 7411 rulemaking, the federal courts would have no warrant to employ the federal common law of nuisance to upset the Agency's expert determination.

EPA's judgment, we hasten to add, would not escape judicial review. Federal courts . . . can review agency action (or a final rule declining to take action) to ensure compliance with the statute Congress enacted. . . . [The] Clean Air Act directs EPA to establish emissions standards for categories of stationary sources that, "in [the Administrator's] judgment," "caus[e], or contribut[e] significantly to, air pollution which may reasonably be anticipated to endanger public health or welfare." . . . "[T]he use of the word 'judgment' . . . is not a roving license to ignore the statutory text. . . . It is but a direction to exercise discretion within defined statutory limits." . . . EPA may not decline to regulate carbon-dioxide emissions from powerplants if refusal to act would be "arbitrary, capricious, an abuse of discretion, or otherwise not in accordance with law." . . . If the plaintiffs in this case are dissatisfied with the outcome of EPA's forthcoming rulemaking, their recourse under federal law is to seek Court of Appeals review, and, ultimately, to petition for certiorari in this Court.

Indeed, this prescribed order of decisionmaking—the first decider under the Act is the expert administrative agency, the second, federal judges—is yet another reason to resist setting emissions standards by judicial decree under federal tort law. The appropriate amount of regulation in any particular greenhouse gas-producing sector cannot be prescribed in a vacuum: As with other questions of national or international policy, informed assessment of competing interests is required. Along with the environmental benefit potentially achievable, our Nation's energy needs and the possibility of economic disruption must weigh in the balance.

The Clean Air Act entrusts such complex balancing to EPA in the first instance, in combination with state regulators. Each "standard of performance" EPA sets must "tak[e] into account the cost of achieving [emissions] reduction and any nonair quality health and environmental impact and energy requirements." . . . EPA may "distinguish among classes, types, and sizes" of stationary sources in apportioning responsibility for emissions reductions. . . . And the Agency may waive compliance with emission limits to permit a facility to test drive an "innovative technological system" that has "not [yet] been adequately demonstrated." . . . The Act envisions extensive cooperation between federal and state authorities. . . .

It is altogether fitting that Congress designated an expert agency, here, EPA, as best suited to serve as primary regulator of greenhouse gas emissions. The expert agency is surely better equipped to do the job than individual district judges issuing ad hoc, case-by-case injunctions. Federal judges lack the scientific, economic, and technological resources an agency can utilize in coping with issues of this order. . . . Judges may not commission scientific studies or convene groups of experts for advice, or issue rules under notice-and-comment procedures inviting input by any interested person, or seek the counsel of regulators in the States where the defendants are located. Rather, judges are confined by a record comprising the evidence the parties present. Moreover, federal district judges, sitting as sole adjudicators, lack authority to render precedential decisions binding other judges, even members of the same court.

Notwithstanding these disabilities, the plaintiffs propose that individual federal judges determine, in the first instance, what amount of carbon-dioxide emissions is "unreasonable," . . . and then decide what level of reduction is "practical, feasible and economically viable." . . . These determinations would be made for the defendants named in the two lawsuits launched by the plaintiffs. Similar suits could be mounted, counsel for the States and New York City estimated, against "thousands or hundreds or tens" of other defendants fitting the description "large contributors" to carbon-dioxide emissions. . . .

The judgments the plaintiffs would commit to federal judges, in suits that could be filed in any federal district, cannot be reconciled with the decisionmaking scheme Congress enacted. The Second Circuit erred, we hold, in ruling that federal judges may set limits on greenhouse gas emissions in face of a law empowering EPA to set the same limits, subject to judicial review only to ensure against action "arbitrary, capricious . . . or otherwise not in accordance with law." . . .

For the reasons stated, we reverse the judgment of the Second Circuit and remand the case for further proceedings consistent with this opinion.

Specific Environmental Hazards

Five other types of environmental degradation were dealt with in somewhat more specifical-ly-focused statutes. The 91st Congress passed the "Poison Prevention Packaging Act of 1970" (PL 91-601) and the "Lead-Based Paint Poisoning Prevention Act" (PL 91-695). The 92nd Congress enacted two substantial regulatory extensions: the "Federal Environmental Pesticide Control Act of 1972" (PL 92-516) and the "Noise Control Act of 1972" (PL 92-574), and it briefly amended the Natural Gas Pipeline Safety Act of 1968—with PL 92-401. And the 93rd Congress added amendments (PL 93-151) to the lead-based paint act just passed by the 91st.

Noise Pollution. President Nixon's signing of the Noise Control Act of 1972 returned to the new area of national government concern that the 1970 Clean Air Amendments had targeted for $30 million worth of "investigation and study." Title IV of that statute (PL 91-406— discussed earlier in this Chapter) had also mandated the establishment of an EPA "Office of Noise Abatement and Control" to do the investigating. Evidently, sufficient evidence had been gathered to convince Nixon that there was a problem and that it was time for corrective action.

Many of the sources—and effects—of water and air pollution are all too visible: the 1969 flames on the Cuyahoga River in Ohio, for example, or the smoke and ash spewing from the chimneys of factories and power plants. The potentially harmful effects of excessive or irritating noises are more insidious—less easy to pin down but perhaps easier to take for granted, as part of the price for living in the modern world. Most of us have grown up in a world where noisy transportation vehicles and blaring communication devices are common-place, and we have not given much thought to the potential ill effects of excessive decibels.

Traditional legal doctrine dealing with claims for injuries resulting from "noise pollution" centered primarily on the concept of "nuisance"—generating unpleasant sounds on one's property, preventing other persons' use and enjoyment of their properties. The person whose activities are causing the offending sounds might be ordered by a court to cease and desist the offending activity or at least to modify it in some way so as to lessen the adverse impact on other persons.[23] In an extreme case, there might be a claim for "trespass" on the victim's land or for a "taking" of the land by a governmental agency generating the nasty noise.[24]

Where the offending sounds are being generated as attempts at communication, the legal analysis becomes even more complicated. The First Amendment to the US Constitution states that "Congress shall pass no law . . . abridging the freedom of speech. . . ." This prohibition against restrictions emanating from the national government has been interpreted by the Supreme Court as also applying to State governments, through the "due process" clause of the Fourteenth Amendment: ". . . nor shall any State deprive any person of life, liberty, or property, without due process of law. . . ."[25] Thus, States and their agencies and political subdivisions are likewise constitutionally limited in the extent to which they can limit the *sounds* of speech, as well as its content.[26]

Additional constitutional issues may be raised if the generator or the "victim" of the objectional noise is a religious building or activity. The First Amendment also prohibits Congress from passing any law "respecting the establishment of religion, or prohibiting the free exercise thereof." As with freedom of speech, these limitations on governmental action also apply to the States, through Fourteenth Amendment "due process."[27] Constitutional challenges might thus be made to special zoning rules for location of church buildings or for prohibitions of other activities near them.[28] Even if not specifically raised in the case as constitutional objections, "religious freedom" concerns may be a factor in deciding whether the interests of a religious community or those of a nearby landowner are to prevail.[29]

So, by 1972, there had already been governmental efforts to control noise pollution—and the attendant litigation arising from enforcement of these additional restrictions on land use. What President Nixon's sponsored legislation added was the weight of the national government on the victims' side of the equation: "The Congress declares that it is the policy of the United States to promote an environment for all Americans free from noise that jeopardizes their health or welfare." He must have felt quite strongly about this particular issue (or at least agreed with those who did so) since he included it specifically in his 1972 environmental message to Congress. Congress may not have needed this extra push, but it did, in fact, pass such a statute—as requested.

What specifically did PL 92-574 say about noise pollution? Three purposes of the Act were stated in section 2(b): effective coordination of the national government's noise-control activities, noise "standards" for products moving in interstate commerce, and public information on the noise levels and noise-reduction features of such products. And further: "The Congress authorizes and directs that Federal agencies shall, to the fullest extent consistent with their authority under Federal laws administered by them, carry out the programs within their control in such a manner as to further the policy declared in section 2(b)." So, all federal agencies are to conduct their programs so as to minimize noise pollution.

Gas Pipeline Safety. PL 92-401 deals with another significant hazard in our modern energy-dependent world: gas pipeline safety. (Even as these words are being written in August 2016, several gas-related explosions have occurred in various parts of the US in recent days! There are obviously some inherent dangers connected with the use of this natural resource.) The 1972 changes are relatively modest in scope: extensions of the program, additional appropriations, and authorization of consultations with State and local agencies by the Secretary of the Interior.

Pesticide Control. In stark contrast, PL 92-516 is a very substantial (some twenty-seven pages) restatement and reworking of FIFRA—the "Federal Insecticide, Fungicide, and Rodenticide Act." Requirements include pesticide registration, use certification, experimental-use permits, registration of "establishments" (i.e., producers), standards for pesticide applicators, and civil and criminal penalties for violations. (Conviction for a knowing violation is a misdemeanor, with a fine up to $25,000 and/or up to one year in prison. This is evidently another statute that is meant to be taken seriously.)

Lead-Based Paint. Even small amounts of lead in the human system can have serious adverse health effects. Children under six are particularly at risk; both physical and mental development can be detrimentally impacted. Millions of homes have been painted with lead-based paints. Over time, absorption sufficient to cause health problems may occur in residents. The most egregious cases involve the ingestion of paint chips by small children. Various levels of government have attempted to deal with the problem, at least since the 1970s.

PL 91-695 was approved on January 13, 1971—very near the official ending of the Second Session of the 91st Congress. It provided grants to local governments "for the detection and treatment of lead-based paint poisoning" and "for the elimination of lead-based paint poisoning," set up a national "demonstration and research program," and prohibited the use of lead-based paint in any residential structures built by or with the assistance of the national government. The State of Massachusetts went a big step further on November 15 of that year in passing a statute requiring property owners to "remove or contain" any "accessible" lead-based hazards in buildings occupied by children under six years of age. One of the early paint-liability lawsuits originated from the application of this State statute.

In an apartment in Peabody, Massachusetts, two small boys ingested paint chips during 1973–1975 and subsequently developed health problems. The defendant-landlord tried to argue that he should not be held liable unless he was proved to have been careless in not removing or covering the lead paint in question. Rejecting that argument, both the trial court and the State supreme court ruled in favor of the two boys, awarding them damages for their injuries and their mother damages for their medical bills that she had paid. The Massachusetts Supreme Court said that the landlord was liable if he did not comply with the statute—

and he had not done so:

> **We agree with the trial judge's determination that an owner of premises may be liable under § 199 without proof either that the owner knew there were materials containing dangerous levels of lead on the premises or that the owner was negligent in not removing the offending materials. Section 199, which is set forth in full in the margin, provides for strict liability, that is, liability without proof of fault beyond the owner's noncompliance with statutory requirements for the removal of materials containing dangerous levels of lead.[30]**

What's involved in this case is, of course, civil liability rather than possible criminal penalties. But the point made should still be clear enough to violators: you are liable if you fail to do what the law requires you to do! There are State high-court decisions on lead-paint liability in at least nineteen other States, plus US Court of Appeals rulings by several "Circuits"—appellate courts for regional groupings of States. Not all State statutes will necessarily be exactly the same, and neither will all States' courts necessarily interpret them the same way, even if they are very similar.

PL 91-695 was thus only a first step, albeit an important one: requiring the national government to stop financing the spread of this particular hazard. Given the high percentage of home purchases financed through government assistance, the potential curb on the use of lead paint seems significant. The application of the national antitrust laws to an alleged local monopoly by New Orleans realtors was justified, in large part, by the fact that many of the home purchases involved were financed through the national mortgage insurers—FHA or VA.[31] In any event, the problem is a serious one, due to the widespread use of lead-based paint in homes constructed before appreciation of the danger involved.[32]

Evidence that the lead-based paint problem is a continuing one can be seen in a small news story that appeared in *The University* [of Michigan] *Record*, (September 12, 2016), p. 2: "A more accurate sensor for lead paint." The article describes a new chemical process that promises more accurate results when testing existing homes for the presence of lead-based paint.[33] Accuracy in that determination would, of course, be very important in States with statutes similar to the one in Massachusetts—imposing civil liability on homeowners who fail to "remove or contain" lead-based paint when required to do so.

Poison Control. PL 91-601 is aimed not at the production and distribution of poisons but rather at their accessibility—specifically, their accessibility by small children who are unaware of the danger. The statute thus requires "childproof" packaging for poisonous substances being made and sold. For many products (medicines, e.g.), that means "childproof" caps on the containers. This extra mandatory product feature thus provides an additional basis for potential liability if injury results from a non-compliant product. This Nixon-era Act previewed, at least to some extent, common-law product-liability developments. A State court decision some eight years later (*Keller v. Welles Department Store*) illustrates the common-law trend-line.

In 1971, Stephen Keller and William Sperry—both two years old—were playing with a gasoline can in the basement of the Sperry home. They opened the can and poured out gasoline—near a gas furnace and a hot water heater. The gasoline ignited, and Stephen suffered severe burns. William's father was not home, and his mother was upstairs. Acting through a guardian, Stephen sued the home builder, the manufacturers of the furnace and water heater, the manufacturer and the seller of the gasoline can, and Mrs. Sperry. The claims against the home builder and appliance manufacturers were settled. The Wisconsin trial court ruled that there were viable claims against the seller (Welles) and the manufacturer (Huffman) of the gasoline can, and those defendants appealed that ruling. The Wisconsin Court of Appeals discussed the liability of the maker and the seller for not providing a "childproof" cap for the gasoline can:

> [T]o recover under the theory of strict liability the plaintiff must . . . prove: (1) that the product was in defective condition when it left the possession or control of the seller, (2) that it was unreasonably dangerous to the user or consumer, (3) that the defect was a cause (a substantial factor) of the plaintiff's injuries or damages, (4) that the seller engaged in the business of selling such product . . . and (5) that the product was one which the seller expected to and did reach the user or consumer without substantial change in the condition it was when he sold it. . . .
>
> To state a cause of action under strict liability then, the plaintiff must essentially allege that the product was defective and unreasonably dangerous. In the present case, the complaint clearly alleges that the defendants respectively manufactured or sold a gasoline can which was defective and unreasonably dangerous to children such as the plaintiff. The defect complained of was the failure to design the can with a cap sufficient to prevent children from removing it. . . .
>
> The product at issue here, a gasoline can, was not as safe as was reasonably possible since the cap was not designed in such a way as to prevent young children from removing it. Equipping the gasoline can with a child-proof cap would have rendered the can substantially safer and entailed only a nominal additional cost. The practical value of such a cap may readily be seen since gasoline cans, while not intended to be used by children unable to appreciate the attendant dangers of gasoline, are customarily stored in places accessible to children. . . .

While the defect in the gasoline can was not concealed, this court is unable to conclude, as a matter of law, that the absence of a child-proof cap was an obvious as opposed to a latent condition. Nor do we believe the dangers to unsupervised children from a gasoline can without a child-proof cap are so apparent that the average consumer would be completely aware of them. . . .

The hazards to a child arising from a gasoline can without a child-proof cap are not so readily apparent. A child is not so clearly attracted to this product that an adult would immediately be put on guard to take precautions for the child's safety.

Based on the foregoing discussion, we conclude the complaint stated a cause of action in strict liability.

In order to state a cause of action for negligence, the following elements must be pleaded: "(1) A duty of care on the part of the defendant; (2) a breach of that duty; (3) a causal connection between the conduct and the injury; and (4) an actual loss or damage as a result of the injury." . . . As against both Huffman and Welles, the plaintiff essentially pleaded that the can had a cap insufficient to prevent young children from removing it; that the defendants knew or should have known that it would be dangerous when accessible to children; that Stephen Keller was severely injured, and that the injuries were caused by the negligence of the defendants. . . .

Children are incurably curious about their environment. They learn by interacting with it and by imitating the behavior of people around them. A gasoline can, found primarily in garages, is commonly stored either on the floor or on a low shelf. These are areas readily accessible to children in their "explorations." It is not unforeseeable that a child might attempt to taste the liquid in the can. Nor is it unforeseeable that in the course of playing "mow the lawn" or "gas station," a child might pour the gasoline from the can. Because children are fascinated with fire, the danger arising from such an action is certainly foreseeable. We conclude that because *some* harm was foreseeable, the defendants owed a duty to the plaintiff and the complaint therefore stated a cause of action for negligence.[34]

The defendants are, therefore, potentially liable under both theories, if the facts alleged can be proved in court. As a cautionary note, the author was informed that his great-grandson—when slightly younger than the two boys in the *Keller* case—was quite adept at accessing supposedly "childproof" containers. Hence the quotation marks around "childproof," an adjectival modifier that may be inaccurate to some unknown degree. What the Wisconsin court did not have to decide was the much more difficult question of whether manufacturer and retailer would still be liable even if the can had had a cap that complied with PL 91-601's "special packaging" requirement but which the two little boys had succeeded in removing.

The *Keller* court did use the phrase "childproof," but PL 91-601 does not do so, instead requiring "special packaging." That phrase is defined in Section 2(4) of the Act as meaning "packaging designed or constructed to be significantly difficult for children under the age of five years to open or obtain a toxic or harmful amount of the substance contained therein within a reasonable time and not difficult for normal adults to use properly, but does not mean packaging which all such children cannot open or obtain a toxic or harmful amount within a reasonable time." Presumably, there could be no "negligence" by either distributor of a product which was fully compliant with federal packaging requirements. It would also seem to be difficult to argue that such a product was so "defective" as to be "unreasonably dangerous" to the user. Indeed, it seems illogical to call a product in full compliance with federal standards "defective" at all. Even if the federal standards are interpreted as being mere minimums, in this case, the "negative" part of the "special packaging" definition in PL 91-601 would seem to insulate distributors from liability for products in compliance. Further litigations may resolve any such remaining doubts.

Protecting the Environment

Each of these last Acts discussed is thus dealing with a more specific environmental hazard, but the treatment each Act gives to the problem at hand is quite different. As noted above, the gas pipeline safety statute is merely a brief update on earlier legislation. In contrast, the pesticide Act is a comprehensive revision of the earlier statute. The noise control Act, the poison-packaging Act, and the lead-paint regulation statutes represent initial major intrusions into areas that had been left to State law. President Nixon's leadership on the noise control issue is particularly well-documented in, for example, his State-of-the-Union address and other messages to Congress. With "instrumentalities" of interstate and foreign commerce (trucks, trains, and planes) generating much of the excess noise present in the modern world, it seems most appropriate for the national government to establish some standards for dealing with the problem. And equally so as to the dangers posed by lead-based paint in homes and by easily-accessible poisonous or flammable substances. At the very least, it is surely proper for the national government to state that its agencies will not finance additions to the danger. Although each of these Acts is dealing with only one rather specific aspect of the environment, each topic seems eminently worthy of regulation.

It is President Nixon's record on *improving* our environment—as highlighted by the Acts dealing with noise, lead paint, poisons, and pesticides—as well as *preserving* it (the dozens of new parks and public spaces, the protection [*and* improvement] of water and air quality, and species protection) that earned him the accolades of the "environmental elite." Without in any way minimizing or challenging Theodore Roosevelt's #1 *conservationist* ranking, it seems quite clear that Richard Nixon—and his substantial-majority-Democrat Congresses— deserve the #1 spot for *environmental* protection.

Chapter 4

Nixon Protecting Workers

THERE WERE FEW groups to whom Richard Nixon owed less, politically, than organized Labor. The unions had generally tended to support Democrat politicians and had
been a key component of Franklin D. Roosevelt's New Deal coalition. They had supplied
much of the money and muscle for Harry Truman's 1948 upset win over Thomas Dewey.
(There is, however, a story that unionized trainmen refused to continue operation of Truman's chartered campaign train until they were paid the wages they were owed. Ostensibly,
they were angry over Truman's wartime seizure and operation of the railroads, which at the
time were being subjected to a union strike.[1]) Some union members surely defected in 1952
and 1956 to support the Eisenhower/Nixon tickets, and a few workers must have backed
Nixon even against John F. Kennedy—in view of the closeness of that election. The Johnson
landslide of 1964 saw most workers return to the Democrat side of the political ledger.

By 1968, therefore, the political landscape seemed to have returned to New Deal "normalcy." But two seismic faults lurked beneath the surface: the Vietnam War and the third-
party candidacy of George Wallace. Wallace's candidacy siphoned off about thirteen and a
half percent of the popular vote, so that Nixon barely won a plurality over Humphrey. Nixon
did win a majority in the electoral college, with Wallace carrying five southern States with a
total of forty-five electoral votes. (In contrast, Ross Perot's third-party effort in 1992 resulted
in 19 percent of the popular vote but no electoral votes. He did draw off enough votes to give
the electoral college majority to Bill Clinton, over the incumbent—President George H. W.
Bush.) Without a serious third-party diversion in 1972, President Nixon won a smashing
victory over Senator George McGovern—an honest, decent, thoughtful man and a war hero,
but perceived as a far-left radical.

The blue-collar industrial workers that were then the hard core of organized Labor generally supported the US' involvement in the Vietnam war. Patriotic and nationalistic—many
of them veterans who had served in World War II and/or in Korea (and eventually, in Vi-

etnam itself)—many, perhaps most, blue collars believed in John Wayne's version of Vietnam: that the US was fighting to protect a small nation from being overrun by Communist aggressors and that it was necessary to do so to provide assurance to our allies that we would stand by our commitments. Both George Meany (president of the AFL-CIO) and Peter Brennan (president of the Building Trades Council of Greater New York) were identified as being strong supporters of President Nixon's Vietnam policies.[2] Evidently, many of the "hard-hat" construction workers in Brennan's union felt the same way. On May 8, 1970, two hundred or so "hard-hats" attacked a New York City protest-march against the War and the shooting of four students at Ohio's Kent State University.

Even some members in a union whose leaders opposed the War may have supported President Nixon's policies. And, of course, union leaders did not have the right to speak for nonmembers (although they often presumed to do so). It was to these rank-and-file individual workers—and to the other non-shouters, non-demonstrators—that President Nixon had addressed his November 3, 1969 "silent majority" appeal.

That approach was not entirely illogical since some nonunion workers may have made a conscious choice not to join a union—if they indeed had had a choice. One of the two key weak spots in the US' version of worker unionization is coerced membership: a majority vote in favor of unionization typically means that *all* employees in the designated "bargaining unit" must join the selected union, even if they do not want to do so—or lose their jobs![3] This is the so-called "union shop." As interpreted by the US Supreme Court, however, actual membership is not required; those who do not wish to join are required only to pay "dues"— or at least the portion of dues that represents the costs to the union of representing all the workers in negotiations on wages, hours, and terms and conditions of employment. Nonmembers cannot be forced to pay for a union's political activities (with which they may strongly disagree) or be "fined" by the union for not performing the duties required of union members.[4]

Thus, the Supreme Court has pared down what initially seemed to be statutory authorization for the "union shop" to the minimal requirements of the "agency shop": a majority vote for a union authorizes (*and requires*) it to negotiate employment terms for all employees in the bargaining unit but requires nonunion employees to pay only for the representation services that the union is required to provide for all. One section of the 1947 Taft-Hartley amendments to the 1935 National Labor Relations Act permitted the States to adopt "right-to-work" laws. About half the States—mostly in the South and the West—have done so. (Indiana has had such an act for some time, and Michigan—the birthplace of the United Automobile Workers—recently adopted one, to the surprise of many.) Even without a State right-to-work law, constitutional objections may be raised even to the agency shop, as seen in the Supreme Court's 2014 decision in the *Harris v. Quinn* case, summarized in the following paragraphs.[5]

An Illinois state program permitted Medicare recipients ("customers") to hire a "personal assistant" (PA) to provide in-home care, as opposed to requiring hospitalization. The State paid the PAs, but the customers hired them, trained them, supervised them, evaluated them, and fired them if the work was not satisfactory. First, by executive order and then by statute, Illinois stated that PAs were "public employees" for collective bargaining purposes—only! PAs received none of the State benefits provided to other State employees. Illinois then signed a collective bargaining agreement with a union purporting to represent all PAs; the agreement required PAs who were not union members to pay a fee to the union for representation services. Several PAs challenged the constitutionality of this requirement.

The State and the union relied on the Court's 1977 decision in the *Abood* case involving public school teachers in Detroit, which said that an agency-shop arrangement was permissible for public employees but that the union could not use those funds for political/ideological purposes. Writing the Court's opinion in the *Harris* case, Justice Alito first limited the application of the *Abood* precedent, and then he proceeded to do a very careful analysis of the inconsistency between First Amendment freedom of speech and the forced financial sponsorship of speech with which the payor disagrees.

Abood failed to appreciate the difference between the core union speech involuntarily subsidized by dissenting public-sector employees and the core union speech involuntarily funded by their counterparts in the private sector. In the public sector, core issues such as wages, pensions, and benefits are important political issues, but that is generally not so in the private sector. In the years since *Abood*, as state and local expenditures on employee wages and benefits have mushroomed, the importance of the difference between bargaining in the public and private sectors has been driven home.

Abood failed to appreciate the conceptual difficulty of distinguishing in public-sector cases between union expenditures that are made for collective-bargaining purposes and those that are made to achieve political ends. In the private sector, the line is easier to see. Collective bargaining concerns the union's dealings with the employer; political advocacy and lobbying are directed at the government. But in the public sector, both collective-bargaining and political advocacy and lobbying are directed at the government. . . .

For all these reasons, we refuse to extend *Abood* in the manner that Illinois seeks. If we accepted Illinois' argument, we would approve an unprecedented violation of the bedrock principle that, except perhaps in the rarest of circumstances, no person

in this country may be compelled to subsidize speech by a third party that he or she does not wish to support. The First Amendment prohibits the collection of an agency fee from personal assistants in the Rehabilitation Program who do not want to join or support the union.

The judgment of the Court of Appeals is reversed in part and affirmed in part, and the case is remanded for further proceedings consistent with this opinion.[6]

As impliedly indicated by the more recent *Abood* and *Harris* case examples, the labor-management relations area was already well-covered by legal rules, with the 1935 National Labor Relations Act having been significantly amended in 1947 and 1959 and its various provisions having been interpreted in many cases, by 1969. Thus, there was not much need for further legislation on these matters. Even so, nine of the ninety "worker protection" statutes passed during the Nixon years can be tallied as "labor-management relations," although none approached the scope of the 1947 and 1959 amendments.

The subject-matter of this Chapter is also quite different, in that Congress is legislating at three distinct levels: local employment rules for the District of Columbia, rules for national government employees, and rules for employees generally—including private employees. Over 10 percent of these statutes relate directly to DC's municipal employees (teachers, public safety staff, et al.); nearly 47 percent to federal employees (some specific group thereof, or generally); and about 39 percent to employees generally—including private-sector employees or some part of them. Thus, well over half are "protecting" some subset of national government employees. To that extent, the national government is simply acting as a benevolent employer as to its own personnel, by providing them with pay raises, enhanced benefits, and improved working conditions. So, there were only thirty-five of the ninety Acts discussed here that pertained to non-federal employees, though some of the DC "local" legislation (the minimum wage law, e.g.) might be applicable to private-sector employees working in DC. But of that smaller number, at least four—the Coal Mine Health and Safety Act, the Occupational Safety and Health Act, the Black Lung Benefits Act, and the Employment Retirement Income Security Act—are truly landmark protections for workers.

One final note as to the subject-matter coverage of this Chapter. Where the statute in question outlawed discrimination or promoted diversity in the workplace, it was tabulated in the following Chapter on protecting minorities, rather than in this Chapter. The "minority protection" aspect seemed the predominant motivation for such legislation, and employment discrimination has been one of the major areas of minority disadvantage. (If we counted the Equal Employment Opportunity Act of 1972 and the Rehabilitation Act of 1973 here, rather than in Chapter 6, there would be *six* landmark worker-protection statutes credited to President Nixon. Not a bad record, considering that he got so little credit—or support—from "organized" Labor.)

Protecting Workers—the Nixon Legislative Record

91st Congress, First Session (1969)

- PL 91-4: amends section 301 of Manpower Development and Training Act of 1962

- PL 91-34: revises pay structure of National Park Police

- PL 91-53: revises unemployment tax and employment security system

- PL 91-54: amends Contract Work Hours Standards Act

- PL 91-73: changes age limits for US Park Police

- PL 91-80: amends DC Unemployment Compensation Act

- PL 91-86: amends section 302(c) of Labor-Management Relations Act of 1947

- PL 91-92: authorizes President to designate October 12–19 "National Industrial Hygiene Week"

- PL 91-93: Civil Service Retirement Amendments of 1969

- PL 91-114: increases maximum per diem expense allowance for federal employees

- PL 91-169: amends 1907 Act regulating hours of service by railroad employees

- PL 91-173: Federal Coal Mine Health and Safety Act of 1969

- PL 91-185: amends Central Intelligence Agency Retirement Act of 1964

- PL 91-187: provides additional supergrade positions for federal employees

- PL 91-189: changes policies on use of Civil Service Commission revolving fund

91st Congress, Second Session (1970)

- PL 91-201: amends Foreign Service Act of 1946 regarding retirement & disability system

- PL 91-203: provides temporary prohibition of strikes or lockouts in a then-current railway dispute

- PL 91-215: amends railroad retirement system to provide for supplementary annuities

- PL 91-216: Job Evaluation Policy Act of 1970—amends Classification Act of 1923

- PL 91-226: provides for settlement of a then-current railroad labor-management dispute

- PL 91-231: Federal Employees Salary Act of 1970—provides increases

- PL 91-234: changes number of representatives on National Railroad Adjustment Board

- PL 91-253: equalizes retirement benefits for Public Health Service officers

- PL 91-263: District of Columbia Teachers' Retirement Amendments of 1970

- PL 91-297: increases salaries for DC police, firefighters, and teachers

- PL 91-311: discontinues annual report of settlements of property claims by federal personnel

- PL 91-369: allows time off for overtime worked by Government Printing Office employees

- PL 91-373: extends and improves unemployment compensation system

- PL 91-375: Postal Reorganization Act—includes provisions on labor-management relations

- PL 91-377: increases annuities under Railroad Retirement Act of 1937

- PL 91-418: increases government's contribution of employees' health benefits

- PL 91-509: Policemen and Firemen's Retirement and Disability Amendments of 1970

- PL 91-532: liberalizes definition of "widow" for police and firefighter survivor benefits

- PL 91-541: provides temporary prohibition of strikes or lockouts in current railway dispute

- PL 91-563: amends rules for court leave-time for US and DC employees called for jury duty

- PL 91-596: Occupational Safety and Health Act of 1970

- PL 91-603: Seamen's Service Act—provides for cooperation with United Seamen's Service

- PL 91-626: amends Central Intelligence Agency Retirement Act of 1964

- PL 91-630: permits certain federal employment to be counted toward retirement

- PL 91-648: Intergovernmental Personnel Act of 1970—improves cooperation and training

- PL 91-656: Federal Pay Comparability Act of 1970—authorizes President to adjust rates

- PL 91-658: amends survivor annuities for civil service retirees

- PL 91-669: extends temporary disregard of income in deciding minimum for railroad retirement

92nd Congress, First Session (1971)

- PL 92-17: extends s.10 of 1926 Railway Labor Act to a then-current labor dispute

- PL 92-46: provides 10 percent increase in annuities under 1937 Railway Labor Act

- PL 92-54: Emergency Employment Act of 1970—provides public service employment

- PL 92-121: provides for payment of medical costs of DC disabled police and fire personnel

- PL 92-190: authorizes compensation for five Government Accounting Office positions

- PL 92-194: gives overtime pay to federal part-timers working more than forty hours a week

- PL 92-211: District of Columbia Unemployment Compensation Act Amendments of 1971

- PL 92-223: amends Social Security Act as to payment of death benefits

- PL 92-224: amends Social Security Act with regard to funds for emergency benefits to be paid

92nd Congress, Second Session (1972)

- PL 92-235: provides a settlement procedure for the West Coast dock strike

- PL 92-243: amends civil service retirement rule for adopted child

- PL 92-277: amends 1962 Manpower Development and Training Act

- PL 92-298: Prevailing Rate Equalization Adjustment Act of 1972

- PL 92-303: Black Lung Benefits Act of 1972—extends benefits to certain orphans

- PL 92-329: provides six-month extension of emergency unemployment compensation program

- PL 92-382: provides early retirement for federal firefighters

- PL 92-392: provides system for setting pay-rates for prevailing-rate federal employees

- PL 92-410: provides salary increases for DC police and firefighters

- PL 92-454: provides civil service retirement credit for DC substitute teachers

- PL 92-460: provides a temporary 20 percent increase in railroad retirement annuities

- PL 92-473: revises method of computing wage rates for federal service-contract employees

- PL 92-518: increases DC teachers' salaries and revises retirement benefits

- PL 92-529: waives employee deductions for life insurance during erroneous suspension

- PL 92-543: provides privacy for DC police personnel records

- PL 92-576: amends Longshoremen's and Harbor Workers' Compensation Act

93rd Congress, First Session (1973)

- PL 93-31: amends Central Intelligence Agency Retirement Act of 1964

- PL 93-39: permits immediate retirement of certain federal employees

- PL 93-58: extends Medicare coverage for railroad employees to include kidney disease

- PL 93-69: revises eligibility rules for railroad retirement annuities

- PL 93-95: permits employer payments to union-sponsored legal services funds

- PL 93-136: liberalizes eligibility for cost-of-living increases in civil-service retirement annuities

- PL 93-160: all "US national" federal employees to receive health and group life benefits

- PL 93-176: general pay/position classifications to apply to Selective Service System employees

- PL 93-181: improves system for granting leaves to federal employees

- PL 93-203: Comprehensive Employment and Training Act of 1973

- PL 93-210: amends Central Intelligence Agency Retirement Act of 1964

- PL 93-223: amends DC Minimum Wage Act to permit airline employees to exchange days

93rd Congress, Second Session (1974)

- PL 93-246: increases government contribution for health benefits for federal employees

- PL 93-255: amends minimum compensation for Senate committee employees

- PL 93-259: Fair Labor Standards Amendments of 1974—increases minimum wage

- PL 93-260: amends civil service retirement act by redefining widow and widower

- PL 93-273: increases annuities for certain federal employees

- PL 93-340: authorizes withholding for city taxes owed by federal employees

- PL 93-349: increases Postal Service payments to cover increased employee benefits

- PL 93-350: DC police and fire personnel—retirement benefits

- PL 93-363: amends federal employees' health-care to include psychiatrists and optometrists

- PL 93-406: the Employee Retirement Income Security Act of 1974 (ERISA)—actually signed by President Ford, but clearly President Nixon's concept and project, and so included in this analysis.

President Nixon's resignation took effect on August 9, 1974. Public Law 93-369 was approved on August 7. Public Law 93-370 was approved on August 10, so it and all later legislation enacted by the 93rd Congress occurred during the Presidency of Gerald Ford. In this specific case, however, we are making an exception to the August 9 dividing line and including ERISA in the Nixon legislative record. (A little "equity," if you please—just trying to give credit where credit is so clearly due.)

There has been no attempt made in this text to sort out which pieces of legislative work-in-process as of August 9 were ultimately passed by the 93rd Congress before their term of office ended—and for which, arguably, President Nixon should be given credit as generator or sponsor. That sort of analysis would call for an extreme level of subjectivity and, therefore, also a high risk of possible bias and untrustworthy conclusions. Further, having attempted to give credit on such basis for some laws passed after resignation, this book's author would surely be challenged by critics for not having proven by similar analysis that the President should be given credit for the laws passed *prior* to resignation. That type of inquiry would seem to require the application of massive human and material resources—several levels of intensity above what is available here.

Thus, for simplicity and clarity, the August 9 date has been used to demark "what counts" here and what doesn't. In the case of ERISA, however, it is simply impossible to do so. This important piece of worker protection legislation has President Nixon's fingerprints all over it, even though it was not finally approved by Congress until some two weeks after he resigned and was therefore signed into law by President Ford. President Nixon made the promise to workers to protect their retirement funds, and the legislation was adopted. The resulting Employee Retirement Income Security Act of 1974 is clearly one of the most important worker protection laws of all time—and it's President Nixon's handiwork. President Ford himself acknowledged as much in his signing statement, as noted in more detail later in this Chapter.

Worker Statutes—a Closer Look

Labor-Management Relations

As noted above, despite the extensive legislative and administrative rulemaking already in place by 1969, there were still nine labor-management relations Acts passed by the Nixon-era Congresses: six Acts by the 91st Congress, two by the 92nd, and one by the 93rd. Only two of the nine dealt with what might be described as traditional labor-management problems. One unfair tactic used by employers in earlier times was the setting up of a "sponsored" union controlled by the employer, to avoid organization of the real thing. National labor law tried to deal with this—in part—by prohibiting employer payments to unions. Section 302(c) of the 1947 Labor-Management Relations Act (Taft-Hartley Act) does list several exceptions to this prohibition. PL 91-86 added exceptions for employer payments to the union for educational scholarships and for day care centers; it also specified that those topics were *not* thereby made compulsory subjects for union-management bargaining. If an employer *wanted* to make such contributions, they were lawful, but the union could not demand that they be part of contract negotiations. PL 93-95 added an exception for voluntary employer contributions to union legal-services plans.

Four statutes attempted to solve an ongoing railroad labor dispute: PL 91-203 and PL 91-541 prohibited strikes while negotiations were in process; PL 91-226 tried to provide a settlement; and finally, PL 92-17 applied Section 10 of the 1926 Railway Labor Act (RLA) to the dispute. RLA section 10 provides that if the Mediation Board is unable to resolve the dispute, it shall report the impasse to the President, who may then impanel a fact-finding board to make recommendations. Further, no strikes or other changes in the workplace situation are permitted after the fact-finders are chosen and for a thirty-day period after they submit their report to the President. (The obvious hope is that the dispute will be settled during this further "cooling-off" period.) PL 92-235 did provide a settlement for another serious labor dispute, this one involving the West Coast dock-workers.

PL 91-375, the Postal Reorganization Act, contained a section regulating labor relations in the new postal system. PL 91-603 provided for government cooperation with the United Seamen's Service in establishing overseas facilities for US merchant seamen. (A facsimile of PL 91-603, with President Nixon's signature, is featured on the website of the United Seaman's Service AMMLA—American Merchant Marine Library Association.)

District of Columbia Legislation

Thirteen Acts represented Congress legislating for the District of Columbia—much in the manner of a State legislature or a city council. Most had to do with compensation for the District's schoolteachers and police and fire personnel. For teachers: PL 91-263 (retirement); PL 92-454 (retirement); and PL 92-518 (salary and retirement). For police and fire personnel: PL 91-509 (retirement and disability); PL 91-532 (survivor benefits); PL 92-121 (disability); PL 92-410 (salary); PL 92-543 (privacy of records); and PL 93-350 (retirement). PL 91-297 provided salary increases for both teachers and police and fire personnel.

Both PL 91-80 and PL 92-211 amended DC's unemployment compensation statute. Finally, PL 93-223 updated the District's minimum wage law.

Federal-Employees Legislation

Of the three "levels" of worker protection legislation, the laws dealing with employees of the national government were the most numerous—forty-two of ninety, which is a bit less than half the total. Three of these pertained to contract workers (those hired for a specific project): PL 91-54, amending the Contract Work Hours Standards Act; PL 92-392, providing a system for setting pay-rates for such personnel covered under the "prevailing wage-rates" requirement; and PL 92-473, revising the method of computing pay for service-contract employees. The remaining thirty-nine were split between those pertaining to a particular group of federal employees (twenty Acts) and those pertaining to federal employees generally (nineteen Acts).

PL 91-369 allowed "time-off" in lieu of extra pay for employees at the Government Printing Office. PL 92-190 authorized compensation for five positions at the Government Accounting Office. PL 92-382 provided early retirement for "federal firefighters." PL 93-176 applied general pay classifications to Selective Service System personnel. (As noted in Chapter 9 of this book, the Selective Service System was "modified" on President Nixon's initiative—in 1969, by PL 91-124.) PL 93-255 adjusted the minimum compensation for Senate committee employees. PL 93-349 actually increased postal rates to cover the cost of increased benefits for Postal Service staff. The national park police were favored by two Acts: 91-34 (revised pay structure) and PL 91-73 (changed age limits). Interestingly, the 1964 Central Intelligence Agency Retirement Act was "amended" *four* times!: PL 91-185, PL 91-626, PL 93-31, and PL 93-210. PL 91-201 revised the retirement and disability system in the 1946 Foreign Service Act, and PL 91-253 equalized retirement benefits for Public Health Service Officers. Federal employees working under the civil service system were the subject of six changes: PL 91-93 (retirement), PL 91-189 (revolving fund), PL 91-658 (survivor annuities), PL 92-243 (retirement, regarding adopted child), PL 93-136 (cost-of-living increases), and PL 93-260 (retirement—redefining widow and widower).

The nineteen Acts dealing with federal employees in general covered a wide variety of topics: job description (PL 91-187 and PL 91-216); salaries (PL 91-231, PL 91-656, and PL 92-194), per diem expense reimbursement (PL 91-114); health and life insurance (PL 91-418, PL 92-529, PL 93-160, PL 93-246, and PL 93-363); leaves (PL 91-563 and PL 93-181); retirement (PL 91-630 and PL 93-39); annuities (PL 93-273); withholding to pay city taxes (PL 93-340); cooperative training with State and local employees (PL 91-648); and "discontinuance of annual reporting of settlements of employee property disputes" (PL 91-311). Although the last Act sounds a bit out of the ordinary scope of employer/employee matters, all the others seem quite mundane—just everyday adjustments in the workplace relationship. It's perhaps a stretch to speak of them as "worker-protection" legislation, but the adjusting being done seems clearly in favor of the employees involved—so the "protection" involved comes in the easily-recognized form of improved compensation and workplace conditions.

Inclusive Worker-Protection Legislation

In addition to the nine "Labor-Management Relations" Acts discussed at the beginning of this section, there were twenty-six others that covered at least some workers who were not employees of the national government and not working in DC and were, thus, subject to statutes of the District. Four of these—the "landmark worker-protection Acts"—are covered in the next subsection of this Chapter.

Nine of the remaining twenty-two Acts apply to railroad workers: PL 91-169 (hours of service); PL 91-215 (supplementary retirement annuities); PL 91-234 (representation on the

National Railroad Adjustment Board); PL 91-377 (increased retirement annuities); PL 91-669 (minimum retirement income); PL 92-46 (10 percent increase in annuities); PL 92-460 (temporary 20 percent increase in annuities); PL 93-58 (Medicare extension to cover kidney disease); and PL 93-69 (eligibility for retirement annuities).

Unemployment was the specific subject of four Acts: PL 91-53 (revising the system and its supporting tax); PL 93-373 ("extending and improving" the system); PL 92-54 (providing public service jobs); and PL 92-329 (providing an extra six months of emergency compensation). Unemployment problems were the implicit motivation behind PL 91-4 (amendments to the 1962 Manpower Development and Training Act); PL 92-277 (further such amendments); and PL 93-203 (the Comprehensive Employment and Training Act of 1973).[7]

Of the six remaining Acts in this subcategory, the most significant seems to be PL 93-259 (raising the minimum wage to $2.30 per hour, but with different phase-in dates for different categories of workers).[8] PL 92-576 amended the Longshoremen's and Harbor Workers' Compensation Act, which provides compensation for workplace injuries. PL 92-298 specifies a procedure for adjusting wages of contract workers hired on the basis of "prevailing rates." PL 91-92 merely authorizes the President to proclaim October 12–19, 1969, as "National Industrial Hygiene Week." The last two Acts in this grouping, amending the Social Security Act—PL 92-223 (death benefits) and PL 92-224 (emergency benefits)—are included here with some hesitancy since the Social Security System has a broader reach than just "workers" or "employees." However, the fact that nearly all workers are subject to Social Security deductions from their paychecks, and are thus part of the System, seemed to mandate their inclusion.

Landmark Worker-Protection Legislation

In addition to NEPA, the foundation-stone of our national environmental policy, the First Session of the 91st Congress passed one of the landmark worker-protection bills, PL 91-173: the Federal Coal Mine Health and Safety Act of 1969. President Nixon signed it on December 30. (He actually signed NEPA on January 1, 1970.) The purpose of the FCMH&S Act could not have been more clearly stated: "Section 2. Congress declares that—(a) the first priority and concern of all in the coal mining industry must be the health and safety of its most precious resource—the miner. . . ."

PL 91-173 directs the Secretaries of HEW and Interior to "develop and promulgate improved mandatory health or safety standards" and to require mine operators to comply with them. None of these "improved" mandatory health or safety standards can *reduce* the miner's protection under existing standards. (Section 101[b].) Section 4 confirms the Act's application to virtually every mine and miner in the country. Section 103(a) requires "frequent inspections and investigations in coal mines each year." Section 103(b)(1) authorizes entry into mines for such purposes by the Secretary of the Interior or his delegate." Other sections in this sixty-two-page statute provide for court injunctions and penalties.

Determined to do a thorough job on this issue, the 92nd Congress (and President Nixon) added a five-page amendment to PL 91-173 in 1972. PL 92-303—the Black Lung Benefits Act of 1972—extended the coverage of Title IV of the 1969 Act, which provided benefits for miners who had contracted black lung disease from working conditions in the mines. Title IV indicated that its purpose was to provide such benefits to miners "totally disabled" by the disease and to "the surviving dependents of miners whose death was due to such disease"— and also to do so for such injuries occurring in the future. Evidently, there were some difficulties in implementing that intent; hence, the five pages of reaffirmation and details in PL 92-303.

Every rational person must recognize that coal mining is an inherently dangerous and dirty job. That being said, there is no reason why miners should be subjected to unnecessary risks. PL 91-173 and PL 92-303 are thus big steps in the right direction. They also provide us with a great example of a President and a Congress—even though of opposing political parties—acting together to do the right thing for the nation and its citizens (including their spouses and children).

Occupational Safety and Health Act. The "protective" intent of this Act is very clearly stated in Section 2(b): "The Congress declares it to be its purpose and policy . . . to assure so far as possible every working man and woman in the Nation safe and healthful working conditions and to preserve our human resources . . . (3) by authorizing the Secretary of Labor to set mandatory occupational safety and health standards applicable to businesses affecting interstate commerce, and by creating an Occupational Safety and Health Review Commission for carrying out adjudicatory functions under the Act. . . ." The phrase "*affecting* interstate commerce" means that a business which itself is not engaged in interstate commercial activity but whose operations somehow impact interstate commerce is also subject to OSHA standards. Under that sort of expansive interpretation of the national government's authority, many (if not most) smaller businesses are included—along with the giant internationals and everything in between. The classic example of "affecting" is the case of *Wickard v. Filburn*.

To try to solve the problem of ruinously low farm prices during the Depression years, the national government established production limits for US farmers. Roscoe Filburn had a small farm near Dayton, Ohio, on which he raised and sold chickens and their eggs. He had grown a small amount of wheat each year, primarily for his own use. For the 1941 crop year, he was told his wheat acreage allotment was 11.1 acres. Roscoe actually planted twenty-three acres and then harvested an "extra" 239 bushels of wheat from the excess 11.9 acres. The Department of Agriculture fined him 49 cents a bushel for the excess wheat production—

$117.11. Roscoe sued in the US District Court for the Southern District of Ohio, and he won. The District Court enjoined the Secretary of Agriculture (Claude Wickard) from enforcing the fine. Wickard appealed to the US Supreme Court, and he won the appeal. Writing for the Supreme Court, Justice Jackson said that even small operations such as Roscoe's chicken farm could be regulated by Congress.[9]

Most legal areas defining and regulating private relationships—property law, contract law, tort (civil injury) law, et al.—were left to the States. So was much criminal law— murder, robbery, assault, arson, etc.[10] The national government was given the power to define the civil and criminal rights and wrongs in certain areas—interstate and foreign commerce, the postal system, "intellectual property" such as patents and copyrights, and other topics. All powers not assigned to the national government remained with the States or with the people at large. This division of governmental functions was expressly stated in the Tenth Amendment to the national Constitution.

Under this federal/state split of authority, the allocation of responsibilities for workplace injuries had been left primarily to the several States. State case-law rules generally recognized that an employer had a legal duty to provide a reasonably safe workplace for its employees or at least to warn them of any unsafe conditions which they would not be likely to discover for themselves.[11] Failure to comply with this requirement would (presumably) mean that the employer was liable for damages resulting to the employee. As interpreted in too many cases, however, an employer could avoid liability by proving that the jobsite was "reasonably" safe or that the injured employee should "reasonably" have discovered the danger. Where the work was obviously dangerous—mining, lumbering, construction, et al.— courts developed an employer defense called "assumption of risk," meaning that the injured employee had accepted the risk of injury by voluntarily coming to work and, therefore, could not collect damages. Two other rules from general tort law were also frequently applied: "contributory negligence" (the injured party was also careless in doing what s/he was doing when the injury occurred, or the injury was at least partially caused by a "fellow servant" (another employee). Application of any of these three tort-law defenses meant that recovery of money damages for the injury was prevented or at least substantially reduced. The bottom line was that, in many cases, on-the-job injuries were not fully compensated for by the employer.

Employers were not necessarily satisfied with this rule set, however. In the relatively rare case where an employer was proved negligent in maintaining a safe workplace, and none of the tort-law defenses applied, an injured employee might recover a large amount over and above the actual financial loss sustained—for "pain and suffering" and the like. The amount of such "mental" damages was generally left to the jury, which might prove quite sympathetic to the injured employee. This sort of open-ended liability was somewhat difficult to calculate in advance and thus to provide for in the business's operating budget.

The workers' compensation system was an attempt to provide a fairer and more certain set of rules for dealing with on-the-job injuries. All (or nearly all) employees suffering such injuries should receive compensation for actual economic losses, including permanent bodily harm—but in specified amounts or within specified calculations.[12] The costs of such payments would come from a state-administered "insurance" fund to which employers would be required to make payments based on their businesses' injury record. In exchange for the insurance feature, employees gave up the right to sue their employer unless the employer had intentionally caused the injury. Employees could still sue third parties who had contributed to causing the injury—manufacturers and sellers of allegedly defective products, for instance. (Many "product liability" lawsuits allege this sort of workplace-use theory of liability.) Typically, a state agency is set up to administer the program, including administrative judges to determine disputed claims.

Unfortunately, employee injuries and deaths continued to occur in significant numbers. The workers' compensation system did not mandate safe workplaces; it simply provided remedies for injuries sustained. Without the potential of large jury awards, a company's "risk manager" might calculate that it made economic sense to forego the costly capital changes that would be required to make a workplace truly as safe as reasonably possible—and to instead just pay the insurance cost for the now-standardized compensation benefits. Some manufacturers were certainly doing so in deciding how to respond to allegations that their products were unsafe, with Ford Motor's decision not to recall and modify the fuel tank on its Pinto model being perhaps the most egregious example. (That case provided the main factual basis for the 1991 movie *Class Action,* starring Gene Hackman.)

Thus, the continuing concern for doing something to prevent more accidental injuries, with PL 91-596 as the national government's response. Three national agencies now have primary responsibility for implementing OSHA's mandate—the Occupational Safety and Health Administration, which sets and enforces standards; the Occupational Safety and Health Review Commission, which reviews enforcement priorities and actions; and the National Institute of Occupational Safety and Health, which conducts research on workplace hazards and prevention. As noted above, OSHA potentially applies to the vast majority of businesses in the US, but there are specific exemptions for the self-employed and for family farms.

Recognizing that at least some readers will not be satisfied by my brief self-serving statements at the beginning of this Chapter—trying to justify my inclusion of ERISA as part of the Nixon legislative record—permit me to elaborate just a bit. I certainly realize that its inclusion here, although it was not, in fact, signed by Nixon, is "inconsistent" with the structure of the analysis I am attempting to present. However, I derive some comfort from the oft-quoted words of Ralph Waldo Emerson: "A foolish consistency is the hobgoblin of little minds, adored by little statesmen and philosophers and divines."[13]

Richard Nixon is indeed *a*—if not *the*—father and "Godfather" of ERISA. While consumed by Vietnam, the USSR, "Red China," and the Middle East—and assailed by a hostile press and the "intellectual elite"—he somehow still found time and intellectual energy to address Congress three separate times with special messages on the need for further protection of employee pension benefits.[14]

In his March 13, 1970, message, the President reminded Congress that he had sent them legislative recommendations—seven months previously—dealing with Manpower Training, Unemployment Insurance, and Occupational Safety, and he hoped that "they will be enacted promptly and sent to me for signature." He then proposed an additional employee protection: the "Employee Benefits Protection Act," covering "four major areas": "First, the Federal government would require that persons who control employee benefit funds must deal with those funds exclusively in the interest of employee beneficiaries. . . . Second, the reporting and disclosure provisions would be broadened and strengthened by requirements which call for additional information. . . . Third, changes would be made to implement the newly imposed management responsibility and the newly strengthened reporting provisions. . . . Fourth, the Act would foster a body of uniform Federal law in employee benefits protection." He urged the Congress "to give urgent priority to this fourth part of the program—the Employee Benefits Protection Act."

President Nixon's message of December 8, 1971, contained a "five-point program" to "reform and expand private retirement programs," which included "4. The Employee Benefits Protection Act which I proposed to the Congress in March of 1970 should promptly be enacted into law." Points 1–3 were "new legislative proposals": "1. Employees who wish to save independently for their retirement or to supplement employer-financed pensions should be allowed to deduct on their income tax returns amounts set aside for these purposes. . . . 2. Self-employed persons who invest in pension plans for themselves and their employees should be given a more generous tax deduction than they now receive. . . . 3. A minimum standard should be established in law for the vesting of pensions—i.e., for preserving pension rights of employees even though they leave their jobs before retirement." And finally, to determine whether there was a need for further legislation, "5. I have directed the Departments of Labor and the Treasury to undertake a one-year study to determine the extent of benefit losses under pension plans which are terminated."

Even as the "wallowing in Watergate" must have been overloading his physical and mental capacities, the President persisted in his efforts to protect and enhance the pension benefits of American workers. His April 11, 1973, message proposed two bills (to be submitted shortly thereafter)—a "Retirement Benefits Tax Act" and an "Employee Benefits Protection Act." The "tax" side of the package "would embody the following five major principles: 1. A minimum standard should be established in law for preserving the retirement rights of employees who leave their jobs before retirement. . . . 2. Employees expecting retirement benefits under employer-financed defined benefit pension plans should have the security of knowing that their vested benefits are being adequately funded. . . . 3. Employees who wish to save independently for their retirement or to supplement employer-financed pensions should be allowed to deduct on their income tax returns amounts set aside for those purposes. . . . 4. Self-employed persons who invest in pension plans for themselves and their employees should be given a more generous tax deduction than they now receive. . . . 5. Workers who receive lump-sum payments from pension plans when they leave a job before retirement should be able to defer taxes on those payments until retirement."

On the "protection" side, Nixon's message said: ". . . the bill we are proposing would establish for the first time an explicit Federal requirement that persons who control employee benefit funds must deal with those funds exclusively in the interest of the employee participants and their beneficiaries. . . . Present reporting and disclosure requirements would also be broadened to require of benefit plan administrators a detailed accounting of their stewardship similar to that rendered by mutual funds, banks, and insurance companies. . . . To back up these changes, the new law would give additional investigative and enforcement powers to the Secretary of Labor and would permit pension fund participants and beneficiaries to seek remedies for breach of fiduciary duty through class action suits. . . . Finally, the Employee Benefits Protection Act would foster the development of uniform Federal laws in employee benefit protection, complementing but in no way interfering with State laws that regulate banking, insurance, and securities."

Noting that he had made a major proposal on benefits protection some three years earlier, President Nixon hoped that Congress would move "rapidly" to enact reform legislation, so as "to make 1973 a year of historic progress" in this area. Of course, as we now know, that hope was not fulfilled. That is to say, the requested action was not taken by Congress in 1973 but in 1974!

The House of Representatives passed the bill on February 28, 1974, and the Senate on March 4, 1974. But the Senate made some changes, so a "conference committee" was necessary to resolve the differences. The Joint Conference Committee presented its compromise bill on August 12—just *three days* after Richard Nixon's resignation took effect! The compromise bill was agreed to by the House (407 to 2) on August 20 and by the Senate (85 to 0) on August 22. President Ford's signing of the bill into law was delayed until September 2— Labor Day, 1974. In his signing statement, he said: "The act has its genesis in a message to the Congress by President Nixon on December 8, 1971." (Six days later—September 8, 1974—President Ford issued ". . . a full, free, and absolute pardon unto Richard Nixon for all offenses against the United States which he, Richard Nixon, has committed or may have committed or taken part in during the period from January 20, 1969, through August 9, 1974.")

Employee Retirement Income Security Act. So, ERISA (PL 93-406) was finally passed after what one commentator called "a long and arduous process."[15] Prior to the imposition of these national standards, employee benefits law was a mixture derived from labor law (imposing a duty to bargain over "terms and conditions of employment") and state contract law (interpreting the terms agreed on in the collective-bargaining agreement). If health-care or pensions were agreed on, the terms and conditions under which they were available could vary widely. Termination provisions were particularly troublesome.

The closing of Studebaker Corporation's auto plant in South Bend, Indiana provided a clear and compelling example of the gaps in the then-existing system. The employees had been members of the United Auto Workers, which had negotiated a "defined benefit" pension plan on their behalf; the company was to make contributions to the plan sufficient to provide a specified level of pension coverage for retirees. When the plant closed in December 1963, Studebaker and the UAW agreed on an arrangement for the plan's termination. The +/– 3,600 workers who were already retired or still active but were already sixty years old and eligible for retirement would receive their full pension benefits for life, taking some $21.5 million of the funds then in the plan. The 4,000 or so workers who had vested pension benefits based on ten years of service would have second claim on the remaining $2.5 million—enough to provide about 15 percent of the benefits earned. The remaining 2,900 with not-yet-vested rights in their pensions would receive nothing at all.[16] This seemingly harsh result was, in fact, exactly what the pension plan provided, and it had been knowingly agreed to by the UAW.[17] The union not only recognized that the plan distinctly favored older workers at the expense of younger ones with less seniority, but the union had decided to have it work that way, so as to induce older workers to retire—and thus make jobs for younger workers more available and more secure. Even so, the forfeiture of "earned"—but not yet "vested"—benefits was perceived by many as unfair.

With what seemed to be such an appealing case for protective legislation, why would the process be "lengthy and arduous"? The complexity of the issues involved (including the taxation issues) of course required very careful analysis and detailed draftsmanship. One would expect many company managements to object to further government intrusions into their prerogatives. But there was also a further hurdle—at least initially. As professor Wooten tells us: "In the decade before Congress passed ERISA, most of organized labor opposed comprehensive pension reform legislation."[18] Therefore, large segments of both direct participants in the unionized labor relations process were saying that they did not want further government participation as to workers' pensions.

As the Vice President, Nixon had, of course, been exposed to the efforts of the Eisenhower administration to improve oversight of pension plans. A "Pension Plans Disclosure Act" had been passed in 1958, and a bill to improve that regulatory package was pending when Ike's term ended. Also awaiting passage had been a proposal allowing self-employed persons to establish pensions.[19] And as it turned out, a similar situation existed at the end of President Johnson's tenure—in May 1968, the Labor Department had sent Congress "a detailed legislative proposal," which had not yet been enacted. However, Wooten says that "The bill that became ERISA was a later iteration of [that] Labor Department bill."[20] So, the JFK/LBJ team had also been interested in pension reform—but without legislative success.

The ins and outs and ups and downs of President Nixon's successful struggle to achieve pension reform are recounted at some length in Professor Wooten's study. For example, he notes the use of the new IRS rules on trustees' self-dealing (adopted to implement Nixon's 1969 Tax Reform Act) to solve some of the tax complications arising from pension administration.[21] He also describes the reformers' shift in strategy: "We discovered that the secret to passing reform legislation is the press."[22] Congress held public hearings, focusing on "horror stories," such as the Studebaker fiasco. Some combination of public support, persistence, and (hopefully) the merits finally carried the day—but just after one of the leading players had "retired."

In his signing statement, President Ford summarized ERISA's provisions by stating the following:

There are seven essential parts to this legislation:

—first, it establishes major standards for employee participation in private retirement plans. . . .

—second, and perhaps most important to those already under private pension plans, the new law establishes equitable standards for the "vesting" of retirement benefits. . . .

—third, the act requires that the fiduciaries who control the pension funds act as reasonable and prudent [wo]men, discharging their duties solely in the interest of protecting the beneficiaries of the fund;

—fourth, the law will impose a high standard upon the operation of plans by making mandatory full disclosure of all information concerning the operations of the employer's retirement plan;

—fifth, the tax laws will be revised to provide more nearly equal treatment to different kinds of plans. . . .

—sixth, as a final backstop to private plans, a federally sponsored, privately financed Pension Benefit Guaranty Corporation will be set up to pay an adequate retirement benefit to those whose private pension funds have foundered and are not adequate for the beneficiaries; and,

—seventh, the act will establish a limited form of portability of pension benefits by allowing workers to transfer some of their pension benefits to other plans or to their individual retirement accounts.

Protecting Workers

If some of the above sound distressingly familiar to President Nixon's messages to Congress, well, that's the point of the exercise. Nixon clearly had a program intended to protect workers—both their physical safety on the job and their financial well-being after retirement. And his goals were accomplished. His "landmark" legislation in this area went far beyond anything that Presidents Eisenhower, Kennedy, or Johnson—for all their endorsements by the intellectual elites—were able to produce.

Chapter 5

Nixon Protecting Minorities

T HE FOCUS OF THIS Chapter is necessarily quite different. Rather than a mostly blank legislative background (e.g., environmental protection) or an incomplete one (e.g., worker protection), minority rights were already protected by significant constitutional and legislative provisions—the Fourteenth Amendment, the 1964 Civil Rights Act, the 1965 Voting Rights Act, and others. There was still room for additional congressional fine-tuning, to be sure, but the most blatant manifestation of discrimination was not the result of an "absence of Law." It was the result of an absence of the will—and the *ability*—to see that "the Law" was enforced.

When Richard Nixon took office as President in 1969, a decade and a half after a unanimous US Supreme Court had ruled that racially segregated public schools violated the Constitution, just 186,000 of the 3 million African-American children in the South (6.2 percent) attended schools that were desegregated.[1] To be sure, the Court had said that its decision was to be implemented with "all deliberate speed,"[2] and the intensities of the Cold War had absorbed much of each President's attention and effort. Nevertheless, for nearly fifteen years, it seemed that the emphasis was on the adjective "deliberate," rather than the noun "speed." All of JFK's soaring rhetoric and LBJ's promises of a "Great Society" had barely dented racial segregation in public schools, especially in the South. Decisions by federal trial courts ordering the busing of children from one school to another to integrate enrollments hardly contributed to an improved education for anyone. Leaving aside the resulting drain on scarce school funds and the increased risks and strains imposed on the bused children (both black and white), the "integrated" schools that resulted often resembled war zones.[3] What was needed, in other words, was the executive/administrative skill to enforce the Supreme Court's 1954 decision—but without disrupting the schools' educational mission.

It seems fair to say that President Nixon's positive accomplishments in domestic policy—including his promotion of civil rights—have not been generally publicized or recognized. Joan Hoff's book is one notable example (previously mentioned), as she ranks those successes as more significant than Nixon's world-changing foreign policy triumphs.[4] More specifically, for purposes of this Chapter, Dean Kotlowski's thorough and meticulously-footnoted study *Nixon's Civil Rights* presents a more complete view and a more balanced evaluation.[5] Kotlowski notes that Nixon's administration, using the Justice Department but working effectively and quietly behind the scenes, had some 90 percent of African-American children in the South attending integrated schools in 1970/1971—the *second* school-year after he had become President! "In this sense, Nixon was the greatest school desegregator in American history."[6]

That Nixon accomplished this momentous task—one that had eluded Ike, JFK, and LBJ (for all the high-flown rhetoric over the intervening years)—with a minimum of violence and public confrontations also says a great deal about his leadership ability and his willingness to use it. What *did* he do? As summarized by H.W. Brands, "He put the prestige of the White House behind efforts to bring together black and white leaders of the South to devise local implementation plans, and he supported them with federal money to facilitate the amalgamation of the dual school systems—and in fact asked for much more money than Congress proved willing to give."[7] The fact that Nixon was able to do with words what had previously only been done (and then only to a very limited extent) with troops and court orders certainly seems to indicate that we had elected something more than the shallow scoundrel painted by most of the opposition. Just to "put the frosting on the cake," so to speak, he did it while maintaining his good working relationships with most of the South's leaders.

This is not to say that President Nixon solved our discrimination problems—or even this important aspect of them—completely and permanently. Indeed, there are indications that there has been a resurgence of school segregation. A 2005 study edited by John Charles Boger and Gary Orfield indicates a disturbing tendency toward segregated *classrooms*—even if the overall population of a school may be integrated.[8] Not all of Nixon's efforts to deal with discrimination were completely successful—the so-called "Philadelphia Plan" (to speed integration of the building trades workforce), for example. And not all of his proposals were adopted: his "Family Assistance Plan" (to reform the welfare system) was never adopted by Congress. Despite the last-minute addition of "sex" to the prohibitions against discrimination in Title VII of the 1964 Civil Rights Act, women still faced major disadvantages in the workplace.

Nonetheless, by any fair standard, President Nixon's record on civil rights is impressive. His leadership in desegregating schools, his advocacy for minority hiring in the building trades, his promotion of minority businesses and colleges, his approval of the 1971 Act (PL 91-122) assuring Latino participation in government assistance programs and of the 1972 Equal Employment Opportunity Act (PL 92-261), his strong support of Native American self-determination, and his insistence that affirmative action programs should include women as well as minority groups. That list seems quite weighty for a President who has often been described as "not caring much about domestic policy." Perhaps Professor Hoff's evaluation of the relative importance of Richard Nixon's contribution is the more valid ranking after all?

In any event, over 100 Public Acts passed during the Nixon presidency were identified as dealing in some way with protecting minorities. For present purposes, "women" were classified as a "minority"—even though they are a statistical majority. Gender discrimination has been (and continues to be) an ongoing problem. Where a particular statute could have been categorized either as "minority protection" or "worker protection," it was placed in the former column. What seems the more specific categorization was preferred, and of course, in addition, discrimination in the workplace has been a very important aspect of minority disadvantages.

Our list of Acts for the "minorities protection" category ends on July 25, 1974, with the passage of PL 93-358—the last of the "minorities protection" grouping prior to President Nixon's resignation on August 9.

Protecting Minorities—the Nixon Legislative Record

91st Congress, First Session (1969)

- PL 91-61: establishes National Center on Educational Media and Materials for the Handicapped

- PL 91-64: compensates the Indians of California for land erroneously taken

- PL 91-69: Older Americans Act Amendments of 1969

- PL 91-75: disposition of Court of Claims judgment for Confederated Salish and Kootenai Tribes

- PL 91-100: US holds land in trust for Three Affiliated Tribes of Fort Berthold Reservation

- PL 91-103: lands placed in trust for Standing Rock Sioux Tribe

- PL 91-104: US holds land in trust for Cheyenne River Sioux Tribe

- PL 91-112: US holds land in trust for Indians of the Pueblo of Laguna

- PL 91-115: amends act authorizing transfer of tribal land on Rosebud Sioux Indian Reservation

- PL 91-125: authorizes expenditures for National Council on Indian Opportunity

- PL 91-149: US holds land in trust for Southern Ute Tribe

- PL 91-181: establishes Cabinet Committee on Opportunities for Spanish-Speaking People

91st Congress, Second Session (1970)

- PL 91-229: provides loans to Indian tribes and corporations

- PL 91-240: sets inheritance rules for Cherokee, Chickasaw, Choctaw, and Seminole tribes, OK

- PL 91-251: authorizes transfer of Fort Belknap reservation irrigation unit to landowners in unit

- PL 91-259: disposition of judgment funds of the Confederated Tribes of Umatilla Reservation

- PL 91-264: furthers economic development of Hopi Indian Tribe

- PL 91-274: amends authorization of sale of inherited land interests on Tulalip Reservation

- PL 91-275: amends authorization of leases of land in Yavapai-Prescott Reservation

- PL 91-283: disposition of judgment funds of the Sioux Tribe of the Fort Peck Reservation

- PL 91-285: extends Voting Rights Act of 1965 regarding discriminatory tests, et al.

- PL 91-290: extends restrictions on lands of the Quapaw Indians, OK

- PL 91-335: disposition of judgment funds of the Tlingit and Haida Indians, AK

- PL 91-361: Department of Interior appropriations, including use of certain tribal funds

- PL 91-362: US holds land in trust for Washoe Tribe

- PL 91-364: disposition of judgment funds for Weas, Piankashaws, Peorias, Kaskaskais Tribes

- PL 91-386: repeals 1959 Act regarding final disposition of the affairs of the Choctaw Tribe

- PL 91-400: disposition of judgment funds for Hualapai Tribe

- PL 91-401: disposition of judgment funds for Citizen Band of Potawatomi Indians

- PL 91-403: reimburses Ute Tribe for Uintah irrigation project

- PL 91-404: disposition of judgment funds for Sac and Fox tribes, OK

- PL 91-413: disposition of judgment funds for Yakima Tribes

- PL 91-416: amends Act regarding Navajo irrigation project

- PL 91-417: disposition of judgment funds for Chemihuevi Tribe

- PL 91-420: disposition of judgment funds for Ute Tribes

- PL 91-442: amends Joint Resolution on employing handicapped to include all such persons

- PL 91-471: US holds land in trust for Yankton Sioux Tribe

- PL 91-478: conveys certain federally-owned land to Cherokee Tribe, OK

- PL 91-489: US holds land in trust for Makah Tribe

- PL 91-495: authorizes each of Five Civilized Tribes of OK to popularly elect a principal officer

- PL 91-501: US holds land in trust for Eastern Band of Cherokee Indians

- PL 91-521: appropriations for the Civil Rights Commission

- PL 91-523: adjusts State jurisdiction over criminal offenses in Indian Country

- PL 91-542: disposition of funds for Nez Perce Tribe

- PL 91-550: US holds land in trust for Pueblo de Taos Tribe

- PL 91-557: authorizes agreement to settle claim of Soboda Band of Mission Indians

- PL 91-593: provides for "National Employ the Older Worker Week"—first full week May 1971

- PL 91-610: extends for one year programs under Vocational Rehabilitation Act

- PL 91-627: amends 1946 Act regarding inheritance in Yakima Tribes

92nd Congress, First Session (1971)

- PL 92-28: extends targeted purchasing program to products made by the severely handicapped

- PL 92-29: disposition of judgment funds for Iowa Tribe of OK, KS, NE

- PL 92-30: disposition of funds for Snohomish, Upper Skagit, Snoqualmie, Skykomish Tribes

- PL 92-59: disposition of judgment funds for Pembina Band of Chippewa Indians

- PL 92-64: appropriations for the Civil Rights Commission

- PL 92-122: appropriations for Cabinet Committee on Opportunities for Spanish-Speaking People

- PL 92-123: authorizes declaration of 1971 as "Year of World Minority Language Groups"

- PL 92-128: prohibits establishment of detention camps

- PL 92-164: disposition of judgment funds for Pueblo of Laguna

- PL 92-182: authorizes land sales on Kalispel Reservation

- PL 92-186: US holds land in trust for Summit Lake Paiute Tribe

- PL 92-187: requires equal treatment of married women employees as to benefits and allowances

- PL 92-189: authorizes grants for the Navajo Community College

- PL 92-203: provides for settlement of Alaska Natives' land claims

- PL 92-206: apportions funds for payment of judgment for Shoshone Tribes

- PL 92-220: amends the District of Columbia's election act

92nd Congress, Second Session (1972)

- PL 92-244: disposition of judgment funds for Confederated Tribes of Colville Reservation

- PL 92-253: disposition of judgment funds for Confederated Salish and Kootenai Tribes

- PL 92-254: disposition of judgment funds for Blackfeet and Gros Ventre Tribes

- PL 92-258: amends Older Americans Act of 1965—low-cost meal projects, et al.

- PL 92-261: Equal Employment Opportunity Act of 1972—expands and strengthens 1964 Act

- PL 92-265: extends life of Indian Claims Commission

- PL 92-295: disposition of judgment funds for Jacarilla Apache Tribe

- PL 92-309: disposition of judgment funds for Miami Indians of Indiana and Oklahoma

- PL 92-312: authorizes land sales by the Southern Ute Indian Tribe

- PL 92-318: amends the 1965 Higher Education and Elementary & Secondary Education Acts

- PL 92-353: extends by ninety days the time for filing lawsuits by Indian tribes or groups

- PL 92-377: regulates inheritance for Confederated Tribes of Warm Springs Reservation

- PL 92-379: approves cancellation of certain charges by Klamath Indian irrigation project

- PL 92-427: US holds land in trust for Confederated Tribes of Warm Springs Reservation

- PL 92-431: authorizes longer-term leases on Indian lands outside reservation in NM

- PL 92-435: US holds land in trust for Fort Belknap Indian Community

- PL 92-438: disposition of judgment funds for Havasupai Tribe

- PL 92-439: disposition of judgment funds for Cheyenne-Arapaho Tribes of OK

- PL 92-441: US holds land in trust for Lac du Flambeau Band

- PL 92-442: disposition of judgment funds for Shoshone-Bannock Tribes

- PL 92-443: regulates inheritance for Nez Perce Tribe

- PL 92-456: disposition of judgment funds for Delaware Tribes

- PL 92-458: provides payment of certain pre-war bank claims by Japanese-American citizens

- PL 92-461: disposition of judgment funds for Yavapai Apache Tribe

- PL 92-462: disposition of judgment funds for Pueblo de Acoma

- PL 92-467: disposition of judgment funds for Kickapoo Indians

- PL 92-468: disposition of judgment funds for Yankton Sioux Tribe

- PL 92-470: authorizes acquisition of village site for Payson Band of Yavapai-Apache Indians

- PL 92-472: authorizes land sales on Coeur d'Alene reservation

- PL 92-480: US holds land in trust for Stockbridge Munsee Indian Community

- PL 92-485: extends time for filing lawsuits by Indian tribes, bands, or groups

- PL 92-488: US holds land in trust for Burns Indian Colony

- PL 92-496: extends life of Civil Rights Commission; its powers to apply to "sex" discrimination

- PL 92-515: enables physically-disabled persons to participate fully in DC's social/economic life

- PL 92-555: disposition of judgment funds for Mississippi Sioux tribes

- PL 92-557: disposition of judgment funds for Assiniboine Tribes

- PL 92-586: disposition of judgment funds for Osage Tribe of OK

93rd Congress, First Session (1973)

- PL 93-10: provides second week in March 1973 as "National Employ the Older Worker" week

- PL 93-29: Older Americans Comprehensive Services Amendments of 1973

- PL 93-37: appropriations for Indian Claims Commission

- PL 93-76: increases authorization for purchase of products/services produced by handicapped

- PL 93-92: amends District of Columbia's election act

- PL 93-102: amends Act terminating supervision over Klamath Indian Tribe

- PL 93-105: authorizes President to proclaim August 26, 1973, as "Women's Equality Day"

- PL 93-112: Rehabilitation Act of 1973—replaces the Vocational Rehabilitation Act

- PL 93-134: distribution of funds to pay judgments of Indian Claims Commission

- PL 93-174: provides for commissioning of women in US Coast Guard Reserve

- PL 93-195: Choctaw-Chickasaw-Cherokee Boundary Dispute Act—determines rights

- PL 93-197: Menominee Restoration Act—reestablishes tribe as federally-recognized, sovereign

93rd Congress, Second Session (1974)

- PL 93-262: Indian Financing Act of 1974—support for economic development

- PL 93-265: publication of materials on constitutional rights of Indians

- PL 93-285: US holds mineral interests in trust for Chippewa Cree Tribe

- PL 93-286: amends law relating to sale of lands on Spokane Indian Reservation

- PL 93-296: amends Public Health Service Act by establishing a National Institute on Aging

- PL 93-351: amends 1965 Older Americans Act by authorizing nutrition program appropriations

- PL 93-358: appropriations for purchase of products/services produced by handicapped persons

Minority Statutes—a Closer Look

This Chapter requires some further adjustments of our paradigm for the treatment of each grouping. To begin with, significant legislation had already been signed into law, and landmark court decisions had further defined minorities' rights. It seemed that the greatest need was not for more "law" but for more effective enforcement of the laws already in place.

Secondly, the overwhelming majority of the 100-plus Acts in this category that reached President Nixon's desk (90 of 121) concerned "Indians"—Native Americans. Further, of that vast majority, by far the largest subcategory (34 of the 90—nearly 40 percent) concerned payment of claims to various tribes that had proved their cases in court. That one subcategory thus accounted for almost 30 percent of the entire "minorities" total. These "claims-disposition" statutes were also nearly all very brief—less than one page each, for the most part. The pure statistics for this Chapter are thus somewhat misleading.

A major reason for what may appear to be an overemphasis on legislation concerning one minority group is due to the unique legal status of Native Americans.[9] Indian tribes were originally treated—at least for some purposes—as separate "nations," and various treaties were negotiated with different tribes over the years. While many of these were violated as the white settlers continued to push across the continent,[10] some are still in force—and recognized as binding by the courts. The State of Michigan's criminal prosecution of Albert LeBlanc provides an interesting example of this early "treaty" approach, summarized in the following paragraphs.

In 1836, representatives of the US government and the Chippewa and Ottawa tribes signed a treaty that ceded to the US almost 14 million acres in what is today part of the State of Michigan (about 37 percent of its land area). However, the treaty reserved hunting rights and preserved the fishing rights that had been agreed on in an 1820 treaty. In a later treaty, in 1855, the tribes had agreed to a money payment "in lieu and satisfaction of all claims" based on prior treaties—again excepting the 1820 fishing rights.

Albert LeBlanc, a Chippewa, was fishing in the reserved area in 1971, when he was arrested for fishing without a Michigan fishing license and for using a gill net—prohibited by State law. He was convicted of both offenses in the trial court, and the convictions were affirmed by a Michigan Circuit Court. LeBlanc then filed a further appeal with the Michigan Court of Appeals, asserting his fishing rights as a Chippewa. The State claimed that the Chippewas had given up their fishing rights by agreeing to the 1855 treaty. The Court of Appeals agreed with LeBlanc as to the fishing license—he didn't need one since the 1820 treaty rights were still valid. But even his treaty rights were subject to State regulation, if the regulation was necessary to preserve fishing stocks. That part of the case was sent back to the lower courts for further findings on "necessity." As Judge Brennan explained:

The Treaty of 1855 was designed to consolidate the Federal government's obligations to the Indians and provide mutually agreeable substituted forms of performance. Nothing on the record indicates that the parties ever intended to eliminate the Chippewas' fishing rights by this clause. In reaching the conclusion that the issue of fishing rights was considered by the parties to this treaty, the district court

placed much reliance on the fact that Article 3 specifically excepted from its application the fishing rights at Sault Ste. Marie, secured to the Chippewas by the Treaty of 1820. Such a conclusion, however, ignores the special circumstances surrounding that particular grant of fishing rights. . . .

A perpetual right of fishing and encampment at Sault Ste. Marie was secured by the Treaty of 1820 to the Chippewas who, by this same treaty, ceded certain lands at Sault Ste. Marie to the United States. Although the right to fish at this particular site was highly prized by the Chippewas, the construction of a canal on the ceded lands virtually destroyed the grounds for encampment and severely injured the fishing. The Chippewas were, at the time the 1855 treaty was signed, demanding large sums of money from the Federal government as compensation for the destruction of their rights under the 1820 treaty. It was to preserve this claim against the United States that Article 3 contained the exception referred to above. To read any more into this "exception" clause is to give effect to a technical interpretation of the treaty rather than to interpret it as it would have been understood by the Chippewas—the method of interpretation we are bound to follow.[11]

The various tribes thus may be subject to different sets of rules, especially as to property rights. Court decisions over the years as to the legal status of Indians have not been fully consistent, and there still seems to be room for differing interpretations. The trend has been in favor of increased tribal self-government on reservations, but there were—and are still—variations.[12] The Indian Citizenship Act of 1924 purported to make all Indians citizens of the United States—and thus presumably eligible to vote, subject to whatever uniform requirements are required by State and national laws. Indians' rights to be treated fairly, without being subject to discrimination on the basis of race or national origin, are protected by the Civil Rights Act of 1964. (Which brings us back to this Chapter—PL 92-261, the Equal Employment Opportunity Act of 1972, which, as noted later in this Chapter, significantly expanded and strengthened the 1964 Act.)

Some portion of the congressional emphasis on "Indians" (or "Native Americans") in our data is surely due to the fact that they were then, and are still, a minority in need of assistance. Some 2 million persons currently fall within the definition, with about one-fifth still living on over 500 "reservations" covering a total of over 5 million acres (about the size of the State of Idaho). Most reservations are quite small, but twelve are geographically larger than the State of Rhode Island. The largest (the Navajo Reservation) is about the same size as West Virginia.[13] Recent statistics indicate that about one-fourth of Native Americans are living on incomes below the official "poverty" line; for those on reservations, the below-poverty rate ranges from one-third to two-thirds. One estimate indicates that some 40 percent of reservation housing is overcrowded and that less than half of the housing has plumbing connected to a public sewer. So, this particular set of "minority" issues is one with which legislators and administrators have been dealing since Europeans first "discovered" the North American continent and started to settle there. Equally obviously, it is a problem-set that is still far from solution.[14]

The temporal sequencing of this group of statutes is also quite different. While the Second Session of each Congress is usually more productive in finalizing bills—because much of the preparation for passage occurs during the First Session—the contrast in this grouping is stark indeed. The First Session of the 91st Congress passed twelve bills in this category; the Second Session, thirty-seven. In the 92nd Congress, the count was sixteen in the First Session and thirty-seven in the Second. The sharp fall-off in these statutes during the 93rd Congress is also noteworthy: twelve bills passed in its First Session, seven in the Second. The explanation for the 93rd Congress's lack of production in this category is not clear. Of course, the fact that we are only considering production prior to August 9 for the 93rd's Second Session skews the numbers to a considerable degree since the later months of each Congress's two-year term tend to be the time when most of the legislative "crops" come in. "Wallowing in Watergate" may also have been partially to blame—but similar steep declines in legislation from the 93rd were not observed for our other categories.

"Indian"-Specific Statutes

In view of their hugely disproportionate part of the numerical total of the "minority-protection" statutes, this group of ninety Acts is given separate treatment and priority of place. For discussion purposes, the "Indian" statutes have been further divided into six sub-groupings.

The most numerous subcategory has already been mentioned—"disposition of funds" in satisfaction of legal claims to various tribes (thirty-four Acts). This is, in fact, a greater number than that of all the statutes pertaining to other specific "minorities" and to minorities generally (thirty Acts). Together, these two subcategories account for over half of the legislative production concerning minorities during the Nixon years. The next largest subcategory for legislation pertaining to Native Americans was acknowledgement of "landholding in trust" by the national government for the benefit of particular tribes (seventeen Acts) and miscellaneous other "land-management matters" (also seventeen Acts). "Inheritance" rules for reservation inhabitants (four Acts) could also have been included in this latter category, but inheritance of property seemed to be a highly specialized set of issues, deserving of specific statement. Five Acts dealt with various aspects of "tribal government." Specific national "government assistance" to various tribes included ten Acts.

Disposition of Funds. The incredible total of "minorities protection" statutes clearly owes much to the inclusion of the thirty-four Acts "disposing" of funds generated by legal claims by various tribes, which had been successfully litigated and resulted in judgments in their favor. The first thirty-three of these were from the 91st Congress (91-75, 91-259, 91-283, 91-335, 91-364, 91-400, 91-401, 9-404, 91-413, 91-417, 91-420, and 91-542) and the 92nd Congress (92-29, 92-30, 92-59, 92-164, 92-206, 92-244, 92-253, 92-254, 92-295, 92-309, 92-438, 92-439, 92-442, 92-456, 92-461, 92-462, 92-467, 92-468, 92-555, 92-557, and 92-586). Congress evidently—at last—recognized the considerable amount of valuable time and talent that this statutory confirmation/allocation process was consuming. The 93rd Congress thus passed PL 93-134, which established a uniform procedure for "disposition" of such judgment funds, through the Secretary of the Interior. For future Congresses, PL 93-134 would therefore result in the elimination, as unnecessary, of about 2 percent of the Nixon-years' legislative production.

Land in Trust. Indian reservation-land ownership rules are, to say the least, extremely complex. The reservation itself is considered "federal" land—part of the 500-million-plus acres of the US owned by the national government, as noted in Chapter 3. So, ultimately, national law applies to those geographical units. But the national government has delegated legal authority to the tribes living on the reservations—to varying degrees and with varying exceptions. (Specific tribes may also have certain treaty rights even as to non-reservation land, as seen in the *LeBlanc* case summarized earlier in this Chapter.) State land-use laws and regulations—and taxes—are thus (generally) not applicable on reservations.[15]

One (evidently frequently-used) method of stating this federal/tribal combination is the declaration of a "trust" relationship. The "trust" is a long-standing legal relationship in which one party—the "trustee" holds ownership of the trust property for the benefit of another party—the "beneficiary." A trust may be established by either of the parties or by a third party—a parent, for example, who transfers ownership of certain property to a financial institution, to use for the support and education of a child. (In this sort of situation, the legal term for the parent is the "settlor.")

Seventeen of our 121 statutes are statements of this "trust" type of relationship. Ten such were passed by the 91st Congress: 91-100, 91-103, 91-104, 91-112, 91-149, 91-362, 91-471, 91-489, 91-501, and 91-550. The 92nd Congress produced six: 92-186, 92-427, 92-435, 92-441, 92-480, and 92-488. For whatever combination of reasons, only one such "trust" declaration—PL 93-285—occurred during that part of the 93rd Congress that ended on August 9, 1974. They are uniformly very brief—merely declaring the existence of the trust in question. Fourteen of them are less than a page long. Three range in length between two and three pages: 91-112, 91-550, and 92-427. The relatively minor length variations derive from the different descriptions for the properties being placed in trust. As described in the Tables of Contents for each volume of statutes, at least fifteen different tribes or parts of tribes are mentioned. "Sioux" groupings are identified in three Acts: 91-103, 91-104, and 91-471.

Land Management. Of the seventeen Acts in this group, eight authorize land sales or leases: 91-115, 91-274, 91-275, 92-182, 92-312, 92-431, 92-472, and 93-286. PL 92-431 has to do with leases of non-reservation Indian lands; the other seven all concern reservation land. Two statutes—PL 91-478 and PL 92-470—provide for tribes' acquisition of additional land: the former, from the national government; the latter, for a "village site for the Payson Band of Yavapai-Apache Indians."

There are three Acts dealing with irrigation projects: PL 91-251, PL 91-416, and PL 92-379. Two statutes settle legal disputes: PL 91-557 and PL 93-195. PL 91-290 extends certain restrictions and tax exemptions on reservation lands of the Quapaw Indians in Oklahoma—for an additional twenty-five years. Finally, PL 93-102 authorizes the Secretary of Agriculture to acquire by "condemnation" (forced government purchase, per the terms of the applicable treaty) all the forest land of the Klamath tribe, for addition to the Winema National Forest—for a maximum price of $70,000,000.

Given the apparent frequency with which various types of reservation-land management problems seem to be occurring, it might be worthwhile for Congress to investigate some further delegation of decision-power to the Secretary of the Interior. Provision could be made for some sort of annual or semi-annual reporting to the appropriate congressional committees, perhaps also with "major decisions" being subject to congressional approval.

Inheritance. There were only four statutes identified as being in this category, but, as noted earlier, this is such a special and personal area of property concerns that it was felt to deserve separate tallying and categorization. State laws provide the rules for determining who receives a decedent's property. If one wishes to change these presumptive heirs, State law specifies what needs to be done to do so—via the requirements for making a valid will, in each State. But State law (generally) does not apply on Indian reservations. So, who succeeds to the rights of a deceased tribe member living on a reservation?

The answer to that question involves national law, subject to the amount of delegation of congressional authority that has been given to a particular tribe for the governance of its reservation. So, these four Acts—PL 91-240, PL 91-627, Pl 92-377, and PL 92-443—are examples of the national government exercising its State-like authority to regulate the distribution of decedents' estates (especially as to interests in tribal lands).

PL 91-240 applies to decedents' estates of members of the Cherokee, Chickasaw, Choctaw, and Seminole tribes in Oklahoma. It provides that, after five years, when a member of any of those tribes has been determined by a court or by the Secretary of the Interior to have died without any heirs, that person's interest in tribal lands shall "escheat" (revert back) to the tribe. The other three Acts all contain the same basic provision, but as to three different tribes: the Yakima, the Confederated Tribes of the Warm Springs Reservation in Oregon, and the Nez Perce of Idaho. No interest in tribal lands will be distributed to the heirs of a member of those tribes if the tribe pays the heir/s the fair market value of that interest, but a surviving spouse does have a one-half life estate interest in that property. (Presumably, the right of occupancy for his/her lifetime.)

This very small sample is thus illustrative of the level of detail and individualistic concern of Congress's management of the lives and fortunes of Native Americans.

Tribal Government. This category also comprises a very small sample—only five Acts: PL 91-386, PL 91-361, PL 91-523, PL 93-197, and PL 93-265. Again, this small grouping seemed to require separate identification and discussion, if only to illustrate the level and extent of congressional supervision of tribal governance (at least, at that point in history).

Four of these Acts are less than one page each in length. Only PL 93-197 is somewhat longer (not quite four pages). That statute restores the Menominee of Wisconsin to tribal status and thus requires some additional language to make sure that everyone's rights are protected, including those who relied on the validity of the original tribal termination. That same final point was also addressed in PL 91-386, a brief repeal of an earlier statute (PL 86-190) that rearranged the ownership of the Choctaw tribe's mineral rights. After stating the repeal, 91-386 added section 2, which stated that the repeal would not affect any rights acquired under the earlier act or any legal action arising under it that was pending as of the effective date of the repeal.

Two statutes deal with legal proceedings. PL 93-265 merely authorizes appropriations of "such sums as may be necessary" for enforcement of the prohibition against acts of "violence or intimidation" contained in PL 90-284: the Civil Rights Act of 1968—which includes extensive coverage of Indian constitutional rights and self-government. And PL 91-523 excludes certain areas of "Indian country" in Alaska from the provision that criminal offenses in Indian country by or against Indians can, generally, be prosecuted under State law. (State criminal law generally applies in "Indian country.")

Perhaps the most important Act of this subgroup is PL 91-495, which gives the "Five Civilized Tribes" in Oklahoma the right to democratically choose their leaders. The five tribes are identified as the Creek (of Muscogee), the Cherokee, the Chickasaw, the Choctaw, and the Seminoles. For the Chickasaw, the official executive is the "governor"; for the other four tribes, it is the "principal chief." The current executives were permitted to serve until the end of twelve months or the duration of their terms, whichever occurred first. Any vacancies (resignation, death, etc.) occurring during those periods would be filled under the new elective procedures. Interestingly, the electoral procedures adopted for the various tribes were still subject to approval by the Secretary of the Interior.

Governmental Assistance. In addition to whatever financial and institutional support was being provided in the overall budgeting/appropriations process, there were also twelve Acts dealing with more specific types of allocations for Indian welfare. PL 91-361, for example, contained specific sections dealing with various "support" projects, as part of the Department of Interior's funding for the fiscal year ending on June 30, 1971: "Education and Welfare Services"—$219,615,000; "Resource Management"—$64,622,000; "Construction"—$19,885,000; "Road Construction"—$20,200,000; "Tribal Funds" (to be used for Indian employees, children, et al.)—$3,000,000; and "Administrative Provisions"—an unspecified total amount from BIA funds, for exhibits, vehicles, etc. PL 91-125 was a brief Joint Resolution, authorizing appropriations for the National Council on Indian Opportunity.

PL 93-262 (the Indian Financing Act of 1971) was an important initiative: "AN ACT To provide for financing the economic development of Indians and Indian organizations. . . ." Several programs and policies were included—an "Indian Revolving Loan Fund," loan guaranty and insurance, interest subsidies and administrative expenses, and Indian business grants. These mechanisms were to be employed "to help develop and utilize Indian resources, both physical and human, to a point where the Indians will fully exercise responsibility for the utilization and management of their own resources and where they will enjoy a standard of living from their own productive efforts comparable to that enjoyed by non-Indians in neighboring communities."[16] This "economic development" emphasis was characteristic of President Nixon's theory of dealing with minority-group problems: economic strength and independence were necessary for minority citizens' advancement. (It's also worth noting that this significant step forward was taken in April 1974. Even in the midst of the developing Watergate scandal that would result in the end of the Nixon presidency, the Nixon-era Congress was still grinding out progressive legislation.) A more specific application of this same approach can be seen in PL 91-264, which grants to the Hopi Tribal Council "certain powers of self-determination," so that it is free to develop the "Hopi Industrial Park."

Three of the Acts in this subcategory allocated funds to specific tribes, for various projects or adjustments. PL 91-64 repaid California Indians for the value of land that had been mistakenly used as an offset against a judgment in favor of the tribe against the national government. PL 91-403 restored Ute tribal funds that had been used to build, operate, and maintain the Uintah Irrigation Project in Utah. The third tribe-specific financial adjustment was PL 92-189: an authorization of grants for the Navajo Community College.

Three Acts passed by the Second Session of the 92nd Congress dealt with the Indian

Claims Commission: PL 92-265, which extended the life of the Commission; and PL 92-353 and PL 92-485, both of which extended the time periods within which Indian claims were asserted must be filed with a court. (This so-called "Statute of Limitations" rule provides that claims not filed with a court within a specific time period after the claims arise are not thereafter enforceable in court; in other words, the claim is legally barred.) PL 93-37 provided further funding for the Commission.

Finally, PL 92-203 (the Alaska Native Claims Settlement Act) seems to fit best in this subcategory. It certainly contains provisions having to do with "tribal government" and "land management," but those features seem outweighed by its fundamental purpose: the recognition and "settlement" of the claims of Alaskan Native Americans. (One could also argue that its scope and historical significance justify placing it in a "category" of its own.)

Alaska is by far the largest of the States, containing over 420 million acres. (It's more than one-fifth the size of the "lower forty-eight"—all by itself.) Of that huge area, however, the national government holds about 65 percent—some 270 million acres. The State of Alaska owns another 100-plus million acres—a bit less than 25 percent. So, when the ANCSA grants 44 million acres to the Alaskan tribes (just over 10 percent of Alaska's total land mass), that's a very significant "claims settlement"!

According to Tom Wicker, much of the credit for the administration's recognition of the 100-year-old tribal claims and the passage of the ANCSA must go to John Ehrlichman and his staff. Ehrlichman overcame Secretary of the Interior Morton's objections to the administration's bill by telling Morton that the President wanted it passed, and then he in fact got the President's "actual approval." The original bill had provided for 10 million acres and $500 million; those figures were increased to the 44 million acres noted above and $962.5 million.[17]

Clearly, Congress was spending considerable time and effort dealing with Native American concerns. Just as obviously, much of resulting legislation stemmed from acting as a sort of "State" government, delegating powers to—but still supervising to some extent—its "local governments." The analogy is, of course, decidedly imperfect, but the need to legislate on the same sort of local matters does seem to explain the sizable body of Indian-specific congressional legislation.

Be that as it may, the Nixon-era Congresses did also pass six civil-rights statutes pertaining to minorities generally (historically disadvantaged groups) and twenty-four others relating to specific groups. These six generally-applicable civil-rights Acts (PL 91-285, PL 91-521, PL 92-64, PL 92-220, PL 92-261, and PL 93-92) would, of course, also apply to Native Americans, as a racial/ethnic minority—as does the Civil Rights Act of 1964, our major piece of anti-discrimination legislation. In fact, Title VII of the 1964 Act, prohibiting discrimination in employment, even contains a clause *permitting* discrimination in favor of

Indians: "Nothing contained in this title shall apply to a business or enterprise located on or near an Indian reservation with respect to any publicly announced employment practice of such business or enterprise under which an employment preference is given to any individual because he is an Indian living on or near a reservation." (Note that the "preferential discriminating" permitted is not limited to Indian-*owned* businesses but also includes any business located on or near a reservation. Indian tribes were, however, excluded from the 1964 Act's definition of "employers" who were prohibited from using the enumerated discriminations.)

The origin of this legislatively-sanctioned employment preference is Section 12 of the Indian Reorganization Act of 1934, which required—not just permitted—such favorable treatment for "qualified" Indians, by the "Indian Office" (the predecessor to the Bureau of Indian Affairs—the BIA). The 1964 Civil Rights Act had originally applied only to private employers; it was the 1972 Act—our Nixon-signed PL 92-261—that added governments to the list of employers who were prohibited from practicing employment discrimination. In 1972, Mancari and several other BIA employees filed a lawsuit in US District Court in New Mexico, claiming that such discrimination by the BIA was no longer lawful because the provisions of the 1964 Civil Rights Act (as amended by our PL 92-261) had impliedly repealed Section 12 of the 1934 Act. A panel of three District Court judges agreed with Mancari's group. A request for review of that decision was filed directly with the US Supreme Court. All nine Supreme Court Justices agreed that the District Court was wrong: there had been no implied repeal of the Indian-preference rule, and that rule did not violate the Due Process Clause of the Fifth Amendment to the US Constitution. Writing for the Court and relying in part on the fact that the 1964 Act itself provided for Indian preference in employment, Justice Blackmun said:

These 1964 exemptions as to private employment indicate Congress' recognition of the longstanding federal policy of providing a unique legal status to Indians in matters concerning tribal or "on or near" reservation employment. The exemptions reveal a clear congressional sentiment that an Indian preference in the narrow context of tribal or reservation-related employment did not constitute racial discrimination of the type otherwise proscribed. In extending the general anti-discrimination machinery to federal employment in 1972, Congress in no way modified these private employment preferences built into the 1964 Act, and they are still in effect. It would be anomalous to conclude that Congress intended to eliminate the longstanding statutory preferences in BIA employment, as being racially discriminatory, at the very same time it was reaffirming the right of tribal and reservation-related private employers to provide Indian preference. [Plaintiffs'] assertion that Congress implicitly repealed the preference as racially discriminatory, while retain-

ing the 1964 preferences, attributes to Congress irrationality and arbitrariness, an attribution we do not share. . . .

Contrary to the characterization made by [plaintiffs], this preference does not constitute "racial discrimination." Indeed, it is not even a "racial" preference. Rather, it is an employment criterion reasonably designed to further the cause of Indian self-government and to make the BIA more responsive to the needs of its constituent groups. It is directed to participation by the governed in the governing agency. . . . Congress has sought only to enable the BIA to draw more heavily from among the constituent group in staffing its projects, all of which, either directly or indirectly, affect the lives of tribal Indians. The preference, as applied, is granted to Indians not as a discrete racial group, but, rather, as members of quasi-sovereign tribal entities whose lives and activities are governed by the BIA in a unique fashion.[18]

Thus, this intentional "discrimination" in favor of Indians—a sort of statutory affirmative action—has survived challenges based on Title VII of the 1964 Civil Rights Act and on the Due Process Clause of the Fourteenth Amendment. It seems a very small compensation for the many years of broken promises, but it is at least a small step in the right direction.

Non-"Indian" Statutes

As noted at the beginning of this Chapter, there were thirty Acts that did not pertain specifically to Native Americans and their problems. Six of these were generally applicable to minority groups (those who have traditionally been subject to disadvantages of one sort or another), and twenty-four pertained to specific groups.

Generally-Applicable Acts. The extension of non-discrimination protection to the millions of employees who work for our national, State, and local governments, even if it had done nothing more, would make the Equal Employment Opportunity Act of 1972 (PL 92-261) the most important of the twenty-nine "non-Indian" minority-protection statutes passed during the Nixon years. But of course, that is not all that PL 92-261 contains. At least as important (and arguably even more so, since government employees already had significant legal protection against unjust treatment via the Due Process Clause of the Fourteenth Amendment), the 1972 EEOA's amendments provided real enforcement power to the Equal Employment Opportunity Commission. A "paper tiger" was transformed into "a sleeping giant—awakened, and filled with a terrible resolve" (paraphrasing Japanese admiral Yamamoto's oft-quoted comment after he learned of the timing of the attack on Pearl Harbor).

Prior to PL 92-261, if the EEOC determined—after investigation—that there were reasonable grounds to believe that a prohibited employment discrimination had occurred, and it thought that a lawsuit was necessary to correct the problem, it had to refer the case to the Department of Justice. Of course, the DOJ has many other responsibilities and its own agenda, and it might or might not pursue a particular case with the same speed and vigor as the EEOC. The victim of the alleged discrimination could file his or her own lawsuit after receiving a "right-to-sue" letter from the EEOC, but that private lawsuit would be at the alleged victim's cost. That financial barrier to a private remedy is made even more burdensome by the fact that significant portions of those legal expenses must be paid *in advance*, before there has been a decision on the merits of the complaint. If the lawsuit is successful, the victim might be reimbursed for at least part of the attorney fees and court costs involved. But, if not successful, the unsuccessful plaintiff would have to personally absorb those outlays. By giving the EEOC the power to bring its own lawsuits in the US District Court, PL 92-261 provides for direct and vigorous prosecution of claims that its investigation has determined are meritorious. (Or at least, for the possibility thereof.) With this second group of additions to the 1964 Act, PL 92-261 must be viewed as one of the most important of the entire total of 1,671 statutes enacted during the Nixon presidency.

Also of great significance is PL 91-285—the Voting Rights Act Amendments of 1970, extending the effectiveness of the Voting Rights Act of 1965. Making sure that all our citizens have their voting rights guaranteed is surely of primary concern. PL 91-285, however, is merely extending protection already in effect for a further period—somewhat arguable, perhaps, but not of the same magnitude of policy innovation as the additions in PL 92-261.

PL 91-521 and PL 92-64 merely authorize appropriations for the Commission on Civil Rights. Acting in an analogous role to a State legislature, Congress uses PL 92-220 and PL 93-92 to amend the DC voting act regarding filing of certain petitions and the primary election for DC's delegate to Congress.

Handicap Protection. Of the four subgroups of statutes applying to specific minorities, the most numerous were the Acts applying to persons with handicaps. Eight fell in this subcategory: PL 91-61, PL 91-442, PL 91-610, PL 92-28, PL 92-515, PL 93-76, PL 93-112, and PL 93-358.

Three of the eight provided for preferential purchase of products and services produced by the handicapped: PL 92-28, which expanded the policy beyond products produced by the blind to include those produced by others with severe handicaps; and PL 93-76, which increased the authorization for such purchases for 1974, and PL 93-358, which approved authorizations for 1975 and beyond.

PL 91-61 provides for a National Center on Media and Materials for the Handicapped. (For a person with limited eyesight, for example, recordings of books or plays can be an important source of entertainment.) As early as 1945, a statute had proclaimed the first week in October each year as "National Employ the Physically Handicapped Week"; and PL 91-442 extended that proclamation to apply to all handicapped workers. PL 91-610 amended the Vocational Rehabilitation Act by extending for one year the authorization for its programs. (The Smith-Fess Act of 1920 had established a joint federal-state program for the rehabilitation of workers injured in injury or occupation, to be funded by equal contributions from both governments and by any other public or private contributions—the latter on condition that there could be no discrimination in payment of benefits on the basis of membership or nonmembership in any private organization. The vocational rehabilitation program was made permanent by section 531 of the Social Security Act of 1935.) PL 92-515 guarantees various protections for blind and physically disabled persons in the District of Columbia to enable them "to participate fully in [its] social and economic life"—including the right of a blind person to have access to museums and the like, with a guide dog, without having to pay an additional admission fee for the dog.

PL 93-112—the Rehabilitation Act of 1973—is clearly the most important statute in this subgroup. It's a total "reboot" of this piece of national law—repealing the old Vocational Rehabilitation Act and transferring its ongoing programs and funding to the newly-established "Rehabilitation Services Administration" established in the Department of Health, Education, and Welfare. Further, in developing plans and providing services for current and future needs of handicapped persons, priority is to be given to those with the most severe handicaps. The new RSA is to develop ways to deal with architectural and transportation barriers faced by handicapped persons. Discrimination against handicapped persons is prohibited in "any program or activity receiving federal financial assistance," and federal agencies are generally required to submit affirmative action programs for hiring, training, and promoting handicapped persons. There are, of course, many more administrative and procedural details in the nearly thirty pages of this very significant statute.

Older Americans Protection. Of the seven Acts in this subcategory, two merely "provide for the designation" of a "National Employ the Older Worker Week." For PL 91-593, it's the first full week of May 1971; for PL 93-10, it's the second full week of March 1973. PL 93-296—the "Research on Aging Act of 1973"—while also brief, does establish the National Institute on Aging to conduct research on the process and problems thereof.

The other four Acts—PL 91-69, PL 92-258, PL 93-29, and PL 93-351—all involve extensions/amplifications of the programs begun under the Older Americans Act of 1965 (part of LBJ's "Great Society.") PL 91-69, for example, in addition to making certain modifications to such programs, adds a new Title VI to the statute, providing for retired-senior volunteers to be used in various public service positions—including that of "foster grandparents" for children needing counseling and mentoring. PL 92-258 covers programs for low-cost meals and nutrition training for seniors. PL 93-29—the Older Americans Comprehensive Services Amendments of 1973—is (as suggested by the title) a very substantial revision of the 1965 Act. (The original 1965 Act is some eight-plus pages in length; PL 93-29 is thirty-five pages long!) The emphasis is on the establishment of regional centers, providing a variety of services and support: special library services for the elderly—to cite one example. In contrast, PL 93-351 is a bit under two pages long, providing continuing funding, with emphasis on senior nutrition programs.

What seems most notable about the statutes in this section, especially those dealing with the Older Americans Act, is the very wide range of services for the elderly being funded by the national government. One suspects that many people, including many seniors, are not fully aware of everything that the national government is making available for their benefit.

Ethnicity/Language Protection. The five Acts in this group were very brief, averaging just over one page in length. PL 91-181 did take two and one-half pages to establish the "Cabinet Committee on Opportunities for Spanish-Speaking People." Members of the Committee include the heads of seven Cabinet Departments, plus a commissioner from the EEOC, the heads of the Civil Service Commission, the Small Business Administration, and the Office of Economic Opportunity, and a full-time appointed chairman. Its functions are to try to assure that existing federal programs are working effectively for Spanish-speaking citizens and to assist in the development of new programs to meet their special needs. While this is perhaps only a small step, it does seem to be headed in the right direction. PL 92-122 was a very brief follow-up, authorizing appropriations for an additional two years for the Cabinet Committee. PL 92-123—a Joint Resolution authorizing a presidential proclamation—has a much more expansive scope: 1971 is to be designated as the "Year of World Minority Language Groups." No specific action to assist such groups is indicated, but at least their existence is recognized. Perhaps intended is an implicit message that such groups are worthy of assistance and in need of protection and cultivation.

Two Acts—PL 92-128 and PL 92-458—were identified as "ethnicity-protection" statutes. The second is clearly that—providing enforcement for certain pre-World War II bank assets ("certificates of deposit" issued by certain banks) to persons of Japanese ancestry. The index description of PL 92-128 says that it is "AN ACT To amend Title 18, United States Code, to prohibit the establishment of detention camps. . . ." That's not quite what the Act itself says, which is: "No person shall be imprisoned or otherwise detained by the United States except pursuant to an Act of Congress." So, detention is not totally prohibited, just detention not authorized by an Act of Congress. (If Congress says it's o.k., it's o.k.)

There is no reference in the Act itself to any specific ethnicity—so why is it being included in this subgroup? At the time, the most recent example of "detention camps" in the US were those used to house the Japanese-ethnicity persons who had been rounded up by US officials at the beginning of World War II. Members of the 93rd Congress certainly remembered the war years, especially the early months right after the Pearl Harbor attack. Some of them had served in the military during the war, including the war against Japan in the Pacific. Future Vice President (and then President, for the balance of Richard Nixon's term) Gerald Ford—at the time, the Republican Minority Leader in the House of Representatives—was one of them, having served in the Pacific theatre on board the aircraft carrier USS *Monterey*. (President Nixon also served in the US Navy in the South Pacific, as had President Kennedy.) So, the war trauma that had generated the level of fear and anger that led to the detention of Japanese-ancestry persons and the seizure (and theft) of their property was something that many Congressmen knew and understood. All this leads one to assume that the purpose of PL 92-128 was to prevent another such administrative detention of citizens and lawful residents in response to a future crisis. ("9/11"?) The fact that this same 92nd Congress later passed PL 92-458 to make partial restitution to Japanese-Americans for bank assets seized during that same period is an indirect confirmation of this speculative analysis.

Without drifting too far from our central purpose here, one can only hope that that sort of emergency response will never again be seen as necessary, whether the final detention-decision is made by administrative or legislative officials.

Women's Protection. Producing—over the course of some five and one-half years—only five statutes dealing specifically with the various forms of discrimination against women would seem to indicate a lack of concern for the interests of this group. That may indeed have been true for some members of Congress, but it should also be noted that women's interests, especially in fair employment practices, had been dealt with to a significant extent by prior Congresses. The Equal Pay Act of 1963 amended the Fair labor Standards Act so as to prohibit pay differentials based on sex, and Title VII of the 1964 Civil Rights Act had outlawed such discrimination in employment. One of the most blatant and harmful areas of discrimination against women had, therefore, already been addressed by regulatory legislation.

Nevertheless, two of the Acts in this small grouping would have some immediate positive effects. PL 92-187 provided that married women who were employed by the federal government had to receive the same benefits and allowances as those specifically provided for married men. For the several millions of women who were then, and in the future would be, in that category, that Act was important. On a much smaller scale, PL 93-174 provided for the commissioning of women as officers in the US Coast Guard Reserve—another step toward sexual equality in the Armed Forces. To parallel the (last-minute) addition of "sex" as one of the bases of employment differentials prohibited by Title VII of the 1964 Civil

Rights Act, PL 92-496 added "sex" discrimination to the jurisdiction of the Civil Rights Commission, as one of the areas where it could investigate and make recommendations. PL 93-105 merely authorizes the President to proclaim August 26, 1973, as "Women's Equality Day." (It's not at all clear how many people might interpret this as a kind of "Queen *for a Day*" message.)

As it turns out, what has proved to be a very important "protection" statute for women was hidden away as three pages in a 146-page package: Title IX of the Education Amendments of 1972. Title IX, section 901 says: "No person in the United States shall, on the basis of sex, be excluded from participation in, be denied the benefits of, or be subjected to discrimination under any education program or activity receiving Federal financial assistance. . . ." Several exceptions are listed to this broad prohibition. As to admissions, the prohibition is not applicable to private-university undergraduate programs—although it is applicable to *all* graduate and professional programs and to undergraduate programs at public universities. There is a one-year delay (after passage of the Act) before the admissions provision becomes effective, plus an extra phase-in period for schools that are shifting from single-sex admissions. Section 901 does not apply to religious schools if its application would conflict with the school's religious doctrines.[19] Nor is it applicable to the military or merchant-marine academies. Interestingly, section 901(a)(5) also excludes application of the prohibition to any institution of higher education "that traditionally and continuously from its establishment has had a policy of admitting only students of one sex."

Section 901(b) specifies that the statute does not require preferential-admission treatment of one sex to "make up" any statistical imbalance, although statistical evidence can be used to show that there is, in fact, such an imbalance. Section 901(c) provides that where there are several administratively separate schools, colleges, or departments in an educational institution, the prohibition applies to each. (A university could not, for example, "balance off" a preponderance of women in its nursing program by showing that there was a corresponding imbalance of men in its engineering program.) Section 904 explicitly prohibits discrimination against the blind, but it does not require provision of any special services. In its final section (907), Title IX specifically permits an institution's requirement of separate living arrangements in its on-campus housing.

Anyone at all familiar with higher education in the US is surely aware of the massive shift that has occurred in women's enrollment in Law, Business, and—to a lesser extent, perhaps—Engineering. (The author remembers his 1957/58 and 1960/61 law school classes having one or no women in large sections of required or recommended courses; one woman was in several of my first-year classes, and there was one in my Tax Law elective.)[20] Even more obvious is the sea-change in women's sports—in high school as well as college—from twenty-seven men in sports to every one woman to 60/40! That's a revolution! One only has to look at the quadrennial Olympic Games to see how far US women have progressed in sports skills. (The US women's soccer team winning a gold?—previously unbelievable.) We may have difficulty showing a cause-and-effect relationship between Title IX and these results, but even the symbolism of PL 92-318 seems to have had a positive impact.

Moreover, as was also true with racial discrimination, one cannot, in fairness, overlook President Nixon's executive actions to try to deal with gender discrimination. As pointed out by H.W. Brands, "Nixon mandated the extension of affirmative action to women, enormously increasing the scope of the equal rights concept."[21] Even if only a "first step," it was surely a very significant one.

Protecting Minorities

So, what can we say in summation of the Nixon-era legislative record as to the protection of minorities? As has been obvious from the start of our discussion, these three Congresses devoted what might seem to be a disproportionate amount of attention to Native American affairs—perhaps at the expense of other minorities' concerns, perhaps not. Nevertheless, there are in this collection at least four (non-"Indian") landmark accomplishments: PL 92-261—the Equal Employment Opportunity Act of 1972, PL 93-29—the Older Americans Comprehensive Services Amendments of 1973, PL 93-112—the Rehabilitation Act of 1973, and PL 92-318—the Education Amendments of 1972. Even though not every person in every "minority" grouping would benefit from them, each of them does apply to a significant group of persons felt to be in need of protection and assistance.

It is also worth repeating that President Nixon's greatest credit in this area may be due to his executive leadership, not to any legislative role he may have played in the enactment of new statutes. His crowning achievement in this area, as noted at the beginning of this chapter, would seem to be the generally peaceful integration of public schools—through private negotiations rather than with lawsuits and court-ordered busing. And after fifteen years of "deliberate speed," Richard Nixon had the southern schools integrated by the middle of the second school year after he took office: 1968 = 6+ percent of black students attending integrated schools; the end of 1970 = some *90* percent![22] "'President Nixon was magnificent,' [Labor Secretary George] Shultz recalled. 'People went out of there [the Oval Office] on Cloud Nine . . . inspired.'"[23] "'He came in . . . and turned it around,' Shultz remembered. 'I had a lump in my throat.'"[24]

Nor was that the only significant executive action Nixon took to end discrimination. Again, Brands notes that "Nixon was also the first president to push affirmative action. His labor secretary, George Schultz, applied the 'Philadelphia plan' which required contractors doing federal work to hire minimum numbers of black employees, to several cities across the country."[25] Moreover, Nixon was evidently serious about getting concrete results: "To ensure enforcement of federal hiring guidelines, the [Nixon] administration requested, and received, dramatic increases in the staff and budget of the Equal Employment Opportunity Commission."[26] Most commentators may have overly-discounted these efforts to pry open certain job categories for the benefit of minorities—and women—and to encourage entrepreneurship among those groups. In fact, improved access to income opportunities would seem to be the surest key to lifestyle improvements—better housing, education, health-care, and the like. That same sort of thinking appears to have also been the basis for President Nixon's "independence" policy for Native Americans. And the quoted endorsements of his work by two Native American leaders, comparing him to Washington and Lincoln, indicate that his accomplishments were recognized and appreciated.

Even seemingly unrelated, or at best only tangentially related, economic developments may have significant impacts (positive or negative) on certain groups. The point is quite forcefully made in a paragraph in Marc Levinson's history of the Great Atlantic & Pacific Tea Company:

> The spread of supermarkets and the industrialization of food production were good news for families of modest means. They enabled the average American to consume 10 percent more food in 1950 than in 1930, with poorer households showing startling improvements in the quality of their daily diets. . . . American families ate better at far lower cost than ever before, in part because they had to pay much less to move their food from farm to table. The rise of the food chains was especially important to African-Americans. . . . [A] disproportionate number of [the A&P] stores were in older urban areas occupied by working-class blacks during World War II and the years thereafter, providing reasonable prices to shoppers who otherwise faced extremely high food bills from independent inner-city stores.[27]

So "unintended consequences" need not always be negative or destructive. President Nixon was clearly willing to try new approaches, and even that which Congress refused to adopt might have produced significant improvements. With the sort of congressional majorities that FDR and LBJ had, there might be another "New Deal" or "Great Society" on the statute books.

Even as it was, with the congressional "deck" stacked against him and with much of the media and the "intellectual" class emotionally opposed to whatever he advocated, Nixon did sign a number of legislative—and administrative—measures that improved the lives of minority citizens. In sum, in dealing with this set of problems, too, President Nixon did not do a bad job, for someone who "didn't care much about domestic policy."

Chapter 6

Nixon Protecting Consumers

T HERE WERE SOME surprises in this data-set of eighty-six Public Acts. One remembers the 1960s and 1970s as a period of considerable consumer-protection activity, especially in the area of consumer finance. Unfortunately—for present purposes—many of those efforts predate or postdate the Nixon presidential years. While the landmark Consumer Credit Protection Act took effect during Nixon's first year in office (on May 29, 1969), it had actually been passed a year earlier. Thus, Nixon's role was that of implementation ("faithful execution" of the law), rather than creation. Three other important pieces of legislation came to fruition later in 1974, after he had resigned the presidency on August 9: the Equal Credit Opportunity Act (which prohibited discrimination in the granting of credit—hidden away as Title V of PL 93-495), the Fair Credit Billing Act (Title III of PL 93-495), and the Privacy Act (PL 93-579). But for the Watergate tragedy, credit for those three items would also have been placed in the Nixon presidential column.

So much for what's not in this Chapter. What *is* here? At least one important consumer-finance statute is included: the Fair Credit Reporting Act—Title VI of PL 91-508. (The table of contents for the 91st Congress does not include any mention of the FCRA in its brief description of 91-508; and the one-and-a-half pages increasing the FTC's powers are also pretty well concealed as part of PL 93-153's Title IV. Miscellaneous.) There are ten other Acts also identified as consumer-finance-protection statutes. Ten more have to do with investor-protection, and thirteen regulate interest rates in some way. Another fourteen affect the rights of consumers of transportation products and services; and an additional eighteen, the rights of homeowners (buyers or renters). Rather surprisingly, in view of the product-liability revolution occurring in the State courts in the 1960s and 1970s, the largest category (nineteen examples) was "protection of product buyers."

As to the temporal distribution of the eighty-six Acts, the 91st Congress passed thirty-three (eight in its First Session, twenty-five in its Second Session); the 92nd Congress, twenty-eight (eleven and seventeen); and the 93rd Congress, twenty-six (all in its First Session).

In terms of their length (a rough measure of their significance), more than half (forty-eight of the eighty-seven) are "mini-laws"—less than two pages—very brief amendments, proclamations, or similar notations. While the Alaska pipeline statute (PL 93-153) takes up eighteen pages, the section on the FTC's consumer-protection function is only a page and a half of that total. Over one-quarter (twenty-two of eighty-six) are at least a bit more substantial—two to ten pages. Each of the other fifteen is over ten pages in length (nine are actually more than twenty pages long)—indicating significant amounts of "new law."

Since no Acts falling in the "consumer protection" category were identified in the portion of the Second Session of the 93rd Congress ending on August 9, 1974, the following listing concludes with Act 93-239, adopted near the end of its First Session.

Protecting Consumers—the Nixon Legislative Record

91st Congress, First Session (1969)

- PL 91-9: extends time for final report on study of mortgage interest rates

- PL 91-38: extends time for final report on study of mortgage interest rates

- PL 91-51: extends life of National Commission on Product Safety Act

- PL 91-71: extends authority to limit interest rates on time and savings deposits

- PL 91-94: amends Section 19(e) of Securities Exchange Act of 1934

- PL 91-113: Child Protection and Toy Safety Act of 1969

- PL 91-130: increases permitted maximum interest rate on US savings bonds

- PL 91-151: controls interest rates and increases availability of mortgage credit

91st Congress, Second Session (1970)

- PL 91-206: amends Federal Credit Union Act—provides independent agency to supervise

- PL 91-258: provides expansion and improvement of airport and airway system

- PL 91-265: National Traffic and Motor Vehicle Safety Act of 1970

- PL 91-266: prohibits debt adjustment business in DC, except by lawyers or nonprofits

- PL 91-342: amends Federal Meat Inspection Act

- PL 91-344: extends National Commission on Consumer Finance

- PL 91-351: Emergency Home Finance Act of 1970

- PL 91-354: creates a commission to study US bankruptcy laws

- PL 91-385: amends DC Cooperative Association Act, regarding usury

- PL 91-410: amends Section 19(e) of the Securities Exchange Act of 1934

- PL 91-432: temporarily extends FHA's insurance authority

- PL 91-467: amends Bankruptcy Act, as regards discharging of debts

- PL 91-468: provides insurance for accounts of credit union members

- PL 91-473: temporarily extends FHA's insurance authority

- PL 91-508: requires banks to keep certain records; Title VI: Fair Credit Reporting Act

- PL 91-518: Rail Passenger Service Act of 1970—establishes national system

- PL 91-525: temporarily extends FHA's insurance authority

- PL 91-530: provides rules in DC for husband and wife ownership as "tenants by the entireties"

- PL 91-536: provides for validation of DC land deeds with certain minor errors

- PL 91-565: amends Securities Act of 1933

- PL 91-567: amends sections of Securities Exchange Act of 1934

- PL 91-597: Egg Products Inspection Act

- PL 91-598: Securities Investor Protection Act of 1970

- PL 91-620: amends Consolidated Farmers Home Loan Administration Act of 1961

- PL 91-663: Emergency Rail Services Act of 1970—financial assistance to preserve services

92nd Congress, First Session (1971)

- PL 92-8: extends stabilization program for interest rates and cost-of-living

- PL 92-15: extends stabilization program for interest payments on savings deposits

- PL 92-67: amends Egg Product Inspection Act

- PL 92-73: appropriations for Agricultural-Environmental & Consumer Protection programs

- PL 92-75: Federal Boat Safety Act of 1971

- PL 92-133: extends authority to insure farmers' home loans under 1961 Act

- PL 92-165: amends Investment Company Act of 1940

- PL 92-173: amends Consolidated Farmers Home Administration Act to permit emergency loans

- PL 92-200: DC Consumer Credit Protection Act of 1971

- PL 92-213: extends authority of HUD Secretary over interest rates on insured mortgages

- PL 92-221: amends Federal Credit Union Act

92nd Congress, Second Session (1972)

- PL 92-231: amends 1930 Perishable Agricultural Commodities Act as to marketing practices

- PL 92-251: extends term of Commission on the Bankruptcy Laws of the US

- PL 92-262: extends International Coffee Agreement Act of 1968

- PL 92-316: amends Rail Passenger Service Act of 1970—financial assistance to Amtrak

- PL 92-321: amends the Consumer Credit Protection Act

- PL 92-335: extends authority of HUD Secretary over interest rates on insured mortgages

- PL 92-348: National Capital Transportation Act of 1972

- PL 92-359: amends Automobile Information Disclosure Act to extend to US possessions

- PL 92-387: amends Food, Drug, and Cosmetic Act to require a listing of all registered drugs

- PL 92-399: appropriations for Agricultural-Environmental & Consumer Protection programs

- PL 92-503: extends authority of HUD Secretary over interest rates on insured mortgages

- PL 92-513: Motor Vehicle Information and Cost Savings Act—promotes safer vehicles

- PL 92-542: amends Flammable Fabrics Act by authorizing appropriations for enforcement

- PL 92-548: National Traffic and Motor Vehicle Safety Act Amendments of 1972

- PL 92-562: permits court determination of real property title questions

- PL 92-573: Consumer Product Safety Act

- PL 92-591: Emergency Rail Facilities Restoration Act

93rd Congress, First Session (1973)

- PL 93-4: increases limit on face amount of HUD-authorized flood insurance

- PL 93-38: increases limit on face amount of HUD-authorized flood insurance

- PL 93-44: Airport Development Acceleration Act of 1973

- PL 93-56: extends term of Commission on Bankruptcy Laws of the US

- PL 93-61: apportions funds for interstate and federal-aid highway funds

- PL 93-63: extends laws relating to payment of interest on savings deposits

- PL 93-85: extends HUD Secretary's authority over insurance of loans and mortgages

- PL 93-86: Agriculture and Consumer Protection Act of 1973

- PL 93-89: District of Columbia Insurance Act

- PL 93-90: Federal Railroad Safety Authorization Act of 1973

- PL 93-100: extends laws relating to payment of interest on savings deposits

- PL 93-117: extends HUD Secretary's authority over insurance of loans and mortgages

- PL 93-123: extends laws relating to payment of interest on savings deposits

- PL 93-125: Agriculture and Consumer Protection Act of 1973—technical amendments

- PL 93-135: appropriations for Agricultural-Environmental & Consumer Protection programs

- PL 93-146: Amtrak Improvement Act of 1973—further financial assistance

- PL 93-147: prohibits use of federal symbols by debt collectors

- PL 93-153: authorizes an Alaska pipeline and increases FTC's consumer protection powers

- PL 93-157: District of Columbia Rent Control Act of 1973

- PL 93-159: Emergency Petroleum Allocation Act of 1973—requires President to allocate

- PL 93-167: Hobby Protection Act—requires accurate labeling of reproductions of coins, etc.

- PL 93-200: removes restriction on change of bankruptcy referees' salaries

- PL 93-229: amends DC's usury law

- PL 93-234: Flood Disaster Protection Act of 1973—substantially increases limits of coverage

- PL 93-236: Regional Rail Reorganization Act of 1973—services in Midwest and Northeast

- PL 93-239: Emergency Highway Energy Conservation Act

93rd Congress, Second Session (1974)

No Public Laws specifically dealing with "consumer protection" were identified for the part of the Second Session of the 93rd Congress ending on August 9, 1974.

Consumer Statutes—a Closer Look

What were the consumer-protection problems that these eighty-seven Acts addressed? One topic was already mentioned in the introductory remarks at the beginning of this Chapter: the basic structure of the Debtor/Creditor relationship. As noted, the Fair Credit Reporting Act (Title VI of PL 91-508) specifically addressed that part of the deferred-payment dynamic. Ten other Acts also related to this same area. As also highlighted earlier, consumer products of various kinds were the subject of nineteen Acts—the largest subgrouping. Eighteen Acts dealt with aspects of home buying and home ownership; fourteen with buyers/users of transportation services; and ten with purchasers of investment securities or banking services. There were fourteen Acts relating to the charging/payment of interest.

Debtor-Creditor Relationships

The Fair Credit Reporting Act is clearly the most important of the twelve statutes in this group, and it is arguably the most significant of the entire group of eighty-seven. Anyone who is familiar with the industry is aware of the sort of tricks and abusive tactics that are "part of the game." Getting "blood out of turnips" is a nasty business, and it takes a certain kind of person to be effective at it. Paying one's lawful obligations is a moral/ethical necessity, to be sure—but not all non-payers are "deadbeats" and therefore deserving of treatment as such. Unfortunately, it appears that too many in the debt-collection "industry" do not feel that it is worth their time and effort to draw such distinctions. As a result, there seems to be a strong current of "anything goes"—if it generates dollars. It's not quite the kneecap-breakers of the loan sharks, but it has the same psychological effect. This is the sort of abuse that Congress was attempting to prevent with the FCRA, the FDCP Act, and several other efforts in the 1970s.

Although standing alone it would meet our definition of a (presumably less significant) "mini-statute," the brief section of PL 93-153 increasing the FTC's powers has also turned out to be very important. In its Fall 2014 issue commemorating the 100th anniversary of the FTC Act, the journal of the American Bar Association's Antitrust Section contained a strong endorsement of the 1973 amendments. One of that journal's editors, in his contribution, noted that they had been adopted—at least in part—on the basis of recommendations that had been made by a special commission of the ABA. He stated that the 1973 Act "gave the agency authority to seek consumer redress and civil penalties as remedies for serious consumer abuses and an easier path to obtaining preliminary injunctions against threatened or ongoing Section 5 violations." And further, "The strengthened ability to obtain preliminary injunctions, together with the Hart-Scott-Rodino Antitrust Improvements Act of 1976 [passed after Jerry Ford assumed the presidency], transformed merger enforcement generally and the FTC's central role in it in particular."[1]

What about the other ten statutes in this category? Five of them—91-354, 91-467, 92-251, 93-56, and 93-200—make minor changes in the bankruptcy rules. PL 91-266 prohibits "debt adjustment" in DC except by lawyers or nonprofit associations, and PL 92-200 gives DC its own "Consumer Credit Protection Act." PL 91-344 simply extended the reporting date for the National Commission on Consumer Finance, and 92-321 made a minor amendment to its charter. PL 93-147 prohibits the use of federal symbols by debt collectors (another nasty little deception).

Interest Rates

There's nothing terribly complicated about the Acts in this subgroup. The first two (PL 91-9 and PL 91-38) merely extend the date for the final report of the Commission to Study Mortgage Interest Rates. PL 91-71 provides a three-month extension for the authorization of limits on savings account interest rates. Apparently, the reasoning behind 91-71 was that banks' lower cost of funds would enable them to make mortgage and other loans at lower rates. That rationale was stated somewhat more specifically in PL 91-151, which provided a further extension. Congress must have felt their policy was working (or at least that it would if in place long enough) because they passed eight other similar statutes—PL 92-8, PL 92-15, PL 92-213, PL 92-335, PL 92-503, PL 93-63, PL 93-100, and PL 93-123. PL 91-385 amends DC's usury law, as does PL 93-229. Apart from PL 91-151 (seven-plus pages), these tinkerings with the interest-rate market are all very brief notations—less than two pages in length, six of them actually less than a page each. (A quote borrowed from literary and political criticism and based on Aesop's fable of *The Pregnant Mountain* seems relevant here: "The mountain has labored and produced a mouse.")

Investors

A few words of explanation are required here, in light of what may seem to be a degree of overlap between one of the Acts placed in this category and those in the immediately preceding one. The brief description of PL 91-130 indicates that it has something to say about "interest," so why is it in this section rather than the last one? The preceding group of "interest" regulations all seemed directed toward the protection of borrowers and credit buyers—against being forced to pay excessive interest charges. In contrast, PL 91-130 *increases* the maximum interest rate permitted for US savings bonds—clearly a "protection" (benefit) for investors in such bonds, rather than for the payor/Government.

Three Acts were added to improve regulation of credit unions. PL 91-206 establishes an independent agency to supervise credit unions, and PL 92-221 provides further fine-tuning.

Perhaps even more significantly, PL 91-408 extends government insurance coverage to credit union accounts.

The other six statutes in this category all deal with what are generally described as the "securities laws." The Securities Act of 1933 was amended by PL 91-565. PL 91-94, PL 91-410, and PL 91-567 updated the Securities Exchange Act of 1934. The less-widely-known Investment Company Act of 1940 was also modified a bit by PL 92-165. PL 91-598—the Securities Investor Protection Act of 1970—is clearly the most significant package of changes in this group. It established a separate corporation (the SPIC) to which all securities brokers must belong. Their membership fees fund a kind of insurance, guaranteeing payment of customer accounts in the event of a broker's bankruptcy—up to $500,000 per account. That was clearly a very important new protection for investors.[2]

Transportation Services

In this subset of fourteen statutes, Congress is attempting to serve the passengers/consumers of the nation's highway, rail, and air networks. Concern for the operation of the nation's passenger trains clearly dominates these efforts. Eight of the fourteen statutes deal with railroads in some way, but there are differences in focus and detail. Passenger service is the specific subject of the two Acts relating to Amtrak (the national rail passenger system)—PL 92-316 and PL 93-146—and of the Rail Passenger Services Act of 1970—PL 91-518. Each of the Amtrak statutes is about seven pages in length; the RPSA contains about fourteen pages of substance. PL 92-348 extends the research effort on high-speed ground transportation, which usually involves "bullet" (i.e., high-speed) passenger trains. PL 93-90 merely provides additional funding for railway safety, which clearly benefits passengers as well as freight cargos and train crews. Two shorter (three/four pages each) Acts—91-663 and PL 92-591—apply to rail operations generally, as does the very lengthy (thirty-eight page) Regional Rail Reorganization Act of 1973—PL 93-236, which targets the rail systems of the Northeast and the Midwest.

Considerably less attention was paid to the nation's highways, perhaps because they were functioning more effectively and did not raise congressional concerns. Four brief Acts involved highway usage: PL 91-265, PL 92-548, PL 93-61, and PL 93-239. (PL 93-61 contained less than one page of "new law"; the other three were about two pages each.) While one of the two statutes reworking our airline system also was only two pages long (PL 93-44), the other (PL 91-258) spanned some thirty-four pages, with the objective of expanding and improving the system. It also provided for certain user fees—perhaps not entirely a positive in the eyes of many "frequent fliers."

Homeowners

For many of us, a home purchase is the single largest financial transaction of our lifetime. This is perhaps less true today than it once was, as higher education costs and motor vehicle prices have risen dramatically. If one purchased a home in 1969, say, and was still living there when a new SUV was bought in 2006, one might observe that the vehicle cost more than twice the price of the house! And, of course, if one rents dwelling-space rather than buying it, the lump-sum comparison looks rather different. Nevertheless, whatever the comparisons to other expenditures, the home-purchase is an important part of many consumers' financial commitments. Congressional action to facilitate and protect home ownership is therefore significant to many citizens (who may also be voters).

It is, then, not surprising that Congress takes time to work on home-ownership issues. Each of the three Nixon Congresses sent several Acts to him for his signature: six from the 91st Congress, five from the 92nd, and seven from the 93rd (all passed in its First Session). The spirit of this subgrouping of eighteen Acts is illustrated rather well by the "purpose statement" in the first, and longest (fourteen pages), of them—PL 91-351, the "Emergency Home Finance Act of 1970": "AN ACT To increase the availability of mortgage credit for the financing of urgently needed housing, and for other purposes."

The 91st Congress also passed three very brief (one-month at a time) extensions of the Federal Housing Administration's insurance authority from November 1 to December 1, 1970, to January 1 of 1971: PL 91-432, PL 91-473, and PL 91-525. Near the end of that Second Session, they also enacted a brief amendment to the 1961 Consolidated Farmers Home Administration Act, increasing its loan maximum from $60,000 to $100,000 (PL 91-620). The 92nd Congress extended the FMHA's duration indefinitely (PL 92-133) and authorized it to issue insured emergency loans (PL 92-173). The 92nd and the 93rd Congresses each passed a small amendment relating to mortgage insurance (PL 92-503, PL 93-85), and the 93rd also added two pages regarding house insurance (PL 93-117). Both Congresses also dealt with flood insurance (PL 92-213, PL 93-4, PL 93-38, and PL 93-234—this last Act being quite extensive, nearly ten pages long).

Congress also exercised its powers as an analog to a State legislature for the District of Columbia, by passing four pieces of legislation dealing with DC-specific real estate matters. PL 91-536 had to do with the validity of deeds to land situated there. PL 92-562 authorized local courts to hear "quiet-title" actions, i.e., lawsuits to determine ownership of land in DC. PL 93-89 regulated the insurance industry in DC. And PL 93-157 regulated rentals of DC real estate. The first two of these Acts were very brief—one page or so. It took nearly four pages for the "tune-up" of the DC rental rules. The changes to DC insurance regulations consumed over eight pages in the statute book.

Products Liability

The introductory comments to this Chapter expressed surprise at the extent of congressional activity—in the 1970s—related to this particular sub-topic. The reason for the surprise is that State legislatures first, and then State courts, had already conducted their own product-liability "revolution": traditional legal rules on liability for injuries caused by defective products had been drastically revised, starting in the early 1960s, in favor of consumers, users, and adversely-affected third parties. These liability rules were covered in the areas of Contract Law, Tort Law, and Sales of Goods Law. Jurisdiction over these topics had been reserved to the States by implication (since the national government had only the powers that had been delegated to it by the Constitution) and also—expressly—by the Tenth Amendment: "The powers not delegated to the United States by the Constitution, nor prohibited by it to the States, are reserved to the States respectively, or to the people."

The State legislatures led the way forward, by adopting the Uniform Commercial Code, which had been drafted by the Commissioners on Uniform State Laws and presented to the States for adoption in 1952. Although adoptions were initially slow in coming, by 1967, the District of Columbia and all the States except Louisiana were on board. Article Two of the UCC, dealing with Sales of Goods (tangible, movable personal property), made some significant changes in the law of "warranty"—a seller's obligation for the quality of goods sold.

Section 2-313 (of UCC Article Two) defined an "express warranty" as: "any affirmation of fact or promise made by the seller to the buyer which relates to the goods and becomes part of the basis of the bargain" or "any description of the goods which is made part of the basis of the bargain" or "any sample or model which is made part of the basis of the bargain." Even more significantly, Section 2-316 (1) stated that: "words or conduct relevant to the creation of an express warranty and words or conduct tending to negate or limit warranty shall be construed wherever reasonable as consistent with each other; but subject to the provisions of this Article on parol or extrinsic evidence (Section 2-202) negation or limitation is inoperative to the extent that such construction is unreasonable."

In plain English, if the seller makes a promise about the goods, but the written contract signed later contains a disclaimer ("There are no warranties on the within-described goods."), the attempted disclaimer is legally ineffective, and the seller is liable if the goods do not fulfill the promise made. Presumably, that means that the only way for the seller of goods to avoid being held liable for a breach of that promise is to call off the whole deal (with the agreement of the buyer) and restart the negotiations—this time without the promise in question. (A *possible* avoidance tactic might be to include a statement in the written contract that it is the complete and final statement of the agreement, thus potentially eliminating any term not in that document—any "parol"/extrinsic evidence.)

Of equal importance is Section 2-302 (1) of Article Two: "If the court as a matter of law finds the contract or any clause of the contract to have been unconscionable at the time it was made the court may refuse to enforce the contract, or it may enforce the remainder of the contract without the unconscionable clause, or it may so limit the application of the unconscionable clause as to avoid any unconscionable result." What does this mean? What is "unconscionable"? The basic idea is that the questioned term is grossly unfair and unjust. Usually, this is the result of a gross disparity in bargaining power—the individual consumer versus the multinational conglomerate; a "take-it-or-leave-it" situation: "You want the new car, sign the contract!" Of course, in the fine print of the contract is the seller's disclaimer of any quality guarantee on the heavily-advertised $40,000 vehicle—it's not even warranted to be "merchantable"—of fair or average quality, reasonably suited for the normal purposes for which such goods are used (the UCC's implied warranty in Section 2-314).

The UCC makes a third very significant change to the traditional warranty rules: a *partial* abrogation of the requirement of "privity" of contract in order to bring a lawsuit for breach of contract, i.e., breach of warranty. UCC section 2-318 mandates that any warranty made to the buyer of the goods is automatically extended, at least, to members of the buyer's family, or household, or guests in the buyer's home. The States are given the power to choose either of two more extensive options: any individual third party is also covered by the seller's warranties, or any third party (including legal fictions such as corporations or limited liability companies) is also covered. Further, Section 2-318 specifies that this liability for third-party injuries from breach of warranty cannot be disclaimed by language in the contract.

Several of the points are illustrated by the New Jersey case that is generally credited with starting the product liability revolution: *Henningsen v. Bloomfield Motors, Inc.*[3] Claus Henningsen purchased a new car as a Mother's Day present for his wife, Helen. Ten days later, she was driving it when she heard a loud noise from the front of the vehicle. She said it felt as if something had cracked. The car could not be controlled; the steering wheel spun in her hands, and the car ran into a brick wall. She sustained injuries, and the car was seriously damaged. When Helen and Claus sued the seller-dealer and the manufacturer (Chrysler Motors), the defendants argued that Helen had no case since she had entered into no contract at all with either of them. They also argued that Claus had no case against Chrysler for the same reason—i.e., no "privity" of contract (since he bought the car from Bloomfield Motors, not from Chrysler)—and no case for money damages against Chrysler or Bloomfield since his purchase contract contained a clause saying that he agreed that the dealer's only liability was to replace defective parts—at the factory! The trial court refused to enforce the disclaimer, so the defendants appealed. The New Jersey Supreme Court made short work of their arguments:

[W]arranties originated in the law to safeguard the buyer and not to limit the liability of the seller or manufacturer. It seems obvious in this instance that the motive was to avoid the warranty obligations which are normally incidental to such sales. The language gave little and withdrew much. In return for the delusive remedy of replacement of defective parts at the factory, the buyer is said to have accepted the exclusion of the maker's liability for personal injuries arising from the breach of the warranty, and to have agreed to the elimination of any other express or implied warranty. An instinctively felt sense of justice cries out against such a sharp bargain. . . .

The warranty before us is a standardized form designed for mass use. It is imposed upon the automobile consumer. He takes it or leaves it, and he must take it to buy an automobile. No bargaining is engaged in with respect to it. In fact, the dealer through whom it comes to the buyer is without authority to alter it; his function is ministerial—simply to deliver it. The form warranty is not only standard with Chrysler but, as mentioned above, it is the uniform warranty of the Automobile Manufacturers Association. . . .

The gross inequality of bargaining position occupied by the consumer in the automobile industry is thus apparent. There is no competition among the car makers in the area of the express warranty. Where can the buyer go to negotiate for better protection? Such control and limitation of his remedies are inimical to the public welfare and, at the very least, call for great care by the courts to avoid injustice through application of strict common-law principles of freedom of contract. . . .

For the most part the cases that have been considered dealt with the right of the buyer or consumer to maintain an action against the manufacturer where the contract of sale was with a dealer and the buyer had no contractual relationship with the manufacturer. In the present matter, the basic contractual relationship is between Claus Henningsen, Chrysler, and Bloomfield Motors, Inc. The precise issue presented is whether Mrs. Henningsen, who is not a party to their respective warranties, may claim under them. In our judgment, the principles of those cases and the supporting texts are just as proximately applicable to her situation. We are convinced that the cause of justice in this area of the law can be served only by recognizing that she is such a person who, in the reasonable contemplation of the parties to the warranty, might be expected to become a user of the automobile. Accordingly, her lack of privity does not stand in the way of prosecution of the injury suit against the defendant Chrysler.

147

The context in which the problem of privity with respect to the dealer must be considered, is much the same. Defendant Bloomfield Motors is chargeable with an implied warranty of merchantability to Claus Henningsen. There is no need to engage in a separate or extended discussion of the question. The legal principles which control are the same in quality.[4]

In addition to forcefully interpreting the UCC provisions, State courts also developed a new theory of product liability: strict liability in tort. Tort liability traditionally required proof of negligence: failure to exercise reasonable care in designing, testing, producing, or distributing the product. The lack of care by a manufacturer or seller is a fact question for the trial jury and is often difficult to prove. Exactly what went wrong with the product to cause the injury? Moreover, a manufacturer may have a statistical defense: if 300,000 products have been made, sold, and used without adverse consequences, is there any negligence if the 300,001st malfunctions and causes injury? Presumably not! Statistically, that is one fine track record.

Traditionally, the application of "strict liability" was confined to persons who engaged in ultra-hazardous activities, where there were inherent dangers that could not be avoided even with the exercise of reasonable care as well as to persons who exposed the public to extra risks by keeping wild animals in their possession. Throughout the 1960s and into the 1970s, State courts gradually applied this doctrine to persons who had distributed products containing a defect that made the product inherently dangerous. This case is clearly advantageous to the injured party: "It's your product. It contained a defect that made it dangerous when it left your control. That defect caused my injury. My damages are $X." That formulation is much more likely to result in liability since the statistical argument is basically irrelevant. The fact that nearly all products are not defective does not matter since all that is required to impose liability is that *this one* was defective when it left the defendant's control.

Several States have taken strict product liability to a new level (higher or lower, depending on one's perspective). In cases where several manufacturers have produced their own versions of a product, and it cannot be determined which one adversely affected the injured party, these courts impose a "market-share" liability. An extreme version of that legal rule was applied in a New York case involving several drug companies.

Mindy Hymowitz had been prescribed the drug DES. Years later, she developed serious injuries caused by the drug. Medical records were long gone, and she could not remember which company's (or companies') product/s she had taken. One of the companies claimed that she could not have taken their drug since it had not been marketed through the channels that had gotten the drug to Mindy. Writing for a four-to-three majority of the New York Court of Appeals (that State's highest court), Chief Judge Wachtler dismissed that "we didn't do it" defense:

> **To be sure, a defendant cannot be held liable if it did not participate in the marketing of DES for pregnancy use; if a DES producer satisfies its burden of proof of showing that it was not a member of the market of DES sold for pregnancy use, disallowing exculpation would be unfair and unjust. Nevertheless, because liability here is based on the over-all risk produced, and not causation in a single case, there should be no exculpation of a defendant who, although a member of the market producing DES for pregnancy use, appears not to have caused a particular plaintiff's injury. It is merely a windfall for a producer to escape liability solely because it manufactured a more identifiable pill, or sold only to certain drugstores. These fortuities in no way diminish the culpability of a defendant for marketing the product, which is the basis of liability here.[5]**

And so, it seems we have come to the end of the road as to the development of strict liability for dangerous products. We began with the requirement that the injured party prove that the defendant manufactured or distributed the product causing the harm, that it was dangerously defective when it left the defendant's control, that it did indeed cause the harm complained of, and that the injured party has sustained damages. Some courts then liberalized those requirements by imposing proportionate liability if the specific producer of the product injuring this plaintiff could not be identified, but this defendant did produce or market some of it. The final nail is hammered into the defendant's liability "coffin" by the New York Court of Appeals: a defendant who produced/marketed some of the product in question is proportionately liable even if it can prove that it could not have been *its* product that injured *this* plaintiff. From the producer's standpoint, the "justice" produced by this decision probably seems a bit "rough" indeed. On the other hand, "consumer protection" surely has received a big boost. Even in terms of trying to negotiate a settlement of the claim, plaintiff's hand has been significantly strengthened by the *Hymowitz* decision. Confronted with this reality, it seems that "retreat" (settlement) would be the better part of "valor" (defend in court).

So, with all these major changes in place, what product-liability matters did the Nixon Congresses find that still needed further legislation at the national level? The first item in this category for the 91st Congress was a very brief amendment (PL 91-51) extending the life of the existing National Commission on Product Safety Act until June 30, 1970. Their only other contribution during their First Session was PL 91-113: the Child Protection and Toy Safety Act of 1969. The power of the Secretary of Health, Education, and Welfare over hazardous products was extended to include children's toys. A finding that a particular toy contains an electrical, mechanical, or thermal hazard subjects that item to listing as a hazardous product. Distributors of the product must then repurchase it—for the purchase price! If the distributor wants the product back in exchange for the purchase price, the buyer's expenses in returning it must be reimbursed.

PL 92-75—the Federal Boat Safety Act—was a similar effort to ensure boat safety, but via a different approach. It provided for establishment of a national boat-safety program, national standards for construction and performance of boats, and a "more flexible" regulatory program. PL 92-542 merely authorized appropriations for 1973 for enforcement of the Flammable Fabrics Act. Similarly, five Acts—PL 92-73, PL 92-399, PL 93-86, PL 93-125 (correcting errors in PL 93-86), and PL 93-135—authorized appropriations for "consumer protection" programs by the Department of Agriculture.

PL 92-573—the Consumer Product Safety Act—was the final step in the statutory progression from the National Commission, through toys and boats, to any dangerous consumer product (with several large exceptions: automobiles, cigarettes, guns, planes, et al.). The CPSA created the Consumer Product Safety Commission (CPSC) and transferred to it (from HEW) the responsibility for dealing with hazardous consumer products. The CPSC can itself make a decision as to whether a product should be banned from the market (subject to later court review, if challenged by the product's supplier), or the Commission can file a proceeding in court itself and let the court make the initial determination. The validity of an initial administrative decision was challenged in the following case example.

Linda Weill, a schoolteacher, had developed a finger-painting product for use by young children. Colors were combined with a shaving-cream substance in aerosol spray cans. The hydrocarbon propellants used in the cans were highly flammable. After testing, the CPSC ruled that the product was a banned hazardous product, and the Commission filed a lawsuit in Connecticut to seize the product inventory located there. Linda's company (X-Tra Art) then filed a lawsuit in California, asking that the CPSC's decision be reviewed and that the CPSC be ordered not to take any further action against the product. The US District Court in California dismissed X-Tra Art's lawsuit, and they appealed. In affirming the ruling of the lower court, the US 9th Circuit Court of Appeals thought that companies' rights were adequately protected against administrative abuse by the opportunity for court review of the CSPC's initial decision, stating:

> **Under the FHSA, any substance, or mixture of substances, that is flammable or combustible is a "hazardous substance" if it may cause substantial illness or injury as a proximate result of foreseeable use. . . . A toy, or other article intended for use by children, is a "banned hazardous substance" if it "is a hazardous substance, or bears or contains a hazardous substance in such a manner as to be susceptible of access by a child." This subsection, applicable to products intended for children, de-**

fines a "banned hazardous substance" in terms that do not require a formal classification by regulation, if the product contains a hazardous substance accessible to children. . . .

Here the Commission is accountable for instituting the condemnation proceeding. Under the statutory scheme established, where the Commission opts to proceed in court on an allegation that the substance is a banned hazardous substance, the issue should be litigated by the manufacturer in that forum. As the Fourth Circuit explained: "where the Commission elects to [go directly to court] in a Section 1265 proceeding, the issue of whether the [product] is, in fact, a 'banned hazardous substance' is a question to be later determined in a hearing on the merits in the condemnation proceeding." Such procedure does not violate the requirements of due process.[6]

Some agricultural products are subject to federal inspection programs, illustrated in this subgroup by PL 91-342 (meat), PL 91-597 (eggs), and PL 92-67 (eggs). Some are even subject to international agreements of various kinds, as shown by PL 92-262, extending the duration of the international coffee agreement until September 30, 1973. In an "emergency" situation, government agencies may preempt normal marketplace activities, by taking steps to regulate the distribution of certain products, e.g., petroleum—seen here as the Emergency Petroleum Allocation Act of 1973 (PL 93-159). PL 92-231, which increases the sanctions for violation of the marketing system established in the 1930 Perishable Agricultural Commodities Act, is another example.

Even without the official declaration of an emergency, the national government has the power to regulate interstate and foreign commerce. Other statutory examples from the Nixon years include PL 92-359 and PL 92-513 (required motor vehicle information) and PL 92-387 (required listing of approved drugs). Finally, the Hobby Protection Act (PL 93-167) protects collectors, by prohibiting the manufacture or importation of imitation "political items" (posters, pins, emblems, and the like) or imitation coins or other "numismatic items" (monetary representations) which are not clearly labeled as such. The former must be marked with the date of manufacture; the latter, with the word "copy." Any violation of the Act is an "unfair method of competition" under the Federal Trade Commission and is subject to enforcement by that agency. Items imported in violation are subject to seizure and forfeiture under the customs rules.

Protecting Consumers

So, how well did President Nixon's legislative efforts care for the interests of consumers? This seemingly straightforward question carries a decided risk of serious bias. Hopefully, the reader is, at this point, somewhat familiar with the contents of our earlier Chapters. President Nixon's marvelous, earth-changing (for the better!—cleaner, healthier, more beautiful, more sustainable) environmental efforts were "all-star" by anyone's standard! His continued support for new legislation to protect workers physically and financially was no less important. And his executive leadership that put nearly nine of ten Southern schoolchildren in integrated schools within a year and a half of his inauguration—after fifteen years of "deliberate speed"—and did so without widespread disruption, achieved a significant social goal.

By comparison, the consumer protection output looks quite modest. To be sure, we have examined several pieces of legislation in this Chapter that were certainly nice additions to the US Code—well worth doing. The Fair Credit Reporting Act and the Consumer Product Safety Act are two such examples. So is the Securities Investor Protection Act. As noted above, the well-hidden page-and-a-half section of PL 93-153 that substantially strengthened the FTC's power to protect consumers has turned out to be very significant, even though it may not have generated much "press" at the time. The Acts to improve the rail and air transport systems were surely appropriate and important, even though not as headline-grabbing as protecting the coral reefs in the Pacific Ocean. And several others have been noted.

So, the President and the three Congresses were finding consumer issues that needed clarity or improvement, and they were adopting the laws they thought necessary. Again, it's worth restating that President Nixon had to have Democrat support to get any legislation at all passed. With all the carping criticism from the far Left and the often-savage attacks in much of the media, it's something of a miracle that he was able to get anything done, let alone all the great work that we've seen in prior Chapters—and the continuing help for consumers expressed in the Acts covered here.

Chapter 7

Nixon Protecting Veterans

I T SHOULD COME AS no surprise that a large number of the legislative enactments during the Nixon years related to military-service personnel. While the US involvement in the Vietnam War caused deep and intense divisions among us, a significant majority still seemed to feel that we owed something to those who had been drafted (mostly) to provide the human capital to do the job. For those who sustained injuries while serving the US, we certainly had a moral obligation (as well as a legal one—presumably) to make sure they received medical treatment and disability services. It's true that some of the "protesters" against the War—safe and snug in their college campuses or civilian jobs—evidently were not sharp enough to distinguish between the policy-making suits in DC and all the Willies and Joes and Janes trying to survive in the jungles of Southeast Asia. Thankfully, most members of Congress were able to perceive that difference, at least to the extent of maintaining and expanding legislative support for those who had rendered military service or were still doing so.

A review of the congressional output during the Nixon presidency yields a total of 100 Public Acts concerning "veterans." (As was true for the agencies concerned in earlier Chapters, regular annual appropriations bills are not included in these counts.) While in the broadest sense these Acts all have to do with veterans' "benefits" of one sort or another, some limited categorization has been done—hopefully, to aid our analysis. For example, fifteen statutes specifically targeted personnel who were POWs (prisoners of war) or MIAs (missing in action). Eight concerned the authority and procedures of the Veterans Administration (VA). For want of a more precise term, the fifteen "recognition" statutes in some way acknowledged or honored veterans' status. The very large (sixty-two Acts) residual category—"pay and benefits"—does contain a number of identified subcategories: "pay," "medical" benefits, "disability" benefits, et al.

The 91st Congress accounted for almost half the total: thirty-one Acts passed in its First

Session (1969) and fourteen in its Second Session (1970). The output of the 92nd Congress was split half-and-half: sixteen Acts in each Session. The 93rd Congress produced eleven such statutes in its First Session and twelve in its Second Session. (Remember, however, that the "productivity" count for the Second Session of the 93rd Congress stops on August 9, 1974, with President Nixon's resignation.)

About three-fourths of these Acts can be described as "mini-statutes"—less than two pages in length. Given the fact that most veterans' programs were already in place in 1969 and only needed adjustments and updating, this lack of length should not be surprising. A bit more than one-sixth of the total (eighteen Acts) have a length between two pages and ten pages. Only five Acts are over ten pages long. Even in this context of numerous already-established programs, however, Congress passed eleven statutes that they saw fit to specifically title and date: the Veterans' Education and Training Act of 1970, the Veterans' Housing Act of 1970, the Disabled Veterans' and Servicemen's Automobile Assistance Act of 1970, the Veterans' Compensation and Relief Act of 1972, the Vietnam Era Veterans' Readjustment Assistance Act of 1972, the VA Medical School Assistance and Health Manpower Training Act of 1972, the National Cemeteries Act of 1973, the Veterans' Health Care Expansion Act of 1973, the Veterans' Insurance Act of 1974, the Aviation Career Incentive Act of 1974, and the Veterans' Disability Compensation and Survivor Benefits Act of 1974. Each of these will be discussed later in this Chapter, in context, with the other Acts from the appropriate category.

Protecting Veterans—the Nixon Legislative Record

91st Congress, First Session (1969)

- PL 91-20: provides special pay for submarine officers with nuclear propulsion qualifications

- PL 91-22: liberalizes eligibility requirements for adapted-housing loans for disabled veterans

- PL 91-24: makes certain technical corrections to US Code, Title 38—Veterans' Benefits

- PL 91-32: insures reservation of all disability compensation evaluations in effect for twenty years

- PL 91-45: cedes concurrent jurisdiction over Fort Harrison VA Center to Montana

- PL 91-96: increases veterans' dependency and indemnity compensation

- PL 91-101: eliminates six-month limitation on veterans' nursing-home care

- PL 91-102: allows VA Administrator to furnish medical care for non-service disabilities

- PL 91-111: declares national day of prayer for American POWs in Vietnam

- PL 91-178: amends Title 38 to promote care of veterans in State veterans' homes

- PL 91-179: adjusts retirement pay to reflect Consumer Price Index

- PL 91-180: continues for two years the duty-free status of overseas gifts from combat personnel

- PL 91-183: increases military personnel's per diem travel-expense allowances

91st Congress, Second Session (1970)

- PL 91-198: permits naval flight officers to command certain other naval activities

- PL 91-199: increases number of officers eligible to serve on promotion-selection boards

- PL 91-200: removes $10,000 limit on amount of deposit for POWs and MIAs

- PL 91-210: provides round-trip to home port for military on ships under repair elsewhere

- PL 91-219: Veterans' Education and Training Act of 1970

- PL 91-235: provides favorable income-tax status for personnel detained by North Korea

- PL 91-241: liberalizes requirement for recoupment by VA of disability compensation

- PL 91-262: redefines "child" to include adopted child as a "dependent" and increases benefits

- PL 91-278: authorizes the Coast Guard to lease off-base housing for personnel

- PL 91-289: amends 1948 War Claims Act to include Vietnam POWs

- PL 91-291: sets a $15,000 maximum for Servicemen's Group Life Insurance; expands eligibility

- PL 91-302: allows special thirty-day leave for those who extend tours in hostile-fire areas

- PL 91-338: extends VA's authority to maintain an office in the Philippines

- PL 91-376: increases veterans' disability compensation

- PL 91-394: permits ordering of any retired Navy officer to be commander of USS *Constitution*

- PL 91-396: provides for headstone or marker for unmarked grave of any Medal of Honor winner

- PL 91-397: provides that US flag may be presented to parents of any deceased serviceman

- PL 91-402: clarifies promotion rules for US Coast Guard officers

- PL 91-421: VA facility at Bonham, TX designated as Sam Rayburn Memorial Veterans Center

- PL 91-456: provides for flying US flag over battleship *Utah*, honoring those entombed within

- PL 91-484: enlisted members taking officer appointment shall not receive lower pay

- PL 91-486: provides cost-of-living allowances for personnel overseas or in Hawaii or Alaska

- PL 91-487: provides for payment of death-related expenses even if no remains are recovered

- PL 91-496: strengthens VA program for sharing services of medical specialists

- PL 91-500: presumes that veterans seventy-two and older are unable to pay hospital and domiciliary care

- PL 91-506: Veterans' Housing Act of 1970—provides or guarantees loans for mobile homes

- PL 91-529: requires family allowance be paid even if dependents do not reside with serviceman

- PL 91-533: requires family allowance be paid even if serviceman residing in military housing

- PL 91-534: requires family allowance be paid to POWs, MIAs, and others detained in Vietnam

- PL 91-584: authorizes family education and loan benefits for POWs, MIAs, and internees

- PL 91-588: increases rates and income limitations for veterans' pensions

- PL 91-666: Disabled Veterans' and Servicemen's Automobile Assistance Act of 1970

92nd Congress, First Session (1971)

- PL 92-6: declares "National Week of Concern for Prisoners of War/Missing in Action"

- PL 92-58: provides special health-care benefits for certain surviving dependents

- PL 92-66: authorizes VA Administrator to sell, to third parties, direct loans made to veterans

- PL 92-69: authorizes VA Administrator to exchange medical information

- PL 92-93: incorporates Paralyzed Veterans of America

- PL 92-95: provides mortgage protection life insurance for disabled veterans in adapted housing

- PL 92-129: amends 1969 Military Selective Service Act and provides for special military pay

- PL 92-169: provides promotion rules for service personnel in a "missing" status

- PL 92-176: permanent authorization of special allowances for personnel-evacuation expenses

- PL 92-183: designates San Antonio hospital as "Audie L. Murphy Memorial Veterans' Hospital"

- PL 92-185: defines "widow," "widower," "child," and "parent" for servicemen's life insurance uses

- PL 92-188: permits using dividends to purchase additional paid-up service life insurance

- PL 92-193: permits conversion of National Service Life Insurance to modified life plan

- PL 92-197: increases veterans' dependency and indemnity compensation

- PL 92-198: liberalizes provisions for payment of veterans' disability and death pension

- PL 92-212: adds two years duty-free status for gifts sent by those in combat zones

92nd Congress, Second Session (1972)

- PL 92-248: declaration of "National Week of Concern for Prisoners of War/Missing in Action"

- PL 92-279: no taxation of income of service and civilian personnel who are POWs or MIAs

- PL 92-315: extends servicemen's life insurance to cadets and midshipmen at service academies

- PL 92-328: Veterans' Compensation and Relief Act of 1972—more compensation for disabled

- PL 92-341: increases maximum grant for specially adapted housing for disabled veterans

- PL 92-418: amends Internal Revenue Code as to tax-exempt status of veterans' organizations

- PL 92-422: authorizes a memorial for WWII "Seabees" (naval Construction Battalions)

- PL 92-425: establishes a Survivor Benefit Plan for armed forces personnel

- PL 92-455: equates pay for Coast Guard Chief Petty Officers with that in other services

- PL 92-469: increases size and weight limits for military mail for members outside US

- PL 92-477: authorizes payment for movement of house trailers and effects for certain MIAs

- PL 92-481: extends grants of thirty-day leave for volunteer extenders-of-duty in combat zones

- PL 92-482: continues incentive pay for MIAs during period of hospitalization and rehabilitation

- PL 92-540: Vietnam Era Veterans' Readjustment Assistance Act of 1972—education and training

- PL 92-541: VA Medical School Assistance and Health Manpower Training Act of 1972

- PL 92-596: authorizes MIAs to accumulate leave without limitation

93rd Congress, First Session (1973)

- PL 93-26: amends promotion rules for MIAs

- PL 93-43: National Cemeteries Act of 1973—establishes national system under VA control

- PL 93-64: makes permanent the dependent allowances under 1940 Dependents Assistance Act

- PL 93-75: amends loan guaranty program for veterans

- PL 93-82: Veterans Health Care Expansion Act of 1973—better medical & nursing-home care

- PL 93-170: provides round-trip to home port for military on ships being inactivated elsewhere

- PL 93-177: increases monthly disability and death benefits and dependency compensation

- PL 93-185: increases interest paid on permanent fund for Soldiers' & Airmen's Home

- PL 93-208: permits VA to continue educational payments during emergency school closures

- PL 93-213: authorizes travel allowances for certain service personnel on leave

- PL 93-232: authorizes President to proclaim March 29, 1974, as "Vietnam Veterans' Day"

93rd Congress, Second Session (1974)

- PL 93-257: provides funeral transportation and living expenses to families of deceased POWs

- PL 93-261: makes "urgent supplemental appropriation" for VA, for FY ending June 30, 1974

- PL 93-267: permits stepmothers and adoptive mothers to join American War Mothers

- PL 93-274: revises pay structure for medical officers in uniformed services

- PL 93-277: revises special pay bonuses for armed forces enlisted personnel

- PL 93-289: Veterans' Insurance Act of 1974—increases maximum for life insurance to $20,000

- PL 93-292: provides for US flag presentation for deceased members of Ready Reserve

- PL 93-293: increases rates for vocational rehabilitation, educational assistance, and training

- PL 93-294: Aviation Career Incentive Act of 1974—special pay for enlisted air-crew members

- PL 93-295: Veterans Disability Compensation and Survivor Benefits Act of 1974

- PL 93-321: makes "further urgent supplemental appropriation" for VA for FY June 30, 1974

- PL 93-337: puts a ten-year limit on educational program assistance for veterans, wives, and widows

Veterans Statutes—a Closer Look

As noted earlier in this Chapter, the major purpose in creating the categories and subcategories for the one hundred Acts covered here was to provide some idea of the relative frequency with which various types of benefits or beneficiaries were addressed. The issues relating to POWs and MIAs were of considerable significance during the Vietnam War, both in official and public discussions of war policy and in the eventual negotiations with North Vietnam to end the war. The problems faced by these service personnel and their families were different enough to warrant specific provisions for their protection and were so recognized by Congress. Hence, the separate category. Acts dealing with the organization and procedures of the Department of Veterans Affairs (VA), while ultimately intended to improve the delivery of benefits, also seemed appropriate for a specific grouping. Some statutes seemed to be a sort of official "Thank You"—a recognition of the existence of our armed forces and the personal sacrifices they and their families have made for the US. Finally, it seemed worthwhile to single out various subcategories ("medical," "disability," etc.) from the large residual "pay and benefits" category, not only to highlight those two most obvious and necessary benefits but also to show that there was significant legislative activity on a number of other topics.

POWs/MIAs

After several years of unsuccessful attempts, negotiations to end the Vietnam War were finally undertaken, and they eventually resulted in the signing of the Paris Peace Accords on January 27, 1973. One point on which President Nixon insisted was North Vietnam's return of US POWs; 591 persons were repatriated in accordance with the Paris agreement. However, various sources had listed totals of POWs and MIAs at 2,200 to 2,500. Even after the North resumed hostilities and completed its conquest of the South in 1975, families of the missing continued to push for further investigation and accounting. Normalization of US/Vietnam relations did permit the identification and return of over 700 "remains." According to Wikipedia, 1,621 of our personnel still remained unaccounted for as of March 23, 2016.

The end of direct American military participation and the increased intensity of anti-war sentiment would thus seem to explain a large part of the fall-off in congressional action in this area during the 93rd Congress (one statute in each Session: PL 93-26 and PL 93-257). By contrast, the 91st Congress passed six statutes, and the 92nd passed seven.

What were the subjects concerning POWs and MIAs that Congress addressed? The 91st and the 92nd Congresses each passed "recognition" statutes, reminding the rest of us of the sacrifices that were being made. PL 91-111 declared a national day of prayer for POWs in Vietnam (November 9, 1969); PL 92-6 declared a national week of concern for POWs and MIAs (March 21–27, 1971); PL 92-248 combined the two ideas—March 26–April 1, 1972, as a national week of concern, with Sunday, March 26 as a national day of prayer.

The other five Acts passed by the Second Session of the 91st Congress dealt with a variety of topics. PL 92-200 removes—for POWs and MIAs—the $10,000 maximum limit on special military savings accounts. (Subsection [d] of section 1035, US Code Title 10 makes these accounts exempt from claims of creditors, including the US Government, and from forfeiture after a court-martial.) PL 91-235 extended favorable income-tax status ("serving in a combat zone") to the servicemen illegally detained ("POWs"—of a sort) by North Korea in 1968. PL 91-289 amended the 1948 War Claims Act to provide an additional $60 per month compensation for Vietnam POWs. PL 91-534 required that a family-separation allowance of $30 per month be paid to POWs, MIAs, and others detained in Vietnam. PL 91-584 authorized family education and loan benefits for POWS, MIAs, and internees.

One additional Act in this category was adopted by the First Session of the 92nd Congress: PL 92-169, which provides that the promotion of a member of the uniformed services "while he is in a missing status is fully effective for all purposes, even though the Secretary concerned determines . . . that the member died before the promotion was made." Section 2 of the Act also amended Section 402(a) of US Code Title 38 ("With respect to a veteran who died in the active military, naval, or air service, his pay grade shall be determined as of the date of his death."), by inserting "or as of the date of a promotion after death while in a missing status" before the ending period.

In addition to PL 92-248, the Second Session of the 92nd Congress adopted four other Acts benefitting POWs and MIAs. PL 92-279 exempted both military and civilian personnel from paying income taxes while they were prisoners or missing. As an alternative to government-paid moving expenses for "household and personal effects," PL 92-477 provided that the government would pay moving expenses for a house trailer for dependents of POW/MIA personnel who had had that status for more than one year. (Presumably, this would facilitate a family's move from an assigned base location to one near the family's original home—or other preferred location.) PL 92-482 guaranteed MIAs that their pay and allowances would continue while they were such and that any incentive pay to which they were entitled would also be continued during any period of hospitalization and rehabilitation, up to one year. PL 92-596 permits MIAs to accumulate unlimited leave-time during their "missing" period.

PL 93-26 is the only Act in this category passed by the First Session of the 93rd Congress (April 27, 1973). For some reason, it merely repeats the language of PL 92-169, omitting section 2 of that 1971 Act, which amended Section 402(a) of Title 38. (In 1991, sections 401–423 of Title 38 were renumbered as sections 1301–1323. Section 402[a], as amended by PL 92-169, was still included—as section 1302[a]—as of February 11, 2017.) As of August 9, 1974, the Second Session had added only PL 93-257, which provided funeral transportation and housing for families of deceased POWs.

VA (Veterans' Administration)

Two of these eight statutes had to do with the operation of VA offices. PL 91-45 provided that the State of Montana would exercise concurrent jurisdiction over the Fort Harrison VA Center located in that State. PL 91-338 authorized VA maintenance of an office in the Philippines until July 3, 1974. Two others could have been placed in the "recognition" category but seemed more appropriately counted here since they concerned the naming of VA facilities. PL 91-421 designated the Bonham, Texas VA office as the "Sam Rayburn Memorial Veterans' Center." (Rayburn was the Speaker of the House of Representatives from 1940 to 1961, except for the four years 1947–1949 and 1953–1955, when the Republicans were the majority party in the House. Bonham was Rayburn's hometown.) PL 92-183 named the new VA hospital then being built in San Antonio the "Audie L. Murphy Memorial Veterans' Hospital," honoring the most decorated US serviceman in World War II.

Two other "VA" Acts passed in the First Session of the 92nd Congress were more substantive in content. PL 92-66 authorized the VA to sell the real estate mortgages it had accepted on housing purchased by veterans to marketplace investors. (The cash generated by such sales would then presumably be available to provide funding for additional home purchases by other veterans.) PL 92-69 permitted the VA to exchange medical information with other health-care providers—the objective being the coordination and improvement of diagnosis and treatment.

Finally, the Second Session of the 93rd Congress responded to what was evidently a significant increase in the demand for VA benefits. PL 93-261 provided an "urgent supplementary appropriation" of $750 million for readjustment benefits. Shortly thereafter, PL 93-321 added another $100 million as a "further urgent supplementary appropriation" for compensation and pensions. These additional funds were clearly an important substantive benefit for veterans, not just an "administrative" VA matter.

Recognition

Fifteen Acts were placed in this category. Some applied primarily or exclusively to those who had completed their active military service, some to persons still on active service, and some statutes applied to both groups.

Nearly half of the total were passed by the Second Session of the 91st Congress. PL 91-198 permitted naval flight officers to command certain other naval activities. PL 91-199 increased the number of officers eligible to serve on promotion-selection boards. PL 91-394 authorized the Secretary of the Navy to order any retired naval officer to serve as commander of the historic USS *Constitution* ("Old Ironsides"—the oak-hulled frigate that won a symbolically-important naval engagement against the British ship *Guerriere* during the War of 1812). PL 91-396 ensured that a headstone or marker would be available for the grave of any deceased who had won the Congressional Medal of Honor. PL 91-397 stated that a US flag could be presented to the parents of any deceased serviceman. PL 91-402 clarified the promotion rules for officers in the US Coast Guard. Finally, 91-456 provided for the flying of the US flag over the sunken remains of the battleship *Utah* and the sixty-four crew members who were trapped inside when she was torpedoed and sank—in Pearl Harbor, Hawaii—on December 7, 1941.

The 92nd Congress enacted two statutes dealing with veterans' organizations. PL 92-93 incorporated the Paralyzed Veterans of America, and PL 92-418 amended the Internal Revenue Code to provide tax-exempt status to veterans' organizations. The Second Session also added PL 92-422, which permitted public land in the District of Columbia to be used for a memorial to the US Navy's World War II *c*onstruction *b*attalions—the "Seabees."

One of the longest statutes in this group (nearly fourteen pages) is PL 93-43: the National Cemeteries Act of 1973. The Act establishes a National Cemetery System for the burial of deceased veterans (and certain family members), sets up its administrative framework, defines eligibility, provides for markers and memorials, and authorizes land management and control. It also legislates conformity with a large number of related statutes, via amendment or repeal. The First Session of the 93rd Congress also authored two other "recognition" Acts: PL 93-185, which increased the interest rate for the permanent fund established for the Soldiers' and Airmen's Home, and PL 93-232, authorizing President Nixon to proclaim March 29, 1974, as "Vietnam Veterans' Day."

The two "recognition" statutes passed by the 93rd Congress's Second Session may seem rather trivial to some unaffected people, but they were certainly important to the veterans and families who benefitted from the definitional extensions. PL 93-267 permitted the stepmothers and adoptive mothers of veterans to join the American War Mothers. (For the author, this Act hits very close to home: a very dear friend lost her Army-veteran adopted son in 2016. I was privileged to attend his military funeral service.) PL 93-292 provides for US flags to be presented to the families of deceased members of the Ready Reserve and twenty-year members of the Reserve.

Pay and Benefits

One of the very first of these "veterans" statutes is in a category all its own. PL 91-24 is not really providing additional benefits but is merely intended to make certain "technical corrections" in a number of provisions of US Code Title 38—Veterans' Benefits. (Editing existing statutes for inconsistencies, reference numbers, and the like.) The "legislative intent" of such Acts is more accuracy and clarification than addition or amendment.

Pay. Twelve Acts relate directly to some aspect of military pay. PL 91-20 authorized special pay for submarine officers with nuclear propulsion capabilities. (President Carter's naval training and career predated this statute, but it seems he would have qualified for this "special pay" had he still been in the service in 1969.) PL 91-96 provided additional "dependency and indemnity" compensation for veterans.

The Second Session of the 91st Congress passed four more "pay"-directed statutes. PL 91-484 ensured that enlisted personnel accepting promotions to officer rank would not be paid a lower salary than they had been receiving. PL 91-486 enacted cost-of-living allowances for personnel stationed overseas, or in Hawaii or Alaska. Both PL 91-529 and PL 91-533 dealt with family allowances: the first required such payments even if the dependents did not live with the service personnel receiving the payments; and the second, even if the recipient was living in military housing.

The 92nd Congress added three "pay" statutes. Most of PL 92-129 concerned changes to the Selective Service Act of 1967. (PL 92-129 was the two-year extension of the military draft, requested by the Administration even as troops were being withdrawn from Vietnam.

The Act was passed on September 22, 1971, after a filibuster in the Senate by opponents was finally halted. Early in 1973, Secretary of Defense Melvin Laird announced that no further registrants would be called up, fulfilling President Nixon's campaign promise to end the Draft.) The Act appears here because it also contained a brief section providing for an incentive bonus to be paid to volunteers and recognized "optometrists" for special medical-personnel pay. PL 92-197 followed the 1961 Act—PL 91-96—by further increasing service personnel's compensation for family support ("dependency and indemnity"). The Second Session passed only one Act in this category—PL 92-455, which provided that Coast Guard Chief Petty Officers would receive the same pay as those of similar rank in the other armed services.

Three more Acts were provided by the Second Session of the 93rd Congress. PL 93-274 revised the pay structure for medical officers serving in the military. (This Act also resonates with the author. My father had just received his commission as a Lieutenant-Colonel in the Army Medical Corps when he was killed in an auto accident in September 1954. [He had served as a medical officer at the Ravenna (Ohio) Army Arsenal during World War II and the Korean War.] Had he still been on active service in 1974, he would have been one of the beneficiaries of PL 93-274.) PL 93-277 updated the special bonuses available to enlisted personnel. The final statute in this set is PL 93-294, the Aviation Career Incentive Act of 1974, which provided special incentive pay for those serving as enlisted aviation crew members.

Medical. Rather surprisingly, perhaps, only seven of these veterans' statutes pertained primarily to medical benefits. One suspects that this relatively small number is at least partly due to the language in the basic authorization for such benefits. If all "necessary and appropriate" medical services are to be provided, there is no particular need to pass new statutory authorizations when new or improved treatments become available. The attending medical staff make their determinations, and the coverage for the required medications and services is already in place. Nevertheless, seven Acts were felt necessary by a majority of Congress—and President Nixon.

Five of the seven Acts were passed by the 91st Congress (1969/1970) while the Vietnam War was still being fought with intensity. PL 91-101 eliminated the six-month limitation on nursing-home care. (There were surely many cases where such care was necessary and appropriate beyond a rather arbitrary limitation period.) PL 91-102 allowed the VA to furnish medical care for non-service disabilities; at least partly, by analogy, this was simply like an "employer's" decision to try to ensure a healthy and productive "workforce." PL 91-178 promoted the use of State veterans' homes as providers of medical care; and this, too, seems a valuable expansion of available choices for patients. PL 91-496 made a small linguistic change in the relevant statutory section, with the intent of facilitating the institutional sharing of the services of medical specialists ("mutual use"). PL 91-500 created a statutory presumption that any veteran receiving a VA pension was "unable to defray the expenses of necessary hospital or domiciliary care," so that such persons did not have to provide a sworn statement to that effect in order to receive VA care.

The 92nd and 93rd Congresses each added only one "medical" Act. PL 92-58 provided that certain dependents of a veteran who dies while eligible for "hostile fire" pay will continue to receive their health-care benefits until age twenty-one. The dependents covered by this provision are those suffering from "mental retardation," "serious physical disability," or "extraordinary physical or psychological condition." PL 93-82—the Veterans' Health Care Expansion Act of 1973—is the second-longest of the ninety-nine Acts identified as veterans' statutes (nearly eighteen pages). Its ambitious objectives are outlined in its purpose statement: "To amend Title 38 of the United States Code to provide improved and expanded medical and nursing home care to veterans; to provide hospital and medical care to certain dependents and survivors of veterans; to provide for improved structural safety of Veterans' Administration facilities; to improve recruitment and retention of career personnel in the Department of Medicine and Surgery; and for other purposes."

Disability. Eleven statutes were identified in this subcategory, including three of the named and dated Acts listed in this Chapter's introduction. Each of the three Congresses passed one of those titled Acts. PL 91-666, the Disabled Veterans' and Servicemen's Automobile Assistance Act of 1970, was actually approved by President Nixon on January 11, 1971. The VA would pay the purchase price for an automobile (up to $2,800) and then provide adaptive equipment necessary to enable its safe operation. Veterans sustaining the loss of one or both feet, or one or both hands, or certain eye injuries—as a direct result of an injury while engaged in active service—were eligible to participate in the program. PL 92-328, the Veterans' Compensation and Relief Act of 1972, provided a further increase in disability payment rates—beyond those in 1970's PL 91-376. PL 93-295, the Veterans Disability Compensation and Survivor Benefits Act of 1974, mandated still further increases in disability payment rates.

The 91st Congress enacted four other "disability" statutes. PL 91-22 liberalized eligibility requirements for disabled veterans wishing to obtain adapted-housing loans. PL 91-32 ensured that disability compensation evaluations would be retained for twenty years. PL 91-241 correlated payment of disability compensation with the disability severance pay due on termination of service. PL 91-376 had already increased disability payment rates once, as noted above.

The First Session of the 92nd Congress passed two other Acts in this category. PL 92-95 provided mortgage-payment insurance for disabled veterans living in adapted housing. PL 92-198 facilitated payment of veterans' disability and death pensions. The Second Session added PL 92-341, which increased the maximum amount available to veterans for specially adapted housing from $12,500 to $17,500.

One more of these Acts was passed by the 93rd Congress. PL 93-177 increased the monthly rates of "disability and death benefits and dependency and indemnity compensation."

Insurance. In addition to the Acts placed in other categories but which also mentioned insurance, six statutes were identified whose primary focus was insurance. PL 91-291 expanded eligibility for Servicemen's Group Life Insurance and increased the available coverage amount to $15,000.

The 92nd Congress passed four insurance laws. PL 92-185 redefined the beneficiaries of SGL Insurance. PL 92-188 permitted the SGL Insurance owner to use policy dividends to buy additional paid-up insurance coverage. PL 92-193 permitted conversion of life insurance policies to "modified-life" plans. PL 92-315 extended availability of life insurance coverage to West Point cadets and Naval Academy midshipmen.

The Second Session of the 93rd Congress passed PL 93-289 as one of the titled and dated statutes—the Veterans' Insurance Act of 1974. It simply increased the maximum available life insurance coverage to $20,000.

Education. The 1944 "GI Bill of Rights" included significant educational benefits for veterans who had been on active duty. Over 2 million veterans used these benefits to attend college, and some 5.5 million used them for various training programs. With the greatly increased cost of higher education, the education benefits earned through military service continue to be a key recruiting tool, emphasized in various media solicitations.

Six education laws were identified, including three named and dated ones. The Second Session of the 91st Congress passed the Veterans' Education and Training Act of 1970 (PL 91-219): "to increase the rates for vocational rehabilitation, educational assistance, and special training allowance paid to eligible veterans. . . ." The Second Session of the 92nd Congress produced PL 92-540, the Vietnam Era Veterans' Readjustment Assistance Act of 1972, which included education and training benefits, and PL 92-541, the VA Medical School Assistance and Health Manpower Training Act of 1972, which established an ambitious program for the development of medical schools and training of health professionals.

The 93rd Congress added three more education updates. PL 93-208 allowed the VA to continue veterans' educational benefit payments during emergency closures of the schools being attended. PL 93-293 provided further rate increases for vocational rehabilitation, educational assistance, and training. PL 93-337 extended the maximum period for payment of veterans' educational benefits from eight to ten years.

Travel. The travel benefits provided by the five statutes in this category are directed toward currently-serving active-duty personnel, rather than those who have already completed their military service. The opportunity to see new places and to be exposed to new peoples and new customs has always been another key part of military service. Indeed, it has been used as a recruiting tool: "Join the Navy and see the world." Some of the benefits described in these laws are rather closely tied to the military mission; others have more the flavor of "employee" perks.

PL 91-183 increased the per diem travel-expense allowance for military personnel. PL 91-210 authorized payment of travel expenses for round-trips to home port for military on ships undergoing repairs elsewhere. PL 92-176 was a very brief amendment to an earlier law that had authorized payment of dependents' expenses when evacuation of a post was necessitated. By just deleting the end-date in the original statute, PL 92-176 made the authorization permanent.

Finally, the First Session of the 93rd Congress made two other adjustments to military travel rules. PL 93-170 duplicated the round-trip-to-home-port authorization of PL 91-210 for military on board ships that were being inactivated elsewhere. And PL 93-213 provided travel allowances for certain service personnel on leave. (That does sound like an "employee perk.")

Leave. "Leave," in a very different context, was the primary subject in two other Acts. PL 91-302 renewed the authority to provide a special thirty-day leave for personnel who extended their tour of duty in "hostile-fire" areas. (That seems a very modest recompense for such an extension, but it at least recognizes the high level of commitment to the mission involved.) PL 92-481 continued for another year the authority to make such grants of thirty-day leave for personnel who voluntarily extended their duty in "hostile fire" zones.

Mail/Gift. Another traditional military "perk" is the privilege of mailing letters and sending packages at reduced or nominal rates. Three statutes dealt with that process. PL 91-180 extended for two years combat personnel's privilege of sending duty-free gifts back to the US. PL 92-212 added another two years to that same privilege. PL 92-469 increased the size and weight limits for military mail being sent from outside the US.

Pension. Perhaps surprisingly, only two Acts dealt with veterans' pensions. Here again, this may be due to the fact that their pension system had been in place for some time and was evidently working well enough that there was no great demand for changes.

Both statutes were passed by the 91st Congress, one by each Session. PL 91-179 adjusted retirement pay to reflect the Consumer Price Index. In the inflationary US economy of the 1970s, that was a potentially significant change and an important protection of retired veterans' standard of living. PL 91-588 was also an upward adjustment in veterans' favor: increased rates and income limitations for veterans' pensions.

Housing. The VA's housing program contains a number of different features. The basic part of the program is a guarantee by the VA for (a large) part of the home mortgage. Along with this reassurance to the mortgage lender that it will be paid, the VA loan process has some important protections for the veteran/home-buyer. The VA does not require a down payment, but the lending bank may do so. Because of the VA's guarantee, the buyer does not have to pay for private mortgage insurance. The VA has established limits on what "closing costs" can be added to the price of the home, and it permits pay of those extra costs by the seller if the parties so agree. Lenders are prohibited from charging a penalty for paying off the mortgage early. It may also be possible to obtain help from the VA if difficulties arise in making the mortgage payments.

This VA program has been up and running for some time and has enabled thousands of veterans to own homes who might not have been able to do so otherwise. Evidently, it has been working satisfactorily—only three Acts were identified as "housing"-directed. The most significant of the three was one of the named and dated statutes—PL 91-506: the Veterans' Housing Act of 1970. Although only six-plus pages in length, this Act is significant because it extended the VA mortgage-guarantee program to the purchase of mobile homes. While this may sound rather trivial to some people, "manufactured housing" is typically much less expensive than "stick-built" homes and is, therefore, the only viable option for many low-income families.[1]

PL 93-75 merely directed the VA Administrator to consult and coordinate with the Secretary of Housing and Urban Development in establishing interest rates for VA-guaranteed loans. PL 91-278 had nothing to do with the VA mortgage-guarantee program; it authorized the Coast Guard to lease off-base housing for its personnel.

Dependents. In addition to whatever mentions were made in other Acts ("medical" statute PL 92-58, for example), four pieces of legislation were specifically targeted at veterans' beneficiaries. PL 91-262 redefined "child" so as to include adopted children as "dependents." PL 91-487 provided for payment of death-related expenses even if no remains are recovered. PL 92-425 established a Survivor Benefit Plan for armed forces personnel. And PL 93-64 made the dependent allowances under the Dependents' Assistance Act of 1940 permanent.

Agent Orange—the "Undiscovered Heritage" of Vietnam

As noted above, the issues surrounding our MIAs and POWs from the Vietnam War have persisted into the twenty-first century. It did not seem appropriate (or possible) to discuss the record of the Nixon presidency in dealing with veterans without at least acknowledging that there was also an unknown residue of other long-range problems—dating back to the earliest days of US involvement, under President Kennedy. With the opposing forces relying on the dense jungles for cover to mask the movement of troops and supplies, the US military engaged in large-scale aerial applications of herbicides, to try to expose trails and bases. Defoliants were also used to destroy food crops sustaining the enemy guerillas. Whether unknown or unappreciated at the time, these various chemical compounds had serious health consequences for humans.

One of the worst of the consequences was "Agent Orange": 2,4-dichlorophenoxyacetic acid. Veterans—and civilians—who had been exposed to it could develop various forms of cancer, as well as injuries to different organs and bodily functions. When these medical conditions started to appear in significant numbers in the later 1970s, Presidents Ford and Carter (both also having military service backgrounds) occupied the White House, President Nixon having had to resign in August 1974.

For several years, court litigations seemed to be the major mechanism for trying to deal with these chemically-induced but service-related injuries.[2] Such lawsuits might be filed by one injured veteran, or by several with similar claims, or by one or more representatives (allegedly) on behalf of a whole group—a "class action." Initially, of course, there had to be some proof that the chemical in question could have caused the plaintiffs' injuries. (As that proof was developed, and it was discovered that some domestic consumer products also contained the specified poison, there were also consumer lawsuits against the chemical manufacturer.[3])

Since many of the medical conditions complained of might also be the result of other genetic or environmental factors, it was also deemed necessary that the plaintiff-veteran prove exactly when and where it was that s/he had been exposed to Agent Orange, or whatever the claimed source was. Needless to say, in "the fog of war," this may be very difficult to do—if not nearly impossible. Finally, then, there was congressional action. Agreeing with the large Democrat majorities in both House (270 to 164) and Senate (56 to 44), President George (H. W.) Bush signed PL 102-4: the Agent Orange Act of 1991 (AOA).[4]

To overcome the practical difficulties in proving a specific veteran's exposure to chemicals, the AOA created a statutory presumption: **"(3) For the purposes of this subsection, a veteran who, during active, military, naval, or air service, served in the Republic of Vietnam during the Vietnam era and has a disease referred to in paragraph (1)(B) of this subsection shall be presumed to have been exposed during such service to an herbicide agent containing dioxin or 2,4-dichlorophenoxyacetic acid, and may be presumed to have been exposed during such service to any other chemical compound in an herbicide agent, unless there is affirmative evidence that the veteran was not exposed to any**

such agent during that service." In other words, the injured veteran did not have to prove that s/he was exposed to agent orange or one of the other chemicals; instead, that was assumed from the nature of his or her medical condition. To avoid payment of medical/disability payments, the government would have to prove that s/he had *not* been exposed to these chemicals while serving in Vietnam.

Protecting Veterans

While a war is in progress and a nation's young citizens are suffering, bleeding, and dying, there is generally an emotional appeal for "supporting our troops." The nature and intensity of that "support" may vary considerably, depending on a number of factors. Is there a significant majority of the populace that feels that the war is necessary and that it is being waged successfully, using appropriate strategies and tactics? World War II, for example, is generally characterized as a "good" war, with a high level of public support. Even so, there were some dissenting voices raised when England (and later the US) started targeting civilian areas of German cities for massive bombing raids. There were also questions (particularly after the fact) about the morality/legality of the use of atomic bombs against Hiroshima and Nagasaki and of the Allies' insistence on "unconditional surrender" by the Germans and Japanese.

With the lapse of some seventy years, some of the gory details that total victory necessitated seem to have been set aside. The *Time* magazine issue of October 12, 2012, included "A Special Advertising Section" called "Milestones in the History of US Higher Education." One such page was for "1944": "President Franklin D. Roosevelt signs the **GI Bill** to help World War II veterans further their education. The bill fuels the growth of the middle class by making colleges and universities more affordable to people from all socioeconomic backgrounds. Nearly half the 16 million World War II veterans benefit by the time the original bill ends in 1956. Later bills enacted during the wars in Korea, Vietnam, Iraq, and Afghanistan help millions more veterans pay for higher education."[5] (The page also contained a marvelous picture of FDR, looking strong, handsome, and healthy.) Whatever its political origins and however it was viewed at the time, the GI Bill is clearly one of the greatest pieces of social legislation ever passed by Congress.

The fact that this celebratory advertisement notes that similar educational benefits were provided for veterans of the Vietnam War is significant. Many of us remember with dismay the "protestors" who disrespected those who were returning from the jungles of Southeast Asia—many with missing or malfunctioning body parts—and even the flag-draped coffins of those who had paid the ultimate price. Whatever the merits or demerits of the war itself, it was hardly fair—or "moral"—for the stay-at-homes to put the blame for the war's horrors on those who had been sent by the rest of us to carry out the nation's policies. Perhaps even more discouraging to those returning veterans, however, may have been the level of seeming indifference that many of us exhibited toward them. There was nothing like the V-E Day and V-J Day celebrations of 1945. All too often, there weren't even the "thank you for your service" acknowledgements of what they had done and what they had suffered.

So, what sort of a job did President Nixon and those three Congresses do for our veterans? On an overall basis, this body of work seems quite similar to their collection of consumer statutes: no big, splashy, world-changing revolutions but, nonetheless, some nicely-balanced efforts to take care of the returnees. The big difference from the consumer legislation was, of course, the presence of the strong contending emotional forces: the "support-our-troops" positive emotion versus the "war criminals" and "baby-killers" rhetoric of the extreme Left. On any given legislative proposal concerning veterans, the relative strength of these two might change, thus adding an extra calculation to legislative strategy—and possibly, output.

As a focal point for this brief evaluation, let's reexamine the eleven "titled" Acts noted at the beginning of this Chapter. Presumably, one reason for applying a title to an Act is to identify the topic with which it is concerned—to announce that the subject has been dealt with by the legislative action. In that sense, at least, Congress seems to be indicating the Act's relative importance. So, just as in 1944/1945 with the GI Bill, "education and training" for returning veterans is an important concern (PL 91-219—the Veterans' Educational and Training Act of 1970 and PL 92-340—the Vietnam Era Veterans' Ready Assistance Act of 1972).

PL 92-541—the VA Medical School Assistance and Health Manpower Expansion Act of 1972—is also concerned with "education," but from a different perspective. Rather than the education of veterans per se, its main thrust is directed at increasing the supply of doctors and other medical professionals available for the treatment of veterans—at VA facilities and elsewhere. That same general objective (improvement of health-care for veterans) also motivates PL 93-82—the Veterans' Health Care Expansion Act of 1973. Two additional statutes—PL 92-328 (the Veterans' Compensation and Relief Act of 1972) and PL 93-295 (the Veterans' Disability Compensation and Survivors' Benefits Act of 1974) provided additional financial compensation for injuries sustained. PL 91-666—the Disabled Veterans' and Survivors' Automotive Assistance Act—made funds available for the purchase of a vehicle (*and* any needed modifications for its safe and effective operation). As noted earlier, PL 91-506—the Veterans' Housing Act of 1970—added mobile homes as a further option for veterans' special financing arrangements. And PL 93-289—the Veterans' Insurance Act of 1974—raised the maximum available life insurance coverage to $20,000.

The remaining two statutes are quite different in nature. PL 93-43—the National Cemeteries Act of 1973—established an overall administration for veterans' cemeteries. Arlington National Cemetery is a beautiful tribute to the bravery and sacrifice of our service personnel. So is the Cemetery of the Pacific in Hawaii. But there is not room for all in these two locations, so other locations have been provided around the country—near Battle Creek, Michigan, for example. Many deceased veterans' families feel strongly about having a military funeral and a military burial in one of these "official" final resting places. The 1973 statute recognizes that desire and provides some uniform standards for such recognitions.

PL 93-294 is the Air Career Incentive Act of 1974, and as the title clearly indicates, it is an attempt to encourage enlisted air crews to make a career of their service. High-tech planes and equipment require highly-trained personnel, so the loss of air crews raises military costs significantly. Sometimes, a bit of financial "recognition" can change the decision-equation.

In sum, then, President Nixon and the 1969–1974 Congresses seem to have taken good care of veterans. While they may not have authored any single piece of legislation that matched the GI Bill in objectives and scope, they did extend and update its basic policies. They enacted a significant number of statutes—some very specific and therefore usually quite brief but some broader in scope. The range of concerns is wide: medical care, housing, transportation, insurance, disability compensation, education, and survivor benefits—even burial privileges. In light of the intensity of anti-war feelings during those years, the level of accomplishment seems very satisfactory.

Chapter 8

Nixon Protecting Citizens

A LTHOUGH THEY MAY BE directed at rather specific problems, and thus not affect all of us equally, the statutes in this Chapter are generally not themselves intended to target the usually identified "interest groups." They are closer in nature to the legislation dealing with the environment: some of us may, in fact, benefit more than others from the implementation of the programs involved, but that is not really the primary purpose of the law. The basic idea behind most, if not all, of these enactments is what the Preamble to the United States Constitution calls to "promote the general Welfare" (and "secure the blessings of liberty to ourselves and our posterity"). This is thus a large (229 Acts) and diverse batch of legislative outputs.

As was true for the statutes covered in Chapters 3 through 7, many of the Acts addressed in this Chapter are "mini-laws" of less than two pages (140 of 229—61 percent). At the other extreme is the massive (195-page) 1970 reorganization of the District of Columbia's court system, followed in size by the 164 pages of 1972 Social Security amendments, the 145 pages of educational amendments in 1972 (Title IX of which has already been discussed in Chapter 6), and 74 pages on educational assistance modifications (1971). The fifth-longest Act took 62 pages to delegate substantial self-government to the District of Columbia, in 1973. A 1970 criminal-law statute occupies sixth place, and a 42-page farm-credit statute ranks seventh. In all, there are fifty-seven Acts having lengths from two to ten pages, and thirty-one of over ten pages. (The "seven longest" will be more specifically identified in the context of our subject-matter discussion, later in this Chapter, following the complete chronological listing of all 229.)

Protecting Citizens—the Nixon Legislative Record

91st Congress, First Session

- PL 91-6: extends time for filing reports under 1965 Correctional Rehabilitation Study Act

- PL 91-21: consents to New Hampshire/Vermont Interstate School Compact

- PL 91-37: amends incorporation act for National Education Association

- PL 91-39: amends 1966 Act on National Commission on Reform of Federal Criminal Laws

- PL 91-63: conveys real property to Washington International School, Inc.

- PL 91-78: extends rural housing programs and FHA insurance authority

- PL 91-79: Disaster Relief Act of 1969—additional assistance for reconstruction

- PL 91-83: permits land in Maryland to be used for highway purposes

- PL 91-87: authorizes President to designate November 16–22, 1969 as "National Health Week"

- PL 91-90: authorizes added funds for John F. Kennedy Center

- PL 91-91: requests President to call for a "Day of Bread" and "Harvest Festival"

- PL 91-95: Emergency Insured Student Loan Act of 1969

- PL 91-97: Educational Television and Radio Amendments of 1969

- PL 91-110: directs Secretary of Agriculture to permit school's use of land in Lee County, SC

- PL 91-116: amends Food Stamp Act of 1964—$610,000,000 for FY 1970

- PL 91-120: National Science Foundation Authorization Act, 1970

- PL 91-123: Appalachian Regional Development Act Amendments of 1969

- PL 91-124: Selective Service Amendment Act of 1969—modifies system

- PL 91-143: National Capital Transportation Act of 1969

- PL 91-152: Housing and Urban Development Act of 1969

- PL 91-159: consents to CT-NY Railroad Passenger Transportation Compact

- PL 91-174: requests President to proclaim January 1970 as "National Blood Donor Month"

- PL 91-176: authorizes appropriations for President's Council on Youth Opportunity

- PL 91-177: Economic Opportunity Amendments of 1969—continuation of programs

91st Congress, Second Session

- PL 91-202: releases restrictions on Texas land so it can be used for State highway

- PL 91-207: amends National School Lunch Act

- PL 91-208: amends Public Health Service Act—makes grants for graduate training

- PL 91-209: amends Public Health Service Act—extends program to domestic migrant workers

- PL 91-211: Community Mental Health Centers Amendments of 1970

- PL 91-212: Medical Library Assistance Extension Act of 1970

- PL 91-213: establishes Commission on Population Growth and the American Future

- PL 91-214: added funds for Library of Congress James Madison Memorial Building

- PL 91-222: Public Health Cigarette Smoking Act of 1969 (Surgeon General's warning)

- PL 91-227: authorizes land exchange for US Public Health Service Hospital at New Orleans

- PL 91-230: extends elementary and secondary education assistance programs

- PL 91-248: amends National School Lunch and Child Nutrition Act of 1966

- PL 91-253: Public Health Service retirement made equal to that of other uniformed services

- PL 91-256: authorizes intra-District transfers by DC blood banks

- PL 91-260: amends Elementary and Secondary Education Act—adjusts loan interest rate

- PL 91-280: transfers acquisition authority for office equipment to Librarian of Congress

- PL 91-281: amends authority over buildings and grounds of Library of Congress

- PL 91-295: provides special milk program for children, under 1966 NSLCN Act

- PL 91-296: Medical Facilities Construction and Modernization Amendments of 1970

- PL 91-304: amends Public Works and Economic Development Act of 1965

- PL 91-334: gives witness-subpoena power to President's Commission on Campus Unrest

- PL 91-340: added appropriations for Pan American Institute of Geography and History

- PL 91-345: National Commission on Libraries and Information Science Act

- PL 91-346: National Foundation on the Arts and the Humanities Amendments of 1970

- PL 91-347: conveys land to Board of Public Instruction, Okaloosa County, Florida

- PL 91-356: National Science Foundation Authorization Act of 1970

- PL 91-358: District of Columbia Court Reform and Criminal Procedure Act of 1970

- PL 91-374: provides relief assistance to Hood River County, Oregon

- PL 91-380: Office of Education Appropriation Act, 1970

- PL 91-381: provide for medals in honor of 100th anniversary of Ohio Northern University

- PL 91-405: establishes Commission on the Organization of DC's Government

- PL 91-431: Emergency Communities Facilities Act of 1970

- PL 91-433: provides for designation of "Day of Bread" and "National Harvest Week"

- PL 91-434: authorizes President to designate October 5–9 as "National PTA Week"

- PL 91-444: extends research on high-speed ground transportation

- PL 91-445: authorizes President to proclaim "National Volunteer Firemen's Week"

- PL 91-447: amends rules for free legal representation of criminal defendants

- PL 91-449: amends Federal Aviation Act of 1958, regarding offenses on board aircraft

- PL 91-452: Organized Crime Control Act of 1970

- PL 91-453: Urban Mass Transit Assistance Act of 1970

- PL 91-458: provides for control of hazardous materials on railroads

- PL 91-464: Communicable Disease Control Amendments of 1970

- PL 91-475: provides exemption from court "attachment" for property of nonresidents of DC

- PL 91-481: authorizes free subsistence for certain air-evacuation patients

- PL 91-488: changes requirement of consent for DC adoption of persons under age twenty-one

- PL 91-490: authorizes voluntary admission for treatment of retarded persons (in DC)

- PL 91-492: authorizes residential community treatment for persons on probation or parole

- PL 91-493: authorizes toll bridge over Rainy River for village of Baudette, MN

- PL 91-507: requests President to proclaim January 1971 as "National Blood Donor Month"

- PL 91-513: Comprehensive Drug Abuse Prevention and Control Act of 1970

- PL 91-515: Heart Disease, Cancer, Stroke, and Kidney Disease Amendments of 1970

- PL 91-519: Health Training Improvement Act of 1970

- PL 91-520: authorizes construction of Saint Lawrence River toll bridge

- PL 91-527: Drug Abuse Education Act of 1970

- PL 91-531: amends DC Public Assistance Act of 1962, regarding relatives' responsibility

- PL 91-535: amends DC Alcoholic Beverage Control Act

- PL 91-543: prescribes rules for service of summonses for jury duty in DC

- PL 91-551: adds members to Board of Regents of Smithsonian Institution

- PL 91-561: provides relief for the State of Hawaii

- PL 91-572: Family Planning Services and Population Research Act of 1970

- PL 91-587: expands authority of Gallaudet College to offer elementary education for the deaf

- PL 91-591: authorizes receipt of gifts for National Agricultural Library

- PL 91-592: authorizes President to proclaim May 9 to June 20 as weeks of MS Society's appeal

- PL 91-600: Library Services and Construction Amendments of 1970

- PL 91-606: Disaster Relief Act of 1970

- PL 91-616: Comprehensive Alcohol Abuse Prevention, Treatment, and Rehabilitation Act of 1970

- PL 91-623: Emergency Health Personnel Act of 1970

- PL 91-629: increases appropriations for Smithsonian Institution

- PL 91-644: Omnibus Crime Control Act of 1970—amends 1968 OCC and Safe Streets Act

- PL 91-657: Practice of Psychology Act—regulates practice of psychology in DC

- PL 91-662: removes prohibitions against importing contraceptives

- PL 91-671: amends Food Stamp Act of 1964

- PL 91-690: modifies nursing service requirement for qualification as a hospital

- PL 91-696: makes grants to medical schools and hospitals for programs in family medicine

92nd Congress, First Session

- PL 92-12: provides additional financing source for rural telephone program

- PL 92-13: increases appropriations for Commission on Marihuana and Drug Abuse

- PL 92-19: removes limits on remedies of owners of lost or stolen bearer securities

- PL 92-23: authorizes President to proclaim June 1 as "Medical Library Association Day"

- PL 92-25: extends time for filing report by Commission on DC government organization

- PL 92-26: designates last week of July as "National Star Route Mail Carriers Week"

- PL 92-31: Juvenile Delinquency Prevention and Control Act Amendments of 1971

- PL 92-32: extends school breakfast and special food programs

- PL 92-40: extends special Social Security assistance program for citizens returned from abroad

- PL 92-43: provides for observance of "Youth Appreciation Week"

- PL 92-48: Office of Education and Related Agencies Appropriation Act, 1972 (FY 1972)

- PL 92-52: extends student loan and scholarship program under Public Health Service Act

- PL 92-85: sets rules for minors' inheritance in DC

- PL 92-86: National Science Foundation Authorization Act of 1972 (FY 1972)

- PL 92-88: District of Columbia Administration of Estates Act

- PL 92-90: amends rules for DC's subsidy for school children's transportation fares

- PL 92-92: applies DC's penalty for assault on police officer to include assault on fire personnel

- PL 92-94: standardizes procedures for testing utility meters in DC

- PL 92-117: provides periodic distribution to States of unclaimed postal savings deposits

- PL 92-124: authorizes participation in Metropolitan Police Band by other law enforcement

- PL 92-148: conveys certain land to University of North Dakota

- PL 92-152: authorizes cooperation with Western Hemisphere nations on animal diseases

- PL 92-153: assures that every needy schoolchild will receive a free or reduced-price lunch

- PL 92-157: provides for increased personnel in health-care professions

- PL 92-158: Nurse Training Act of 1971

- PL 92-173: amends 1961 Act to authorize insured emergency farm loans

- PL 92-181: Farm Credit Act of 1971—provides for cooperative system of financing

- PL 92-192: requests the President to proclaim 1972 as "International Book Year"

- PL 92-196: District of Columbia Revenue Act of 1971

- PL 92-202: District of Columbia Appropriation Act, 1972 (FY 1972)

- PL 92-205: provides for weather modification reporting by federal government agencies

- PL 92-209: provides financial assistance for disaster damage to nonprofit medical facilities

- PL 92-218: National Cancer Act of 1971—strengthens National Cancer Institute

92nd Congress, Second Session

- PL 92-225: Federal Election Campaign Act of 1971

- PL 92-255: Drug Abuse Office and Treatment Act of 1972

- PL 92-269: changes minimum age for jury service from twenty-one to eighteen

- PL 92-280: Interstate Compact on Mental Health Act—authorizes DC to join compact

- PL 92-289: authorizes President to designate May 1972 as "National Arthritis Month"

- PL 92-293: authorizes Attorney General to provide care for narcotic addicts on probation

- PL 92-294: National Sickle Cell Anemia Control Act

- PL 92-305: redesignates National Institute of Arthritis, Metabolism, and Digestive Diseases

- PL 92-318: Education Amendments of 1972—amends 1963 Vocational Education Act, et al.

- PL 92-324: enhances financing for Rural Telephone Bank

- PL 92-327: authorizes DC to join motor-vehicle fee agreements with Virginia and Maryland

- PL 92-337: makes supplemental appropriation for disaster relief

- PL 92-344: District of Columbia Appropriation Act, 1973 (FY 1973)

- PL 92-345: extends special grants for maternal and child health services

- PL 92-349: National Capital Transportation Act of 1972

- PL 92-358: effectuates 1967 Convention of Paris for Protection of Industrial Property

- PL 92-360: extends Federal Civil Defense Act of 1950

- PL 92-361: adds appropriations for highway emergency relief—floods and other disasters

- PL 92-363: authorizes President to name third Sunday in October as "National Shut-In Day"

- PL 92-368: authorizes designation of highest State appellate court as a depositary library

- PL 92-372: National Science Foundation Authorization Act of 1973 (FY 1973)

- PL 92-373: provides copies of Congressional Record to certain US courts

- PL 92-381: amends 1968 Juvenile Delinquency Prevention and Control Act

- PL 92-385: authorizes added loan assistance for small businesses damaged during disasters

- PL 92-391: delays effectiveness of 1972 amendments to Guaranteed Student Loan Program

- PL 92-393: makes supplemental appropriations to disaster relief

- PL 92-411: authorizes appropriations for Corporation for Public Broadcasting

- PL 92-414: National Cooley's Anemia Control Act

- PL 92-419: Rural Development Act of 1972

- PL 92-420: Narcotic Addict Rehabilitation Amendments of 1972

- PL 92-423: National Blood Vessel, Lung, and Blood Act of 1972—training and research programs

- PL 92-424: Economic Opportunity Amendments of 1972—continuation of programs

- PL 92-433: continues and expands child nutrition programs

- PL 92-449: Communicable Disease Control Amendments Act of 1972

- PL 92-450: authorizes President to proclaim October 1, 1972, as "National Heritage Day"

- PL 92-452: authorizes President to proclaim Thanksgiving week as "National Family Week"

- PL 92-457: authorizes President to proclaim February 11, 1973, as "National Inventors' Day"

- PL 92-491: provides conveyance of DC land to the National Firefighting Museum

- PL 92-494: authorizes annual contributions to International Agency for Research on Cancer

- PL 92-495: District of Columbia Public Utilities Reimbursement Act of 1972

- PL 92-508: requests President name October 15 week "National Drug Abuse Prevention Week"

- PL 92-511: provides for joining the International Bureau for Protection of Industrial Property

- PL 92-517: National Capital Area Transit Act of 1972

- PL 92-519: District of Columbia Implied Consent Act

- PL 92-531: changes pay for National Commission on Financing of Postsecondary Education

- PL 92-546: adds two members to National Historical Publications Commission

- PL 92-554: extends grants for State and local programs dealing with treatment for alcoholism

- PL 92-563: National Advisory Commission on Multiple Sclerosis Act—establishes NACMS

- PL 92-566: extends copyrights expiring before December 31, 1974, to that date

- PL 92-569: amends Fishermen's Protective Act of 1967—reimburses owners for wrongful taking

- PL 92-579: limits time for filing claims against DC landowners for premises injuries

- PL 92-585: Emergency Health Personnel Act Amendments of 1972

- PL 92-595: Small Business Investment Act Amendments of 1972 .

- PL 92-603: amends Social Security Act

93rd Congress, First Session

- PL 93-6: extends life of Commission on Highway Beautification

- PL 93-13: maintains financial support for child nutrition programs

- PL 93-21: authorizes President to designate May 1973 as "National Arthritis Month"

- PL 93-24: amends loan program under Consolidated Farm & Rural Development Act

- PL 93-32: restores rural electric and telephone direct-loan programs

- PL 93-35: extends National Commission on Financing of Postsecondary Education

- PL 93-42: authorizes President to proclaim June week as "National Autistic Children's Week"

- PL 93-45: Health Programs Extension Act of 1973

- PL 93-67: authorizes appropriation for John F. Kennedy Center for the Performing Arts

- PL 93-73: amends National Sea Grant College and Program Act of 1966

- PL 93-83: Crime Control Act of 1973

- PL 93-91: District of Columbia Appropriation Act of 1974 (FY 1974)

- PL 93-92: amends DC Election Act, regarding filing for Delegate from DC

- PL 93-96: National Science Foundation Authorization Act, 1974 (FY 1974)

- PL 93-113: Domestic Volunteer Service Act of 1973

- PL 93-133: National Foundation on the Arts and Humanities Amendments of 1973

- PL 93-140: authorizes certain programs of DC government

- PL 93-150: National School Lunch and Child Nutrition Act Amendments of 1973

- PL 93-154: Emergency Medical Services Systems Act of 1973

- PL 93-198: District of Columbia Self-Government and Governmental Reorganization Act

- PL 93-202: postpones implementation of fee schedule for Headstart program

- PL 93-204: authorizes insured loans for fire safety equipment for nursing homes

- PL 93-222: Health Maintenance Organization Act of 1973

- PL 93-233: provides a 7 percent increase in Social Security benefits

- PL 93-241: amends DC's child-adoption system

93rd Congress, Second Session

- PL 93-247: Child Abuse Prevention and Treatment Act

- PL 93-256: extends time period for presumptive disability payments under Social Security

- PL 93-268: amends DC corporate taxation provisions

- PL 93-269: carries over appropriations for education expenditures through June 30, 1975

- PL 93-270: Sudden Infant Death Syndrome Act of 1975

- PL 93-272: amends DC self-government act regarding neighborhood councils

- PL 93-281: Narcotic Addict Treatment Act of 1974

- PL 93-282: extends appropriations for alcoholism and alcohol abuse programs

- PL 93-288: Disaster Relief Act Amendments of 1974

- PL 93-326: National School Lunch and Child Nutrition Act Amendments of 1974

- PL 93-334: repeals compulsory smallpox vaccination requirement for DC school students

- PL 93-335: extends food stamp eligibility for SSI program beneficiaries

- PL 93-343: authorizes legal education fellowship program through Commissioner of Education

- PL 93-347: continues food stamp and special milk programs

- PL 93-353: Health Services Research, Health Statistics, and Medical Libraries Act of 1974

- PL 93-354: National Diabetes Mellitus Research and Education Act

- PL 93-355: Legal Services Corporation Act—transfers program to new corporation

- PL 93-361: extends approval time for Federal Rules of Criminal Procedure

- PL 93-366: amends Federal Aviation Act of 1958, regarding aircraft piracy

Citizens Statutes—a Closer Look

Here again, it seemed self-evident that a set of categories was necessary as a framework for discussion of this vast array of legislative production. Prior to the establishment of a separate Department of Education in 1979, the Department of Health and Human Services was titled the Department of Health, Education, and Welfare. Those three "general-service" functions seemed to be a good starting-point for this Chapter's categories. As it has turned out, those are three of the four most frequently occurring statutory topics: "Health"—sixty-seven Acts, "Education"—thirty-two Acts, and "Welfare"—twenty-four Acts. Reviewing the list, legislation dealing with the District of Columbia is an obvious recurrence. That category turned out to be the third most numerous, at twenty-six Acts. (There are at least five other Acts that also involve DC in some way but were placed in another category that seemed more closely related to the main thrust of the statute.)

One of President Nixon's major campaign themes was the promise to restore "law and order"—after the riots, assassinations, and general turmoil of the 1960s. (The Preamble to our Constitution also lists "insure domestic Tranquility" as a reason for the establishment of the national government.) As noted in this Chapter's introduction, two of the six longest Acts relate to criminal law. "Safety"—of Citizens, in their persons and homes—was used as the label for a category that includes the law-and-order matters and other related concerns. Twenty Acts were placed in this category.

Even a cursory examination of the several pages containing the 229 items indicates a repeated mention of "child," or "youth," or "minor." Legislation directed at those persons did seem to merit a separate "Child/Youth" grouping, even though a statute might also be concerned with the Health, Education, Welfare, etc. of the minor child. Judgment calls had to be made as to which feature was the primary focus of the particular Act. The ultimate test in "category-juggling" occurred in the placement of PL 93-334, which repealed DC's vaccination requirement for school children. Health? Education? Child? The "DC" category was chosen, as the Act is an excellent example of congressional legislation on a topic traditionally assigned to the States—simply because, in this case, Congress is making the policy decision as the "State Legislature" or "City Council" for DC.

As another inter-Chapter illustration of the "categorization" problem, the two Acts dealing with the creation and maintenance of a "Youth Conservation Corps" were initially placed in this Chapter but subsequently moved to the "Conservation" category in Chapter 3. Obviously, different readers might make different decisions on a number of these overlapping-topics statutes. Our final count allocated nineteen Acts to the "Child" category.

A related analytical question concerned the level of refinement to which the data should be subjected. Stopping with the above six categories left a rather unwieldy "miscellaneous" group of forty-one Acts. Some further parsing seemed to be called for. Four more groups were defined: "Arts"—eight Acts, "Business"—nine Acts, "Farm/Rural"—eight Acts, and "Transportation"—nine Acts. That left only seven statutes in what is believed to be a more realistic residual category.

Health

By any standard, the level of concern for the health of the nation's population shown by the Nixon-era legislative process is impressive. Fifteen statutes directed against specific diseases! Ten more targeting substance abuse! Another ten, supporting health-care professionals! And yet another ten, developing health-care programs! The total count here is sixty-seven Acts somehow related to "health"—admittedly, some less so than others. One could question the inclusion of the five statutes appropriating funds for the National Science Foundation—PL 91-120, PL 91-356, PL 92-86, PL 92-372, and PL 93-96. Financial support of so-called "applied" research directed at finding a cure for cancer would certainly seem to qualify as health-related. Purely "scientific" inquiry into the origin and behavior of natural phenomena such as earthquakes, tidal waves, volcanic eruptions, and meteors may not be specifically intended to make the world safer for human existence, but the knowledge thus produced can certainly be applied to do so. Our human condition has been, and presumably will continue to be, improved by "unintentionally" discovered information.

Similarly, objections can be raised against another of the "Health" subcategories: the various requests for presidential "Proclamations." Ten such have to do with health issues: PL 91-87 (National Health Week—November 16–22, 1969); PL 91-174 (National Blood Donor Month—January 1970); PL 91-507 (National Blood Donor Month—January 1971); PL 91-592 (Multiple Sclerosis Society's appeal—May 9 to June 20, 1971); PL 92-23 (Medical Library Association Day—June 1, 1971); PL 92-289 (National Arthritis Month—May 1972); PL 92-363 (National Shut-In Day—third Sunday in October 1972); PL 92-508 (National

Drug Abuse Prevention Week—week of October 15, 1972); PL 93-21 (National Arthritis Month—May 1973); and PL 93-42 (National Autistic Children's Week—a week in June 1973). None of these in itself specifically provides treatment to persons suffering symptoms, but a public-service announcement might motivate someone to donate blood or to financially support a research program—or at least, to check on one's own personal health status. Raising public awareness of the existence and nature of a health problem, and conceivably thus building support for the use of public funds to try to deal with the problem, surely seems to be a legitimate congressional function.

Perhaps most impressive of all the subgroups identified here is the targeting of "Specific Diseases": fifteen statutes focusing national efforts on eradicating, or at least minimizing, these serious threats to human health. Cancer was the target of PL 92-218 (strengthening the National Cancer Institute) and PL 92-494 (making annual contributions to the International Agency for Research on Cancer). PL 92-294 created a Public Health Service program to deal with sickle-cell anemia, and PL 92-414 provided assistance to programs for the diagnosis, prevention, and treatment of Cooley's anemia. The 1970 amendments to the Public Health Service Act (PL 91-515) covered heart disease, cancer, stroke, and kidney disease. The similar Act passed in 1972 (PL 92-423) included heart, blood vessel, lung, and blood malfunctions. Separate 1972 Acts applied to arthritis (PL 92-305) and to multiple sclerosis (PL 92-563). The National Diabetes Mellitus Research and Education Act (PL 93-354) was passed in 1974. Communicable diseases in general were the subject of (the very brief) PL 91-464, the Communicable Disease Control Amendments of 1970, and of (the more substantial) PL 92-449, the Communicable Disease Control Amendments of 1972.

Not to be forgotten, mental illness concerns were recognized by PL 91-211, the Community Mental Health Centers Amendments of 1970, and by PL 92-280, the Interstate Compact on Mental Health Act, establishing the program and authorizing DC to join with any State that wished to participate. A related law, PL 91-490, authorized (in DC) the voluntary admission for treatment of mentally retarded persons. PL 92-152 completes this listing. It authorized the Secretary of Agriculture to cooperate with Western Hemisphere nations to prevent the spread of certain animal diseases that are potential threats to US food supplies. (The purpose of the Act seems clearly to be the human consequences of the named diseases, rather than the health of the animals involved.)

The Nixon-era Congresses also devoted substantial efforts to the national health problems related to "Substance Abuse." No less than six Acts attempted to deal with some aspect of drug abuse: PL 91-513, the Comprehensive Drug Abuse Prevention and Control Act of 1970; PL 91-527, the Drug Abuse Education Act of 1970; PL 92-13, increasing appropriations for the Commission on Marihuana and Drug Abuse; PL 92-255, the Drug Abuse Office and Treatment Act of 1970; PL 92-420, the Narcotic Addict Rehabilitation Amendments of

1972; and PL 93-281, the Narcotic Addict Treatment Act of 1974. Despite their rather impressive-sounding titles and purpose statements, however, four of these were "mini-statutes" of less than two pages each: PL 91-513 (not very "comprehensive"), PL 92-13, PL 92-420, and PL 93-281. PL 92-255 was indeed a serious (twenty-page) addition to the mechanisms for dealing with the problem; a special office in the executive branch was established to coordinate and supervise anti-drug efforts. PL 91-527 took a bit over three pages to authorize grants for educational materials and programs explaining the dangers connected with drug abuse.

Only one of the three statutes concerning alcohol abuse was a "mini-statute": PL 92-554. PL 91-616, the Comprehensive Alcohol Abuse Prevention and Treatment Act of 1970, if not exactly what one might normally call "comprehensive," was at least of substantial length (seven-plus pages) and established a National Institute to support and coordinate State efforts in this area. Nearly twice the length of PL 91-616, PL 93-282 extended national appropriations for anti-alcoholism and drug-abuse programs.

PL 91-222, the Public Health Cigarette Smoking Act of 1969, established a national policy on the marketing and advertising of cigarettes—including the required health warning from the US Surgeon General: "Warning: The Surgeon General Has Determined That Cigarette Smoking Is Dangerous to Your Health."[1] (Confronted by the fact that cigarette smoking continued to be widespread, subsequent regulators also terminated the use of "friendly" characters in cigarette advertising—"Joe Camel" and the Western cowboy "Marlboro Man," for example. Most recently, more extreme regulations attempted to force the inclusion of graphic and frightening images on cigarette packages but were prevented by the courts from doing so—in the name of constitutional "free speech."[2])

While the "Health Personnel" grouping did include three "mini-statutes"—PL 91-208, PL 91-690, and PL 92-52, these were more than balanced off by three Acts of over ten pages each—PL 91-519, PL 92-157, and PL 92-158. PL 91-623, PL 91-657, PL 91-690, and PL 92-585 were each two to ten pages in length. Of the "mini-statutes," PL 91-208 provided grants for training in Public Health subjects, and PL 92-52 extended the Public Health Act programs for student loans and scholarships. PL 91-690 modified the "nursing service" requirement for qualification as a hospital.

The predominant theme of the other seven Acts in this subcategory was increasing the supply of health-care personnel—through support for education and training, for example. PL 91-519 (the Health Training Improvement Act of 1970), PL 91-696 (providing grants to medical schools and hospitals for the development of "family medical" programs), PL 92-157 (providing financial support for additional health-care education and research facilities), and PL 92-158 (the Nurse Training Act of 1971) are illustrative of the "educate more personnel" approach. Both PL 91-623 (the Emergency Health Personnel Act of 1970) and PL

92-585 (the Emergency Health Personnel Act Amendments of 1972) tried to alleviate personnel shortages in various areas around the country by assigning health-care officers there and encouraging other health-care workers to locate there. PL 91-657 regulated the practice of psychology in the District of Columbia.

Seven of the ten items pertaining to health-care "Programs" were "mini-statutes." Some of them simply extended coverage of an existing program, such as PL 91-209 (extending the Public Health Service Act to domestic migratory workers), PL 91-481 (authorizing free subsistence for air-evacuation patients), PL 91-492 (authorizing residential community treatment for persons on probation or parole), and PL 92-345 (continuing the special grants for maternal and child health-care services). Their brevity should not, however, be allowed to prevent the potential importance of these small statutory changes to the persons positively affected thereby.

The other three "mini-statutes" in the "Programs" subgroup were more in the nature of administrative-policy changes. PL 91-6 extended the time for filing reports under the 1965 Correctional Rehabilitation Study Act. PL 91-256 authorized intra-District exchanges of supplies by DC blood banks. And PL 91-662 removed the prohibition against importation of contraceptives from other nations.

PL 93-222, the Health Maintenance Organization Act of 1973 (at twenty-two-plus pages, the longest Act in this subgroup), represented an important new health-care initiative.[3] HMOs are such a commonplace part of our health-care dialogue and planning these days that we are apt to forget that they did have a beginning, and much of their early development occurred during the Nixon years—with the passage of the 1973 HMO Act. PL 91-572, the Family Planning Services and Population Research Act of 1970, established the Office of Population Affairs (as part of the HEW Department)—to expand, improve and coordinate family-planning services and research. Finally, PL 93-45, the Health Programs Extension Act of 1973, extended (through FY 1974) appropriations authorizations for the Public Health Service Act, the Community Mental Health Centers Act, and the Developmental Disabilities Services and Facilities Construction Act.

The remaining group of seven Acts has to do with "Facilities." (PL 92-157 also aimed at facility construction—but with the main purpose being education and training of additional health-care personnel, rather than for provision of health-care services to the public.) The "size" distribution (i.e., the length of the statutes) in this collection is not replicated in any of the other six subcategories in this section of the Chapter. There are three "mini-statutes" in the group: PL 91-227, PL 92-209, and PL 93-204. But there are also three Acts of over ten pages each: PL 91-296 (eighteen pages), PL 93-154 (eleven pages), and PL 93-353 (eleven pages). PL 91-212 used four-plus pages, for the Medical Library Assistance Extension Act of 1970.

PL 91-227 authorized an exchange of lands in New Orleans, to enable the construction of a new Public Health Service Hospital there. PL 92-209 provided for financial assistance for reconstruction of private nonprofit medical-care facilities damaged or destroyed by a major disaster. PL 93-204 amended the National Housing Act so as to provide insured loans to nursing homes for the installation of fire safety equipment.

As to the three longer Acts—PL 91-296 amended the Public Health Service Act by revising, extending, and improving its hospital construction program—most notably, by adding "modernization" after "construction" to its intended coverage. (Today's hospitals are a far cry from the facilities at the 1940s Bedford [Ohio] Hospital that the author visited on several occasions with his physician-father. "Modernization" is at least as important today as original construction, particularly in light of the tremendous technological advances that have occurred in the intervening years.) PL 93-154, the Emergency Medical Services Systems Act of 1973, provided "assistance and encouragement" for the development of comprehensive area emergency medical services systems. The final "plus-ten" Act in this subcategory, PL 93-353 revised health services' research programs and extended the program of assistance to medical libraries.

Education

For whatever combination of reasons, while this is the second largest category of Acts in this Chapter, 70 percent of them (22 of 32) are "mini-statutes" of less than two pages each, three more are just over three pages, and another two are each five pages in length. By way of contrast, this group also includes the third longest Act (145-plus pages)—PL 92-318—and the fourth longest (74-plus pages)—PL 91-230, which extended elementary and secondary education assistance programs. Perhaps a partial explanation for this somewhat odd length distribution is that most of the serious substantive changes that Congress felt were needed were put into the two very long statutes, so that as other legislative topics arose, they were mostly taken care of by relatively minor updatings and clarifications.

The thirty-two Acts included here were grouped into four more specific topics and a very general "Office and Amendments" catch-all category. Rather surprisingly, the largest (eight items) of the specifics was "Libraries"—including the Smithsonian Institution. Next in line, with six items, was "Institutions." The "Loans" category consisted of five statutes, and "Land" had four items. The general category had nine entries, including the two very extensive Acts referred to above.

For a professional educator, it's of course very encouraging to see Congress spending some time and effort (and funds) dealing with "Libraries." Of the eight Acts included here, however, only two had to do with libraries generally—PL 91-345, the National Commission on Libraries and Information Science Act, and PL 91-600, the Library Services and Construction Amendments of 1970. PL 91-345 created the National Commission, which is charged with studying the US' national and State libraries and making recommendations for improvement. PL 91-600's purpose clause said that it was intended to help State library systems provide services and to help with the development of the inter-library loan arrangement. These two Acts were, however, the only ones with more than two pages of content.

Three statutes concerned the Library of Congress. PL 91-214 provided additional funding for the construction of the James Madison Memorial Building as part of the Library of Congress complex. PL 91-280 and PL 91-281 gave the Librarian of Congress authority over the Library's office equipment as well as buildings and grounds, respectively. PL 91-591 authorized the National Agricultural Library to receive gifts. The Smithsonian Institution was the subject of PL 91-551 (additional members of its Board of Regents) and PL 91-629 (increased appropriations).

Five of the six items dealing with "Institutions" were less than two pages in length. The sole exception was PL 91-21, which used eighteen-plus pages to consent to the Interstate School Compact between New Hampshire and Vermont. PL 91-37 was a brief amendment of the incorporation act for the National Education Association. PL 91-340 provided additional funding for the Pan-American Institute of Geography and History. PL 91-381 authorized medals to commemorate the 100th anniversary of Ohio Northern University. PL 91-434 asked the President to designate October 5–9, 1970, as "National PTA Week." And PL 91-587 permitted Gallaudet College (in DC) to offer elementary education for deaf children.

Similarly, only two of the five Acts in the "Loan" category were over two pages: PL 91-95 needed just a bit over two pages for the "Emergency Insured Student Loan Act of 1969." The Act stated that special bonuses could be paid to lenders of insured student loans, if the market returns on such loans were so low that lenders might refuse to make them and students thereby denied access to higher education. PL 93-269 (guaranteeing that student loan funds authorized for fiscal years 1973 and 1974 would be available through June 30, 1975) took about two and a half pages.

The other three Acts pertaining to student loans were all "mini-statutes." PL 92-391 delayed the implementation of the 1972 amendments to the guaranteed student loan program. PL 93-73 extended the "Sea Grant" program of maritime studies by establishing annual appropriations through June 30, 1976, and made certain technical corrections. PL 93-343 authorized a legal education fellowship program through the Commissioner of Education.

Each of the four Acts in the "Land" subcategory was under two pages in length. PL 91-63 conveyed land in DC to the Washington International School, Inc. PL 91-110 directed the Secretary of Agriculture to permit specified South Carolina lands under his jurisdiction to be used for a local school. Similarly, PL 91-347 conveyed land located in Okaloosa County, Florida to that county's board of public instruction. Finally, with PL 92-148, Congress transferred certain federal land to the University of North Dakota.

The residual "Office and Amendments" grouping included two appropriations Acts for what was then the Office of Education, located within the then-Department of Health, Education, and Welfare—PL 91-380 and PL 92-48. The impressively-titled "Educational Television and Radio Amendments of 1969" (PL 91-97) took less than a page to provide additional funding for the Corporation for Public Broadcasting and related facilities. In stark contrast, PL 91-230, "AN ACT To extend programs of assistance for elementary and secondary education, for other purposes," was a comprehensive revisiting of the national government's education programs. Its opening sentence/paragraph/section (after the "Be it enacted" phraseology, actually numbered "Sec. 2. [a]") was a very profound statement of purpose and is worth quoting in full:

Sec. 2. (a) It is the policy of the United States that guidelines and criteria established pursuant to title VI of the Civil Rights Act of 1964 and section 182 of the Elementary and Secondary Education Amendments of 1966 dealing with the conditions of segregation by race, whether de jure or de facto, in the schools of the local educational agencies of any State shall be applied uniformly in all regions of the United States whatever the origin or cause of such segregation.

That language, all by itself, would seem to qualify PL 91-230 for inclusion in Chapter 6— "Protecting Minorities." Its inclusion in the present Chapter does not in any way minimize its crucial significance as part of the Nixon administration's program for the elimination of segregation.

Other parts of PL 91-230 also dealt with the need for educational programs to include children who were neglected, handicapped, or delinquent—and thus disadvantaged. Likewise, the special situation of the children of migratory farm workers had to be recognized and provided for. Of course, much of the great bulk of the Act had to do with the specific details of program development and administration, but it was still important to restate the basic principles of inclusion and equality at the beginning.

PL 91-230 was approved on April 13, 1970. PL 91-260, approved May 21, 1970, changed one of the percentages in the amended education statute from "10%" to "6%."

Two years later, the 92nd Congress revisited national education policies with PL 92-318, which contained a set of amendments twice the size of PL 91-230. Several existing laws were amended, at least to some degree. There were further adjustments to the 1965 Elementary & Secondary Education Act. There were relatively minor changes to the Vocational Education Act of 1963, the General Education Provisions Act, and the "Impact Aid" Act of 1950 (PL 81-874). Significant provisions concerned the 1965 Higher Education Act, including sections dealing with college libraries, "developing institutions," grants to emeritus professors to encourage teaching, and student support. (The sections dealing with the 1950 Impact Aid Act also have relevance to Chapter 6 of this book—"Protecting Minorities"— since they substantially reworked the provisions for ensuring the education of Native American children.)

PL 92-531 used a half-page to amend the compensation arrangements (appropriately enough) for the National Commission on Financing of Postsecondary Education. PL 93-35 took a bit more paper to extend the life of the NCFPE. PL 93-202 required less than half a page to delay implementation of a fee schedule for the "Headstart" program for preschool children.

Welfare

There are, of course, several varieties of "welfare" programs. "Relief" is often used as a rough synonym for welfare: being "on welfare" meaning the same thing as being "on relief" or "on public assistance." Coupled with the word "disaster," however, "relief" has a slightly different meaning: publicly funded emergency assistance to deal with a specific happenstance event that causes serious economic and social consequences. With the benefit of these overlapping definitions/connotations, "relief" is the largest subcategory in this section: nine Acts of the twenty-four included here. Four Acts specifically dealt with the food stamp program, and four others specifically related to Social Security benefits. Two concerned the government's economic opportunity programs, and two more requested presidential proclamations. The remaining three are in the "miscellaneous" subgroup.

Five of the nine Acts in the "Relief" category specifically referenced "disaster relief": PL 91-70, PL 91-606, PL 92-337, PL 92-393, and PL 93-288. Three others were targeted at a designated geographic area—PL 91-374 (Hood River County, Oregon), PL 91-531 (the District of Columbia's public assistance program [limiting liability for reimbursement to spouse for relief payments to spouse, and parent for relief payments for minor child]), and PL 91-561 (the State of Hawaii). PL 92-385 authorized additional loan assistance to small businesses that had suffered losses during disasters.

The four "food stamp" statutes are PL 91-116 (providing $610,000,000 for the program, for FY 1970); PL 91-671 (redefining eligibility rules and including "non-related individuals over age 60 who are not residents of an institution or boarding house, but are living as one economic unit sharing common cooking facilities and for whom food is customarily purchased in common"); PL 93-335 (extending the food stamp eligibility of "supplemental security income recipients" for an additional twelve months); and PL 93-347 (continuing the Agriculture Department's free food distribution program until July 1, 1975).

The four items dealing more generally with the Social Security system include the huge (164-plus pages) set of amendments in PL 92-603. Some idea of the wide scope of the Act can be gained by sampling a few of its specifics. There are forty-five sections dealing with "Old-Age, Survivors, and Disability Insurance." Included are sections increasing benefits for surviving spouses (Section 102) and defining a child's benefits based on a grandparent's income (Section 113), benefits for certain employees of the government of Guam (Section 128), and benefits for certain World War II detainees (Section 142). Another 116 sections covering "Medicare, Medicaid, and Maternal and Child Health" follow. Briefer coverage is given to the provisions for "Supplementary Security Income for the Aged, Blind, and Disabled."

PL 93-233 devotes some twenty-eight pages to authorization of a 7 percent increase in Social Security benefits and related matters. The other two Acts are each less than one page in length. PL 92-40 extended the special Social Security assistance program for citizens returning from overseas. And PL 93-256 extended the timeframe for presumptive disability payments under Social Security.

PL 91-177, the Economic Opportunity Amendments of 1969, continued the EO programs for health and medical support, food distribution, "Headstart" (for children), and others—and also inaugurated an "alcoholic recovery" program. PL 93-424 provided a further continuation of the various EO efforts.

Somehow, the 91st Congress found time to enact two requests for presidential proclamations of a "Day of Bread"! PL 91-91 asked for a designation of Tuesday, October 28, 1969, as a "Day of Bread" and of the last week of October 1969 as "Harvest Festival." PL 91-433 did the same in 1970: Tuesday, October 6, 1970, as the "Day of Bread" and October 4–10, 1970, as "National Harvest Week." (One has to wonder if there are ever any "Nay" votes on this sort of sloganeering.)

The three remaining Acts in this category include one with significant content and two "mini-statutes." PL 91-123, the Appalachian Regional Development Act Amendments of 1969, modified the funding and administration of the 1965 Act dealing with Appalachia. PL 91-304 and PL 91-431 are half-page-each amendments to the 1965 ARD Act and to the 1970 Emergency Communities Facilities Act.

District of Columbia

The twenty-six Acts placed in this group seemed to fit rather neatly into just three subcategories: "DC Government" (ten items), "DC Public Programs" (twelve items), and "DC Private Law" (four items). The first group includes Acts dealing with the structure and powers of the DC government itself; the second, with the various municipal functions it performs; and the third, with its functions as a quasi-State legislature—adopting laws for the governance of private relations. (As an [non-Nixon-era] example of the third subgroup, Congress decided which parts of the Uniform Commercial Code—governing many areas of private law— would be applicable in DC.)

Five of the ten "Government" Acts related to changes in the structure of DC's unique governmental system. PL 91-405 established the Commission on the Organization of the Government of the District of Columbia—and provided that DC could elect a "delegate" to the US House of Representatives who could participate in the debates but *not* vote on proposed legislation. PL 92-25 merely extended the time limit for the filing of that Commission's report. PL 93-92 set up the primary election procedure for selection of candidates for DC's delegate to Congress. PL 93-198 was the culmination of the Commission's study and recommendations: the sixty-two-page statute that reorganized the DC government. The new structure roughly parallels that of the national government, with a mayor and a thirteen-member Council elected for four-year terms of office. Section 302—delegating "Legislative Power" to the Council—is the key part of the law, worth quoting in full:

Except as provided in sections 601, 602, and 603, the legislative power of the District shall extend to all rightful subjects of legislation within the District consistent with the Constitution of the United States and the provisions of this Act subject to all the restrictions and limitations imposed upon the States by the tenth section of the first article of the Constitution of the United States.

Section 601 reserves ultimate legislative power to Congress, in much the same way that State governments reserve ultimate power over their legislatively-created city governments. Section 602 prohibits the Council from contradicting the provisions of PL 93-198 itself and from legislating on nine specified subjects (including the imposition of a local tax on property of the United States or any State, thus exempting considerable acreage in the District). Section 603 specifies that the Act is not intended to change the existing law as to the roles of "Congress, the President, the Federal Office of Management and Budget, and the Comptroller General" in preparing and approving DC's total budget. Section 10 of Article I of the US Constitution prohibits the States from individually exercising what are exclusively national governmental functions, such as making treaties with other nations, establishing its own monetary system or army and navy, taxing imports or exports, and the like. Finally, PL 93-272 was a brief clarifying amendment on the establishment of advisory neighborhood councils—if a majority of DC voters decided that they wanted them.

Three Acts—PL 92-202, PL 92-344, and PL 93-91—were congressional appropriations of funds to augment the District's budget.

PL 92-124 permitted participation in the Metropolitan Police Band by personnel from other District law enforcement/administration agencies. PL 93-140 authorized certain DC governmental activities—health-care for indigent persons, emergency expenditures, et al.

Three of the "Public Programs" statutes had to do with mass transit: PL 91-143, the National Capital Transportation Act of 1969; PL 92-349, the National Capital Transportation

Act of 1972—which amended the 1969 Act, adding several features; and PL 92-517, the National Capital Area Transit Act of 1972, which authorized the Washington Metropolitan Area Transit Authority to acquire local bus lines, as part of the public mass transit system. Two others related to motor vehicle rules: PL 92-327 authorized DC to enter into motor-vehicle fee agreements with Maryland and Virginia; and PL 92-519, the District of Columbia Implied Consent Act, provided that persons operating motor vehicles in DC had, by doing so, impliedly consented to being tested for blood-alcohol content.

States typically regulate the distribution of alcoholic beverages. PL 91-535 amended DC's Alcoholic Beverage Control Act. States also, of course, levy various sorts of taxes on persons who reside in the State, or work there, or own property or conduct business there. PL 92-196, the District of Columbia Revenue Act of 1971, imposed a tax on transfers of real estate and tangible and intangible personal property as well as a separate tax on business inventories. PL 93-268 amended DC's corporate tax law.

Cities may have various regulations dealing with public utilities and may even operate some of them (water supply, for example). PL 92-94 requires uniform procedures for testing utility meters used in DC. PL 92-495 is a more benign "regulation": it provides reimbursement to DC utilities that were caused extra expenses by the city's urban renewal programs. Cities also control the use of their public lands. PL 92-491 permits the building of a firefighters' museum on city property. Local government agencies exercise considerable control over public schools, so DC authorities—ultimately, Congress—decide on the requirements that must be met for school attendance. PL 93-334 repealed the smallpox vaccination requirement that had been imposed on DC school children.

All four Acts in the third category are "mini-statutes" of one page or less. PL 91-475 exempted DC property of nonresidents of DC from "attachment" (seizure and sale, to pay debts) by DC courts. PL 92-85 regulated inheritance by minors, in estates of less than $1,000. PL 92-88 regulated the administration of small (up to $2,500) decedents' estates. PL 92-579 limited the time for filing of lawsuits against DC landowners for injuries occurring on their DC properties.

Safety

All but one of the twenty Acts included here have a rather direct relationship to the "law and order" theme that was a key part of President Nixon's 1968 election campaign. (PL 91-458 regulated the railroad transportation of hazardous materials—a "safety" concern, to be sure, but hardly categorized as a "law and order" problem.) Of course, the statutes deal with different aspects of "law and order," but even so, the temporal distribution of effort seems a bit strange. Nine of the twenty were passed by the Second Session of the 91st Congress, including one of the seven longest Acts in this entire Chapter. By contrast, the 92nd Congress produced only six "mini-statutes" related to these "Safety" problems, and the 93rd Congress only four such Acts—but three of those were over ten pages. No obvious explanation appears to account for this rather skewed sequencing.

The three titled and dated statutes legislating substantive criminal law stand out clearly as a subgroup: "law and order" by definition. PL 91-452, the Organized Crime Control Act of 1970, is undoubtedly the most important of the three. It mandated the periodic appointment of a "special grand jury" by each US District Court located in a district with over 4 million population or as to which the US Justice Department certifies the necessity thereof due to criminal activity. It granted general immunity from criminal prosecution to any witness summoned to testify before US courts, certain agencies, or Congress—where the witness claims the constitutional privilege against self-incrimination. (Presumably, then, the witness cannot refuse to testify since they cannot be criminally prosecuted. One must wonder, however, if Congress has the constitutional power to also immunize such a witness against the possibility of *State* criminal prosecution based on the information thus disclosed.) The Act also created a new federal crime: conspiracy to obstruct State or local criminal processes "with the intent to facilitate an illegal gambling business," and it established a "Commission on the Review of the National Policy Toward Gambling."

Most well-known of the Act's provisions are the "RICO" sections, dealing with Racketeer Influenced and Corrupt Organizations. (RICO offenses have been used as plotlines in numerous film and TV episodes.) "Racketeering activity" is defined by a lengthy list of criminal offenses. Any property used for or obtained through racketeering activity is subject to forfeiture on conviction for a RICO violation, in addition to penalties of criminal fines and/or twenty-five years in prison. Persons injured by RICO violations can collect triple damages from the offender. PL 91-452 also regulates the manufacture and distribution of explosive materials, with criminal penalties for violations. Finally, the Act established a National Commission on Individual Rights, as a monitor on the implementation of these new anti-crime programs.

PL 91-644—the Omnibus Crime Control Act of 1970—was a thirteen-page package of amendments to the similarly-titled 1968 Act, which provided national government assistance to State and local law-enforcement agencies. The amendments included changes to assistance-program administration; facilities construction; grants for planning, training, and research; criminal appeals by the national government (as prosecutor); protection of members of Congress and the President; and operations of the wiretap commission. PL 93-83—the Crime Control Act of 1973—was a further and rather comprehensive (twenty-two page) reworking of many of the same topics, including the repeal of the 1965 Law Enforcement Assistance Act.

Seven statutes relate to courts and court procedures. The range of their scope is the greatest of any group analyzed: from the 195-page restructuring of the DC courts, through twelve-plus pages on the Legal Services Corporation and four-plus on free lawyers for criminal defendants, to four Acts of less than one page each—PL 91-39, PL 91-543, PL 92-269, and PL 93-361.

Needless to say, the District of Columbia Court Reform and Criminal Procedure Act of 1970 (PL 91-358) was essentially a book in itself. Covering court structure, power to hear various types of cases, and criminal procedure, it's the sort of material that the several States put in their constitutions, statutes, and court rules. PL 93-355 transferred the legal services program to a newly-formed government corporation. PL 91-447 modified the rules for providing free legal assistance to criminal defendants. (This constitutional right for defendants in "non-capital" cases originated in the US Supreme Court's decision in *Gideon v. Wainwright*, 372 US 355 [1973].)

Two of the "mini-statutes" extended deadlines concerning federal criminal law reform. PL 91-39 gave the National Commission on Reform of Federal Criminal Laws an extra year in which to report on their work—and a funding increase from $500,000 to $850,000. PL 93-361 gave Congress extra time (until August 1, 1975) to approve the criminal procedure changes ordered by the Chief Justice of the US Supreme Court. The other two related to service on federal juries. PL 91-543 restated the procedures for notifying jurors that they had been called to serve. PL 92-269 lowered the age of eligibility for jury service to eighteen—from twenty-one.

Three Acts dealt with transportation "safety" and criminal conduct that might cause harm to persons or property. PL 91-449 was a brief amendment to the 1958 Federal Aviation Act, to try to implement an international treaty dealing with criminal acts on board airplanes. Evidently realizing that PL 91-449 was inadequate, the Second Session of the 93rd Congress revisited the problem in 1974, with PL 93-366—a much more comprehensive redefinition of air piracy and US authority to deal with it. As noted above, PL 91-458 dealt with railroad transportation of hazardous materials.

Two very brief items dealt with the other major local-government "safety" group: fire personnel. (Some local governments have combined firefighters and police into a "Safety Department.") PL 91-445 authorized the President to proclaim "National Volunteer Firemen's Week." PL 92-92 provided that the criminal penalties for assaulting a police office would also apply to assault on fire personnel. (Fire personnel as well as police were subject to assault during the urban riots in several cities during the 1960s—Detroit, for example.)

Two other short statutes provided for distribution of materials to certain courts. PL 92-369 added each State's highest court as a "depositary library" for the receipt of federal government publications. PL 92-373 indicated that copies of the *Congressional Record* would be sent to certain US courts.

The last three of this group—all "mini-statutes"—have to do with a very broad range of "safety" issues. PL 91-334 gave the President's Commission on Campus Unrest the power to subpoena witnesses to testify at its hearings. (Having "been there"—on the sidelines at the on-campus riots at Eastern Michigan University in the spring of 1970—the author can attest to the seriousness of the campus "unrest" during that period.) PL 92-293 authorized the US Attorney General to provide care for narcotic addicts on probation. Finally, PL 92-360 extended the 1950 Civil Defense Act ("Duck and cover!"—the "defense" against a nuclear attack promoted in 1950s TV ads.)

Child/Youth

What stands out most clearly in this statutory collection is Congress's concern for child nutrition. As part of President Johnson's "Great Society" package, Congress had passed the National School Lunch and Child Nutrition Act of 1966. Of the eighteen "child/youth" statutes identified here, half of them concerned that same topic. The 91st Congress passed three such Acts—PL 91-207 and PL 91-248, amending the 1966 Act, and PL 91-295, which focused more specifically on the milk program. The 92nd Congress added three more—PL 92-32, which was directed at school breakfast programs; PL 92-153 (school lunches); and PL 92-433, dealing with child nutrition generally. Not to be outdone, the 93rd Congress also chipped in three short items—PL 93-13 (additional funding for child nutrition); PL 93-150 (a so-titled 1973 set of amendments to the 1966 NSL&CN Act); and PL 93-326 (another, smaller set of NSL&CN 1974 amendments). Only three of these (PL 91-248, PL 92-433, and PL 93-150) were over two pages in length.

Five of the other nine were also "mini-statutes"—less than two pages in length. PL 91-176 provided funding for the President's Council on Youth Opportunity. PL 91-488 changed the requirement of consent for the adoption of persons under age twenty-one in the District of Columbia. (It thus could have been placed in the "DC" category.) PL 92-31 dealt with federal programs on juvenile delinquency, making small changes in funding and rehabilitation programs and in the membership of the interdepartmental council concerned with the topic. PL 92-43 designated the week starting with the second Monday of November 1971 as "Youth Appreciation Week" and requested the President issue a proclamation to that effect. PL 92-90 adjusted an effective date in the statute pertaining to DC's subsidy for transporting children to school.

PL 92-381 was a more substantive attempt to combat juvenile delinquency, by providing assistance to courts, schools, and community programs established to deal with the problem. It authorized the Secretary of Health, Education, and Welfare (as the Department was then titled) to issue grants for construction of special facilities, provision of services, or personnel training. The original program, as it had been administered from 1968 to 1971, was sharply criticized by a 1977 report to the House Committee on Education and Labor. PL 92-381 appears to have been a first attempt at improving the implementation of these statutory interventions. PL 93-415, the Juvenile Justice and Delinquency Prevention Act of 1974, was later passed by the Second Session of the 93rd Congress and signed by President Gerald Ford—after President Nixon had resigned—and thus is not included in the count for present purposes. Further changes were also made in subsequent years. (This seemingly excessive concern with "juvenile delinquency" was not unique to the 1970s. Todd Gitlin, one of the early leaders of the "Students for a Democratic Society," refers to the "Fifties panic over juvenile delinquency" and the Senate Subcommittee on Juvenile Delinquency hearings in the 1960s, in *The Sixties: Years of Hope, Days of Rage*, [New York: Bantam Books, 1993], at pp. 215–216.)

PL 93-241 established a "Board of Public Welfare" for DC and made further changes in the treatment and possible adoption of orphaned/abandoned/homeless children. PL 93-247 provided funding for "a demonstration program for the prevention, identification, and treatment of child abuse and neglect" and established a "National Center" for that purpose. PL 93-270 set up financial assistance for research on "sudden infant death" syndrome.

Arts

Two of the eight statutes dealing with "Arts" were brief requests/authorizations for presidential proclamations. PL 92-192 asked that 1972 be declared "International Book Year"; PL 92-450 asked that October 1, 1972, be announced as "National Heritage Day."

Two other statutes allocated funds to the Kennedy Center for the Performing Arts. PL 91-90 raised one allocation from $15,500,000 to $23,000,000 and another from $15,400,000 to $20,400,000. PL 93-67 provided ("for services necessary") up to $2,400,000 for the fiscal year ending June 30, 1974, and up to $2,500,000 for the FY ending June 30, 1975. Similarly, PL 92-411 gave the Commission for Public Broadcasting $40 million for the FY ending June 30, 1973, plus up to another $25 million for its grant programs.

The 1965 Act setting up the National Foundation on the Arts and the Humanities was amended by a pair of four-page statutes—PL 91-346 (1970) and PL 93-133 (1973). Finally, the National Historical Publications Commission was modified by the addition of two members—in PL 92-546.

Business

Although only nine in number, there is a considerable range of scope/substance in these Acts. The first (PL 91-152) and last (PL 93-113) chronologically are each over twenty pages in length, while six of the other seven are "mini-statutes" of under two pages. PL 92-595 is a bit longer, at three-plus pages.

PL 91-152 was designated the "Housing and Urban Development Act of 1969."[4] The original 1965 HUD Act was a key part of President Johnson's "Great Society" program, which was announced in his magnificent commencement address at the University of Michigan, on May 22, 1964. (LBJ's speech is well worth watching and can be found online.) The 1969 Act essentially extended and expanded the original—e.g., "$1,000,000,000" in funding increased to "$2,500,000,000." The HUD programs also benefitted the "consumers" of homes—buyers and renters—as well as the businesses involved in providing the homes. (The author actually received a low-cost loan, through the "Model Cities" part of the "Great Society" program—for home improvements on an older residence in Ann Arbor, Michigan.)

At the other end of the timeline, PL 93-113—the Domestic Volunteer Service Act of 1973—established an innovation program to provide small businesses with consulting services, provided by persons with significant business training and experience. Similarly, PL 92-595—the Small Business Investment Act Amendments of 1972—was designed to facilitate business ownership by persons "whose participation in the free enterprise system is hampered because of social or economic disadvantages." (This latter Act could have been placed in Chapter 5—"Protecting Minorities"—since it illustrated one of President Nixon's key policy positions: promoting minority economic growth as an important part of the solution to minorities' disadvantaged position in society.)

Two of the five "mini-statutes" in this category were considerably more significant than their length would indicate. Both related to the US' joining an international agreement for the protection of "intellectual property" (patents, copyrights, trademarks, et al.). PL 92-358 related to the Paris Convention for Protection of Industrial Property, and PL 92-511 to the International Bureau for Protection of Industrial Property. PL 92-457 merely authorized the President to proclaim February 11, 1973, as "National Inventors' Day." PL 92-566 extended to December 31, 1974, the copyright protection for intellectual works whose protection would otherwise expire before that date. The only one of the five that did not somehow relate to intellectual property was PL 92-569—an amendment to the 1967 Fishermen's Protective Act—giving reimbursement for wrongful takings of property.

Farm/Rural

With the fortieth anniversary of Franklin Roosevelt's Tennessee Valley Authority (TVA) arriving in 1973, parts of rural America were still struggling to modernize during the Nixon years. (Twenty years earlier, as Nixon was running for Vice President on the Eisenhower ticket in the summer of 1952, the author's family moved into an old farmhouse in northeastern Ohio that lacked running water and indoor plumbing. A difficult few weeks ensued, while modifications were made. The point for present purposes being that it was not just the

Tennessee Valley that was "developmentally challenged.") As a result, there may be a certain level of unbelief in reading some of the legislative products of the Nixon-era Congresses. But the farm/rural problems were surely real enough for those who were forced to endure them.

A large part of the TVA's mission was to make electricity—and all the modern devices that operated from it—available to the inhabitants of the Valley. That did happen there, of course, but not all at once and not necessarily in all other areas of the nation. So, there was the 92nd Congress—in 1971 and 1972—providing extra financing for rural telephone programs (PL 92-12 and PL 92-324). And again, in 1973, the 93rd Congress "restored" rural electric and telephone programs (PL 93-32).

The TVA was also tasked with leading the economic development of that area of Appalachia—and development did occur. But it's clear from the legislative record of the Nixon years that the rural development job nationwide had also been less than fully accomplished. PL 92-419, the Rural Development Act of 1972, was the fifteenth-longest of the 229 Acts covered in this Chapter. It expanded the loan and grant programs available to farmers and relabeled the 1961 Act as the "Consolidated Farm and Rural Development Act." PL 92-173 had already amended the 1961 Act to authorize *insured* emergency farm loans; PL 93-24 was a further (very brief) amendment to the emergency loan programs under the amended CFRDA.

As noted above in the brief parenthetical reference to 1950s Ohio, rural housing had also been a long-standing problem. The Nixon-era Congresses (91st and 92nd, anyway) also took note of this shortfall. PL 91-78 was only a very brief statute that extended rural housing programs and the Federal Housing Authority's mortgage insurance function. But PL 92-181, the Farm Credit Act of 1971—noted in the Chapter introduction as the seventh longest Act of the 229 in this Chapter, at forty-two-plus pages—was a substantial addition to the government's financing programs for farm/rural developmental activities.

Transportation

"Transportation" as a category seems a rather clear call, but there is of course considerable overlap here with transportation *businesses*. Many, if not all, businesses also rely on the delivery of goods and services via one form of "transportation" or another—or several. So, does the national government's assistance in the construction and maintenance of an airport system belong in *this* category or instead as aid to the airline industry? After some reconsideration, PL 91-258, the Airport and Airway Development Act of 1970, was placed in the "Consumers" Chapter, rather than here. Those facilities are being used by businesses, individuals, and governmental units. In contrast, PL 91-159, the congressional consent to the Railroad Passenger Transportation Compact between Connecticut and New York, seems clearly to belong here. (It's a *transportation* compact, after all!) And PL 92-453—the Urban Mass Transit Assistance Act of 1970—looks like another easy call.

The other seven Acts all relate to motor vehicle transportation via highways. PL 91-83 and PL 91-202 permit State governments to use federal land, in Maryland and Texas, respectively, for State highways. The Second Session of the 91st Congress was particularly active in this area, passing PL 91-444 (extending research on high-speed transportation), PL 91-493 (authorizing a toll bridge over the Rainy River in Minnesota), and PL 91-520 (another toll bridge—over the St. Lawrence River). PL 92-361 increased funding for restoration of highways after floods, landslides, and similar disasters. On a less serious note, PL 93-6 extended the life of the Commission on Highway Beautification.

Miscellaneous

If not properly entered in any of the above ten categories, what exactly were the topics covered by the seven "remnants"? Two of these Acts were fractional-page commemorations. PL 92-452 authorized the President to proclaim Thanksgiving week 1972 as "National Family Week." PL 92-26 designated the last week of July 1971 as "National Star Route Mail Carriers Week." ("Star Route" carriers are the private contractors who deliver most rural mail, along specified routes.).

Three others made small adjustments in various government programs. PL 91-124, with the impressive title "Selective Service Amendment Act of 1969," took one sentence to repeal a section of the 1967 Selective Service Act that had authorized the President to provide draft exemptions for otherwise-eligible men with certain critical skills. PL 92-117 provided for periodic distribution to States ("escheat" to the Government) of unclaimed postal savings balances. PL 92-205 required federal government agencies to report any weather-modification activities. (This last Act might possibly have been placed in Chapter 3, as an "environmental" measure.)

The remaining two statutes are somewhat more substantive. PL 91-213 establishes a "Commission on Population Growth and the American Future"—to try to anticipate problems and to consider ways to deal with them. Clearly, the most significant enactment in this group is PL 92-225, the Federal Election Campaign Act of 1971, intended to "promote fair practices in the conduct of election campaigns for Federal political offices." Although its effectiveness was later questioned, the 1971 FECA was at least an important step forward in trying to deal with the potentially corrosive effect of money on political elections.[5] There are, of course, some serious constitutional questions raised by the "spending limits" approach to the problem. As early as 1978, the Supreme Court ruled that a Massachusetts statute that prohibited corporations from funding messages relating to ballot referendums was unconstitutional.[6] (The problem is not only the denial of the corporations' freedom to publish the message but, equally—perhaps even more—distastefully, the denial of the voters' right to hear the message and to evaluate its worth for themselves.) After some four decades as part of the US Code, much of FECA's policy approach was rejected when the Supreme Court decided, in the *Citizens United* case, that a prohibition of corporate political expenditures was an unconstitutional impairment of First Amendment freedom of speech.[7]

Protecting Citizens

So, what's the verdict on the Nixon years' efforts to "promote the general welfare" and "secure the blessings of liberty"? President Nixon put considerable emphasis during his campaigns on reestablishing "law and order."[8] His legislative output certainly fulfilled that pledge, with the comprehensive reform of the DC court system, the Organized Crime Control Act, and the Omnibus Crime Control Act. The residents of DC also received a significant extension of their "liberty" as citizens to participate in the selection of their city's political leadership. And the "welfare" of all citizens (present *and* future) was potentially enhanced by the 1972 Social Security changes—and other statutes.

What about the other two parts of "HEW"—the generic citizens' benefits trilogy: "Health" and "Education"? The number of health-related statutes passed by Nixon's three Congresses (some 30 percent of the "citizens-protection" category) is truly impressive; so is the scope of their coverage. Fifteen specific diseases were targeted for action, and several other Acts dealt with substance-abuse threats to human health. (It's worth noting at this point that at least one knowledgeable reporter commented that ". . . the Nixon administration, perhaps more than any since, proved to be highly effective in combatting drugs."[9]) While there may not be an "EPA-level" innovative statute in this group, PL 93-222—the Health Maintenance Act of 1973—certainly comes close.

Although it was the subject of fewer than half as many Acts as "Health," and even though some two-thirds were "mini-statutes," "Education" was by no means short-changed during the Nixon administration. Uniform, nationwide application of "guidelines and criteria" prohibiting racial discrimination in public schools was forcefully reaffirmed in PL 91-230; likewise, the need for programs to include children subject to special disadvantages. Considerable "fine-tuning" of national educational policies and procedures was also done by PL 92-318 (the third-longest Act in that Chapter).

Chapter 9

Summary and Conclusions

S O, WHAT ARE WE to say in attempting to summarize and evaluate the Nixon legislative record? We know that he made some awful decisions—or at least tolerated the making of them—to get elected and reelected. Those have been rather fully and repeatedly documented and discussed. We know that he used foul and demeaning language in White House meetings. That's on the taped record and, again, has been repeatedly discussed and denounced. Whatever the root causes of these errors, they have weighed heavily on the negative side of the Nixon "equation."

But what about the positive side of the balance? Richard Nixon was our President for some five and one-half years. We elected him to the job twice—once by a very narrow margin, but the second time by one of the largest majorities ever. (Franklin D. Roosevelt carried 46 of 48 States in the 1936 election; Nixon won 49 of 50 in 1972—and so did Ronald Reagan in 1984.) How well did President Nixon do the job we elected him to do? Presumably, we constructed our government to do for us, as our representative, those things which we cannot do for ourselves or for which we need some assistance in the doing. As our system has developed, it is the President who is the main agenda-setter, the chief proposer of policies and programs. It is he also who is the major public advocate of the government's proposals; he's the one with the "bully pulpit." Of course, the job of governing the US cannot be done by one person. Congress is assigned the job of actually turning proposals into proposed statutes, which must be passed by both houses of Congress in identical form and then signed by the President. (If the President refuses to sign the proposed bill—"vetoes" it—it can still become law if Congress repasses it by a two-thirds majority in each house.) The congressional leaders of both parties are, therefore, also key variables in deciding what legislative business gets done or not done.

The 1,671 Acts that became part of the law of the United States while Richard Nixon was our President are surely not to be solely attributed to the fact that he was President when they were so added. But it seems equally clear that the fact of their passage is some evidence of the extent to which the lawmaking function was being fulfilled with him as a leading part of the process. In simpler terms, while Nixon may not deserve *all* the credit for their passage, he must certainly be given *some* of it. Just how much of the credit he deserves is, of course, the key question. How does one decide that?

That kind of allocation would seem to involve the ultimate level of subjectivity—the sort of personal ax-grinding that has been the hallmark of negative Nixon evaluations over the years. Is there any hope for a bit more objectivity from these pages? Having already "disqualified" my own evaluations by confessing that I voted for Mr. Nixon four of five times (being too young in 1952), let me propose a comparative analysis of presidential "effectiveness."

Let us examine President Nixon's "legislative productivity" in comparison with that of eight other modern-day Presidents during their first five and one-half years (up to August 9 of their sixth year in office). Included are the four years of FDR's fourth term, of which Harry Truman served as President for all but the first eleven weeks, added to the first year and six-plus months of HST's own term, and the similar JFK/LBJ combination for years 1961–1966. The two vice-president-as-successor combinations are included for information and for comparison. In each case, there was certainly a significant holdover of staff—at least initially. Moreover, there was also some effort to continue policies of the deceased (and popular) President, and even to some extent, to reemphasize them. (Truman's insistence on "unconditional surrender" by Japan and Germany in 1945,[1] for example, not to mention LBJ's determination to "win"—or at least, not to "lose"—the Vietnam War.) Recognizing that these "succession" combinations involve some very different political dynamics, their inclusion in the analysis seemed preferable to their exclusion. In any event, the fact that their data-points fit rather neatly into the historical timeline seems to underscore the main observation: that the trends in congressional statutory productivity proceed regardless of White House occupant or party control of Congress.

There are, of course, inherent objections to this "productivity" approach. Mere numerical counts of statutes enacted and signed do not take account of the length, significance, or wisdom of the Acts counted. Moreover—and perhaps even more significantly—they do not account for the permutations and combinations of what would seem to be key factors in the legislative process. Of most importance, for example, which party controls the two houses of Congress and by how much: the President's party or the opposition? In one sense, then, the argument is that apples are being compared to oranges. (Or at least, that red delicious apples are being compared to golden delicious to pink ladies to galas to braeburns.)

We did not attempt to tabulate all 1,671 Acts that became law during Richard Nixon's presidency. We have examined over 830 of them—almost exactly half: somewhat fewer than 100 each relating to protection of Workers and Consumers, 100 or a bit over for Veterans and Minorities, and over 220 each for the Environment and for Citizens. Many of these were very brief—less than a page or under two pages. Only a very few of the 1,671 Acts might be considered landmark legislation. So, we are using the 1,671 total Acts as representing President Nixon's "productivity." In the same way, we are simply using the gross totals of Acts that became law during the similar five-and-one-half-year periods for FDR, FDR/HST, Dwight Eisenhower, JFK/LBJ, Ronald Reagan, Bill Clinton, George W. Bush (Bush II), and Barack Obama. Using just the numerical data in this way of course takes a great "leap of faith."

Even these crudest of raw data produce some surprising—perhaps shocking—results. Having been elected with huge majorities in both 1932 and 1936, FDR's legislative productivity (2,205 Acts during the first five-plus years) is *not* the highest of our eight examples. The popular impression of the legislative blizzard that was the New Deal seems to be a bit overdone. The shocking statistic is President Eisenhower's total of 2,426—more than that during the trial-and-error period of the early New Deal, and far and away the highest of any of the seven post-war presidencies compared! The Eisenhower years have generally been viewed as a period of quietness, even somnolence. Supposedly, not much was happening. Eisenhower was playing a lot of golf and napping—still having heart attacks that required Richard Nixon to be on close stand-by alert. It turns out that, somehow, the General was getting a lot done, or at least *seeing that* it got done. (Perhaps some re-evaluation of the Eisenhower presidency is also overdue.)

And, in fact, FDR's first sixty-six weeks of the "New Deal" is not even the second-highest total productivity period. That runner-up position goes to the FDR/HST combination—FDR serving only the first eleven weeks of his fourth term, with Harry Truman as President for the remainder and then being elected in 1948 for his own full four-year term. The 1945-through-August 9, 1950, pairing produced 2,320 Public Acts. (PL 79-30 is recorded as having been approved on April 12, 1945—the date FDR died; the other 2,290, starting with PL 79-31 on April 16, were added while Truman was President.)

We all remember Lyndon Johnson's "Great Society" plan, so it is not completely surprising that the JFK/LBJ combination has the fourth-highest legislative-Act total: 2,079. What *is* unexpected is that about half of their total was already in place when President Kennedy was assassinated and LBJ became President. So, there was no great avalanche of laws due to the Great Society. (JFK, too, may have gotten more done than he is generally given credit for.)

By comparison, the "Reagan Revolution" was quite modest in terms of legislation: 1,454 Acts adopted during his first five and one-half years. Although some important statutes were passed, overall "productivity"—by this measurement—took a significant drop under Bill Clinton: 1,021 Acts during his similar period. George W. Bush's first five-plus years saw a slight deviance from the downward progression: 1,142 Acts passed (a 10 percent *increase* from the Clinton Congresses' total). The historical decline resumed with our final subject ex-chief-executive: only 815 Acts passed for Barack Obama (by this numerical measure, the least productive of all—but what else would one expect from an elected leader with virtually-zero executive experience?)

In the interest of fairness, then, let's now try to factor-in the congressional situation. Richard Nixon faced substantial opposition—Democrat majorities during his *entire* presidency (down 14-10-14 votes in the Senate; down some 50-75-50 votes in the House). By comparison, for much of his presidency, FDR *owned* Congress! There were then only ninety-six Senators—FDR had sixty of them in the 73rd Congress, seventy-two in the 74th Congress, and seventy-eight in the 75th Congress! (The sixteen Republican Senators—there were several "Independents" of various flavors—during 1937 and 1938 must have looked like an AA meeting or a Weight Watchers group.) In the House, the Democrat majorities were about 3 to 1 from 1933 through 1936 and approached 4 to 1 in the 75th Congress! (The eighty-eight Republican representatives in 1937/38 probably didn't need more than one Greyhound Bus to go to a baseball game together.)

If FDR had wanted Congress to pass a law commanding the sun to rise in the East, they probably would have done so—at least during the early years—and he would have signed it![2] The law presumably would not have had the desired astronomical effect, but the point is that it would have been passed and signed. (FDR's longer-term congressional "problems" apparently lay in the opposite direction—trying to ride herd on legislative stampedes: Wikipedia tells us that FDR vetoed an incredible *635* bills over the course of his twelve-plus years as President! Congress may have been overeager to please him, or trying to tell constituents that they were contributing to solving the problems of depression and war, or motivated by unknown factors.[3] In any event, they seem to have sent a lot of unwanted legislation his way.)

After initially omitting the Truman years in this analysis, it seemed necessary to include them. If the JFK/LBJ combination was worthy of inclusion for comparative purposes, the FDR/HST pairing had an even stronger case for admission. FDR was reelected for his fourth term in November 1944, to be sure, but he had served only eleven weeks of it when he died on April 12, 1945. Harry Truman was the President for the remaining 197 weeks and then for his own full four-year term. Truman inherited FDR's Democrat congressional majorities from the 1944 election, but the Republicans swept the field in 1946, gaining thirteen Senate seats and fifty-seven in the House. He was confronted with a (very) hostile Congress for the next two years. The brief Republican tidal wave receded substantially in 1948, with Truman upsetting Thomas Dewey's second run for the presidency and the Democrats regaining control of both Houses of Congress (54 of 96 in the Senate and 263 of 435—plus one "American Labor" ally—in the House).

President Eisenhower did have slim Republican majorities in both Houses for his first two years but then had to deal with comparably slim Democrat majorities for the next four years. For the JFK/LBJ combination, there were huge Democrat majorities all six years: roughly 2 to 1 in the Senate, and +/– 80 or 90 vote majorities in the House from 1961 through 1964, and then about 2 to 1 House majorities during 1965 and 1966. As a significant variation, Ronald Reagan had Republican majorities in the Senate for all of his first six years, but there were Democrat majorities in the House—a situation similar to Obama's during 2011–2014. Bill Clinton had to deal with a still different congressional lineup: his first two years saw big Democrat majorities in both houses, then he had to work with Republican majorities for the next four years. George W. Bush benefitted from Republican majorities all six of his first years, although they were very thin for his first four years.

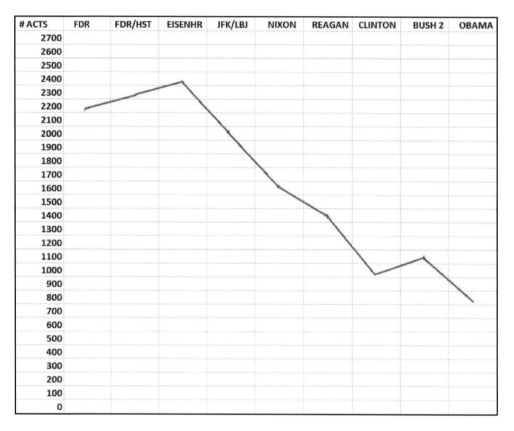

Figure 9.1. Number of Acts per Presidency

And what of the Congresses under our final White House occupant in this analysis: Barack Obama? President Obama was particularly vocal in attempting to justify his lack of progress on the nation's unfinished business by stating that "the Republicans in Congress won't work with me." In fact, Obama enjoyed substantial Democrat majorities in *both* houses of Congress for his first two years and Senate majorities for *all six* years tabulated (six votes in 2011/2012, ten votes in 2013–2014). He used that congressional control to play "cram-down" politics during his first two years—passing his bloated (900+ [mostly unread?] pages) health-care act, for example, with *none* of the 178 House Republicans voting in favor. They were joined by thirty-four House members of the Democrat Party; the final House vote was very close—219 for, 212 against. Is it possible that this sort of "hardball" legislating during the first two years may have "poisoned the well" as far as Republican cooperation was concerned? If Obama was determined to pass controversial legislation that was opposed by substantial minorities, including some members of his own party, might the Republican leadership and members have decided that their only choice was determined opposition?

Of course, the majority side wins. But accepting the legitimacy of that majority-yes vote means that one must also accept the legitimacy of a majority-no vote. It seems incredibly presumptuous to claim that my "Yes" vote in favor of my proposed policy is somehow morally superior to your "No" vote opposing it. It would seem that opposing what one sees as bad legislation (i.e., ineffective, wasteful, damaging, etc.) is as much the moral and legal duty of our elected representatives as is supporting what one sees as good legislation. Gratuitously labeling any opponents as "obstructionists" and blaming them for the lack of progress in dealing with public problems hardly seems conducive to overall legislative productivity. Part of effective leadership—indeed, perhaps the largest part—consists in finding that "middle ground" on which a majority agrees that action can be taken. With our system of President/Senate/House approval being required to produce legislation, it is obvious that very high levels of leadership skills are necessary if the system is to function effectively.

The numerical data presented above suggest that President Eisenhower's executive/administrative/political abilities may have been significantly underestimated by most historical analyses to date. "Ike" has generally been credited with superlative quasi-political skills in holding together the military coalition that prevailed in World War II in North Africa and Western Europe. But, for whatever combination of reasons, he has received too little acclaim for his eight years of presidential leadership—keeping the "Free World" free, and peaceful, and (generally) prosperous. It may indeed be time for serious re-examination of "the Eisenhower years."

One cannot help but wonder how much of this low-key, soft-sell methodology Richard Nixon recognized and absorbed as Ike's Vice President. The "hands-across-the-aisle," working-with-the-opposition-majority results make the question all too obvious. Nixon is generally given credit as a master politician, and it certainly seems that he learned a thing or two from the General.[4] Clearly, President Nixon had a much tougher "legislating" job than President Eisenhower. Objectively, the legislative "deck" was stacked against him—sizeable

Democrat majorities in both Houses for his entire presidency. Subjectively, the "stack" was even higher. "Ike" was the beloved war hero; everybody "liked Ike." President Nixon was subjected to nearly continuous personal attacks throughout his public life—negativities greedily, even joyously, published and republished in much of the media. One wonders how he managed to survive—personally, as well as politically—the ongoing onslaught. That he not only survived but accomplished as much as he did, for as long as he did—both domestically and internationally—says a great deal about the man's toughness and courage (*and* leadership ability).

So, while President Nixon was playing *détente* with the USSR—keeping the nuclear missiles in their silos and subs and remaking the modern world—by bringing China back into the system, he was also participating quite effectively in the US' internal lawmaking process. And he was doing so despite the Democrat majorities in both houses of Congress during his entire presidency. By contrast, FDR hardly ever had to worry much about finding "common ground" with Congress. With the Democrat majorities he had, "common ground" was pretty much whatever he said it was. (He did fail with his plan to "pack" the Supreme Court with enough handpicked extra Justices to guarantee that none of his legislative efforts would be declared unconstitutional. That effort to neuter the Court was too much even for many of FDR's own party.) In contrast, President Nixon could produce no legislation at all unless there was Democrat support for the proposal. He *had* to find "common ground."[5] He clearly excelled at doing so—at least as indicated by the number of Acts produced during his tenure, which place him "fifth," exactly consistent with the chronological progression of these nine case studies.

While President Nixon's productivity seems quite impressive when compared to that of the other eight periods in this data-set, it seems less so when matched against that of the JFK/LBJ combination that immediately preceded him. His 1,671 total represents a "fall-off" of some 20 percent from their combined 2,079. Of course, both JFK and LBJ enjoyed large Democrat majorities in both Houses of Congress throughout their terms. They also had some significant public-psychology advantages working in their favor: the magic of "Camelot," the outpouring of grief following JFK's assassination, and LBJ's experience and credibility derived from his extensive service in Congress—topped off by media coverage that was, for the most part, worshipful. Whether the combined effect of these factors is sufficient to explain the full differential is, of course, problematic. The fact that the JFK/LBJ total itself represents a productivity decline of about 14 percent from Eisenhower's record may indicate that there are other factors at work. It has been suggested that removal of some of the leadership's control mechanisms has made it much more difficult to maintain party unity.[6] Individual Senators and Representatives have become much freer agents. (Senator Ted Cruz immediately springs to mind as a current example.[7])

As we check through the examples post-Nixon, we see the overall downward trend continuing. Reagan's first five-and-a-half years saw enactment of 1,454 statutes—a decline of about 13 percent. Bill Clinton's comparable period produced 1,021 new Acts: down nearly 30 percent from Reagan's total! The Bush II Congresses at least halted the decline (1,142 Acts passed to Clinton's 1,021.) But then there was a further 29 percent loss of legislative output under Obama, to a mere 815 Acts—about one-third of the Eisenhower years' total!

Of course, it may just be that Congress has ceased passing hundreds of flyspeck, small-detail items and concentrated on the big, important programs and projects that really need doing. That would seem to be a desirable development, if indeed true. Intuitively, that explanation seems hard to accept. It would require the sort of collective, collaborative, rational decision-making that seems in very short supply these days. The jury is still out on this question, waiting perhaps for the sort of comprehensive qualitative content-evaluation that would require a massive commitment of time and resources—far beyond the scope of this preliminary inquiry.

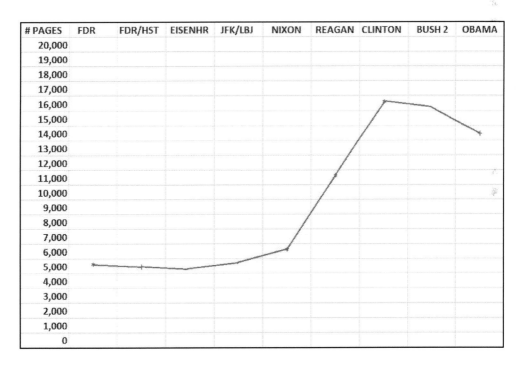

Figure 9.2. Total Number of Act Pages per Presidency

There is, however, another data-set that provides some basis for a more balanced analysis. Although also merely quantitative, rather than qualitative, a comparison of the total pages of statutes produced by Congress during each of the five-year-plus periods studied yields some very interesting insights. Using the number of statutes passed, our ranking of those nine periods was Ike, FDR/HST, FDR, JFK/LBJ, Nixon, Reagan, GWBush, Clinton, Obama. But for the Ike/FDR–HST/FDR and BushII/Clinton (close) "reversals," a historical progression of decline in the number of statutes passed is observable. When we compare the total pages of the Public Acts passed in each of these nine periods, however, the comparative rankings are almost exactly reversed! ("So the last shall be first, and the first last. . . ." *Matthew*, 20-16.)

The 2,426 Acts passed by the Eisenhower Congresses took up just under five thousand pages—the lowest total of the nine case-studies. So, the ranking for that period (1953–1958) did indeed go from "first to last." Using the total-pages standard, the FDR/HST combination goes down from second to eighth; FDR's ranking for 1933–1938 drops from third to seventh. The JFK/LBJ combo drops from fourth to sixth. Nixon ranks fifth on both scales—exactly in historical sequence. Reagan rises from sixth to fourth. Clinton moves from eighth to first! Bush II (also over 16,000 total pages of Acts) rises from seventh to runner-up. And Obama leaps from last/ninth to third—undoubtedly helped by the massive verbiage of "Obamacare." What was a downward trend line from Ike through Obama becomes (at least, overall) an upward trend line, using this different measuring-stick.

It is important to note, however, that while the congressional-product page totals for the first five-plus years under the three most recent Presidents are each roughly equal to the total pages for the similar periods under our first three examples *combined* (FDR, FDR/HST, and Ike), the trend-line for the latest three is itself slightly *downward*—again. The page-total for the Clinton years is 16,751; for Bush II, 16,145; and for Obama's Congresses, 15,436. While the relative sizes of these two decreases are much smaller than those occurring earlier, they at least would seem to suggest the presence of another factor in the "congressional-production" dynamic.

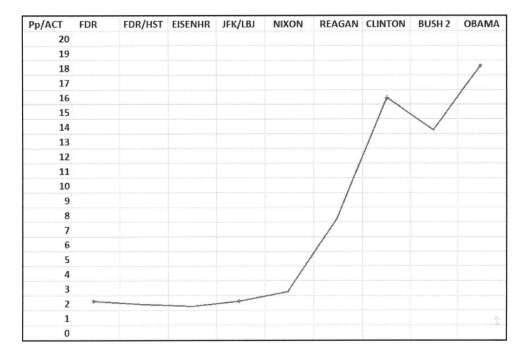

Pp/ACT	FDR	FDR/HST	EISENHR	JFK/LBJ	NIXON	REAGAN	CLINTON	BUSH 2	OBAMA
20									
19									
18									
17									
16									
15									
14									
13									
12									
11									
10									
9									
8									
7									
6									
5									
4									
3									
2									
1									
0									

Figure 9.3. Average Number of Act Pages per Presidency

One other quantitative measure of comparative congressional "productivity" over this span of some eighty-plus years (1933–2014) seemed obvious: the average page-length of the statutes passed. Using this metric, the general historical trend-line is up, as was the case using the total pages in the statutes passed in each of these temporarily-equivalent periods. But, because the number of Acts passed during each period was trending downward, the upward trend for the average page-length was much sharper. The page-average per Act for the first four presidential examples are all under 3.00: FDR 2.59, FDR/HST 2.37, Ike 2.09, and JFK/LBJ 2.84. There is an increase for the Nixon Congresses of a bit more than one-third, to 4.06 pages per Act. By this measure, congressional "productivity" doubles under Reagan (8.12 pages per Act) and then *doubles again* for the Clinton Congresses (16.42 pages per statute)! The average goes down two-plus points for the Bush II Congresses (14.14) but then hits its high point under President Obama at 18.94 pages per statute. So, by this standard, the Obama Congresses move from last to first; the Clinton years are second highest in average statutory page-length; and Bush II Congresses are third. The next three examples are in their reverse historical order: Reagan fourth, Nixon (again) fifth, and JFK/LBJ sixth.

As indicated above, the rankings of the first three presidencies in historical sequence show a declining average page length per statute. A similar contrary trend also characterized the rankings for total pages of legislation and for total number of Acts passed. So, there may be some unidentified factor that influenced the reversal of the trend-lines during the Eisenhower years. In any event, these alternate data-sets clearly indicate that Congress has indeed progressed from passing many, many mini-laws to concentrating on fewer but more substantial pieces of legislation. Whether one agrees or disagrees with the substantive content of the fewer but larger outputs, this trend would appear to be a significant positive development.

Perhaps the most important observation one might make about these three data-sets is the remarkable overall consistency of the historical trend-lines. From the chronologically first six-year period to the second and from the second to the third, the number of Acts adopted rises, and the number of pages adopted and average pages per Act both decrease. From Eisenhower to Obama, the overall trend-lines reverse: generally, downward for the number of Acts passed, upward for the total number of pages of law enacted and for the Acts' average length. The clearly observable differences in presidential skill-sets and policy preferences do not seem to have had any major impacts on either historical progression. Nor, evidently, did the various permutations and combinations of the two parties' control of the House and the Senate. Even more puzzling is the apparent lack of effect of the major economic and social crises—both domestic and international—during this time-span. Presidential assassinations (one successful and two attempted), two impeachments (one threatened, one with Senate acquittal), another President dying in office from "natural causes," wars, and "9/11": none of these seems to have produced the sort of zigs and zags that we see in the numerous pictures of the stock market averages or the price of crude oil.

So, what, if anything, can these objective measurements tell us about President Nixon's performance as our chief executive for five years and seven months? At first blush, perhaps not much—by each measure, he is right where he belongs in the historical sequence spanning eighty-plus years. But on second thought, doesn't this, in fact, say a great deal about his presidency?

Logically, one might have expected to find a significant drop-off in legislative productivity during the Nixon years, as he (and the nation) were "wallowing in Watergate" for the latter part of his presidency—and distracted (to say the least) by Vietnam and its aftermath throughout his White House years. But somehow, despite all the vilification and general media negativity that characterized most of his years as President, Richard Nixon's signature is on as many pieces and pages of Public Acts as his historical placement in this set of nine presidential examples would warrant. Somehow, President Nixon and those Congresses continued doing the country's political business at or near the "going rate." Again, this is not necessarily a validation of the substantive content of the laws that were passed, except for the fact that they were produced by a Republican President and a House and Senate with significant Democrat majorities. There was at least a very considerable amount of legislation on which *both* parties could agree—*and* felt necessary—*and* actually added to the statute-books!

That one bottom-line, net result—all by itself—would seem to indicate that there was a significant positive side to the Nixon presidential years and that some of the credit for those advances must be assigned to him.

Without forgetting the serious risks inherent in attempting a qualitative evaluation of the legislative output of the Nixon presidency, the author's not even making the attempt would seem to be a greater offense. Hopefully, some of the likely partisan bias will be offset by remembering that President Nixon's statutory additions were produced in combination with three Democrat-majority Congresses. Tooting one's own horn for legislation adopted when your party has large majorities in both houses of Congress *and* the presidency might readily be assumed to be a bit "partisan" in content. Claiming *some* credit for being able, as President, to "reach across the aisle" to large congressional majorities of the opposing party, find common ground, and adopt measures thought necessary simply asks for recognition of a considerable level of competence, judgment, and *nonpartisanship*.

So, what can usefully be said, at this point, by way of summary and evaluation? First, the study did not include the entire legislative record for the Nixon years. Appropriations bills were generally omitted, for example, so there is no basis here for claiming that overall military financing was adequate or inadequate. We are looking at the Acts dealing with the Environment, Workers, Minorities, Consumers, Veterans, and Citizens. Second, to some extent, there has been a chapter-by-chapter evaluation as part of the discussion of specific Acts. Third, we are looking at these statutes with the benefit of forty-plus years of hindsight—the nth degree of "Monday-morning quarterbacking." With these caveats, let's see what seems worthwhile in the Nixon legislative record.

Protecting the Environment

Our first area for specific examination was environmental protection legislation, and one reason for that was the overwhelmingly positive evaluation of President Nixon's policies by the "experts"—the various self-proclaimed champions of the environment. To restate that analysis: in 2012, twelve leading environmental-protection groups rated presidential administrations on their pro-environment records. President Nixon was number two—only Theodore Roosevelt ranked ahead of him overall, and two of the twelve groups rated Nixon number one![8]

Admittedly, many of the 200-plus environmental-protection Acts passed during the Nixon years were very short amendments or corrections. But there were also a number that were groundbreaking and positive steps forward. Heading the list, of course, is NEPA itself: PL 91-190, the National Environmental Policy Act of 1969. Three statutes in the "water regulation" group seem worthy of note: PL 91-224, the Water Quality Improvement Act of 1970;

PL 92-500, the Water Pollution Control Act Amendments of 1972; and PL 92-532, the Marine Protection, Research and Sanctuaries Act of 1972. There are also three in the "species protection" category that deserve mention here: PL 91-135, the Endangered Species Conservation Act of 1969; PL 92-522, the Marine Mammal Protection Act of 1972; and PL 93-205, the Endangered Species Act of 1973.

Although there were surprisingly few "air regulation" statutes, the breadth and depth of PL 91-604, the Clean Air Act Amendments of 1970, require its inclusion in this listing.[9] Three other Acts attempt to prevent injuries from the introduction of poisons into the environment: PL 91-601, the Poison Prevention Packaging Act of 1970; PL 91-695, the Lead-Based Paint Poisoning Prevention Act; and PL 92-516, the Federal Environmental Pesticide Control Act of 1972. Finally, there was long-overdue recognition of an unseen environmental "pollutant" in PL 92-574, the Noise Control Act of 1972.

By any reasonable person's standard, whether expert or amateur environmentalist, this part of the Nixon legislative record represents a significant positive accomplishment. And it's well worth mentioning that he achieved most of these remarkable results as a "minority" (43 percent of the 1968 votes) President, before his leadership was confirmed by the 1972 landslide!

Protecting Workers

While there had been some limited national legislation dealing with environmental protection, and considerable "conservation" regulation prior to the Nixon administration, much of its work in that area involved new subject-matter. By way of contrast, "worker protection" had a long and checkered history—both in the US and internationally.[10] Nonetheless, there were still areas where work needed to be done. While some financial compensation was generally provided for workers who sustained on-the-job injuries, there were considerable variances from State to State in the amounts paid and the coverages provided. Coverage for slow-developing diseases caused by long-term exposure to carcinogens, noxious fumes, and the like was particularly problematical. Moreover, the employer's motivation for providing a safe workplace was based on statistical cost/benefit analysis: cost of eliminating or minimizing the injury-producing condition vs. cost of paying compensation times probability of injuries. Aside from the inherent unfairness of leaving that decision in the hands of the employer, doing so seems to be the height of irresponsibility on the part of government. ("Employees will have safe workplaces *if* their employers decide it's in their own best interests to provide safe workplaces!")

So, the passage of the 1970 Occupational Safety and Health Act was indeed a huge step forward. Employers are now *required* to provide a safe workplace, subject to monitoring by an agency of the national government to ensure that they do so, and liable for fines and, ultimately, for a prison term—for a willful violation causing a death. Hopefully, the last situation would be a rare occurrence, but it does seem to send a strong message.

The First Session of the 91st Congress had already passed (and President Nixon had signed) an important job-safety bill covering coal miners. Since labor costs represent a significant proportion of the price of the final product—in contrast with competing energy sources such as oil and hydro[11]—the cost/benefit approach to employee safety has a strong appeal to mining companies. In addition to the obvious dangers involved in drilling and blasting deep underground, these workers were exposed to inhalation of coal dust. Many of them eventually developed "black lung disease" and other long-term illnesses. In an effort to deal with these problems, the President and Congress agreed on the 1969 Federal Coal Mine Health and Safety Act. Specific coverage for black lung disease injury was added in 1972 by the Black Lung Benefits Act.

Finally, ERISA surely represents a crucial improvement for US workers. With all the additional uncertainties they face in the new "one world" economy—off-shoring, out-sourcing, automation, foreign competition, plant relocation, mergers—anything that can be done to protect their earned retirement benefits is of vital importance. Problems may still remain, and pension benefits can still be lost—but worker protection took a "giant leap" forward with ERISA.

Considering that labor unions had constituted a key part of the Democrat coalition since FDR's New Deal, the accomplishments in this area under a Republican President seem quite impressive. Here again, Nixon's willingness to lead from the Center and to find areas of agreement where the public interest could be advanced are praiseworthy.

Protecting Minorities

As with workers, minorities also provided a major support category for the FDR/New Deal/Democrat political assemblage. These voters as well would hardly be considered part of President Nixon's core constituency. In addition, as noted in Chapter 5, seemingly abundant "laws"—both constitutional provisions and statutes—were already on the books. A unanimous Supreme Court had ruled in 1954 that racially-segregated public facilities were inherently "unequal" and thus unconstitutional.[12] Eighty-some percent of the black schoolchildren in the South were, at the time Richard Nixon became President in 1969, not in segregated schools because of a lack of legislation! What was needed for this problem was the executive/administrative determination and skill to make the "law on the books" the "law in action."

After fifteen years of "deliberate speed" (mostly "deliberate," considerably less "speed") and lots of sparkling rhetoric—and a considerable amount of violence—it was plain old Richard Nixon that got the job done. And he got it done quietly—*and* peacefully—*and* quickly! (As noted in Chapter 5, the percentages for black students in segregated vs. integrated public schools were almost exactly reversed by the end of the 1969/1970 school year.) It was done, without any additional congressional action, by President Nixon and his administrative team—working behind the scenes, without publicity, without recognition, and largely without public credit for this amazing accomplishment. Perhaps he was just "in the right place at the right time." But he put himself there, and when the problem presented itself, he saw what needed to be done and saw to it that it did, in fact, get done.

Landmark legislation—the 1964 Civil Rights Act and the 1965 Voting Rights Act—was already on the books. So were the various provisions of the national and state constitutions, prohibiting invidious discrimination by government and its agencies. The output of the Nixon Congresses in this area was, therefore, predominately group-specific, rather than generic. Legislation protecting or enhancing the rights and status of specific disadvantaged groups thus varied markedly.

Highlighting these differentials is the plethora of statutes (many very brief) dealing with Native Americans. Having assumed considerable responsibility for the welfare of these citizens, the national government needs an appropriate package of statutes and regulations to deal with the kinds of issues that would usually be handled by States and cities. President Nixon's basic approach was to increase tribal self-government for those still living on reservations and to promote economic improvement for all. His efforts were applauded by many—but not all—tribal leaders. Especially noteworthy here was his administration's sponsorship of the 1971 Alaska Native Claims Settlement Act (PL 92-203), for which he was applauded as the first President since George Washington to recognize the government's treaty obligations to Native Americans.

The summary section for the Chapter on protection of minorities did specify four other statutes that seemed especially significant—one generic, three "group-specific." PL 93-29, providing services to older Americans, and PL 93-112, providing rehabilitation for those with injuries or limiting conditions, were important gains for those groups. PL 92-318, the Education Amendments of 1972, is listed because it contains the requirement that women have equal access to public school sports programs. That provision has enabled several generations of young women to further develop their physical, mental, and interpersonal skills. The fourth ("generic") law noted was the 1972 Equal Employment Opportunity Act, which greatly strengthened the enforcement of the 1964 Civil Rights Act—thus improving protection for all those covered by the earlier Act.

Were all "minorities problems" solved by Richard Nixon? Of course not—nor have they been in the forty-plus years since he resigned. Were minorities' rights and privileges better protected in 1973 than they had been at the start of 1969? The answer to that one would appear to be "Yes—definitely!"

Protecting Consumers

As noted in Chapter 6 itself, the legislative record in this area was not quite what had been anticipated. The flurry of consumer-finance protection legislation remembered from this period did not quite mesh with the years of the Nixon presidency—"Truth-in-Lending" before, several Acts just after. The 1970 Fair Credit Reporting Act (Title VI of PL 91-508) was the only statute that fit neatly into this preconception, but it is nonetheless an important addition to the consumer-protection framework. Likewise, even though the courts had used provisions of the 1933 and 1934 securities-regulation acts to protect consumers, the 1970 Securities Investor Protection Act did add significant insurance protection for investors' brokerage accounts. And PL 91-408 did the same for the millions of us who have accounts at credit unions.

Even though it seemed like a bit of "overkill" at the time, the 1972 Consumer Product Safety Act did establish a new national watchdog Commission, with authority over many consumer products. Despite the exemptions for cigarettes, guns, cars, planes, and some other items, consumers have gained an additional advocate against dangerous products. We certainly do not have the time, expertise, or inclination to do our own studies on the vast array of products we are offered daily—in print and picture and by voice. Not only is the array vast, but the complex nature of many of the products themselves makes the traditional "Buyer beware" approach largely nonsensical. Having an administrative advocate for safe consumer products, with staff and resources—and a safety mandate—thus seems like a very good idea.

As an excellent cautionary signal against judging the significance of a piece of legislation solely by its length ("mini-statutes" lack significance), the short section of PL 93-153 stands out. Even the strong endorsement here of those Nixon-sponsored changes may, in fact, understate their significance. Giving the FTC more real power to enforce its consumer-protection mandate may, in fact, be more effective in improving consumer welfare than simply placing additional laws on the statute books.

In this area, too, there were thus several significant accomplishments, even though they may have lacked the game-changing scope (and attendant publicity) of the environmental-protection achievements.

Protecting Veterans

The overall record for veterans-protection legislation seems to parallel that for consumers to a considerable degree. Here, too, there was already significant "Law" on the books—most notably, the post-World War II veterans' benefits statutes. One significant legislative effort was therefore directed toward making sure that the Vietnam veterans and their families received similar packages. The special needs of disabled veterans received specific recognition—PL 91-666, for example, which is the 1970 statute providing for purchase of specially-adapted cars. There was at least one notable "extension" of benefits: the 1970 Veterans' Housing Act (PL 91-506), which applied the VA's home-financing program to manufactured housing/mobile homes.

Special concern, via repeated legislative action, was also shown for the POWs and MIAs—and their families. There were continuing efforts to try to ensure prompt and effective medical care and readjustment programs. For those who had made the ultimate sacrifice, there was the official recognition and "Thank You" provided by the 1973 National Cemeteries Act. To some persons, this last item may seem to be a grossly inadequate symbolism. As someone who has attended several military funerals and burials, I can state that there are also many people who feel quite differently about the worth of these ceremonies. Evidently, so did President Nixon and a majority of the 93rd Congress.

Here again, there is a record of solid, meaningful work—even without the fanfare and revolutionary achievements in some of the other areas.

Protecting Citizens

President Nixon and the three Democrat Congresses of 1969–1974 did enact over 200 statutes characterized in this category. Several of them were quite lengthy, most notably the two dealing specifically with the District of Columbia—reorganizing its court system and giving it substantial self-government. Each of these constituted positive change for the "citizens" (and indeed for all those living and working or just visiting) in DC. Three of the longest Acts were generally-applicable sets of amendments, designed to improve Social Security and educational policies and assistance. Two major crime-control acts were put on the statute books, as well as several dealing with prevention and treatment of substance abuse. Health-care was also a high priority: ten statutes providing various forms of support to health-care professionals and fifteen targeting specific illnesses. Several forward steps were taken to improve nutrition and safety for children. Of course, there was also legislation favoring specific groups of citizens—farmers, for example—or specific social activities, such as travel or commerce.

Remembering that not all the (presumably) generally beneficial legislation dealing with the ongoing functions of government is included in these lists, the "citizen-protection" function of the legislative process seems to have been performed very satisfactorily, with several major accomplishments.

"Grading" the Legislative Output of the Nixon Presidency

When evaluating performance, it's hard for someone who assigned letter-grades to several thousand students over the course of fifty-three years of college teaching not to think of "evaluation" in those terms. Admittedly, the "A-B-C-D-F" sorting, even without "pluses and minuses," implies a precision that may be difficult to explain satisfactorily. (On the other hand, "Pass/Fail" or "Credit/No Credit" seems to be an abdication of a significant part of the teaching function—a cop-out.) Administrative pressure for satisfied "customers" and financial pressure for full classrooms may make it difficult for a non-tenured faculty member to feel comfortable in assigning significant proportions of lower-than-desired grades. Some of the pressure for "grade inflation" may be reduced if numerical indicia of performance can be devised and applied and some reasonable benchmarks established and maintained. Alternatively, perhaps faculty can agree on percentages to be assigned in each grade range—at least for classes taken by large enough numbers of students to justify the probable existence of some variance in performance levels.

Before applying a letter-grade evaluation to the legislative output of the Nixon presidency, it is probably useful to explain the meaning of the letter-grades—at least as understood by the current evaluator. "A" indicates superior performance: on a 100-possible-points standard, at least 85 points but more likely 90 points or more. If one uses "pluses and minuses," the A– might be 85–89 points, the As 90–94, and the A+s 95 or above. "B" means above-average but something less than excellent/outstanding. "C" is generally recognized as average performance. ("Keep your job"—at least until they find someone better and still have a need for your "average" contribution—but no "merit" raises.) "D" is unsatisfactory— a warning of serious performance deficiencies in need of correction. "F" (or "E") equates to failure; you did not do even the absolute minimum to receive credit for "being there." It also needs to be noted that academic courses contain a wide variance in subject-matter and in instructional goals. There are thus wide variances among them as to what "performances" are graded and how those various evaluations are weighed in determining the final grade for the course. Even as between different instructors of the same course, there may be more or less significant grading variances, depending on the school's academic policies.

Having the temerity to reduce the productivity of the "Leader of the Free World" and the 535 members of his contemporaneous Congresses (to say nothing of their supporting staffs) to the incredible simplicity of a scale of letter-grades seems the height of foolish egotism. One is strengthened a bit, however, by the belief that the First Amendment protects foolish speech as well as wise—and expression of all the opinions as to which is which. Further, if this "speech" indeed be foolish, it is at least "bipartisan" foolishness—since the subject-matter being "graded" is such itself. And it at least explicitly recognizes its own potential foolishness—which is more than one can say of much of the prior "grading" of this particular POTUS, Richard Nixon.

But enough of this self-justification! How does this fifty-three-year assigner of course grades rate Richard Nixon on the legislative performance in the six areas studied? What is Richard Nixon's "presidential GPA"?

Based on the summary-evaluations above and the slightly-longer Chapter-highlight paragraphs, "Environmental Protection" rates an A+. So does "Worker Protection." Likewise, "Minorities Protection." The legislative output for each of these topics is seen as "outstanding," "superior," and "excellent"—as good as it gets; as good as we've ever seen; better/much better than usual; perhaps the best we can hope for with our checks and balances and powerful interest groups. As one might surmise from having read those same sets of summaries, "Consumer Protection" and "Veteran Protection" are not rated nearly as high on the scale. The output for "Veterans" seems to fall into the "B" category—distinctly above average but not "game-changing." With the addition of the brief section strengthening the FTC's powers, the Nixon years' production protecting "Consumers" rates a slightly higher "B+." Finally, the "Citizen Protection" statutes rate an "A"—based both on the quantity of "HEW" Acts and on several "game-changers" (most notably, the long-delayed DC home rule law). Using a four-points-for-A scale (A+ = 4.5), the legislative productivity of the Nixon Presidency thus grades out as a 4.0 (A)! As has been noted several times in this book, "Not bad, for someone who 'didn't care much about domestic policy'!"

Available Soon . . .

RICHARD NIXON'S COURT

Pruning the Judicial Branch
(*The Age of Nixon* Series, Book 2)

By George D. Cameron III

DEAR READER:

Thank you for your interest in and purchase of *Richard Nixon's America: The Legislative Record (The Age of Nixon Series, Book 1)*. If you enjoyed this book, please be sure to obtain a copy of *Richard Nixon's Court: Pruning the Judicial Branch (The Age of Nixon Series, Book 2)*, available soon at major book retailers.

Sincerely,

Van Rye Publishing, LLC

From the Publisher

Thank You from the Publisher

Van Rye Publishing, LLC ("VRP") sincerely thanks you for your interest in and purchase of this book.

VRP hopes you will please consider taking a moment to help other readers like you by leaving a rating or review of this book at your favorite online book retailer. You can do so by visiting the book's product page and locating the button for leaving a rating or review.

Thank you!

Resources from the Publisher

Van Rye Publishing, LLC ("VRP") offers the following resources to readers and to writers.

For *readers* who enjoyed this book or found it useful, please consider receiving updates from VRP about new and discounted books like this one. You can do so by following VRP on Facebook (at www.facebook.com/vanryepub), Twitter (at www.twitter.com/vanryepub), or Instagram (at www.instagram.com/vanryepub).

For *writers* who enjoyed this book or found it useful, please consider having VRP edit, format, or fully publish your own book manuscript. You can find out more and submit your manuscript at VRP's website (at www.vanryepublishing.com).

Thank you again!

About the Author

GEORGE D. CAMERON III is Professor Emeritus of Business Law at the Ross Business School of the University of Michigan. He earned B.A. and M.A. degrees at Kent State University and LL.B./J.D. and Ph.D. (Political Science) degrees at the University of Michigan. He taught Law at the college level for fifty-three years—the last forty-three at Michigan. In July 1990, he was invited by the People's Republic of China's Ministry of National Defense to teach at the China University of Political Science and Law. He later made a similar visit to the Helsinki School of Economics and Business. With a Michigan colleague, he taught in the U/M's program with Erasmus University (the Netherlands) and U/M's own programs for MBAs in Hong Kong and Sao Paolo. His three Business Law texts total a combined seventeen editions. Retiring in 2014, he published his revised International Law course-pack as *International Business Law: Cases and Materials*.

Professor Cameron's "value added" has been recognized by his students, his colleagues, and third parties. He received the U/M Business School's first "Best Professor" teaching award in 1982 (with all students eligible to vote). He is one of only two B-School Professors to be so chosen *twice* by vote of all B-School students. *Business Week* identified him in 1986 as a notable professor at the "Top Ten" U/M B-School. And the State of Michigan bestowed an Undergraduate Teaching Award on him in 1990. In 1998, Professor Cameron taught one section of LHC 306 Business Law, named by the *Michigan Daily* as one of the two "Best On Campus" courses. His B-School colleagues honored him with their Teaching Leadership Award in 2003. And the Academy of Legal Studies in Business named him the Distinguished Senior Faculty for 2004—at their conference in Ottawa, Canada.

Freed from his "all-in" commitments to students, Professor Cameron has spent the last several years researching, analyzing, and writing on political topics—specifically, President Nixon and his administration. *Richard Nixon's America: The Legislative Record* is a product of those more recent activities, substantially leavened by earlier academic work and a lifelong interest in political phenomena.

Notes

Foreword

1. For a further discussion of this "left/right" problem and the Nixon/Kissinger "partnership," *see, e.g.,* Robert D. Kaplan, "The Statesman: In Defense of Henry Kissinger," *The Atlantic,* (May 2013), pp. 70–76, 78; Henry A. Kissinger, "Between the Old Left and the New Right," 78#3 *Foreign Affairs* (May–June 1999), pp. 99–116; Richard Nixon, "Dealing with Gorbachev," *New York Times Magazine* (March 13, 1988), pp. 27–30, 66–67, 78–79; John G. Stoessinger, "Henry Kissinger and the Anguish of Power," *Saturday Review* (September 18, 1976), pp. 6–10; E. William Proxmire, "The Legality of US Participation in the Defense of Vietnam, *Congressional Record—Senate,* (March 10, 1966), pp. 5274–5279. The Kaplan article is an especially perceptive review and evaluation of Kissinger's work with Presidents Nixon and Ford.

The Nixon-Kissinger partnership is also extensively analyzed by Tom Wicker, in *One of Us: Richard Nixon and the American Dream*, New York, NY: Random House, Inc., 1995—paperback edition, especially Chapter 11: "Channels."

In his 1999 study, historian Melvin Small expresses a very positive evaluation of Nixon's handling of relations with China and the USSR, e.g.: ". . . in the long run, his Soviet diplomacy was a success"; ". . . Nixon took justifiable pride in his China policy"; "He was completely in charge of the China policy . . ."; and "In old-fashioned, Great Power diplomacy with his two Communist rivals, Nixon and his foreign policy team displayed skill and acumen." Small, *The Presidency of Richard Nixon,* (University Press of Kansas, Lawrence, KS, 1999), pp. 118 & 125. However, Small was not as impressed with the Nixon, Kissinger, et al. record in dealing with the rest of the world. In his last sentence of Chapter 4 (immediately following the "skill and acumen" quote), he concludes: "Their foreign policy record with the rest of the world was not as successful—or as admirable." *Ibid.,* p. 125.

2. Theodore H. White, *Breach of Faith: The Fall of Richard Nixon,* New York: Atheneum Publishers/Reader's Digest Press (1975), p. 334.

3. Tom Wicker also notes this "track record" in his Preface to *One of Us: Richard Nixon and the American Dream, op. cit., supra*, endnote 1, at p. xiii.

4. *See, e.g.*, Seymour Hersh, *The Dark Side of Camelot*, Boston: Little, Brown and Company (1997); Ted Schwartz, *Joseph P. Kennedy*, Hoboken, NJ: John Wiley & Sons, Inc. (2003); Christopher Hitchins, "Feckless Youth," *Atlantic Monthly*, (September 2006), pp. 108, 110, 112–115; Caitlin Flanagan, "Jackie and the Girls," *The Atlantic*, (July/August 2012), pp. 133–138, 140, 142; Edward Klein, *Unlikeable: The Problem with Hillary*, Washington, DC: Regnery Publishing (2015); Russell Baker, "The Heights of Charm," *The New York Review of Books*, (September 29, 2016), pp. 4, 6. (The Flanagan article is a particularly telling indictment of JFK.)

5. "I did not have sexual relations with that woman, Ms. Lewinsky"—Clinton's finger-wagging denial of the affair, on national TV—later recanted when he was forced to testify under oath.

6. Hoff rates Nixon's domestic accomplishments as the most important, ahead of the foreign policy work. ("[M]ost of his lasting achievements are in domestic, rather than foreign, affairs—as this study documents. . . .") Joan Hoff, *Nixon Reconsidered*, New York: Basic Books, 1994, at p. 4.

Acknowledging that (at least to an extent) "Hoff has a point," Melvin Small provides us with his own lengthy list of President Nixon's domestic accomplishments:

> The extension of the Voting Rights Act, postal reorganization, the end of Selective Service, the Clean Air Act, the Water Pollution Control Act, the establishment of the Environmental Protection Agency (EPA), the Consumer Product Safety Act and the establishment of an Office of Consumer Affairs in the White House, expansion of the national park system, the Occupational Safety and Health Act (OSHA), the Rail Passenger Service Act that established AMTRAK, the eighteen-year-old vote, the State and Local Fiscal Assistance Act (revenue sharing), the beginning of the federal "war" against cancer, and dramatic increases in federal support for the arts. The list could go on. . . .

(Small, *op. cit., supra*, p. 157)

In his brief summary of the Nixon years—a "Postscript" to the account of Nixon's return to power—his close advisor Pat Buchanan covered specifics from both sets of accomplishments:

> Nixon was the first President since Zachary Taylor in 1849 to take office without carrying either house of Congress. . . .

Yet the years that followed that 1969 inaugural would be a time of extraordinary accomplishment. By spring of 1973, all US troops were out of Vietnam, the POWs were home, every provincial capital was in Saigon's hands. Having mined Haiphong harbor and bombed Hanoi, Nixon had ended the war with honor, as he had promised. Americans had walked on the moon. Nixon had negotiated SALT I and the ABM treaty, the greatest arms limitation treaties since the Washington Naval Agreement. He had ended decades of hostility between the United States and the People's Republic of China dating to Mao's revolution and the Korean War. He had put an end to the draft and signed into law the eighteen-year-old vote, put four justices on the Supreme Court, including Chief Justice Warren Burger and future Chief Justice William Rehnquist. He had created the Environmental Protection Agency, the Occupational Safety and Health Administration, the National Cancer Institute. Though routinely denounced for a "Southern Strategy," by the time he left office he had desegregated the schools of the South and been rewarded in 1972 with the greatest landslide in modern history, winning 62 percent of the votes and 49 states, creating the New Majority that would dominate presidential politics until 1992. He would go on to rescue Israel from defeat in the Yom Kippur War, end Soviet domination of Egypt, and convert that largest of Arab nations into a de facto American ally for four decades, from Sadat through Mubarak.

Had Nixon stepped down in January 1973 he would be ranked as one of the great or near-great presidents. . . .

(Patrick J. Buchanan, *The Greatest Comeback*, [New York: Crown Forum, 2014], pp. 365–366)

Unfortunately, as we know, the "Olympic Gold" of Nixon's first term was followed by the "agony of defeat" during the second term—despite, or perhaps because of, the landslide of 1972.

Introduction

1. Evans, Rowland and Robert D. Novak, *Nixon in the White House: The Frustration of Power*, (New York: Random House, 1971). Tom Wicker also provides a perceptive view of Nixon's preference for foreign policy (greater intellectual challenge, more opportunity to do great things, less interference from other US power centers, et al.) in Wicker, *One of Us: Richard Nixon and the American Dream, op. cit., supra*, Foreword, endnote 3, at pp. 418–421. But he also quotes Nixon, from his autobiography (*RN: The Memoirs of Richard Nixon*, [New York, NY: Grosset & Dunlap, 1978]), as stating that "I was determined to be an activ-

ist President in domestic affairs." Wicker, *ibid.*, p. 412. This statement appears on page 512 in the "1969" chapter of the 1978 paperback edition of *RN*. It is a restatement of an earlier Nixon comment on page 437: "I wanted to be an activist President in domestic policy, but I wanted to be certain that the things we did had a chance of working." *RN, op. cit.*, pp. 437–438.

2. Richard Reeves cites several examples of this approach. Reeves, *President Nixon: Alone in the White House*, (New York, NY: Simon & Schuster, 2002). Wicker also discusses some of the reasons for the selection of the various domestic policy managers—Moynihan, for example, on page 406: "a witty and convivial academic, a Harvard professor"; his thinking was "refreshing and stimulating"; he provided "something of the desired bipartisan cast." Wicker, *op. cit., supra*, endnote 1. *See also*, Reuel Marc Gerecht, "For Your Eyes Only" (review of Moynihan's *Secrecy: The American Experience*, Yale University Press, 1999), *The New Republic*, February 8, 1999, pp. 37–39; and George Will, "The wisdom of Pat Moynihan," *Ann Arbor News*, October 3, 2010, p. A20.

3. Nixon biographers generally seem favorably impressed by his FAP/GAI initiative, even though it was not successful (and thus is not really part of this book's study of his years of legislative outputs). *See, e.g.*, Joan Hoff, *Nixon Reconsidered*, (New York, NY: Basic Books, 1991), pp. 121–137; Evan Thomas, *Being Nixon: A Man Divided*, (New York, NY: Random House, 2015), pp. 249–250. John A. Farrell, however, quotes chief of staff Bob Haldeman's diary as recording that Nixon wanted the plan killed as too expensive and wanted the Democrats blamed for killing it. Farrell, *Richard Nixon: The Life*, (New York, NY: Doubleday, 2017), p. 382. That "quote" requires rebuttal since the President's own version of what happened to his revolutionary proposal provides a quite different impression of who "wanted" what for the FAP:

> [A]fter a brief round of praise from columnists, editorialists, and academics, the liberals turned on the plan and practically pummeled it to death. They complained that the dollar amounts were not enough and the work requirements were repressive. In fact, FAP would have immediately lifted 60 percent of the people then living in poverty to incomes above that level. This was a real war on poverty, but the liberals could not accept it. Liberal senators immediately began to introduce extravagant bills of their own that had no hope of passage. . . .
>
> The interest groups reacted no more admirably. The National Welfare Rights Organization, purportedly representing the interests of welfare recipients, formed an alliance with the social workers, who were threatened with extinction, and denounced the plan.

NWRO called it an "act of political repression" and accused the administration of conspiring to starve children. The plan was even called "racist," despite the fact that immediately upon passage it would have provided roughly 40 percent more money to blacks living in fourteen Southern states—and in 1969 slightly more than half the black population lived in the South. . . .

We fought hard. On April 16, 1970, thanks in large part to the leadership of Jerry Ford with help from [Democrat] Wilbur Mills, FAP passed the House. But the Senate Finance Committee, with Southern conservatives in key positions and no coordinated endorsement from the liberals, kept the plan on ice. . . .

During the fall, I put pressure on the Senate Finance Committee, but my efforts failed. On November 20, the committee voted the measure down, 10-6. In 1971, the House again passed the bill and again the Senate Finance Committee bottled it up.

(*RN, op. cit., supra*, pp. 528–529)

It sounds as if the President gave up on FAP only after he became convinced that his further efforts would be futile. It also seems as if he had a valid reason for believing that the liberal Senators' efforts to "hijack" FAP with their own bloated versions may have solidified Southern Senators' opposition to the whole idea. Stating the Haldeman quote without explaining whose version of the FAP President Nixon may have been referring to and the hard fight that he and the minority House Republicans had made for his version of FAP seems to deny credit for this very important initiative. (*See also*, Warren Weaver, Jr., "Welfare Reform Is Again Rejected by Senate Panel," *New York Times*, [November 21, 1970], p.1.)

In fairness to Farrell, he does also list several of Nixon's major progressive achievements: "Tax reform for low- and middle-income individuals, increased aid for education, a bigger food stamp budget, a 20 percent hike in Social Security payments, and the new annual cost-of-living allowances became law with his approval during his first term." (Farrell, page 375.)

4. Roth, Bennett, "Bush Likely to Unleash Veto over Stem Cells," *Houston Chronicle* (reprinted in *Grand Rapids Press*, July 19, 2006, p. A3).

5. Grimmelikhuijsen, Stephan, Lars Tummers, and Sanjay K. Pandey, "Promoting State-of-the-Art Methods in Public Management Research," 20 *Intl. Public Mgmt. J.*, 7–10 (2017).

6. Having opened the second paragraph of his study of Nixon's White House years with the negative statement, "Nixon was an unpleasant human being," Melvin Small proceeds to explain how that conclusion may affect different analyses in different ways: "For historians of his

presidency, as distinct from biographers, the challenge is to pay attention not just to what he stated in public or murmured in private but to what he accomplished in domestic and foreign politics and his broader influence on American political institutions and culture." *The Presidency of Richard Nixon*, (Lawrence, KS: University Press Kansas, 1999), p. xiii. For many Nixon critics, that distinction seems to have been difficult, if not impossible, to maintain.

Chapter 1. Inheriting the Sixties

1. The daunting challenges posed by Vietnam's geography are forcefully described by Martin Windrow in *The Last Valley: The Battle That Doomed the French Empire and Led America into Vietnam*, Da Capo Press, 2004. The book is a riveting account of the battle at Dien Bien Phu.

More than 500 years earlier (1418–1428), the Chinese empire had suffered a similar humiliation at the hands of rebel Le L'oi, who founded a Vietnamese dynasty that lasted 360 years. He lost battles but escaped, and he ultimately won independence despite what Gavin Menzies describes as "a massive [Chinese] commitment of combat troops." Menzies says this was "the first serious defeat the Ming dynasty had ever experienced." Gavin Menzies, *1421: The Year China Discovered America*, William Morrow (2002), at page 51. It's difficult to name another small nation with a similar record of military success against some of the great powers of the world—China, France, and the US—whatever the particular circumstances of the specific struggle.

For an alternate analysis and "might-have-been" of the Dien Bien Phu battle, *see* Hilaire du Berrier, *Background to Betrayal: The Tragedy of Vietnam*, Belmont, MA: Western Islands, 1965: "The public in the West was never told that the Communist army of Ho chi [sic] Minh was virtually destroyed at Dien Bien Phu while winning its Pyrrhic victory." (caption under picture #3—"A grim-faced lieutenant of the Foreign Legion peers out of a shelter in beleaguered Dien Bien Phu."); "It was established that a one-hour strike by American planes could have saved the beleaguered garrison and changed the course of history. On five separate occasions, such a strike was discussed, but each time, reasons were found to rule out American rescue from the air." (du Berrier, at p. ix.)

Tom Wicker also discussed this "abstention" decision in *One of Us: Richard Nixon and the American Dream*, (New York, NY: Random House, Inc., 1995—paperback edition), pp. 144–147:

> Eisenhower was never willing to commit the US fully in support of the French war to retain Indochina. Early in 1954, with that war on the verge of failure, the president did agree to provide ten B-26 bombers, with two hundred airmen to service (but not to fly)

them—less than half what the desperate French had requested.

The president was wary of being dragged too far into a war that he feared would be bloody and endless and would identify the US with colonialism. . . .

Still . . . Eisenhower . . . was doing more to help than he publicly disclosed. . . . [H]e had ordered the so-called Civil Air Transport—an airline secretly owned by the CIA and later renamed Air America—to help supply Dienbienphu. . . .

Meanwhile, the French army chief of staff, Paul Ely, had concocted with [US] Admiral Radford something called "Operation Vulture"—an American air strike against Giap's siege force at Dienbienphu. . . .

When Nixon and others then argued in an NSC [National Security Council] meeting on April 9 for a conventional air strike, Eisenhower rejected that idea too.

2. It even came to upstage the struggles for civil rights, although many saw important connections between the two causes—both were attempts by people to gain control over their own lives, and both were directed against the elitist class governing the economically-advanced Western nations. For a perspective from the political far-left, see *The Sixties: Years of Hope, Days of Rage*, by Todd Gitlin—one of the first presidents of Students for a Democratic Society (SDS). Founded at the University of Michigan in Ann Arbor, by Alan Haber and a few other "radicals," SDS grew to become one of the most prominent protest groups during that period. In the words of Carl Oglesby (another of SDS's presidents—also [like the author] by way of Kent State, Ann Arbor, and the University of Michigan), SDS was "explicitly democratic, reformist, and nonviolent." Carl Oglesby, *Ravens in the Storm: A Personal History of the 1960s Antiwar Movement*, New York: Scribner (2008), at page 314. Oglesby also states that he "was among those who most insistently pushed SDS into antiwar politics" (page 315). Throughout his memoir, however, he maintains his commitment to nonviolence and openness. For this consistency, he was finally banished from the organization that he had done as much as anyone to build into an important national force.

While the University of Michigan was certainly one of the centers of the 1960s' protest-activism, it was also the place where candidate John F. Kennedy announced the idea that became the Peace Corps—in an evening speech on the front steps of the Michigan Union, on October 14, 1960. A small commemorative plaque was embedded in the union's steps, and the U/M has continued to be a major supplier of volunteers to the Peace Corps. (I missed JFK's evening speech, but I'm quite sure that I was there the next morning to see him leave. I also remember seeing and hearing Vice President Nixon doing a whistle-stop at the Ann Arbor railroad station during the 1960 campaign.)

3. *See, e.g.*, "Senator Eugene McCarthy: Courage-Integrity-Honor" (brochure), McCarthy for President Committee; Eugene J. McCarthy, "Topics: Thoughts on the Presidency" (pamphlet), from *The New York Times*, March 30, 1968; "Eugene McCarthy on the Record" (booklet), Coalition for a Democratic Alternative, (New York, NY: 1968); "The Democrats' Best Candidate" (reprint), from *St. Louis Post-Dispatch*, (April 28, 1968).

4. Louis Menard describes his rather different memory of the event in "Been There: The Presidential Election of 1968," *The New Yorker*, (January 8, 2018), pp. 69–75.

5. For an eyewitness account of what really happened (not what was "officially" reported), *see* John Schultz, *No One Was Killed: The Democratic National Convention, August 1968*, Chicago: The University of Chicago Press (1969). The official description of the carnage as a "police riot" seems wholly misleading after Schultz describes the synchronized, clearly-organized clubbing and beating by detachments of police, not only of the crowds of demonstrators but especially the news reporters with their notebooks and cameras. The police weren't individuals running amok; they were following orders.

6. For some examples of that refurbishing of HHH, see the (self-described) "probing," "highly controversial," "unauthorized" biography by Allan H. Ryskind, *hubert* [sic], New Rochelle, NY: Arlington House (1968); especially Chapter 22 The "New" Humphrey I, Chapter 23 The "New" Humphrey II, and Chapter 24 The "New" Humphrey III.

7. Michael Nelson provides a particularly persuasive explanation of this ticket-splitting—by two major differentials between the parties. Republican presidential candidates were generally perceived as being better at dealing with national issues—foreign policy and cultural values (and less subject to "special interests")—while the more pro-government Democrats were more likely to respond to local and special problems. And secondly, Republicans were a much more "homogeneous" group—economically, socially, and racially—and could, therefore, more easily agree on an acceptable national candidate than the fragmented Democrats, who were a coalition of many groups, some of which had conflicting interests that led to bitter divisions over presidential candidates and party platforms. Nelson, *Resilient America: Electing Nixon in 1968, Channeling Dissent, and Dividing Government*, Lawrence, KS: University Press of Kansas (2014), pp. 245–248.

8. In what I thought was probably the most perceptive and provoking passage in his 687-page text, Tom Wicker wondered how Nixon could possibly have come as close as he did to winning in 1960 (or perhaps, to actually have won, with an honest vote-count in Illinois and Texas):

Despite all the unfavorable developments of the campaign . . . despite handicaps that would have sunk most candidates, the sometimes-derided, sometimes-despised Nixon, a suspect candidate for a minority party, matched virtually vote for vote the remarkable performance of Kennedy and the Democrats. . . .

What explains, then, the fact that this insecure and embittered man, this introvert withdrawing more and more within himself, a repressed intellectual . . . forcing himself into the fancied mold of a typical middle-class American, so nearly won the presidency of the United States over one of the most attractive candidates ever to seek it?

(Wicker, *op. cit.*, *supra*, endnote 1, p. 251)

I think that question still lacks an answer.

9. Those "Eastern establishment" leaders were roundly denounced by Senator Everett McKinley Dirksen of Illinois at the 1952 Republican convention as having led the party to defeat—by nominating Thomas Dewey of New York as the GOP presidential candidate. Dewey lost to President Franklin Roosevelt in 1944 (FDR's fourth election as President) and then lost to Harry Truman in a stunning "upset" in 1948. Dirksen's accusation is quoted by Tom Wicker on page 84 of *One of Us: Richard Nixon and the American Dream*, *op. cit.*, *supra*, endnote 1: "We followed you before, and you took us down the path to defeat. Don't do it to us again."(Note that Wicker used the "membership" phrase in the biography's title.)

More recently, the Main Street/Wall Street stresses have been a significant feature of the Trump takeover of the Republican Party. *See*, *e.g.*, Brian Bennett and Justin Worland, "Beyond the Base," *Time*, (October 22, 2018), pp. 30–35; and Sam Tanenhaus, "Trump's Thought Leaders," *Time*, (October 22, 2018), pp. 36–41. Nancy Isenberg also provides an interesting perspective on the role of "class" in US politics; *see* the "Preface to the Paperback Edition" in *White Trash: The 400-Year Untold History of Class in America*, (New York, NY: Penguin Books, 2017), pp. *xiii–xxiv*. *See also*, Adam Tooze, *Crashed: How a Decade of Financial Crises Changed the World*, (New York, NY: Viking/Penguin Random House LLC, 2018), pp. 457–463: "Across the country, class, not race, was the most important determinant of an American's life chances, and the big story of [Obama's] second term as president was rural white working-class despair." (p. 457.) Hillary Clinton's lack of perception of the scope and depth of that despair was surely a major factor in her loss in the 2016 election. (I hasten to add that she was not alone in missing the boat on that piece of reality. When I informed my colleagues at our November 7, 2016, emeritus luncheon in Ann Arbor that, based on what I had seen the day before, driving across the State, "something was happening" in Michigan, several of them pooh-poohed the idea. "Hillary was up by twelve points in the polls." "Trump was a bad joke." If he was, the "joke" was on Hillary—and her supporters.) *See*, Katie Reilly, "Lessons for 2018 from One of America's Most Tumultuous Years [1968]," *Time*, (December 25, 2017–January 1, 2018), pp. 92–93.

Another presidential candidate dismissed by the pseudo-intellectual "elites" as a joke ("a grade-B movie actor"), Ronald Reagan benefitted from a similar working-class disaffection to carry 44 of 50 States in the 1980 election. *See, e.g.*, Timothy D. Schellhardy, "Midwest Mood: Carter's Support Slides In a Blue-Collar Town That Backed Him in '76" [Warren, Ohio], *Wall Street Journal*, (June 2, 1980), pp. 1, 23.

10. *See, e.g.*, Russell Kirk, *The Political Principles of Robert A. Taft,* New York, NY: Fleet Press Corp. (1967); *The Roots of American Order*, Wilmington, DE: ISI Books (1974); *The American Cause*, Wilmington, DE: ISI Books (2002); *The Politics of Prudence*, Wilmington, DE: ISI Books (1993); *The Conservative Mind: From Burke to Eliot*, Seventh Revised Edition, Washington, DC: Regnery Publishing Inc. (2001). (Kirk's former home in Mecosta, Michigan, is about a one-hour drive from my retirement home in Newaygo.)

11. Vladislav Zubok explains (at least part of) Khrushchev's motivation by noting the Soviet leader's extreme discounting of JFK's abilities: "The [1960] victory of John F. Kennedy heartened Khrushchev because his bête noir, Richard Nixon, lost. Yet he also became convinced that Kennedy was a light-weight, a spoiled rich young man, unready for serious confrontation. . . . Khrushchev felt he could intimidate the new president by his brinkmanship tactics." Vladislav M. Zubok, *A Failed Empire: The Soviet Union in the Cold War from Stalin to Gorbachev*, Chapel Hill, NC (2007), p. 139.

Khrushchev had, of course, already experienced a mano-a-mano confrontation with Nixon—in the well-publicized "kitchen debate" at the 1959 opening of the American National Exhibition in Moscow. Nixon evidently gained substantial political benefit from the iconic photo "depicting Nixon's long finger poking into Khrushchev's chest." Wicker, *One of Us: Richard Nixon and the American Dream, op. cit., supra,* endnote 1, at page 220. *See also,* George W. Healy, Jr., *Mission with Nixon*, New Orleans, LA: The Times-Picayune Publishing Company (1959)—brochure.

12. I must confess that I do not remember being that afraid of a possible nuclear exchange during the "Cuban Missile Crisis." Whether that was from ignorance, or fatalism, or bravado, or mere self-centeredness, I don't know. At the time, I was fully occupied with my teaching duties at Cleary College in Ypsilanti, Michigan—the six fifty-minute classes a day, five days a week, four or five different preparations, and for some terms a seventh (evening) class. In hindsight, that hardly seems a sufficient excuse for what now appears to be a shockingly cavalier attitude toward a potentially world-ending event.

13. Robert A. Cairo, "The Transition: Lyndon Johnson and the Events in Dallas," *New Yorker*, (April 2, 2012), pp. 32–49. Cairo reported that, as the Dallas *Morning News* for November 22, 1963, headlined Texas Senator Ralph Yarborough's "snub" of Lyndon B. Johnson, the Senate Rules Committee was conducting an investigation in DC—into Johnson's alleged financial irregularities. There was also a parallel investigation ongoing at *Life* magazine, which had already published part of the story and was trying to decide whether to publish an immediate update or hold the added information for a longer feature item. (Cairo's full article is a great account of LBJ's transformation from a "hangdog"-looking "second banana" into a calm and determined leader with presidential qualities.)

14. One question asked with some frequency of those of us who ("sort-of") survived the 60s is: "Where were you when JFK was assassinated?" In my case, it was the campus of Eastern Michigan University, in Ypsilanti, Michigan—assisting with students' pre-registration for the winter semester (January–June) 1964. For whatever reason/s, however, I do not have any sharp recollection of the day's details in Ypsilanti.

15. Considerable newsprint has been expended in the debate over whether LBJ's continuous but gradual "doubling down" on Vietnam by increasing US troop levels from several thousand (presumably non-combat) "advisors" to some half-million soldiers and marines constituted a "continuation" of JFK's policy on Vietnam. Indeed, there has been significant disagreement as to what JFK's Vietnam policy was.

16. One of those Great Society programs was "Model Cities"—to promote urban development. Several years after my 1967 purchase of the Ann Arbor home that my family would occupy for the next fifty years, we received a low-interest loan from that program for some necessary remodeling work. (The house had been built in 1914.)

17. In 1965, I was privileged to be part of a delegation from Eastern Michigan University (led by our then-president, Harold Sponberg) that went to DC to consult with our representative from what was then the Michigan Second District, Weston Vivian. I do not recall specific details of our discussions, but I do remember also meeting with our junior Senator, Donald Riegel—and being very favorably impressed by his command of the issues with which we were concerned. Without producing the exact numbers of which dollars paid for which facilities, I do know that Eastern Michigan University subsequently embarked on a very vigorous facilities-construction effort: a new library, a new large classroom building, new dormitories, and more.

Even though the event occurred in 1970—not in the 60s—I feel that I cannot leave this building-the-university story without adding a very sad and discouraging footnote on Eastern

Michigan University's "days of rage." I have a vivid memory of standing in the University Police building with President Harold Sponberg, Faculty Senate President and Economics Professor Charles Helppie, and most of the university's senior administrative staff, listening to the smashing of the large glass windows of the new campus buildings that had been constructed with the funds that EMU had received through the 1960s legislation. It was heartbreaking, especially so, I think, for President Sponberg. He had been so successful in his quest to enhance our campus and our image, and here were these "Vandals," sacking "Rome"! For me, even though it was then 1970, I had had a "close encounter" with the spirit of the 1960s.

It's also worth noting that I had a very close personal relationship to the 1970 shootings at Kent State University. I had four wonderful years there as an undergraduate (1953–1957) and had actually taken the "Introduction to Business" class in North Hall, which the rioters had burned down prior to the shootings, and I had returned in 1958/59 as a graduate student and graduate assistant in Political Science. (As noted in endnote 2, *supra*, Carl Oglesby— later an SDS president—was also a student at Kent State during 1953–1955, before he went to New York and then came back to finish a degree at the University of Michigan. I do not, however, recall any one-on-one interaction with him at either location, although he appears in the KSU yearbooks I have for 1954 and 1955.) For a rather different perspective on the Kent State shootings, *see*, Pauline Toole, "Déjà vu—seven years after," *Michigan Daily*, (October 28, 1977), p. 4. *See also*, "Ann Arbor aids design of Kent State memorial," *Ann Arbor News*, (April 5, 1986), p. A1; "KENT STATE REMEMBERED," *Ann Arbor News*, (May 5, 1986), p. C2.

18. Darrow (1857–1938), the famous trial lawyer who defended *Eugene v. Debs*, "Big Bill" Haywood, Loeb and Leopold, and John Scopes, was born in Ohio—like the author, and also attended the University of Michigan Law School. Darrow, however, did not complete degree requirements but left school to study with a lawyer and then passed the bar exam and began his legal career. One of his best-known cases was the Scopes "Monkey Trial" in Tennessee. Despite Darrow's withering cross-examination of the State's lawyer, William Jennings Bryan, whom Darrow had called as an "expert witness" on the Bible, Scopes was convicted of violating Tennessee's statute that prohibited the teaching of evolution. He was sentenced to pay a fine of $100. His conviction was reversed on appeal. *Scopes v. State*, 276 S.W. 57 (TN 1925); 289 S.W. 363 (TN 1926).

19. Alan Glenn, "The Battle of Ann Arbor," *The Ann Arbor Chronicle*, (June 16–20, 1969), online. The discussion here relies heavily on Glenn's reportage. For whatever reasons, I have no specific recollections of this chain of events.

20. *Ibid.*

21. "This Week in U-M History Oct. 14–20: 1969," *The University Record*, (October 14, 2019), p. 5.

22. Camilla Roper and Capt. J. H. Evans, "North Hall: 1900–2014," online. Here again, I have no personal recollection of this shocking event and no real way of knowing why I do not.

23. *Ibid.*

24. In his 317-page indictment of the "tragedy" (Vietnam and Watergate) that constituted the essence of the Nixon presidency, Tim Weiner allocates one paragraph on page 8 and one footnote on page 185 to the Weathermen. Tim Weiner, *One Man Against the World*, New York: Henry Holt and Company, 2015. The footnote states that the Weathers "set off thirty-eight bombs during the Nixon years; the FBI made no arrests." It also indicates that three top FBI officials—director Patrick Gray, #2 Mark Felt (the "Deep Throat" tipster of Watergate), and intelligence chief Ed Miller—were indicted for illegal evidence gathering and that Felt and Miller were convicted but later pardoned by President Reagan.

In fairness to Weiner, even though his picture of the Nixon years is heavily focused on the negatives, he still makes an occasional complementary comment. Perhaps the most telling appears on page 258, where he describes President Nixon as "one of the most talented and tenacious presidents of the twentieth century"—but in the context of describing him as a convincing liar!

25. "From the Archives: Hearing History," *Eastern Magazine*, (Spring 2018), p. 46.

26. "This Week in U-M History: 1966," *The University Record*, (September 24, 2018), p. 5.

27. Patrick J. Buchanan, *The Greatest Comeback: How Richard Nixon Rose from Defeat to Create the New Majority*, (New York: Crown Publishing Group, 2014), p. 64

28. Interestingly, many of the 60s' "radicals" also—eventually—"came home." *See*, Peter F. Drucker, "Report on the Class of '68," *Wall Street Journal*, (February 3, 1978), p. 10: "The class of '68 has . . . turned into the most probusiness class among college generations in many decades."; *and* Trudy Rubin, "Radicals Have Changed Since The '60s," *Ann Arbor News*, (June 10, 1973), p. 50.

Chapter 2. Legislating and Litigating in the United States

1. Evidently using some not-widely-publicized verbal manipulations, in 1996, Congress passed—and President Clinton signed—the "Curt Flood Act," which invalidated the employment contract restrictions to which Curt Flood had objected. The Act did not, however, reverse the 1922 ruling as to the inapplicability of the Sherman Act. Had Congress somehow acquired the power to regulate baseball's hiring practices, even though the 1922 Supreme Court decision had not been overruled? It's possible to argue that the 1922 case was impliedly overruled by the 1937 Supreme Court validating congressional regulation of labor relations. But that argument would have been available in 1972 as well, and the 1972 Court specifically declared its reaffirmation of the 1922 opinion.

2. In *Schechter Poultry Corp. v. United States*, 295 US 495 (1935), the Supreme Court did state that Congress had gone too far in delegating its legislative authority to the National Recovery Administration. The National Industrial Recovery Act—arguably the centerpiece of FDR's "New Deal"—was declared unconstitutional. Chief Justice Hughes wrote the opinion for a unanimous Court; Justices Cardozo and Stone added concurring comments. Four-plus months earlier, Hughes had written a sort of "preview" opinion for eight Justices (Cardozo dissented), holding that the NRA's "code" for the oil industry was not valid because it had not been adopted by required procedures. (*Panama Refining Co. v. Ryan*, 293 US 388.) However, the Court has subsequently approved "delegations" that have been quite broad.

3. For another example (citing *Belmont* several times), see *United States v. Pink*, 315 US 203 (1942).

4. It is surely presumptuous to suggest criticism of a Supreme Court Justice and former president of the American Bar Association—and a fellow student from the University of Michigan Law School. (The record indicates he attended U/M Law but did not receive a degree.) In addition to law school and our first name, we share one other connection: Justice Sutherland died on July 18, 1942—my seventh birthday.

5. Anyone who doubts the absolute power of Joseph Stalin over the lives and fortunes of every soul in the USSR in 1933 is respectfully referred to in Eugenia Semyonovna Ginzburg's "memoir of Stalin's reign of terror": *Journey Into the Whirlwind*, Houghton-Mifflin Harcourt Publishing Co., New York, NY (1975).

6. *See, e.g.*, Anthony Kubek, *How the Far East Was Lost*, New York, NY: Twin Circle Publishing Co., Inc. (1972), *passim*, esp. Chapters VIII, IX, X.

7. Leventhal suffered the heart attack while playing tennis with one of his law clerks.

8. In *Medellin v. Texas*, 552 US 491 (2008), for example, the Court rejected the idea that the President—acting on his own—could make a treaty effective as supreme national law.

9. One of the allegedly corrupt "other unions" investigated was the Amalgamated Meat Cutters & Butcher Workmen of North America, AFL-CIO, to which the author was forced to pay tribute for four years in order to keep the part-time job that was financing his undergraduate education.

10. The author was indeed privileged to have had another—much closer—personal connection with the matters under discussion. I recall standing outside one of the large windows of the "Lawyers Club"—the rather cavernous lounge in the University of Michigan's Law Quad (packed to overflowing on this occasion)—and listening to the high-level give-and-take going on inside between Teamsters' president Jimmy Hoffa and some 300 of my law-student colleagues. The date was April 7, 1960. (*North by Northwest*, starring Cary Grant, was playing at one of the local Ann Arbor theatres.) As reported by the law school's student news sheet, *Res Gestae*, for April 8, Hoffa had been invited "to talk to the Odd Lot Investment Club about union funds." He said little about the scheduled subject but rather reviewed the union's history and recent legal difficulties—and noted the fact that all the Government's horses and all the Government's men had not been able to put a conviction together. I specifically remember his handling of students' questions and comments on the then-recently passed Landrum-Griffin Act (touted as "labor's Bill of Rights"). My recollection is that he was more than a match for his brilliant but (for the most part) woefully inexperienced questioners. The *Res Gestae* story said that "His candid views on the subject delighted the crowd, which also found favor with his forthright approach in facing tough questioning from the floor." The man was clearly much more than the crude brawler usually portrayed.

11. In the film *A Man for All Seasons*, the point is argued as a defense—unsuccessfully—by actor Paul Scofield, as Lord High Chancellor of England Sir Thomas More, during his 1535 trial for treason for refusing to swear the "Oath of Supremacy" acknowledging Henry VIII as head of the Church of England. More was found guilty by the jury and was beheaded.

12. *See, e.g., Freeland v. Liberty Mutual Fire Insurance Co.*, 632 F.3d 250 (6th Cir. 2011), where a summary judgment for Liberty Mutual by the US District Court was reversed on appeal and the case remanded to the District Court for dismissal, on the basis that the $75,000 difference in insurance coverage was held to be "exactly one penny short of the jurisdictional minimum of the federal courts." Betty Freeland is now free to refile her exactly $75,000 claim in the State courts of Ohio. (Liberty Mutual had filed a motion to remove the

case from the Ohio court to the US District Court for the Northern District of Ohio, which granted the motion. Betty's lawyer did not object to the removal, and the US District Judge evidently did not catch the error.)

Chapter 3. Nixon Protecting the Environment

1. http://www2.epa.gov/aboutepa/guardian-origins-epa. Greenpeace and the Union of Concerned Scientists actually rated President Nixon #1!

2. In reporting on the study, Frank Gannon also recognized the distinction: "Whatever his intentions, Nixon would prove every bit as foundational to environmentalism as Roosevelt was to conservationism." *Ibid.* The separation between the two concepts is not complete, however. In fact, there is evidently more linkage between them than many of us suspected. *See, e.g.*, Nicole Casal Moore, "Fewer biofuels, more green space: Climate action researcher calls for urgent shift," *University [of Michigan] Record*, (October 8, 2018), p.6. Michigan research professor John DeCicco concluded that: "For reducing atmospheric CO2, the most efficient use of ecologically productive land is to leave it alone, or reforest it. Let it act as a natural, long-term carbon sink."

In his comprehensive examination of the "Progressive" period, McGerr notes that Roosevelt also "wanted federal support for Western irrigation projects" and that Congress defeated his "drive to reform the management of water resources." Michael McGerr, *A Fierce Discontent: The Rise and Fall of the Progressive Movement in America*, (New York: Oxford University Press, 2005), pp. 166 & 168. McGerr also makes the point that Theodore Roosevelt was not absolutist about "conservation;" rather, he favored efficient development of at least some natural resources. *Id.*, pp. 164–169.

Fundamental fairness and full disclosure also require noting that Theodore Roosevelt was (and is) not without his critics. In his study of US history from 1877 to 1920, Robert Wiebe characterizes him as "[a] man of unlovely traits who relished killing human beings, nursed harsh personal prejudices, and juggled facts to enhance his fame" and a "forceful preacher of the balanced banalities." And further, "No one of his time better understood the operations of American politics, and no one more shrewdly turned his knowledge to the service of personal glory." Robert H. Wiebe, *The Search for Order*, (New York: Hill and Wang, 1967), pp. 189–190. Theodore Roosevelt's famous "Man in the Arena" speech was quoted by former Ohio Supreme Court Justice Andy Douglas in a speech at Toledo Law School in 2017. ("Alumni News," *Toledo Law Transcript*, [Fall 2017], p. 52.) On the minus side of Roosevelt's more recent press, pages C1 and C6 of the Arts section of the *New York Times* of July 18, 2019, had a large feature story on the negative vibes being perceived from the Roosevelt statue in front of the American Museum of Natural History.

For a more systematic debunking of the myth of Theodore Roosevelt as a "liberal reformer," *see* Gabriel Kolko, *The Triumph of Conservatism*, (Chicago: Quadrangle Books, Inc., 1967—paperback edition). Kolko even challenges Roosevelt's credentials as a conservationist: "There can be no doubt that [President] Taft was not a great conservationist—but neither were Roosevelt nor [his Secretary of the Interior] Gifford Pinchot for that matter."! *Ibid.*, p. 165. The partnership between Pinchot's planning and John Muir's pen is also noted in Bill McKibben's more recent review of two books on the early conservationists: "My Land, Your Land," *The New York Review of Books*, (January 16, 2020), pp. 24–25.

3. Richard Nixon, veto message, October 17, 1972. Congress overrode the veto, 52 to 12, with 36 Senators not voting, and 247 to 23, with 160 Representatives not voting and one voting "present." https://greenlaw.blogs.law.pace.edu/2011/04/01/cwa101/

It might be argued that Nixon's veto of this significant piece of environmental legislation shows a *principled* commitment to environmental protection, rather than a "be-in-favor-of-anything-labelled-as-pro-environment" sort of catering to the professional "tree-huggers" of the world.

Just for the record, President Eisenhower also vetoed 1960 amendments to the Federal Water Control Act that authorized increases "from $500 million to $900 million" for construction of sewage treatment works—for which he felt "the local level" of government bore "the principal responsibility." Dwight D. Eisenhower, veto message, February 22, 1960. Here again, perhaps evidence of a principled opposition to budget-busting congressional spending rather than an "anti-environment" decision.

4. Tom Wicker specifically makes this point: "In the 1968 campaign, . . . neither Nixon nor Hubert Humphrey—both men of sensitive political antennae—spoke more than cursorily of environmental concerns, despite Muskie's [the environmentalist Senator from Maine] presence on the Humphrey ticket [as the candidate for Vice President]. Obviously, the candidates felt no need to. Nor were they pressed to speak on the subject by the reporters trailing them." Wicker, *One of Us: Richard Nixon and the American Dream*, (New York, NY: Random House, Inc., 1995—paperback edition), p. 508.

5. http://www.cleveland.com/science/index.ssf/2009/06/Cuyahoga_river_fire_40_years_a.html. Without citing any such striking example of the problem's existence, Michael McGerr says that, as the twentieth century began, "Americans had a sense of economic limits, new in the nation's history. For the first time, there was a widespread understanding that forests, land, and other resources were not infinite." McGerr, *A Fierce Discontent*, *supra*, note 2, p. 149.

6. Theodore H. White, *Breach of Faith: The Fall of Richard Nixon*, (New York: Atheneum Publishers/Reader's Digest Press, 1975), p. 334. In a 2018 biographical piece on Rachel Carson, Jill Lepore claims that the 1962 publication of *Silent Spring* "launched the environmental movement" and "provoked" passage of the environmental legislation in the Johnson and Nixon administrations. Interestingly, she also quotes President Kennedy—at an August 29, 1962, press conference—as knowing that his administration is "already" investigating the long-term effects of DDT, at least partly as a result of Carson's book. Lepore, "The Shorebird," *The New Yorker*, (March 26, 2018), pp. 64–66, 67–72. However, the fact remains that the vast majority of the landmark environmental Acts have Richard Nixon's signature on them, not JFK's and not LBJ's. The two Democrats, with large majorities in both Houses of Congress and with six-plus years of incumbency after "knowing" about DDT, did not put the environmental revolution on the statute books. Richard Nixon, with his several "prompts" to Congress on what needed to be done, did the follow-up negotiating to get the statutes passed—and the setting-up of the EPA and its policies and programs. (Lepore's assertion of JFK's "knowledge" of the DDT problem in 1962 is confirmed in Tim Flannery's review of William Souder's biography of Carson; Flannery also uses the quote from JFK's 1962 press conference. Flannery, "A Heroine in Defense of Nature," *The New York Review of Books*, [November 22, 2012], pp. 21–23.)

7. Nate Rawlings, "Russell Train," *Time*, October 1, 2012, p. 15. The importance of President Nixon's appointments of Train and William Ruckelshaus (his predecessor as EPA director) is confirmed by Tom Wicker: "At least until 1989, when George [H. W.] Bush appointed the environmentalist William K. Reilly to head the EPA, the two Nixon appointees were considered the strongest leaders the EPA had had." Wicker, *op. cit.*, *supra*, note 4, p. 510.

8. Gannon's comment on the study, referenced in endnote 1, recognized the distinction, as noted above.

9. With the advent of the airplane (and space satellites), the *ad coelum* doctrine had to be modified—significantly. *See, e.g.*, the classic case of *US v. Causby*, 328 US 256 (1946), at pages 260–261. Justice Douglas's opinion for the Supreme Court:

> **It is ancient doctrine that at common law ownership of the land extended to the periphery of the universe—*Cujus est solum ejus est usque ad coelum*. . . . But that doctrine has no place in the modern world. The air is a public highway, as Congress has declared. Were that not true, every transcontinental flight would subject the operator to countless trespass suits. Common sense revolts at the idea. To recognize**

such private claims to the airspace would clog these highways, seriously interfere with their control and development in the public interest, and transfer into private ownership that to which only the public has a just claim.

10. *Louisville & N.R. Co. v. Commonwealth*, 166 S.W. 237 (KY 1914).

11. *Louisville Refining Co. v. Mudd*, 339 S.W.2d 181 (KY 1960).

12. *Village of Euclid v. Ambler Realty Company*, 272 US 365 (1926).

13. *Id.*, pages 390–391.

14. *Lucas v. South Carolina Coastal Council*, 505 US 1003 (1992)

15. *Id.*, pp. 1018, 1019, 1027.

16. *Environmental Defense Fund v. Massey*, 986 F.2d 528 (DC Cir. 1993).

17. *Ibid.*, pp. 529, 532, 536. For a recent affirmation of the international scope of environmental concerns—and of the significance of President Nixon's leadership in dealing with them—*see, e.g.*, Associated Press story, "Global Environment: Ozone Layer Healing, UN Study Finds," *Wall Street Journal*, (November 6, 2018), p. A12: "Earth's protective ozone layer is finally healing from damage caused by aerosol sprays and coolants, a new UN study said. . . . The ozone layer had been thinning since the late 1970s. Scientist [*sic*] raised the alarm and ozone-depleting chemicals were phased out world-wide."

While the ozone problem is largely a "post-Nixon" development—as is the apparent (at least partial) remediation—the increased sensitivity to environmental damage and the use of forceful governmental action to deal with it can surely be traced back to his presidency.

18. Water pollution has been, and continues to be, an ongoing problem. *See, e.g.*, Michael H. Brown, "Love Canal and the Poisoning of America," *The Atlantic* (December 1979), pp. 33–40, 42–47. Michigan, identified by Brown as being one of a few States in his most-threatened ("alarming") category as of 1979, witnessed a drawn-out industrial pollution scandal in 2017/2018—which included the dumping of toxic chemicals in various sites over a period of several years. Garret Ellison, "Michigan tops list of PFAs hotspots," *Grand Rapids Press*, (April 22, 2018), pp. 1A–2A. It also saw a controversy over the massive industrial extraction of water from a large in-ground aquifer for bottling and resale. Jeff Alexander, "Nestle bottling plan riles residents," *Grand Rapids Press*, (January 11, 2007), pp. B1–B2; Ken Kolker, "Nestle water case seeps onto docket at Supreme Court," *Grand Rapids Press*, (January 12, 2007), p. B2; Jeff Alexander, "Paradise or Gold Mine?," *Grand Rapids*

Press, (January 14, 2007), pp. B1–B4; Jeff Alexander, "Residents fear damage to river," *Grand Rapids Press*, (January 14, 2007), pp. B1–B4; Peter Luke, "Disorder reigns supreme in court," *Grand Rapids Press*, (January 14, 2007), pp. B1–B6.

The Michigan Supreme Court affirmed the decision of the Michigan Court of Appeals, dismissing the case filed by the "Michigan Citizens for Water Conservation." The members of the plaintiff group had not shown that they had sustained any specifically-personal, individualized injuries caused by Nestle's activities. In legal terms, the MCWC lacked "standing to sue." *Michigan Citizens for Water Conservation v. Nestle Waters N. Am., Inc.*, 737 N.W.2d 447 (MI 2007). Approval by the Michigan Department of Environmental Quality of Nestle's request to increase water withdrawals to 400 gallons per minute (from 250 gallons per minute)—despite over 80,000 public objections being filed—sparked a new protest at the Nestle plant on April 23, 2018. That controversy continues.

For another ongoing water-pollution problem (plastic shopping bags), *see* Ian Frazier, "The Bag Bill: Taking action on a ubiquitous ecological blight," *The New Yorker*, (May 2, 2016), pp. 32–37. An interesting and potentially divisive "species-protection" problem has also been identified by Natalie Angler in "The Killer Cats Are Winning!," *The New York Review of Books*, (September 28, 2016), pp. 34–35. A 2013 study estimated that prowling house-cats kill *each year—just in the US*—"up to 4 billion birds, 22 billion small mammals, 822 million reptiles, and 299 million amphibians." *SILENT SPRING?* One wonders if Ms. Carson owned cats, and whether she let them out of the house. One might also wonder what sort of social policy "balancing" is being done when six Supreme Court Justices are willing to write off a $100 million (uncompleted) public project to save a handful of "snail darters" while our laws evidently permit the genocide of lesser species at the levels reported by Ms. Angler. (These issues are, of course, far beyond the scope of our present study.)

19. These "river-basin" regulations are an early attempt to deal with another ongoing problem—the ecological health of large-scale, multi-State geographical regions. For a suggested alternative approach, *see, e.g.*, William Tucker, "The Next American Dust Bowl . . . and How to Avert It," *The Atlantic* (July 1979), pp. 38–43, 46–49. For a much gloomier (lack of) "progress report," *see* the brief note by Stephen Gandel, "The Moment—7/24/10: Iowa," *Time*, (August 9, 2010), p. 9. He reported that the American Society of Civil Engineers says that the US' infrastructure needed a $2.2 *trillion* upgrade—as of 2010!

20. H.W. Brands, *The Strange Death of American Liberalism*, (New Haven, CN: Yale University Press, 2001), p. 113.

21. *Chevron USA, Inc. v. Natural Resources Defense Council*, Inc., 467 US 837 (1984).

22. *American Electric Power Company, Inc. v. Connecticut*, 564 US 410 (2011). Political debate continues over the best way to deal with "global warming" and even—to some extent—over its very reality. *See, e.g.*, "Most Americans see climate change where they live," *USA Today*, (December 16, 2019), p. 1A. One of the sharpest divisions of opinion occurs with respect to the role of atomic energy, which has been used to generate a significant share of electric power in several countries. The anti-nuclear forces think that this (partial) solution to the global warming problem is worse than the "disease" itself, that it creates more dangers than it mitigates. *See, e.g.*, Bloomberg Opinion Editorial, "A warming world needs nuclear power," *Grand Rapids Press*, (January 13, 2019), Perspective, p. 5; Joseph H. Weber, "The Mail: The Nuclear Alternative," *The New Yorker*, (December 17, 2018), p. 5; "Nuclear Matters" (ad), *Wall Street Journal*, (April 29, 2014), p. A5; Rhiannon Hoyle, "Prices Pull Plug on Uranium Power Play," *Wall Street Journal*, (September 11, 2013), p. C4; Lawrence Makovich & Jone-Lin Wan, "Nuclear Power: Taking A Long View," *Wall Street Journal*, (March 7, 2012), p. A10; Alan Klein & Atul Arya, "Getting to Scale: Renewable Energy in an Era of Austerity," *Wall Street Journal*, (March 7, 2012); Leslie Kwoh, "Chief Leads NRG From Nuclear to Solar, Gas," *Wall Street Journal*, (March 7, 2012), p. B7; William Tucker, "Fukushima and the Future of Nuclear Power," *Wall Street Journal*, (March 6, 2012), p. A19; Rebecca Davis O'Brien, *et al.*, "The Growing Problem of Nuclear Waste," *Parade*, (March 29, 2009), p. 6; Marton Dunai, "Nuclear Industry's Weak Spot," *Wall Street Journal*, (August 12, 2004), p. A8; Timothy J.V. Walsh, "Turning Our Backs: Kyoto's Mistaken Nuclear Solution," 16 *Georgetown International Environmental Law Review* 147 *et seq.* (Fall 2003); Bruce Van Voorst, "Toxic Dumps: The Lawyers' Money Pit," *Time*, (September 13, 1993). Keith Schneider, "Is Nuclear Winter Giving Way to Nuclear Spring?," *New York Times*, (May 12, 1993), S.4 p.4; Jerry Harkavy, "Activists: Nuclear site fire shows perils of old plants," *Ann Arbor News*, (May 1, 1991), p. A6; "The Legacy of Chernobyl: Disaster for the Lapps," *US News & World Report*, (March 23, 1987), p. 36; Matthew L. Wald, "Hanford Reactor Is Troubled Link in Aging Production Chain," *New York Times*, (December 13, 1986), p. 10; Ben A. Franklin, "Key US Reactor To Shut 6 Months For Safety Moves," *New York Times*, (December 13, 1986), pp. 1, 10; Lindsey Gruson, "Nuclear Power Plant Dismantled," *New York Times*, (November 25, 1986), pp. 17, 20; Ben A. Franklin, "The T.V.A. Mothballs Its Nuclear Ambitions," *New York Times*, (June 8, 1986), section 4, p. 6; Anne B. Fisher and Peter Petre, "Nuclear Power After Chernobyl," *Fortune*, (May 26, 1986), pp. 130–132; Barry Rohan, "The high cost of nuclear power," *Detroit Free Press*, (May 4, 1980), pp. 1F–2F; Shirley Hobbs Sheibla, "Three Mile Island Fallout," *Barron's*, (March 10, 1980), pp. 11, 22–23, 30. *Note* the related concerns arising from the increased international emphasis on nuclear weaponry, *e.g.*, W.J. Hennigan "The New Nuclear Poker," *Time*, (February 12, 2018), pp. 20–25; Simon Shuster, "The Missile Factory," *Time*, (February 12,

2018), pp. 26–33; "The nuclear club grows, but new members are shy," *US News & World Report*, (March 23, 1987), pp. 34–35; Joseph Nye, "When is the threshold crossed?," *US News & World Report*, (March 23, 1987), p. 35. For an example of the possible economic consequences of global warming, *see* Justin Worland, "Coffee's Climate Crisis," *Time*, (July 2, 2018), pp. 41–45. For brief "end-of-the-world" interpretations of the problem, *see* Eric Klinenberg, "The Great Green Hope," *The New York Review of Books*, (April 23, 2020), pp. 55–58; Basav Sen, "America is a rogue superpower on climate," *USA Today*, (December 16, 2019), p. 7A; Frank Jordans and Aritz Parra, "UN climate talks end with no deal on carbon markets," *USA Today*, (December 16, 2019), p.4A; Jonathan Mingle, "Our Lethal Air," *The New York Review of Books*, (September 26, 2019), pp. 64–66; Alan Weisman, "Burning Down the House," *The New York Review of Books*, (August 15, 2019), pp. 4, 6, 8; Michelle Nijhuis, "Early Warnings," *The New York Review of Books*, (June 27, 2019), pp. 37–39; Elizabeth Kolbert, "Coal for Christmas," *The New Yorker*, (December 17, 2018), pp. 15–16; Bill McKibben, "Life on a Shrinking Planet," *The New Yorker*, (November 26, 2018), pp. 46–55 (he does mention the WSJ ozone story noted in endnote 16, *supra*); Justin Worland, "Climate catastrophe seen just 12 years away," *Time*, (October 22, 2018), p. 12; "Now You See It," *The New Yorker*, (October 15, 2018), pp. 97–99, and "Fire Alarm," *The New Yorker*, (September 10, 2018), pp. 35–36; Justin Worland, "The earth faces a climate reckoning. So does the plan to save it," *Time*, (December 25, 2017–January 1, 2018), pp. 64–65; Jeffrey Kluger, "The big melt: climate change in the Alps," *Time*, (December 11, 2017), pp. 52–57; Eric Betz, "Meltdown," *Discover*, (June 2017) pp. 36–47; Susmita Dasgupta et al., "Climate Change and Rural Livelihoods in Bangladesh," *World Bank Research Digest*, (Fall 2015), pp. 1, 8; Ian Frazier, "In the Beautiful, Threatened North," *The New York Review of Books*, (March 7, 2013), pp. 37–38; William Nordhaus, "Why the Global Warming Skeptics Are Wrong," *The New York Review of Books*, (March 22, 2012), pp. 32–34; James Fallows, "Dirty Coal, Clean Power," *The Atlantic*, (December 2010), pp. 64–68, 70, 72–76, 78; Joel Kurtzman, "The Low-Carbon Diet," *Foreign Affairs*, (September/October 2009), pp. 114–122; Michael A. Levi, "Copenhagen's Inconvenient Truth," *Foreign Affairs*, (September/October 2009), pp. 92–104; Jessica Seddon Wallack and Veerabhadran Ramanathan, "The Other Climate Changers," *Foreign Affairs*, (September/October 2009), pp. 105–113; Garret Keizer, "Climate, Class, and Claptrap," *Harper's Magazine*, (June 2007), pp. 9–11; Ruth Greenspan Bell, "What to Do About Climate Change," *Foreign Affairs*, (May/June 2006), pp. 105–113; Elizabeth Kolbert, "The Climate of Man—1," *The New Yorker*, (April 25, 2005), pp. 56–62, 64–71. A somewhat more hopeful view was taken by Worland, in "Wind power catches a mountain breeze," *Time*, (June 5, 2017), p. 30; Jeffrey Ball, "Why the Saudis Are Going Solar," *The Atlantic*, (July/August 2015), pp. 72–80; and also, more recently, by Worland, in "Oil Companies See Green," *Time*, (October 8, 2018), pp. 23–24—

oil and gas companies have been "driven . . . to position themselves as part of the solution to addressing climate change."

Presidents are now required to publish a "National Climate Report" every four years. *See, e.g.*, Michael D. Shear and Brad Plumer, "Trump Could Be Forced to Choose Between Science and His Base," *New York Times*, (August 9, 2017), p. A14.

23. For example, in one early "noise-nuisance" case, adjoining landowners in San Francisco, California, complained about the noise, dust and dirt, and safety concerns generated by an asphalt-mixing plant. The plant was part of a street-paving business that had been established in a "light industrial" zone prior to the construction of additional nearby residences. The city's board of health ordered the termination of the entire operation and the demolition of all the buildings. The business sought a court injunction to prevent the city from enforcing the board's decision. The trial court refused to grant such an injunction. On appeal, the California Supreme Court ruled that the city could certainly order the termination of the asphalt-mixing plant—which was causing the "nuisance"—but that the board's order to terminate the entire business and to dismantle all the buildings was excessive. An injunction could issue to prevent the city's enforcement of the excessive part of the board's order. *Eaton v. Krimm*, 18 P.2d 678 (CA 1933).

24. The claim in *Causby*, note 9, above, was that the noise (and lights) from the US government's over-flying planes frightened the inhabitants, interfered with their sleep, and prevented their chicken-ranch operation. The Fifth Amendment to the US Constitution prohibits the national government from "taking" private property for public "use" unless "just compensation" is paid for what is taken—as do at least some State constitutions.

25. *Gitlow v. New York*, 268 US 652 (1925); *Whitney v. California*, 274 US 357 (1927); *Stromberg* v. *California*, 283 US 359 (1931).

26. *Saia v. New York*, 334 US 558 (1948).

27. *See, e.g.*, *West Virginia State Board of Education v. Barnette*, 319 US 624 (1943), ruling that the State could not penalize school children who had religious reasons for refusing to salute the US flag—reversing *Minersville School District v. Gobitis*, 310 US 586 (1940). The *Saia* case (endnote 26) involved the use of a sound truck to broadcast religious messages.

28. *See, e.g.*, *Murphy v. Cupp*, 31 S.W.2d 396 (AK 1930): injunction denied as to construction of church tabernacle as an addition to a Baptist Church located in a residential neighborhood.

29. *See, e.g.*, *McPherson v. First Presbyterian Church of Woodward*, 248 P. 561 (OK 1925):

operation of a gas station would interfere with the holding of religious services in two churches; contra, *Franklin Street Methodist Episcopalian Church v. Crystal Oil and Gas Co.*, 163 A. 910 (PA 1932).

30. *Bencosme v. Kokoras*, 507 N.E.2d 748 (MA 1987).

31. *McLain v. Real Estate Board of New Orleans, Inc.*, 444 US 232 (1980).

32. As the former owner of a 100-plus-year-old house, the author is very appreciative of the problem.

33. The short news item makes a brief reference to a report on the study which had appeared in the *Journal of the American Chemical Society*. The researchers/authors are Gesine K. Veits, Kelsey K. Carter, Sarah J. Cox, and Anne J. McNeil. The reference seems to indicate volume 138 of the J/ACS, at pages 12228–12233—published September 2016.

34. *Keller v. Welles Department Store of Racine, and Another*, 276 N.W.2d 319 (WI App. 1979).

Chapter 4. Nixon Protecting Workers

1. The story is recounted in the made-for-TV movie *Truman*. That version has President Truman literally "passing the hat" for contributions from the press corps accompanying him to pay the train crew so that he could continue his "whistle-stop" presidential campaign.

2. Brennan was, in fact, appointed by President Nixon to be Secretary of Labor in 1973, and he served until replaced by President Ford in 1975. In Brennan's 1996 obituary in the New York Times, Robert McFadden cites the then-Labor Secretary Robert Reich as noting that it was during Brennan's tenure that two landmark worker-protection statutes (ERISA and the 1973 Rehabilitation Act) were passed. Robert D. McFadden, "Peter Brennan, Union Head and Nixon's Labor Chief," *The New York Times*, (October 4, 1996).

A 1979 commentary prompted by Meany's retirement and succession by Lane Kirkland noted that some Labor leaders thought that they should have a larger role in setting the nation's foreign policy. Ben Rathbun, "Organized Labor: Changing of the Guard," *The Atlantic*, (December 1979), pp. 6, 10–14.

3. The other basic weakness in the US' labor/management structure is the traditional union view of the company (or at least its current management) as "the enemy." This was certainly understandable in the bad old days of open physical warfare (the "Battle of the Overpass,"

for example—as the UAW tried to organize Ford Motor workers). Nearly as bad, or perhaps even worse, was the management attitude in the early post-war years of simply giving the unions anything they wanted and then passing the increased costs along to the consumers by raising prices or lowering quality. This "worked" only as long as the US had the only large-scale manufacturers; when European and Asian producers reentered world markets, US companies lost significant market shares—even in the US. It's taken some very hard knocks—the bankruptcy of General Motors and the drastic loss of "market share" by unionized labor, e.g.—to somewhat convince at least some representatives of labor and management that they are all in the same boat. If the boat sinks, all hands lose their rides.

For a passionate (and persuasive) defense of the "employer-as-enemy" position and the concomitant necessity for the (undemocratic) forcing of all to join, *see* James A. Gross, "The NLRB: Then and Now," *Labor & Employment Law*, (Winter 2011), pp. 213–229.

4. *See, e.g., NLRB v. General Motors*, 373 US 734 (1963); *Pattern Makers' League v. NLRB*, 473 US 95 (1985); *Chicago Teachers Union v. Hudson*, 475 US 292 (1986).

5. *Harris v. Quinn,* 134 S. Ct. 2618 (2014).

6. *Ibid.* The (seemingly) final step in this progression of cases was taken by the five-Justice majority of the Court at the end of the 2017/2018 Term, when they at last overruled *Abood*. Justice Alito again did the honors for the majority in *Janus v. A.F.S.C.M.E., Council 31*, 138 S. Ct. 2448 (2018). The fact that it took forty-one years for the Court to correct what appears to be a gross violation of the First Amendment rights of the objecting employees illustrates the importance of Court appointments and the President's responsibility in making the nominations. President Nixon was, of course, acutely aware of this responsibility, as he struggled to find a jurist from the South who could be confirmed. His greatest success was in nominating William Rehnquist, who eventually became Chief Justice and began an overdue reconsideration of several points of statutory and constitutional interpretation. (*See, e.g.*, the *Albrecht* case noted in Chapter 2 [endnote 30].)

7. Rising unemployment raised concerns about the efficacy of the macro-economic "game-plan" adopted by President Nixon's economic team. *See, e.g.*, Sidney L. Jones, *Public and Private Economic Adviser: Paul W. McCracken*, (Lanham, MD: University Press of America, 2000), pp. 218–235. Patrick Buchanan (one of President Nixon's closest confidants) identifies my late colleague Dr. McCracken as one of Nixon's top economic advisers—along with Milton Friedman, Arthur Burns, and Alan Greenspan. Patrick J. Buchanan, *The Greatest Comeback*, (New York, NY: Crown Forum, 2014), pp. 137–138. Paul had been one of three members of Eisenhower's Council of Economic Advisors and was the chairman of

Nixon's CEA. *See, e.g.*, Paul W. McCracken (interview), "The Prospects for 1972 Are Now Markedly Improved," *US News & World Report*, (August 30, 1971), pp. 48–52; Richard M. Nixon, "President's Economic Policy in His Own Words" (radio/TV address & *The Executive Order on Wages, Prices*), *US News & World Report*, (August 30, 1971), pp. 62–65.

In 1971, believing that Nixon's decision to impose wage and price controls to try to deal with inflation was a serious mistake, Paul resigned from the CEA. As reported by Joan Hoff, President Nixon and most of the other members of his economic team subsequently came to agree with McCracken. Joan Hoff, *Nixon Reconsidered*, (New York: Basic Books, 1994), p. 143. For an example of the policy and personality disagreements over economic strategy within the Nixon administration, *see, e.g.*, Bruce Agnew, "Washington Outlook: Connolly vs. Schultz—Again," *Business Week*, (May 19, 1973), p. 44; for an immediate post-Nixon perspective, *see, e.g.*, Herbert Stein, "Grounds for Pessimism," *Wall Street Journal*, (December 12, 1974), p. 18. Some twenty years later, McCracken's views seemed remarkably consistent with those expressed in the 1971 interview: "A Great Time to Be Alive—Economically Speaking," *Twenty-fourth Annual William K. McNally Memorial Lecture*, Ann Arbor, MI: School of Business Administration, The University of Michigan (1991).

8. When the author started his first salaried job as a high school senior in December 1952, with the A&P store in Newton Falls, Ohio, the wage rate was 89.5 cents an hour. (Our meat department employees were represented by the Amalgamated Meat Cutters and Butcher Workmen of North America, AFL-CIO. The other employees belonged to the Retail Clerks union and had a starting wage of 87 cents an hour.) To the best of my recollection, after several raises and having qualified as a "journeyman," when I graduated from college in 1957 and left for law school, I was making $2.34 an hour—plus an extra 25 cents an hour for every hour worked after 6 p.m. (The A&P store in Ravenna, Ohio, to which I had transferred when I started college, closed at 9 p.m., and it was not open on Sundays or most holidays.)

9. 317 US 111 (1942).

10. *United States v. Lopez*, 514 US 549 (1994).

11. The general rule is stated in section 492 of the *Restatement of the Law, Second: Agency 2d*: "A master is subject to a duty that care should be used either to provide working conditions which are reasonably safe for his servants and sub-servants, considering the nature of the employment, or to warn them of risks of unsafe conditions which he should realize they may not discover by the exercise of due care."

The underlying case law is illustrated by *Scott Burr Stores Corp. v. Morrow*, 180 So. 741 (MS 1938):

[W]e have a case here where fellow servants, with the knowledge of the master, had engaged in the negligent habit of leaving the elevator shaft unguarded in such a manner as to show actual knowledge on the part of the master that the place of work was not reasonably safe. . . .

[T]he duty of the master to furnish the servant with a reasonably safe place in which to work was a continuing duty, that is to say, the duty of the master in that regard is not satisfied by putting the place in a reasonably safe condition once and then allowing it to become dangerous while the servant is at work, but he must exercise reasonable care to keep it reasonably safe at all times. . . .

The evidence, although conflicting, was sufficient to go to the jury on the question as to whether the [Store] had exercised reasonable care to discharge its nondelegable duty of keeping the elevator shaft closed, or to provide sufficient light in that immediate locality to avert the danger of employees falling into the same. Of course, the semidarkness of the place, as testified to by [Morrow], and the alleged failure to provide, or the refusal in the interest of economy to permit the use of, sufficient light, is material only to show the degree of care required on the part of the appellant to see to it that the elevator shaft was kept closed when employees were required to pass close by the opening in the discharge of their duties.

We are of the opinion that . . . the judgment [for the employee, Morrow] **should be affirmed.**

(In Mississippi and a few other States—and the US Supreme Court—the party asking for review by the higher court—the "Appellant" or "Petitioner"—is listed first in the title of the appeals court's decision. Morrow sued the Store and won. The company appealed, so it is listed first in the title of the appellate case.)

12. As an example of this approach, the Michigan statute specifies payments for permanent physical injuries (losses of various body parts), based on the injured employee's average weekly wage for the quarter-year immediately preceding the injury: for loss of a thumb, 65 weeks of payments; first finger, 38 weeks; second finger, 23 weeks; third finger, 22 weeks; fourth finger, 16 weeks; great toe, 33 weeks; other toe, 11 weeks; hand, 215 weeks; arm, 269 weeks; foot, 172 weeks; leg, 215 weeks; eye, 162 weeks. Measurements are provided for determining the point at which loss of a "hand" becomes loss of the whole arm, or loss of a "foot" becomes loss of the whole leg—for compensation purposes. Despite its obvious advantages over this sort of "carving up" of injured workers, OSHA had its critics. *See, e.g.*, "Why Nobody Wants to Listen to OSHA," *Business Week*, (June 14, 1976), pp. 64–68, 72;

"Labor Agency Issues Stringent New Rules Limiting Workers' Exposure to Benzene," *Wall Street Journal*, (February 3, 1978), p. 7. (The reality of this financial "dissecting" of the injured worker under the Michigan statute was forcefully brought home to the author in June 2019, when one of his daughter's fingers very nearly lost a section when one of her nursery-school students slammed a heavy metal door against it. The absence of compensation for the excruciating pain attendant to such injuries seems grossly unfair to the injured employee.)

13. Ralph Waldo Emerson, "Self-Reliance," *ESSAYS: First Series* (1847).

14. Richard Nixon, "Special Message to the Congress on Employee Benefits Protection," (March 13, 1970), THE AMERICAN PRESIDENCY PROJECT; Richard Nixon, "Special Message to the Congress on a Pension Reform Program," (December 8, 1971), THE AMERICAN PRESIDENCY PROJECT; Richard Nixon, "Special Message to the Congress Proposing Pension Reform Legislation," (April 11, 1973), THE AMERICAN PRESIDENCY PROJECT.

15. John L. Conway, "The Private Resolution of Employment Benefits Disputes," *Michigan Bar Journal*, (September 2016), pp. 44–46.

16. James A. Wooten, *The Employee Retirement Income Security Act of 1974*, University of California Press, Berkeley, CA, 2004, pp. 51–79; James A. Wooten, "'The Most Glorious Story of Failure in the Business': The Studebaker-Packard Corporation and the Origins of ERISA," 49 *Buff. L.R.* 683 (2001).

17. A similar situation had arisen in Michigan in 1955, when Kaiser-Frazer Corporation shut down its huge Willow Run plant near Ann Arbor. Some 1,100 of the company's nearly 12,000 Michigan employees filed a lawsuit asking the court to terminate the pension trust which had been set up and to distribute the trust's $6 million in funds to the workers. In affirming the trial court's dismissal of the lawsuit, the Michigan Supreme Court relied heavily on the contract language creating the trust. *George v. Haber*, 72 N.W.2d 121 (MI 1955).

18. Wooten, *op. cit.*, *supra*, note 16, p.1. He also tells us that "The labor movement was divided." Some unions were already administering pension funds and may have feared changes. *Ibid.*, pp.7–8. For an example of extreme negativity, *see*, Shirley Hobbs Scheibla, "ERISA Eraser: The Pension Law Can Wipe Out a Company," *Barron's*, (April 12, 1982).

19. *Ibid.*, p. 81.

20. *Id.*, p. 116.

21. *Id.*, p. 155.

22. *Id.*, p. 168.

Chapter 5. Nixon Protecting Minorities

1. James A. Farrell, *Richard Nixon: The Life*, New York: Doubleday (2017), p. 393—citing Dean Kotlowski, *Nixon's Civil Rights: Politics, Principle, Policy*, Cambridge, MA: Harvard College (2001).

2. *Brown v. Board of Education of Topeka, Kansas*, 347 US 483 (1954).

3. According to Sarah K. Mergel, "HEW studies showed that few integrated schools were free from violence." Mergel, *Conservative Intellectuals and Richard Nixon: Rethinking the Rise of the Right*, New York: Palgrave Macmillan (2010), p. 124. She also notes that, while some 74 percent of those surveyed "accepted" integration of the schools, "only 2 percent believed busing was an appropriate means to combat racism." And further, that "the same liberals making desegregation policy in Washington had moved out of the city to send their children to all-white schools. . . . By 1968, there were around 139,000 black students and 9,000 white students in the District's public school system [as opposed to roughly equal numbers before the 1954 *Brown* decision]." *Id.*

4. Joan Hoff, *Nixon Reconsidered*, New York: Basic Books (1994). For a more recent re-weighing of the Nixon years, *see* John A. Farrell, *Richard Nixon: The Life*, New York: Doubleday (2017). Tom Wicker's Nixon biography also does a good job of balancing the positives and negatives. Wicker, *One of Us: Richard Nixon and the American Dream*, New York, NY: Random House, Inc. (1991 & 1995).

5. Kotlowski, *op. cit.*, *supra*, note 1.

6. *Id.*

7. H.W. Brands, *The Strange Death of American Liberalism*, (New Haven, CN: Yale University Press, 2001), pp. 114–115. Wicker's discussion of Nixon's desegregation success is also quite respectful. "[T]he indisputable fact is that he got the job done—the dismantling of dual schools—when no one else had been able to do it. . . . At least after early 1970, it was Richard Nixon's formula, deliberately conceived, meticulously carried out." Wicker, *op. cit.*, *supra*, note 4, at p. 506.

8. Erica Frankenberg and Gary Orfield, editors, *Resegregation of Suburban Schools: A*

Hidden Crisis in American Education, Cambridge, MA: Harvard Education Press (2012). *Cf.*, Kristen Bahler, "Workplaces Are More Segregated Than 40 Years Ago. What Gives?," *Money.Com,* (March 2018), pp. 28–29.

9. For an initial familiarization with some of the legalities involved, *see* Michael D. Petoskey, "The Fundamentals of Federal Indian Law: A Brief Orientation," *Michigan Bar Journal* (May 1986), pp. 438–443; James A. Bransky, "The Political Status of Indian Tribes in Michigan," *Michigan Bar Journal* (May 1986), pp. 444–450; Garfield W. Hood, "Return of the Laughing Whitefish," *Michigan Bar Journal*, (May 1985), pp. 400–404, 406–407; George D. Cameron III, "A Note on the Legal Status of Native Americans," *University of Michigan Business Review*, (September 1979), pp. 27–28; James Mann, "Business Breakout For America's Indians," *US News & World Report*, (May 28, 1979), pp. 68–71. As an example of the possible commercial implications of this special status, *see* George D. Cameron III, "Indian Taxation of Reservation Minerals: A Domestic OPEC in the Making?," *American Business Law Journal*, (Fall 1984), pp. 429–438; Ken Wells, "Cold Cash: North Slope Eskimos Borrow on Oil Taxes To Acquire Amenities," *Wall Street Journal*, (May 16, 1984), pp. 1, 16; "Indian tribes can tax their mineral wealth, high court says," *Ann Arbor News*, (January 26, 1982), p. B9. *See also*, David H. Getches, "Conquering the Cultural Frontier: The New Subjectivism of the Supreme Court in Indian Law," *California Law Review*, (volume 84, 1996), pp. 1573–1663; *Cayuga Indian Nation of New York v. Pataki*, 413 F.3d 266 (2d Cir. 2005); *US v. Sioux Nation of Indians*, 448 US 371 (1980). For a look at the current status of the taxation issue, *see* Tanya Gibbs and Jennifer Saecki, "State Taxation of Tribal Businesses," *Michigan Bar Journal* (August 2019), pp. 30–32.

10. Robert H. Wiebe provides an interesting insight into how some of these treaty violations occurred in the late 1800s: "With neither the will nor the apparatus for continuous supervision, administrators in Washington declared the law at the outset and perhaps checked a few of its results at some later date. . . . [O]nce Congress had acted, power effectively dispersed to the recipients. Even where broad government management seemed imperative, people simply muddled along without it. Settlers in the Western territories . . . were by default forced 'to improvise mining laws, exercise the harsh prerogatives of vigilante justice, preempt lands illegally . . . and shape a confused, unrealistic Indian policy to serve their own ends'." Wiebe, *The Search for Order*, New York: Hill and Wang (1967), p. 32.

Alan Dawley provides a similar analysis: "In the period when Yankee adventurers, grim sodbusters, and US cavalry were dispossessing Indians of their 'free land,' all manner of villainy, treaty breaking, and massacre was justified by blaming the victim for not tilling the soil, abstaining from alcohol, or being Anglo-Saxon." Dawley, *Struggles for Justice: Social Responsibility and the Liberal State*, Cambridge, MA: The Belknap Press of Harvard University Press (1991), p. 29. *Cf.*, "A Life of Disillusionment, Poverty—and Pride Too," *National Observer*, (May 6, 1968), p. 22. For a much more sinister view of the US' Native-Americans policy, *see* Alex Ross, "The Hitler Vortex," *The New Yorker*, (April 30, 2018), pp. 66–73. *See also*, Ian Frazier, "Staying Native," *New York Review of Books*, (August 15, 2019), pp. 37–38: "[D]uring Johnson's and Nixon's presidencies the government noticed that Indian poverty and unemployment had increased under termination [policies]. It switched back to an emphasis on tribal sovereignty and Indian self-determination yet again. Many tribes that had been terminated applied for and won official re-recognition."

As evidence of the continuing relevance of these issues, *see* Bart T. Stupak and Justin Nemeroff, "2015 Acknowledgement Regulations Invalidate Native American Treaties," *Michigan Bar Journal* (August 2019), pp. 22–25; *Little River Band of Ottawa Indians v. National Labor Relations Board*, 747 F.Supp.2d 872 (W.D. MI 2010); and *Wagnon v. Prairie Band Potawatomi Nation*, 545 US 95 (2005). What appears to be a very significant recent win for reservation tribes was reported by Oliver Willis in the *Michigan Independent*, (July 2022), p. 9: "EPA allocates millions under Biden infrastructure law for tribal water access projects."

11. *People of the State of Michigan v. LeBlanc*, 223 N.W.2d 305 (MI App. 1974). *LeBlanc* did not end the controversy; *see, e.g.*, "State pays for study of fishing rights," *Detroit Free Press*, (August 30, 1999), p. 2B; "Groups ask to intervene in fishing rights case," *Ann Arbor News*, (June 3, 1984), p. A21; Tom Opre, "Agreement will guard trout stocks," *Detroit Free Press*, (April 1, 1985), p. 15E; "New DNR director Skoog takes tough stand on fishing rights," *Ann Arbor News*, (September 1, 1983), p. B7; "Judges lock horns over gill nets," *Ann Arbor News*, (March 12, 1981), p. A8; "Chippewa protected from gill net sentence," *Ann Arbor News*, (November 4, 1980), p. A12. In another Michigan case, the "Children of the Chippewa" failed to convince the State courts that the tribes who had negotiated a treaty granting land for the establishment of a university had intended to create a trust by which Native Americans would receive free tuition thereto. *Children of the Chippewa, Ottawa and Potawatomi Tribes v. The University of Michigan*, 305 N.W.2d 522 (Mich. App. 1981). *See also*, William E. Cole, "U-M – Indian treaty case arguments heard," *Ann Arbor News*, (June 13, 1980), p. A-4; and "High court won't hear Indian suit," *Ann Arbor News*, (December 13, 1982), p. A3.

No readily-ascertainable principle for winning or losing appears in similar cases. *See, e.g.*, "What is a tribe?," *The Economist*, (January 4, 1978), pp. 34, 36; Jill Norgren and Petra T. Shattuck, "Still Fighting the Indians," *Juris Doctor*, (October/November 1978), pp. 30, 32, 34; William E. Blundell, "Arizona Indians Win Victory Over US: Refuse $33 Million," *Wall Street Journal*, (December 17, 1981), pp. 1, 14; *New York Times*, "Settlement lets

Indians turn to capitalism," *Detroit Free Press*, (April 6, 1984), p. 13A; "Indian Land Claims Rejected," *New York Times*, (January 18, 1987), Section 1, p. 21; Wallace Turner, "Eskimos Win $10 Million in Lawsuit," *New York Times*, (June 25, 1987), p. 9; "Tribe's Land Claim Voided In Vermont," *New York Times*, (June 18, 1992), p. A12; James E. Roper, "IRS won't honor treaty with Indians," *Ann Arbor News*, (May 24, 1992), p. A7; Lyn Riddle, "South Carolina Settling Catawba Claim," *New York Times*, (November 15, 1992), p. 32.

12. For a discussion of the conflicting currents of assimilation and segregation during the period of "progressive" reform, *see* Michael McGerr, *A Fierce Discontent: The Rise and Fall of the Progressive Movement in America*, New York: Oxford University Press (2003), pp. 202–209. In a much more recent development, a significant proportion of Native Hawaiians have campaigned for federal government recognition of their special status, asking for treatment similar to the Indian tribes in the continental US and Native Alaskans. Rhonda McMillion, "Kamehameha's Children," *ABA Journal*, (January 2008), p. 65. Although Hawaiian Senator Daniel Akaka was not able to get his desired legislation passed prior to his retirement in 2010, the Department of the Interior adopted a rule in September 2016 which seems to achieve his objective—recognition as a semi-sovereign ethnic unit. Presumably, there will be further installments in this story. (The Kamehameha Schools survived a "discrimination" lawsuit when the US Ninth Circuit Court of Appeals ruled that their admissions favoritism of Native Hawaiian children was justified. *Doe v. Kamehameha Schools/Bernice Pauahi Bishop Estate*, 470 F.3d 827 (9th Cir. 2006).)

13. Starting in 1977, an estimated 12,000 Navajos were required to vacate certain lands in favor of the neighboring Hopi tribe. This "settlement" of a long-standing dispute was described as "the United States' largest forced relocation of people since Japanese-Americans were interned during World War II. Over an extended period of time, some members of each tribe had settled on the reservation land of the other tribe." Bill Curry, "Hundreds of Navajos forced off lands," *Ann Arbor News*, (April 10, 1986), pp. B1–B2. Susan Brown describes a similar "traumatic relocation" of a Canadian Ojibway tribe in "Canadian tribe feels itself dying," *Detroit Free Press*, (April 4, 1983), pp. 1A, 15A. The Lake Superior Ojibwe now have their own publication—promoting traditional skills and explaining their treaty rights. *See, e.g., Mazina'igan,* (Spring 2022 issue: 16 pages).

14. One smaller tribe—"with the help of church and university groups"—has taken an innovative approach toward improving its housing conditions. The Mexican Kickapoo of Eagle Pass, Texas, purchased 125 acres about eight miles south of the town, with the intent of living there and integrating further into the larger society. David Maraniss, "Things are changing for the Kickapoo Indians," *Ann Arbor News,* (June 18, 1986), pp. F1–F2.

Native American entrepreneurs have also been quite successful in establishing (legal) on-reservation gambling operations. *See, e.g.*, *Michigan v. Bay Mills Indian Community*, 572 US 782 (2014); *Colombe v. Rosebuud Sioux Tribe*, 835 F.Supp.2d 736 (D. SD 2011); Fox Butterfield, "Indian Casino Revenues Grow to Sizable Segment of Industry," *New York Times*, (June 16, 2005), p. A18; Thomas E. Weber, "Idaho Tribe Uses Loophole to Put Gaming on Web," *Wall Street Journal*, (February 4, 1998), pp. B1, B6; "Las Vegas North: Buying chips from the Chippewa," *US News & World Report*, (February 9, 1987), p. 31; Jacquelynn Boyle, "Tribal bingo's big bucks mean less for state, charitable groups," *Ann Arbor News*, (July 1, 1984), p. A14; Michael Lewis, "Tribe's bingo palace may be bad luck for non-profit groups," *Ann Arbor News*, (May 21, 1984), pp. A1–A2; Susan Brown, "For some Canadian Indians, money just keeps rolling in," *Detroit Free Press*, (April 4, 1983), p. 15A. *See also*, David Treuer, *The Heartbeat of Wounded Knee*, New York, NY: Riverhead Books (2019), Part 6 "Boom City—Tribal Capitalism in the Twenty-First Century." Treuer identifies *Bryan v. Itasca County*, 426 US 373 (1976); *Seminole Tribe v. Butterworth*, 658 F.2d 310 (5th Cir. 1980); and *California v. Cabazon Band of Mission Indians*, 480 US 202 (1987) as the three main court cases providing the basis for tribal-reservation gambling. He had previously discussed the importance of the *Bryan* case in his semi-autobiographical study, *Rez Life* (New York, NY: Grove Press [2012], pp. 225–238), but he also noted that the Supreme Court had ruled only two years later that tribes did not have jurisdiction over non-Indians for offenses committed on reservations (pp. 148–151). (Litigating continues. *See* James A. Keedy, "The History of Indian Legal Services," *Michigan Bar Journal* [August 2019], pp. 26–28; Matthew L.M. Fletcher, "Professionalism in tribal jurisdictions," *Michigan Bar Journal*, [November 2022], pp. 24–28.)

15. For an application of these principles to a current problem-set, *see* Lance Boldrey, "Cannabis on Tribal Lands: An Alternative to Michigan Regulation of Marijuana," *Michigan Bar Journal* (August 2016), pp. 20, *et seq*. Boldrey indicates: "While there is some legal dispute as to whether land acquired in trust by the federal government for a tribe is Indian Country, as a practical matter, such land is typically proclaimed 'reservation' land through 25 USC 467, meaning that most if not all land held in trust for Michigan tribes is Indian Country, and state criminal jurisdiction over tribal members is lacking."

For an update on the marijuana issue, *see* Jeff J. Davis, "Michigan Marijuana Laws: Michigan Tribes Can Participate, but How?," *Michigan Bar Journal* (August 2019), pp. 38–41; Scott F. Roberts and Griffin Kas, "The Michigan Cannabis Industry and the Dormant Commerce Clause," *Michigan Bar Journal*, (June 2021), pp. 20–24; Allison M. Arnold, "Criminal Law Issues After Passage of the MRTMA: Uncertainty Remains," *Michigan Bar Journal*, (June 2021), pp. 26–30; Shyler Engel, "Will Regulated Weed Bring New Coke?,"

Michigan Bar Journal, (June 2021), pp. 32–36; Michelle R.E. Donovan, Jason Canvasser and Danielle M. Hazeltine, "The Evolving CBD and Hemp Market," *Michigan Bar Journal*, (June 2021), pp. 38–43; and Seth Quidachay-Swan, "Researching Marijuana Law," *Michigan Bar Journal*, (June 2021), pp. 52–53. (Obviously, June 2021 was a themed issue on "Cannabis Law." Author Donovan was identified as "a director of the State Bar of Michigan Cannabis Law Section," and the Section's next meeting—at Northern Michigan University on September 3—was announced on page 58.)

On a related problem, *see* Patrick M. Shannon, "A Tribal Court's Response to the Prescription Drug and Opioid Crisis," *Michigan Bar Journal*, (August 2019), pp. 34–36. For a recent example of *State* "paternalism," *see* Norika L. Kida Betti and Cameron Ann Fraser, "Michigan Indian Family Preservation Act at Seven Years," *Michigan Bar Journal*, (November 2019), pp. 32–34.

16. Joan Hoff quotes two Native American leaders as being strongly supportive of President Nixon's policies: Bruce Wilkie, executive director of the National Congress of American Indians (saying that Nixon is ". . . the first US President since George Washington to pledge that the government will honor obligations to the Indian tribes") and Peter MacDonald, Navajo tribal leader (saying that Nixon is ". . . the Abraham Lincoln of the Indian people"). Hoff, *op. cit.*, *supra*, note 4, at p. 28. (Some rather "elevated" company for someone who "didn't care much about domestic policy"!)

Tom Wicker also refers to the Wilkie tribute. Wicker, *One of Us: Richard Nixon and the American Dream*, (New York, NY: Random House, Inc., 1995—paperback edition), pp. 820–821.

More recently, the Ojibwe (Chippewa) author David Treuer expressed similar favorable evaluations of President Nixon's policies regarding Native Americans: "[T]he 1970s turned out to be pretty good years for Indian tribes. Nixon's administration turned out to be a good one for Indian tribes—millions of dollars were appropriated for the Indian Financing Act of 1974 and the money went into insurance, loan, land and business projects." Treuer, *Rez Life*, New York, NY: Grove Press (2012), p. 220. In his later work, *The Heartbeat of Wounded Knee* (New York, NY: Riverhead Books, 2019), Treuer describes Richard Nixon as: "a surprisingly good [P]resident as far as Indian policy was concerned" (p. 278), and later, Treuer is evidently thankful that "federal Indian policy seems to have settled into the track laid down during the Nixon administration: that of self-government, self-determination, and a government-to-government relationship between the federal government and the tribes" (p. 417).

17. Wicker, *op. cit.*, *supra*, p. 520. Needless to say, it has taken a rather extensive set of litigations (398 federal-court cases identified on July 31, 2021) to try to integrate the 1971

ANCSA into the web of special rules applying to Alaska and its native peoples. Seven of the 398 were decisions of the US Supreme Court. Two involved the same dispute, between State regulations permitting hovercraft use on the Nation River and National Park Service rules that prohibited them: *Sturgeon v. Frost*, 577 US 424 (2016) and 139 S. Ct. 1066 (2019). In each decision, a unanimous Court upheld Sturgeon's right to operate his machine; the NPS rules could not be applied since the river was not "public" land (but now rather privately-owned land). Earlier cases upheld the EPA's regulatory authority over Alaska operations (*Alaska Department of Environmental Conservation v. EPA*, 540 US 461 [2004]) and the ICC's authority to regulate rates for use of the Alaska pipeline (*Trans-Alaska Pipeline Rate Cases*, 436 US 631 [1978]). Consistent with its later hovercraft rulings, the Court had decided in 1998 that land that had been conveyed to an "Alaska Native corporation" by the ANCSA was no longer "Indian country" with a semi-sovereign power to collect taxes. *Alaska v. Native Village of Venetie Tribal Government*, 522 US 520. (The State of Alaska had objected to the Village's having that power, which would remove the State's power of taxation—and regulation—as to some 1.8 million acres of land!) All the Justices had also agreed that the US District Court had improperly issued an injunction banning all offshore operations over the Outer Continental Shelf by oil companies that had purchased leases there from the US Department of the Interior: *Amoco Production Co. v. Village of Gambell*, 480 US 531 (1987).

As of this writing, the most recent decision of the Court rather appropriately—and perhaps not all that surprisingly—involved the covid-19 epidemic and the Government's response to it. The specific issue was the legal status of the "Alaska Native Corporations" (ANCs): were they eligible to receive the financial aid provided by the Coronavirus Aid, Relief, and Economic Security Act (the CARES Act)? The Treasury Department asked the Department of the Interior (the administrator of Native American assistance programs) for its opinion, and the DOI said the ANCs qualified as "tribes." The Treasury then set aside $500 million of covid funds for the ANCs. Other tribes (who would receive less money) sued to prevent the payments to ANCs. The US District Court for the District of Columbia agreed with Interior and Treasury, but the US Circuit Court for DC overruled: *Confederated Tribes of the Chehalis Reservation v. Mnuchin*, 976 F.3d 17 (2020). The new Secretary of the Treasury, Janet Yellen, asked for Supreme Court review.

A badly-scrambled set of Justices reinstated the District Court's ruling: Treasury and the ANCs win. Justice Sotomayor's opinion was joined in full by four of her colleagues: Chief Justice Roberts and Justices Breyer, Kavanaugh, and Barrett (two "liberals" and three "conservatives"). Justice Alito agreed with most of Sotomayor's reasoning—Parts I, IIC, IID, III, and IV. But Justice Gorsuch dissented, joined by Justices Thomas and Kagan (two "conservatives" and one "liberal"). They felt that a profit-making (or at least trying-to) corpora-

265

tion was not an "Indian government"—the traditional meaning of "tribe." *Yellen v. Confederated Tribes of the Chehalis Reservation,* 210 L.Ed. 2d 517 (2021).

18. *Morton v. Mancari,* 417 US 535 (1974). While Justice Blackmun's analysis seems reasonable, it may seem somewhat inconsistent with the same court's unanimous (for eight of the same Justices, Justice Brennan not participating) decision just three years earlier in a similar case, challenging two apparently neutral "employment criteria" because they had a "disparate impact" on a "protected class" (African-American employees). In an effort to upgrade the 95-person workforce at its Dan River power plant in Draper, North Carolina, Duke Power Company required that each one either possess a high school diploma or pass an intelligence test; those who met neither requirement would be assigned only to lower-status jobs. Claiming illegal racial discrimination was occurring, thirteen of the fourteen African-American employees filed a lawsuit (*Griggs v. Duke Power Co.,* 401 US 421 [1971]). Both the US District Court and the US Fourth Circuit Court of Appeals ruled in favor of Duke Power, on the basis that there could be illegal discrimination only if the employer's intent to discriminate was proved. No intent, no violation of the 1964 Act. Chief Justice Burger (for the unanimous Supreme Court) disagreed:

> **The Act proscribes not only overt discrimination but also practices that are fair in form, but discriminatory in operation. The touchstone is business necessity. If an employment practice which operates to exclude Negroes cannot be shown to be related to job performance, the practice is prohibited.**
>
> **On the record before us, neither the high school completion requirement nor the general intelligence test is shown to bear a demonstrable relationship to successful performance of the jobs for which it was used. Both were adopted, as the Court of Appeals noted, without meaningful study of their relationship to job-performance ability. Rather, a vice president of the Company testified, the requirements were instituted on the Company's judgment that they generally would improve the overall quality of the work force.**
>
> **The evidence, however, shows that employees who have not completed high school or taken the tests have continued to perform satisfactorily and make progress in departments for which the high school and test criteria [were used]. The promotion record of present employees who would not be able to meet the new criteria thus suggests the possibility that the requirements may not be needed even for the limited purpose of preserving the avowed policy of advancement within the Company.**

The difference in result is presumably explained by the fact that the BIA convinced the

Court that its "Indian preference" criterion was indeed substantially related to successful performance of the BIA positions in question, while Duke Power was not able to do so for either of its two employment criteria. In a different context, much the same sort of justification has been used to successfully defend even *intentional* racial discrimination, i.e., "affirmative action" in university admissions. *See, e.g.*, Thomas J. Bray, "U-M Plaintiffs: 'Two wrongs don't make right,'" *Detroit News*, (August 29, 1999), p. 7B; *Grutter v. Bollinger*, 539 US 306 (2003); and *University of Texas at Austin v. Fisher*, 136 S. Ct. 2198 (2016).

19. A very interesting international comparison on this point is provided by Margaret Scott, "Indonesia: The Saudis Are Coming," *The New York Review of Books*, (October 27, 2016), pp. 56–58. Indonesia is attempting to reconcile its avowed secular and democratic political system with proposed expansions of Saudi-sponsored radical-Islamic schools. *See also*, Margaret Scott, "Indonesia: The Battle Over Islam," *The New York Review of Books*, (May 26, 2016), pp. 37–39.

20. In Fall 1957, the author's handwriting was eminently legible but quite slow in its production. In my first year, I had great difficulty in filling the "blue-books" in which we wrote our essay answers to the law school exams. Taking off a year to complete my course work for a Master's in Political Science, I bought a cheap portable typewriter and taught myself to type ("hunt-and-peck"). When I returned for my second and third years of law school, I took the option of going to the special room with my portable and *typing* my exam answers. I think this was worth at least a half-grade improvement in my exam performances.

But my point here is my memory of the Tax Law exam. I went to the room, got the exam booklet, sat down, set up my typewriter, and was reading the first question when I heard the "brrrrr-t" of an electric portable. A female colleague had already read the first tax question, done her analysis, and was typing her answer. Since I had not even read the first question, it was somewhat dispiriting, to say the least. I think I did get a "C" grade, anyway. ("Gender equality"?)

21. Brands, *op. cit., supra*, p. 115.

22. Farrell, quoting Kotlowski, *supra*, note 1. Wicker also states the 90+ percent figure, in Wicker, *One of Us: Richard Nixon and the American Dream*, *op. cit.*, *supra*, note 4, at page 504.

23. Farrell, *op. cit.*, p. 392.

24. *Ibid.*, p. 393.

25. Brands, *op. cit.*, p. 115.

26. *Ibid.*

27. Marc Levinson, *The Great A&P and the Struggle for Small Business in America*, New York: Hill & Wang (2011), p. 268. Even in small cities and towns, A&P stores tended to be "right downtown." The A&P store in Newton Falls, Ohio, where I started work in December 1952, was in the middle of the one-block "downtown." The Ravenna store to which I was transferred when I started college at Kent State University in September 1953 was across a side street from the Portage County courthouse, which was in the center of town. I was unable to transfer to the A&P store in Kent since that was in a different administrative district of the company, but it was located only one block away from the main downtown intersection of that city.

Nancy Isenberg, in her examination of the continuing existence and significance of class in America, points out the importance of "location" as a marker of class—including the sort of grocery stores available: "Location is everything. Location determines access to a privileged school, a safe neighborhood, infrastructural improvements, the best hospitals, the best grocery stores." Nancy Isenberg, *White Trash: The 400-Year Untold History of Class in America*, (New York, NY: Penguin Books, 2016), p. 317.

Chapter 6. Nixon Protecting Consumers

1. Robert A. Skitol, "1969: The FTC's Mid-Life Crisis and Near-Death Experience," *Antitrust*, (Fall 2014), pp. 23–26.

2. There has been considerable litigation interpreting the 1933 and 1934 Acts, most of it producing favorable results for complaining investors. Notable earlier cases include *Escott v. Barchris Construction*, 283 F. Supp. 643 (S.D. NY 1968) and *Securities Exchange Commission v. Texas Gulf Sulphur*, 446 F.2d 1301 (2d Cir. 1971). A list of subsequent important decisions would surely cite *Chiarella v. Securities Exchange Commission*, 445 US 222 (1980) and *Dirks v. US*, 463 US 646 (1983). What some consider a plethora of such cases has not, of course, remedied all possible harms to investors. Nor did SIPA: a few weeks after Nixon's resignation, efforts were under way in Congress to improve SIPA. Allan F. Hussey, "Strengthening SIPC: That's the Aim of Sweeping New Proposals," *Barron's*, (September 16, 1974), pp. 11, 14–15, 20.

3. *Henningsen v. Bloomfield Motors, Inc.*, 163 A.2d 69 (NJ 1960).

4. *Ibid.*

5. *Hymowitz v. Eli Lilly & Co.*, 539 N.E.2d 1069 (NY 1989).

6. *X-Tra Art v. Consumer Product Safety Commission*, 969 F.2d 793 (8th Circuit 1992).

Chapter 7. Nixon Protecting Veterans

1. Many veterans were already familiar with mobile homes, or "trailers." "Faced with a severe housing shortage, the federal government purchased trailers for soldiers, sailors, and defense workers." Nancy Isenberg, *White Trash: The 400-Year Untold History of Class in America*, (New York, NY: Penguin Books, 2016), p. 241. Isenberg notes that these alternative housing units acquired an unsavory image early on (the inhabitants were labeled "trailer trash") and that the negative view still persists to a considerable degree. *Ibid.*, at pp. 241–247.

2. *In re Agent Orange Product Liability Litigation*, 577 F. Supp. 740 (E.D. NY 1984), 603 F. Supp. 239 (E.D. NY 1985), 611 F. Supp. 1396 (E.D. NY 1985), 818 F.2d 179 (2d Cir. 1987), 689 F. Supp. 1250 (E.D. NY 1988).

3. *See, e.g., Bendix Corp. v. Stagg*, 486 A.2d 1150 (DE 1984). *See also*, Ben A. Franklin, "Scrutiny of Agent Orange Data Allowed," *New York Times*, (November 17, 1987), p. 13.

4. Efforts had also been made to get legislation passed at the State level. *See, e.g.*, "Vietnam veterans press for action on Agent Orange: Rally at Capitol [sic] Building draws 250 vets," *Ann Arbor News* (May 8, 1986), p. A14.

5. *Time,* (October 10, 2012), p. 46.

Chapter 8. Nixon Protecting Citizens

1. As we now know, the package warnings proved to be somewhat less than compelling reasons to stop smoking. Cigarette sales continued at high levels—and still do, some forty years later! So, even the smokers who did manage to kick the habit were still being subjected to "second-hand" smoke—having to inhale the fumes from nearby smokers' use—at work, in restaurants, at sporting events or cultural performances, and elsewhere. Confronted with this continuing problem, concerned persons pressured government agencies and private organizations to adopt policies to ban smoking completely, or at least in certain areas. *See, e.g.*, "San Francisco Officials Cite Success With Law" and Jonathan Friendly, "Plan to Restrict Smoking in New York City Faces Considerable Opposition," *New York Times*, (April 13, 1986), p. 26; Irvin Molotsky, "Washington Bears Down on Smoking: The FTC Took R.J. Reynolds to Task Last Week," *New York Times*, (June 22, 1986), p. 8E.

In 2009, by statute, the Food and Drug Administration was finally given regulatory jurisdiction over tobacco. Smokers, ex-smokers, and even victims of second-hand smoke continued to file lawsuits, some successful, thereby adding to the cost of doing cigarette business.
In 1998, major tobacco companies agreed to a "settlement" with forty-six States and five US
territories, whereby some $246 billion would be paid into a special fund over the following
twenty-five years. Ostensibly, these dollars were reimbursement for the tobacco-caused
health-care costs paid by the States, with the intent that a substantial share of the fund would
be used for anti-smoking efforts, as well as direct public health costs. (Since the settlement
terms had no requirement that the States in fact so use the money, not very much of it was in
fact spent for anti-smoking activities. *See, e.g.*, Andrew Nehring, "State Tobacco Settlement
Funds Go Up in Smoke," Citizens Against Government Waste [May 12, 2016]—accessed
via *Wikipedia*.) Many States did, however, raise cigarette taxes by massive amounts, putting
a much larger financial "penalty" on those continuing to smoke.

2. In one such case, tobacco companies challenged the constitutionality of the FDA's proposed rule requiring inclusion of the graphic images on all cigarette packages. The US District Court in Washington, DC decided the case in favor of the US Food and Drug
Administration, and the tobacco companies appealed that decision. Deciding that the Rule
violated the tobacco companies' constitutionally-protected freedom of speech, the US Court
of Appeals for the District of Columbia reversed (by a two-to-one vote) that trial court decision. The following quotation is from the Appeals Court's written opinion:

> **In the Proposed Rule, FDA lamented that their previous efforts to combat the to-
> bacco companies' advertising campaigns have been like bringing a butter knife to a
> gun fight. According to the FTC, tobacco companies spent approximately $12.49
> billion on advertising and promotion in 2006 alone, employing marketing and ad-
> vertising experts to incorporate current trends and target their messages toward
> certain demographics. . . . The graphic warnings represent FDA's attempt to level
> the playing field, not only by limiting the Companies' ability to advertise, but also
> by forcing the Companies to bear the cost of disseminating an anti-smoking mes-
> sage. But as the Supreme Court recently reminded us, "[t]hat the [government]
> finds expression too persuasive does not permit it to quiet the speech or to burden
> its messengers." . . . The First Amendment requires the government not only to
> state a substantial interest justifying a regulation on commercial speech, but also to
> show that its regulation directly advances that goal. FDA failed to present any da-
> ta—much less the substantial evidence required under the APA [Administrative
> Procedure Act]—showing that enacting their proposed graphic warnings will ac-
> complish the agency's stated objective of reducing smoking rates. The Rule thus**

cannot pass muster under *Central Hudson* [the applicable precedent case from the US Supreme Court]**. The APA directs that we "shall . . . set aside [the] agency action . . . found to be contrary to constitutional right." . . . We therefore vacate the graphic warning requirements and remand to the agency. In so doing, we also vacate the permanent injunction issued by the district court, in furtherance of our obligation to "set aside" the unlawful regulation.**

The full opinion is reported as *R.J. Reynolds v. Food and Drug Administration*, 696 F.3d 1205 (DC Cir. 2012).

Even more recently, the US Court of Appeals for the Eleventh Circuit ruled in tobacco companies' favor in a Florida case (*Philip Morris USA v. Douglas*) involving a State court ruling that, in essence, presumed all cigarettes were "defective" for "product liability" purposes, so that smokers were practically guaranteed a favorable verdict when they sued for smoking-related illnesses. This decision was based on a different clause in the US Constitution—the so-called "supremacy clause" (Article VI, Section 2: This Constitution, and the Laws of the United States which shall be made in Pursuance thereof, and all Treaties made, or which shall be made, under the Authority of the United States, shall be the supreme Law of the Land; and the Judges in every State shall be bound thereby, any Thing in the Constitution or Laws of any State notwithstanding." As the Appeals Court explained:

Fifth, Graham insists that by preempting his strict-liability and negligence claims, we will leave . . . plaintiffs a right without a remedy. Not true. To begin, we express no opinion as to the validity of other . . . claims, for example, fraudulent concealment or conspiracy to conceal. And as we have explained, nothing in our reasoning prevents an injured plaintiff from bringing a state-law tort suit against a tobacco company, provided he does not premise his suit on a theory of liability that means all cigarettes are defective as a matter of law (and provided that he can actually prove his case). Nor does our conclusion necessarily foreclose . . . plaintiffs from bringing state-law strict-liability or negligence claims, so long as they do not rely on the *Engle* [the case ruling that all cigarettes were defective] **jury findings to do so. The subtext of Graham's legal analysis seems to suggest that his claims are immune from preemption simply because the *Engle* litigation has managed to survive for twenty years and has now grown too-big-to-fail. Thankfully, our Constitution lends credence to no such argument. . . .**

Cigarette smoking presents one of the most intractable public health problems our nation has ever faced. It was not so long ago that anyone would walk a mile for a Camel: cigarette smoke once filled movie theaters, college classrooms, and even in-

door basketball courts. For fifty years, the States and the federal government have worked to raise awareness about the dangers of smoking and to limit smoking's adverse consequences to the greatest extent possible, all without prohibiting the sale of cigarettes to adult consumers. To that end, the State of Florida may ordinarily enforce duties on cigarette manufacturers in a bid to protect the health, safety, and welfare of its citizens. But it may not enforce a duty, as it has through the *Engle* jury findings, premised on the theory that *all* cigarettes are inherently defective and that *every* cigarette sale is an inherently negligent act. So, our holding is narrow indeed: it is only these specific, sweeping bases for state tort liability that we conclude frustrate the full purposes and objectives of Congress. As a result, Graham's *Engle*-progeny strict-liability and negligence claims are preempted, and we must reverse the District Court's denial of judgment as a matter of law.

As plaintiffs' attorneys continue to develop liability theories against marketers of cigarettes (and other forms of smoking tobacco), analogous claims are also being made against manufacturers and sellers of "smokeless" tobacco—snuff and chewing tobacco, e.g. Consider the case Gloria Tuttle filed in 1999 against Lorillard and several other tobacco companies. Her husband Bill had died from oral cancer in 1998. He had started using chewing tobacco in 1955—as a young professional baseball player—and continued until he was diagnosed with cancer in 1993. (His favorite brand was "Beech-Nut," manufactured by Lorillard.) Gloria's case alleged the defendants were guilty of negligence, fraud, and civil conspiracy, as well as violations of several Minnesota statutes—the Unlawful Trade Practices Act, the Deceptive Trade Practices Act, the Consumer Fraud Act, and the False Advertising Act. (The US District Court for Minnesota entered summary judgments in favor of all the defendants—2003 US Dist. LEXIS 3721. That decision was affirmed by the US 8th Circuit Court of Appeals—2004 US App. LEXIS 15764.)

3. The payment system under the 1973 HMO Act was criticized by Adam Davidson in "Price Fix," on the Financial Page of *The New Yorker*, May 29, 2017, p. 19.

4. In addition to the very large increase in its funding—via statute—HUD was also undergoing some significant administrative restructuring. *See* Shirley Scheibla, "Housecleaning at HUD: Secretary Lynn Is Pushing Plans for Sweeping Reform," *Barron's*, (June 25, 1973), pp. 5, 19, 21.

5. The constitutionality of the Act was subsequently challenged by several elected officials, candidates, and political organizations, with US Senator James Buckley as the lead plaintiff. The lead defendant was Francis Valeo, the Secretary of the US Senate—an ex-officio mem-

ber of the Federal Election Commission, which the Act had created. The US Supreme Court upheld the Act's limits on contributions to political parties but ruled that the limits on independent personal expenditures to support candidates were unconstitutional restrictions on the freedoms of speech and association. The following extract from the Court's opinion in *Buckley v. Valeo*, 424 US 1 (1976) indicates the majority's analysis:

The intricate statutory scheme adopted by Congress to regulate federal election campaigns includes restrictions on political contributions and expenditures that apply broadly to all phases of and all participants in the election process. The major contribution and expenditure limitations in the Act prohibit individuals from contributing more than $25,000 in a single year or more than $1,000 to any single candidate for an election campaign and from spending more than $1,000 a year "relative to a clearly identified candidate." Other provisions restrict a candidate's use of personal and family resources in his campaign and limit the overall amount that can be spent by a candidate in campaigning for federal office. . . .

The constitutional power of Congress to regulate federal elections is well established and is not questioned by any of the parties in this case. Thus, the critical constitutional questions presented here go not to the basic power of Congress to legislate in this area, but to whether the specific legislation that Congress has enacted interferes with First Amendment freedoms or invidiously discriminates against nonincumbent candidates and minor parties in contravention of the Fifth Amendment. . . .

The Act's contribution and expenditure limitations operate in an area of the most fundamental First Amendment activities. Discussion of public issues and debate on the qualifications of candidates are integral to the operation of the system of government established by our Constitution. The First Amendment affords the broadest protection to such political expression in order "to assure [the] unfettered interchange of ideas for the bringing about of political and social changes desired by the people." . . . Although First Amendment protections are not confined to "the exposition of ideas," . . . "there is practically universal agreement that a major purpose of that Amendment was to protect the free discussion of governmental affairs, . . . of course includ[ing] discussions of candidates. . . ." This no more than reflects our "profound national commitment to the principle that debate on public issues should be uninhibited, robust, and wide-open. . . ." In a republic where the people are sovereign, the ability of the citizenry to make informed choices among candidates for office is essential, for the identities of those who are elected will inevitably shape the course that we follow as a nation. As the Court [has] observed . . .

"it can hardly be doubted that the constitutional guarantee has its fullest and most urgent application precisely to the conduct of campaigns for political office."

The First Amendment protects political association as well as political expression. The constitutional right of association . . . stemmed from the Court's recognition that "[e]ffective advocacy of both public and private points of view, particularly controversial ones, is undeniably enhanced by group association." Subsequent decisions have made clear that the First and Fourteenth Amendments guarantee "freedom to associate with others for the common advancement of political beliefs and ideas," a freedom that encompasses "[t]he right to associate with the political party of one's choice."

It is with these principles in mind that we consider the primary contentions of the parties with respect to the Act's limitations upon the giving and spending of money in political campaigns. Those conflicting contentions could not more sharply define the basic issues before us. Appellees contend that what the Act regulates is conduct, and that its effect on speech and association is incidental at most. Appellants respond that contributions and expenditures are at the very core of political speech, and that the Act's limitations thus constitute restraints on First Amendment liberty that are both gross and direct. . . .

A restriction on the amount of money a person or group can spend on political communication during a campaign necessarily reduces the quantity of expression by restricting the number of issues discussed, the depth of their exploration, and the size of the audience reached. This is because virtually every means of communicating ideas in today's mass society requires the expenditure of money. The distribution of the humblest handbill or leaflet entails printing, paper, and circulation costs. Speeches and rallies generally necessitate hiring a hall and publicizing the event. The electorate's increasing dependence on television, radio, and other mass media for news and information has made these expensive modes of communication indispensable instruments of effective political speech. . . .

The expenditure limitations contained in the Act represent substantial rather than merely theoretical restraints on the quantity and diversity of political speech. The $1,000 ceiling on spending "relative to a clearly identified candidate" . . . would appear to exclude all citizens and groups except candidates, political parties, and the institutional press from any significant use of the most effective modes of communication. Although the Act's limitations on expenditures by campaign organizations and political parties provide substantially greater room for discussion and debate, they would have required restrictions in the scope of a number of past congressional and Presidential campaigns and would operate to constrain campaigning by candidates who raise sums in excess of the spending ceiling. . . .

By contrast with a limitation upon expenditures for political expression, a limitation upon the amount that any one person or group may contribute to a candidate or political committee entails only a marginal restriction upon the contributor's ability to engage in free communication. A contribution serves as a general expression of support for the candidate and his views, but does not communicate the underlying basis for the support. The quantity of communication by the contributor does not increase perceptibly with the size of his contribution, since the expression rests solely on the undifferentiated, symbolic act of contributing. At most, the size of the contribution provides a very rough index of the intensity of the contributor's support for the candidate. A limitation on the amount of money a person may give to a candidate or campaign organization thus involves little direct restraint on his political communication, for it permits the symbolic expression of support evidenced by a contribution but does not in any way infringe the contributor's freedom to discuss candidates and issues. While contributions may result in political expression if spent by a candidate or an association to present views to the voters, the transformation of contributions into political debate involves speech by someone other than the contributor. . . .

In summary, we sustain the individual contribution limits, the disclosure and reporting provisions, and the public financing scheme. We conclude, however, that the limitations on campaign expenditures, on independent expenditures by individuals and groups, and on expenditures by a candidate from his personal funds are constitutionally infirm. Finally, we hold that most of the powers conferred by the Act upon the Federal Election Commission can be exercised only by "Officers of the United States," appointed in conformity with Art. II, § 2, cl. 2, of the Constitution, and therefore cannot be exercised by the Commission as presently constituted.

6. *First National Bank of Boston v. Bellotti*, 435 US 765 (1978).

7. *Citizens United v. Federal Election Commission*, 558 US 310 (2010). The following key paragraphs illustrate the majority's reasoning:

Political speech is "indispensable to decisionmaking in a democracy, and this is no less true because the speech comes from a corporation rather than an individual." ... [T]he worth of speech "does not depend upon the identity of its source, whether corporation, association, union, or individual." ... "[T]he concept that government may restrict the speech of some elements of our society in order to enhance the relative voice of others is wholly foreign to the First Amendment." ... This protection for speech is inconsistent with *Austin*'s antidistortion rationale. *Austin* [a 1990 case] sought to defend the antidistortion rationale as a means to prevent corporations from obtaining "'an unfair advantage in the political marketplace'" by using "'resources amassed in the economic marketplace.'" ... But *Buckley* rejected the premise that the Government has an interest "in equalizing the relative ability of individuals and groups to influence the outcome of elections." ... *Buckley* was specific in stating that "the skyrocketing cost of political campaigns" could not sustain the governmental prohibition. ... The First Amendment's protections do not depend on the speaker's "financial ability to engage in public discussion." ...

The Court reaffirmed these conclusions when it invalidated the BCRA provision that increased the cap on contributions to one candidate if the opponent made certain expenditures from personal funds. ... "Leveling electoral opportunities means making and implementing judgments about which strengths should be permitted to contribute to the outcome of an election. The Constitution, however, confers upon voters, not Congress, the power to choose the Members of the House of Representatives, Art. I, § 2, and it is a dangerous business for Congress to use the election laws to influence the voters' choices." ... The rule that political speech cannot be limited based on a speaker's wealth is a necessary consequence of the premise that the First Amendment generally prohibits the suppression of political speech based on the speaker's identity.

Even if one objects to the Supreme Court's characterization of corporations as "persons" entitled to constitutional protections, the interests of millions of *human* "persons"—employees, stockholders, customers, suppliers, neighbors—are closely tied to the interests of the corporations themselves. Political decisions that are "bad for business" may also have adverse effects on some or all of these human beings. Shouldn't the possibility/likelihood of such evil results be presented to the electorate, in order for there to be a more informed decision? Surely the freedom of speech protected by the Constitution must include the electorate's right to *hear* all arguments, pro and con, on the decision to be made, trusting the electorate to evaluate the weight and accuracy of the "speech." Censoring policy arguments with which one disagrees (because they are too persuasive?) seems somewhat inconsistent with "liberal values" and the concept of a "free marketplace of ideas."

A major opposing argument is forcefully summarized in a recent article by Steven Brill,

"My Generation Was Supposed to Level America's Playing Field. Instead, We Rigged It for Ourselves," *Time*, (May 28, 2018), pp. 32–39. Brill's point is that by extending First Amendment "free speech" constitutional protection to corporate messages, the US Supreme Court has enabled large commercial interests to overly-influence the political process and thus to permit the "Haves" in the US to protect their financial dominance of the society.

For further perspectives on some of the issues involved, *see, e.g.*, Bill McKibben, "The Ultimate Corporation," *The New York Review of Books*, (June 7, 2012), pp. 50–51, 54; Justin Fox, "Stop Spoiling the Shareholders," *The Atlantic*, (July–August 2013), pp. 30, 32, 34; Matthew G. Davis, "From *Buckley* to *Citizens United*," *Michigan Bar Journal*, (January 2014), pp. 30–33; Patrick Radden Keefe, "Limited Liability," *The New Yorker*, (July 31, 2017), pp. 28–30, 32–33.

8. For the connection of Nixon's "Law and Order" campaign theme to the development of the "Victim's Rights" movement, *see* Jill Lepore, "Sirens in the Night," *The New Yorker*, (May 21, 2018), pp. 48–50, 52–55. "'For Law and Order' became a slogan of Richard Nixon's 1968 Presidential campaign. 'As we look at America, we see cities enveloped in smoke and flame,' Nixon said, accepting the Republican nomination. 'We hear sirens in the night.'" *Id.*, p. 49.

9. Tom Wicker, *One of Us: Richard Nixon and the American Dream*, (New York, NY: Random House, Inc., 1995), p. 406.

Chapter 9. Summary and Conclusions

1. Just for the record, it is worth noting that FDR's insistence on "unconditional surrender" of the Axis Powers was challenged at the time by numerous military and diplomatic leaders and severely criticized by later commentators. Especially with respect to Japan, whose navy had been almost totally destroyed and whose homeland was suffering from near starvation and intense aerial bombardment, repeated use of that largely undefined phrase may have aided the die-hard Army clique in Japan. If the allowance for the continuation of the Japanese emperor that was, in fact, finally agreed to had been communicated earlier, the war might have been ended earlier, without the use of the atomic bomb or the Russian entry into the Pacific War. *See, e.g.*, the thorough discussion in Anthony Kubek, *How the Far East Was Lost*, New York, NY: Twin Circle Publishing Co., Inc. (1972), especially Chapters III–VI.

2. Alan Brinkley indicates that the "honeymoon" period was quite brief and that many of FDR's initiatives were met by an increasingly assertive opposition coalition of conservative Democrats (especially from the South) and Republicans. Even the Democrats' sweep of

1936, he says, was "misinterpreted" by FDR and his allies as a mandate to enact their liberal program. Brinkley, *The End of Reform*, New York, NY: Vintage Books (1996), pp. 16–17. Further, he notes that "An increasing popular weariness with the New Deal expressed itself in the growing Republican and conservative strength in congressional elections, a shift in strength that began in 1938 and continued, largely unabated, through the whole of the war." *Ibid.*, p. 139.

3. William Leuchtenberg's analysis of FDR's tenure confirms Brinkley's points. Leuchtenberg says that after the ("somewhat limited") Republican resurgence in the 1938 congressional elections—gains of eighty-one House seats (nearly *doubling* their strength) and eight more in the Senate, including their future leader, Robert Taft of Ohio—Congress was dominated by the Republican-Southern Democrat coalition that had already formed against parts of the New Deal. Leuchtenberg, *Franklin D. Roosevelt and the New Deal*, New York, NY: Harper Perennial edition (2009), pp. 271–274. Describing Taft's role in this "limited" resurrection, Russell Kirk and James McClellan state:

> For fourteen years this man of courage and talent stood on the floor of the Senate chamber to resist the encroachments of the New Deal and the Fair Deal upon old liberties and institutions. Turning any blunder of Roosevelt or Truman into a victory for his party, Taft was to alter the whole drift of American society. It is not that he totally undid New Deal and Fair Deal: rather, he, more than any other man, compelled impulsive reformers to come to terms with reality and with the American pattern of politics. In part abandoned, in part restricted, in part reconciled with the American constitutional and economic system, the New Deal ceased to be a quasi-revolutionary ideology.

> (Kirk & McClellan, *The Political Principles of Robert A. Taft*, New Brunswick, US [2010 edition], p. 28)

Richard Hofstadter comes to the same basic conclusion, albeit from a different angle. He concludes that the New Deal was not really about "reform" but about getting the existing system to function again: "And what of the old Progressive issues? They were bypassed, sidestepped, outgrown—anything but solved. . . . [T]he New Deal was almost completely free of such crusading. To the discomfort of the old-fashioned, principled liberals who were otherwise enthusiastic about his reforms, FDR made no effort to put an end to bossism and corruption, but simply ignored the problem." Hofstadter, *The Age of Reform*, New York: Vintage Books (1955), p. 310.

4. Farrell states that: "In coping with the presidency's demands, Nixon often fell back on the lessons he had learned as Eisenhower's understudy. . . . Like Ike, Nixon sought to govern

from the center. . . ." John A. Farrell, *Richard Nixon: The Life*, New York: Doubleday (2017), p. 372.

Tom Wicker notes that Nixon may also have learned some other lessons from the General:

> The vice president probably noticed also . . . that despite his chief's frequent preachments about allies and collective security, when perceived American interests were at stake, Eisenhower acted alone and with ruthless disregard for allies. . . .

> Watching the Guatemalan operation from the sidelines, Nixon could hardly have failed to see also that when Eisenhower thought it necessary, he did not hesitate to take illegal action—a naval blockade of Guatemala, for example. . . .

> [N]ecessity may have appeared to Nixon, as to Eisenhower, to have legalized a president's illegality. "Well, when the president does it, that means it is not illegal," he later told David Frost. . . .

> (Wicker, *One of Us: Richard Nixon and the American Dream*, [New York, NY: Random House, Inc., 1995—paperback edition], p. 143)

> "The president's far-reaching claim of executive privilege [in 1954, defying Senator Joe McCarthy's efforts to subpoena executive branch persons to testify before his Senate committee] . . . was one of the strongest lessons and precedents to be impressed upon Nixon during his service in the vice-presidency." *Ibid.*, p. 174.

One wonders how much these "other lessons" may have helped to produce the Watergate fiasco—and affected Nixon's handling of it as it developed.

5. Tom Wicker indicates that President Nixon understood very well his need for such a bipartisan approach. In appointing Bryce Harlow as his congressional liaison, he asked Harlow to prepare a list of congressional leaders, including the chair and the ranking member of all committees in both the House and the Senate. According to Harlow, Nixon promised to call each of them, stating: "We are going to get along and get things done together." As Harlow remembered:

> He was quite sincerely counting on them to cooperate. Now, we're talking about some thirty-one committees, two members apiece to be called—sixty-two calls by a man who hardly had time to go to the john, plus a score of other leaders. He had to make some eighty calls to do this project. Each call would take at least five minutes, that is four hundred minutes, which is about seven hours. He did exactly that. He called them all. They were all flattered . . . and promised to cooperate as best they could.

(Wicker, *op. cit., supra*, p. 404)

That sounds like effective leadership!

6. For a fuller discussion of the roots of what he describes as the "chaos syndrome," *see* Jonathan Rauch, "What's Ailing American Politics?," *The Atlantic*, (July/August 2016), pp. 51–58, 60, 62–63. His major point is stated early in the article (p. 53):

> Chaos syndrome is a chronic decline in the political system's capacity for self-organization. It begins with the weakening of the institutions and brokers—political parties, career politicians, and congressional leaders and committees—that have historically held politicians accountable to one another and prevented everyone in the system from pursuing naked self-interest all the time. As these intermediaries' influence fades, politicians, activists, and voters all become more individualistic and unaccountable. The system atomizes. Chaos becomes the new normal—both in campaigns and in the government itself.

> Our intricate, informal system of political intermediation, which took many decades to build, did not commit suicide or die of old age; we reformed it to death. For decades, well-meaning political reformers have attacked intermediaries as corrupt, undemocratic, unnecessary, or (usually) all of the above. Americans have been demonizing and disempowering political professionals and parties, which is like spending decades abusing and attacking your own immune system. Eventually, you will get sick.

Some readers may recall Jeb Bush's accusatory characterization, during one of the early debates—before Bush dropped out of the race—of Donald Trump as a "chaos candidate" who would be a "chaos President" if he were elected. The author has no information on whether Jeb had talked with Rauch or read a draft of the cited Rauch article (or some similar source) prior to making his own "chaos" comment. In any event, even if believed, that characterization did not seem to do candidate Trump much damage. Indeed, one suspects that a little "chaos" was just what many Trump supporters were looking for ("Drain the Swamp!").

7. Rauch also identifies Senator Cruz as an example of the new "independence." *Ibid.*, p. 62. Much of the Rauch analysis is paralleled in political scientist Tascha Mounk's commentary, "Too Much Democracy," *The New Yorker*, (November 12, 2018), pp. 46, 48–51. The "reform-the-system" believers are still active. As one recent example, on November 6, 2018, Michigan voters passed a ballot initiative establishing an independent (and seemingly uncontrolled) commission to perform redistricting for that State's seats in the US House of Representatives.

As early as 1979, Arthur Schlesinger, Jr. identified television and computers as "having a devastating and possibly fatal impact on the traditional structure of American politics." Schlesinger, "Crisis of the Party System: II," *Wall Street Journal*, (May 14, 1979), p. 22. *Cf.*, Dennis Farney, "Inert Body: Congress, Fragmented and Fractious, Gets Less and Less Done," *Wall Street Journal*, (December 14, 1979), pp. 1, 26. While Farney's evaluation was quite common at that time (and to some extent still is), it is certainly called into question by the data presented in this Chapter.

8. As already noted, part of this one/two ranking may be due to Theodore Roosevelt's overall positive rating, while Nixon suffers from the negativity of Watergate and the Vietnam War. Of course, TR also had his critics—as President and more recently. As noted in Chapter 3, endnote 2, Robert Wiebe described TR as—*inter alia*—"A man of unlovely traits who relished killing human beings. . . ." Wiebe, *The Search for Order, 1877–1920*, New York: Hill and Wang (1967), p. 189. TR was also widely depicted as a killer of animals—for sport! In stark contrast, the President ranked "Number Two" by the "experts" (Nixon) signed the three endangered-species Acts listed above, as well as several other protective statutes!

The latest episode in the evaluation of Theodore Roosevelt was reported extensively by the *New York Times* on July 18, 2019 (a very useful—if unknowing—"birthday present" for the author): "A Monument, A Lightning Rod," pp. C1, C6. In view of TR's several seemingly racist statements over the years, objections have been raised to the continuing presence of the TR statue in front of New York's American Museum of Natural History. One cannot help but draw a contrast with President Nixon's significant efforts on behalf of Native Americans and his strong leadership in desegregating Southern schools, as discussed in Chapter 5, *supra*.

9. Its importance as a key part of environmental protection policy was reconfirmed recently in an extensive (and critical) review of the resetting of the EPA's priorities by its then administrator, Scott Prewitt. Margaret Talbot, "Dirty Politics," *The New Yorker*, (April 2, 2018), pp. 38–51. Talbot is good enough to mention President Nixon as the EPA's creator: "The agency was established in 1970 by President Richard Nixon." *Ibid.*, p. 40. The much-maligned Prewitt resigned on July 5, 2018, but his policies may be continued—perhaps even more effectively—by his (temporarily-appointed) successor, Andrew Wheeler. Justin Worland, "Scott Pruitt's successor at the EPA: a similar agenda without the scandals," *Time*, (July 23, 2018), p. 45. One of Wheeler's first major steps was reported by Coral Davenport in the *New York Times* on October 1, 2018, at page A13: "Trump Proposes Major Weakening of Mercury Rules." For a similar "correction" of the agency's policies during the Obama administration, *see*, *e.g.*, "Brushing Back a Lawless EPA," *Wall Street Journal*, (December 23, 2015), p. A12.

More recently, the 1970 Clean Air Act was lauded by Jonathan Mingle as having established "the world's most stringent emissions controls" and as being "a sweeping piece of legislation that required the newly created Environmental Protection Agency to use the best available science to set and enforce limits on six pollutants at levels that would allow "an adequate margin of safety . . . requisite to protect the public health." Unfortunately for the peoples of the world, Mingle concludes that efforts to date have not been sufficient—"the problem of air pollution is far from being solved in the US or anywhere else." Jonathan Mingle, "Our Lethal Air," *The New York Review of Books*, (September 26, 2019), pp. 64–66, 68.

10. The texts by Brinkley, Leuchtenberg, and Hofstadter cited in endnotes 1 and 2, and Wiebe's study noted in endnote 5, *supra*, all discuss labor developments. Various aspects of US labor history are also reviewed in some detail in Alan Dawley, *Struggles for Justice: Social Responsibility and the Liberal State*, Cambridge, MA: Belknap Press (1993); Leon Fink, *Workingmen's Democracy: The Knights of Labor and American Politics*, Champaign, IL: Illini Books (1985); Lawrence Goodwyn, *The Populist Movement: A Short History of the Agrarian Revolt in America*, New York: Oxford University Press (1978); Colin Gordon, *New Deals: Business, Labor, and Politics in America 1920–1935*, New York: Cambridge University Press (1994); and Michael McGerr, *A Fierce Discontent: The Rise and Fall of the Progressive Movement in America*, New York: Oxford University Press (2003). *See also*, Gabriel Kolko's challenge to the typical view of the "Progressive" movement: *The Triumph of Conservatism*, Chicago: Quadrangle Books, (paperback edition, 1967).

11. This industry-to-industry labor-cost disparity has evidently existed since the early twentieth century. Gordon, *op. cit.*, *supra*, note 10, pp. 104, 107. The coal mine operators have, of course, increasingly mechanized their operations to reduce this disadvantage, thus eliminating thousands of mining jobs over the last century.

12. *Brown et al. v. Board of Education of Topeka, et al.*, 347 US 483 (1954).